Dan Kent

ASP.NET

E V O L U T I O N

SAMS 800 East 96th Street, Indianapolis, Indiana 46240

ASP.NET Evolution

Copyright © 2004 by Sams Publishing

All rights reserved. No part of this book shall be reproduced, stored in a retrieval system, or transmitted by any means, electronic, mechanical, photocopying, recording, or otherwise, without written permission from the publisher. No patent liability is assumed with respect to the use of the information contained herein. Although every precaution has been taken in the preparation of this book, the publisher and author assume no responsibility for errors or omissions. Nor is any liability assumed for damages resulting from the use of the information contained herein.

International Standard Book Number: 0-672-32647-7

Library of Congress Catalog Card Number: 2004091250

Printed in the United States of America

First Printing: June 2004

07   06   05   04   4   3   2   1

Trademarks

All terms mentioned in this book that are known to be trademarks or service marks have been appropriately capitalized. Sams Publishing cannot attest to the accuracy of this information. Use of a term in this book should not be regarded as affecting the validity of any trademark or service mark.

Warning and Disclaimer

Every effort has been made to make this book as complete and as accurate as possible, but no warranty or fitness is implied. The information provided is on an "as is" basis. The author and the publisher shall have neither liability nor responsibility to any person or entity with respect to any loss or damages arising from the information contained in this book or from the use of the CD or programs accompanying it.

Bulk Sales

Sams Publishing offers excellent discounts on this book when ordered in quantity for bulk purchases or special sales. For more information, please contact

> U.S. Corporate and Government Sales
> 1-800-382-3419
> corpsales@pearsontechgroup.com

For sales outside of the U.S., please contact

> International Sales
> 1-317-428-3341
> international@pearsontechgroup.com

Associate Publisher
Michael Stephens

Acquisitions Editor
Neil Rowe

Development Editor
Mark Renfrow

Managing Editor
Charlotte Clapp

Project Editor
Tonya Simpson

Copy Editor
Jessica McCarty

Indexer
Mandie Frank

Proofreader
Tonya Fenimore

Technical Editor
Doug Holland

Publishing Coordinator
Cindy Teeters

Multimedia Developer
Dan Scherf

Book Designer
Gary Adair

Contents at a Glance

	Introduction	1
1	Getting Started	3
2	The Online Community Application	11
3	Exploring the Code	25
4	Experimenting with the Code	69
5	Improving the User Interface	91
6	Improving the Modules	135
7	Managing Members	169
8	Keeping Members Under Control	207
9	Improving the Code	247
10	Extending the Application	295
	Index	345

Table of Contents

Introduction 1

1 Getting Started 3

What You Need to Run the Application 3

    Versions of the Application on the CD-ROM 4

    STEP-BY-STEP GUIDE: Installing the Application 4

    Copying the Source Code Files 4

    STEP-BY-STEP GUIDE: Setting Up the Web Application 5

    STEP-BY-STEP GUIDE: Compiling the Source Code 6

    Setting Up the Database 7

    Checking the Application Configuration 8

    Copying the WebControl Client Script Files 9

    Testing the Application 9

Troubleshooting 9

    Access Is Denied `Microsoft.Web.UI.WebControls` 9

    Directory Not Found Exception for `C:\Inetpub\wwwroot\community\global\OJB.NET\repository.xml` 9

    SQL Server Does Not Exist or Access Denied 10

    Could Not Load Type 10

Moving On 10

2 The Online Community Application 11

What Does the Online Community Application Do? 11

    Members 13

    Modules 14

    Global Module Instances 16

    Adding Information to Module Instances 18

    Member Settings 19

    Search 22

Moving On 23

3 Exploring the Code — 25

Terminology — 25
Why Was the Online Community Built the Way It Was? — 26
The Overall Logical Structure — 27
    ASP.NET Pages — 27
    Controls — 28
    Business Services — 28
    Persistent Objects — 29
    `Member` — 30
    `CommunityModule` — 31
    `ModuleView` — 32
    `ModuleInstance` — 33
    `SectionItem` — 34
    `Section` — 34
    The Persistence Service — 35
The Database — 36
The Modules — 37
    The `ModuleBase` Class — 37
How the Code Files Are Organized — 38
    CODE TOUR: `Default.aspx` — 40
    CODE TOUR: `CoreModule.vb` — 47
    CODE TOUR: `DisplayLatestHeadlines.ascx` — 55
    CODE TOUR: `NewsModule.vb` — 57
Search — 60
Security — 66
Moving On — 67

4 Experimenting with the Code — 69

Changing the Style of the Application — 69
    EXPERIMENT: Playing with the Style Sheet — 69
    CODE TOUR: `Navigation.ascx` — 77
    STEP-BY-STEP GUIDE: Adding Icons to the Navigation — 86
Moving On — 89

5 Improving the User Interface — 91

Section Items 91

    CODE TOUR: `Global/Controls/SectionItemHeader.ascx` 91

    STEP-BY-STEP GUIDE: Adding the Number of Images to the Header of `ImageGallery` Module Instances 94

    CHALLENGE: Displaying the Number of Images for Global Instances 95

    IDEA: Customizing the Header for Other Modules 95

    STEP-BY-STEP GUIDE: Adding Icons to Module Headers 96

    CHALLENGE: Distinguishing Global Instances 99

    STEP-BY-STEP GUIDE: Adding a New Icon to Module Instances That Have Been Updated in the Last Week 99

    STEP-BY-STEP GUIDE: Adding New Icons to the Navigation 103

    STEP-BY-STEP GUIDE: Adding an Automated What's New? Page 108

    CHALLENGE: Showing Only Non-global Sections in What's New? 115

    STEP-BY-STEP GUIDE: Displaying the Latest Member to Join 115

    STEP-BY-STEP GUIDE: Allowing Members to Have a Custom Image on Their Page 119

    CHALLENGE: Imposing a Size Limit on Uploaded Images 126

    STEP-BY-STEP GUIDE: Adding Configurable Module Names 126

    CHALLENGE: Display Names for Module Views 132

    STEP-BY-STEP GUIDE: Solving a Problem with the Return Key 132

    CHALLENGE: Adding Default Buttons to Other Controls 134

Moving On 134

6 Improving the Modules — 135

The Send Message Module 135

    CODE TOUR: `SendMessageModule.vb` 135

    CODE TOUR: `Modules/SendMessage/SimpleSendMessageBox.ascx` 137

    STEP-BY-STEP GUIDE: Requiring a Valid Email Address 139

    CHALLENGE: Requiring a Valid Email Address from New Members 142

    STEP-BY-STEP GUIDE: Dealing with Errors 142

    STEP-BY-STEP GUIDE: Allowing a Global `SendMessage` Instance 145

    CHALLENGE: User-Definable Subject Line 148

The News Module 148
    CODE TOUR: `Modules/News/DisplayItem.ascx` 149
    STEP-BY-STEP GUIDE: Formatting News Items Better 152
Entering and Editing News Items 155
    STEP-BY-STEP GUIDE: Validating the Length of the Inputs 157
    CHALLENGE: Automatic Summaries 158
    STEP-BY-STEP GUIDE: Allowing Markup Code 159
    CHALLENGE: Adding More Markup Options 162
    CHALLENGE: Allowing Members to Upload an Image to Accompany Each News Item 162
The ImageGallery Module 163
    STEP-BY-STEP GUIDE: Generating Thumbnails 163
Moving On 167

7   Managing Members   169

Building a Member Administration System 169
    Protecting the Administration System 169
    CODE TOUR: `Global/CommunityPrincipal.vb` 171
    STEP-BY-STEP GUIDE: Adding General Member Management Facilities 172
Helping Users Who Forget Their Passwords 189
    STEP-BY-STEP GUIDE: Automating Password Resetting 190
    CHALLENGE: One-Use-Only Change Password Emails 197
Improving the Registration Process 198
    STEP-BY-STEP GUIDE: Requiring Approval for New User Registrations 198
    CHALLENGE: Email Reminders 205
    CHALLENGE: Requiring Email Confirmation for Registration 205
    IDEA: Requiring Agreement to Terms and Conditions 205
Moving On 206

8 Keeping Members Under Control — 207

Managing Members' Resource Usage … 207
- **STEP-BY-STEP GUIDE:** Setting a Quota for Members' Data … 207
- **CHALLENGE:** Including the Member's Personal Page Image and Text in Her Resource Usage … 223
- **IDEA:** Personalized Resource Quotas … 223

Dealing with Troublesome Users … 224
- **STEP-BY-STEP GUIDE:** Temporarily Banning a Member … 224
- **STEP-BY-STEP GUIDE:** Hiding Deactivated Members' Data … 226
- **STEP-BY-STEP GUIDE:** Deleting a Member … 228
- **STEP-BY-STEP GUIDE:** Logging IP Addresses … 233
- **CHALLENGE:** Updating the Date on Existing IP Addresses … 240

Security Configuration Options … 241
- **STEP-BY-STEP GUIDE:** Changing the Timeout Period … 241
- **STEP-BY-STEP GUIDE:** Remembering Members Between Visits … 241
- **STEP-BY-STEP GUIDE:** Building a Private Community … 243

Moving On … 246

9 Improving the Code — 247

Improving Performance with Caching … 247
- **STEP-BY-STEP GUIDE:** Caching Page Output … 248
- **STEP-BY-STEP GUIDE:** Partial-Page Caching … 250
- **CHALLENGE:** Caching a Dynamic Control … 251

Viewstate … 251
- **STEP-BY-STEP GUIDE:** Pruning the Viewstate … 252

Improving Text-Handling Performance with `StringBuilder` … 253

Eliminating Magic Numbers … 260
- **STEP-BY-STEP GUIDE:** Making the Thumbnail Width Configurable … 264
- **STEP-BY-STEP GUIDE:** Removing the `Community.RandomTextItem` Duplication … 269
- **CHALLENGE:** Removing the `Type.GetType` Duplication in All Module Classes … 270

Reorganizing Code … 271

STEP-BY-STEP:	Breaking Out Databinding Code into a Databinding Subroutine	278
CHALLENGE:	Breaking Out Databinding Code	279

Creating Reusable Code 279
More Efficient Data Access 281

STEP-BY-STEP GUIDE:	Using Custom SQL to Get Recent News Items	283

Retrieving Less Data with Summary Objects 285

STEP-BY-STEP GUIDE:	Using a `NewsItemSummary` Class	286
CHALLENGE:	Implementing Another Summary Class	291

Improving File Naming 292
Moving On 294

10 Extending the Application   295

Adding a New View 295

CHALLENGE:	Improving the `DisplaySingleImage` View	299

Adding a New Module 299

Required Items 299
Optional Items 300

STEP-BY-STEP GUIDE:	Implementing the Persistent Object	300
STEP-BY-STEP GUIDE:	Creating a Business Service Class for the Module	306
STEP-BY-STEP GUIDE:	Implementing the Display Module Control	314
STEP-BY-STEP GUIDE:	Implementing a View to Display Upcoming Events	318
STEP-BY-STEP GUIDE:	Adding a View to Display a Graphical Calendar	320
STEP-BY-STEP GUIDE:	Implementing the View Item Control	326

Making the Calendar Module Work 331

CHALLENGE:	Adding a Delete Event Option	333
CHALLENGE:	Displaying an Error Message	333

Integrating ASP.NET Forums with the Online Community Application 334

STEP-BY-STEP GUIDE:	Integrating ASP.NET Forums	334

Moving On 342

Index   345

About the Author

Dan Kent has been interested in online communities since he first discovered the wealth of information and arguments to be found on Usenet in the mid-1990s. After studying artificial intelligence, he went on to become part of the "dotcom bubble," building online community sites that empowered newcomers to the Web to create a Web presence.

Like many programmers involved in the Web at that time, Dan became another victim of big plans that didn't quite work out. He decided to leave frontline programming and concentrate on passing on some of his know-how. His desire to be involved with books was kindled by some work as a technical reviewer for Wrox, and he went on to join them as a technical editor. While at Wrox, Dan developed the Problem-Design-Solution concept, which pioneered the approach of presenting readers with real-world solutions in the context of a real application. He also worked with the Microsoft ASP.NET team to help programmers learn more about the fantastic technology they created and contributed as an author to the highly respected *Professional ASP.NET Security*, which is now sadly out of print. Two years, four job titles, and far too many books later, Dan decided to leave Wrox. He accidentally timed his exit to perfection—Wrox finally succumbed to the pressures of the post-dotcom market and went out of business on the day that Dan was due to finish work.

Dan was keen to continue to develop the ideas that he worked on while at Wrox and, fortunately, Sams was looking for a new series. Thus, the *Evolution* series was born. Dan now edits the *Evolution* series for Sams, builds sites that support community regeneration, and performs cutting-edge video shows as half of the VJ duo Syzygy.

Dedication

This book is for Jenny.

We Want to Hear from You!

As the reader of this book, *you* are our most important critic and commentator. We value your opinion and want to know what we're doing right, what we could do better, what areas you'd like to see us publish in, and any other words of wisdom you're willing to pass our way.

As an associate publisher for Sams Publishing, I welcome your comments. You can email or write me directly to let me know what you did or didn't like about this book—as well as what we can do to make our books better.

Please note that I cannot help you with technical problems related to the topic of this book. We do have a User Services group, however, where I will forward specific technical questions related to the book.

When you write, please be sure to include this book's title and author as well as your name, email address, and phone number. I will carefully review your comments and share them with the author and editors who worked on the book.

Email: `feedback@samspublishing.com`

Mail: Michael Stephens
Associate Publisher
Sams Publishing
800 East 96th Street
Indianapolis, IN 46240 USA

For more information about this book or another Sams title, visit our Web site at `www.samspublishing.com`. Type the ISBN (0672326477) or the title of a book in the Search field to find the page you're looking for.

Introduction

Have you ever found that you get to the end of a programming book and think, "Great, now I know the syntax, but where do I actually start with building something for real?" Have you ever tried to apply a technique from a book and quickly discovered that things are far more complicated when you are actually implementing code, or that the technique just doesn't work in the real world? If so, you will immediately understand where the *Evolution* series is coming from. If not, you can appreciate the complete application that comes with this book and is free for you to use as the basis of your own development.

The aim of the *Evolution* books is to teach real-world programming techniques in the best way possible—by looking at real applications. You won't find any toy samples or theoretical solutions in *Evolution* books— just real code for the sort of applications that a lot of developers want to build.

The *Evolution* name refers to the idea that, throughout the book, the sample application is improved and extended. It also applies to the fact that, when you have finished reading the book, you can take the code provided and use it as a starting point for an online community of your own.

Each *Evolution* book is based upon a single, fully working application. The application is completely explained so that, even if you haven't built an application on this scale before, you will be able to understand how it works and why it was built the way it was. This book will then show you how to modify the application, customize it to your needs, and add completely new features to it. By the time you finish working through an *Evolution* book, you will know the sample application well enough to make it your own. You also will have seen how a real application works, from the user interface to the data structures.

The sample application that is covered in this book is an ASP.NET online community application. It is designed to be flexible so that it can form the basis of many different communities. For example, it could be used to create a way for friends to stay in touch with each other or for related businesses to network. (I already have two installations of the code base running and a third on the way.)

Online community applications are proving very popular, with all kinds of groups of people using online systems to share information, stay in touch, or meet like-minded people.

We will take a complete tour of the application in Chapter 2, "The Online Community Application," after we have installed everything it requires to run in Chapter 1, "Getting Started."

After touring the application, we will dig into the code to see how the framework of the application works.

The remainder of the chapters will show how to make changes to the application, starting with small tweaks in Chapter 4, "Experimenting with the Code," and building up to adding entirely new features in Chapter 10, "Extending the Application." Over the course of the chapters, we will modify pretty much every part of the application, so you will see how everything works.

Because each chapter makes new changes to the application, building on what was done in the previous chapters, you will get the most out of this book if you read the chapters in order starting from Chapter 1. You will also find that it is good to read this book while in front of a computer that has the sample code on it—there are a lot of places in this book where you will be encouraged to experiment some more with the code.

My final advice for getting the maximum value from this book and the sample application is to experiment! The best way to learn programming techniques is to try them out for real, so don't limit yourself to following the instructions in this book—try out some changes of your own and see what happens!

If you get stuck with anything, whether it is something from this book or a change of your own that would like to implement, I will be happy to help you out on the book forum, which you can find at `www.evolutionbooks.com`.

Getting Started 1

The whole idea behind the *Evolution* series is that you are encouraged to get hands-on with the example application throughout each book. With that in mind, it makes sense that the first thing we will do is install the code for the example application and get it up and running. In Chapter 2, "The Online Community Application," we will take a look at the application to see what it does. Chapter 3, "Exploring the Code," will explain how the application works. From Chapter 4, "Experimenting with the Code," onward, we will make changes to the application.

In this chapter, we will

- ▶ See what basic software is required to run the sample application
- ▶ Install the source code and compile it so that it's ready to run
- ▶ Install some other specific items that the application needs

What You Need to Run the Application

This book assumes that you have the following already installed and working on the computer on which you intend to install the example online community application:

- ▶ Microsoft Windows 2000, Windows Server 2003, or Windows XP Pro
- ▶ Microsoft .NET Framework 1.1
- ▶ Microsoft Visual Studio .NET 2003
- ▶ Microsoft SQL Server 2000 or MSDE

If you do not have Visual Studio or SQL Server and you want to evaluate them while using this book, you can order evaluation copies of them from the Microsoft Web site:

http://msdn.microsoft.com/vstudio/

http://www.microsoft.com/sql/

MSDE is a free alternative to the full SQL Server database engine. It is available for download from the Microsoft Web site. It does not have any user interface components itself, but you can use the tools that come with an evaluation version of SQL Server 2000 (particularly Enterprise Manager and Query Analyzer) to control MSDE. However, you should consider buying the Developer Edition of SQL Server—it is not very expensive, and by using it, you gain the advantage of testing your applications with the full SQL Server engine.

Versions of the Application on the CD-ROM

There are two different versions of the application on the CD-ROM supplied with this book. The first one is the *starting-point application*, in which all of the activities in this book are based. This is the version that you should install first.

The second version is the *final application*, which contains all the alterations made from the book activities. You might want to use this version as a reference to compare the changes that you make. You might also want to install it in order to see what the final application is like.

You can also see the final application online at www.evolutionbooks.com.

STEP-BY-STEP GUIDE:
Installing the Application

To get the example online community application installed, you will need to perform the following steps:

1. Copy the source code files and Visual Studio projects to your computer.
2. Set up the database for the application.
3. Set up the Web application.
4. Copy the client-side scripts for the WebControls that are used by the application.
5. Check that the application is configured correctly for the database.
6. Configure the application to use the correct server for sending emails.
7. Ensure that the file paths in the configuration are correct.
8. Compile the source code to create the application.
9. Test the application.

The activities that follow will guide you through each of these steps.

Copying the Source Code Files

You will find all of the source code files required for the application on the CD-ROM in the back of this book.

What You Need to Run the Application

STEP-BY-STEP GUIDE: **Setting Up the Web Application**

Copy the `Community` folder from the `Starting_Point` folder to somewhere on your hard disk. I keep my code in my `Inetpub/wwwroot` folder in order to keep all of my applications in one place, but there is no reason why you have to do this. (Indeed, many programmers prefer to keep the code in a separate place.)

STEP-BY-STEP GUIDE:
Setting Up the Web Application

To browse to the application and have ASP.NET run it as an application, we need to tell Windows Internet Information Services (IIS) to allow users to access it:

1. Open the Internet Information Services Control Panel (Control Panel > Administrative Tools > Internet Information Services).
2. Open the Web Sites section in the left tree view.
3. Right-click Default Web Site and select New > Virtual Directory.
4. Enter **Community** for the alias. (You can actually make this whatever you like—it is the folder name that you will browse to in order to access the application. It does not have to match the real folder of the application.)
5. Select the folder to which you copied the code. This should be named `Community`.
6. On the Allow the Following page (see Figure 1.1), click Next.

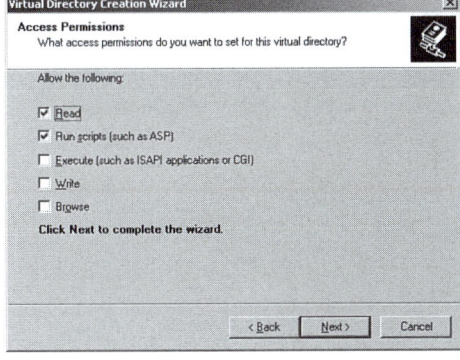

FIGURE 1.1
The Allow the Following page.

We allow the permissions necessary for users to read the application and for ASP.NET to execute, but we do not allow anything more.

7. Click Done.

6 What You Need to Run the Application

STEP-BY-STEP GUIDE: **Compiling the Source Code**

IIS now knows that when a user browses to `http://[yourmachine]/Community`, it should run the application in the `Community` folder that you created.

However, if you browse to `http://localhost/community/`, you will get an error message. This is because the application has not yet been compiled—ASP.NET needs the source code to be compiled before it can run it.

STEP-BY-STEP GUIDE:
Compiling the Source Code

We will now compile the source code to produce the Intermediate Language assemblies that ASP.NET will execute when the application runs.

1. Open Visual Studio .NET and use the Open Solution menu option.

2. Browse to the folder where you copied the source code and open the `Community.sln` solution file. You should now see the solution in the Solution Explorer.

3. Select the Build > Build Solution menu option to compile the code.

If you now browse to `http://localhost/community`, you will see a different error message (see Figure 1.2).

FIGURE 1.2
Database error message.

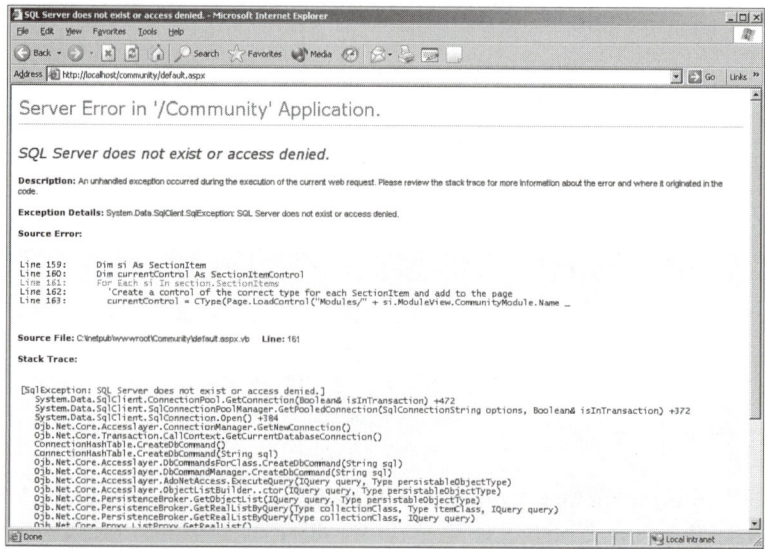

The ASP.NET application is now running, but the database it requires is not set up, so there is a database error. Our next step, therefore, is to get the database installed.

If you have your code in a different location than where I store mine, you will have received a different error message (see Figure 1.3).

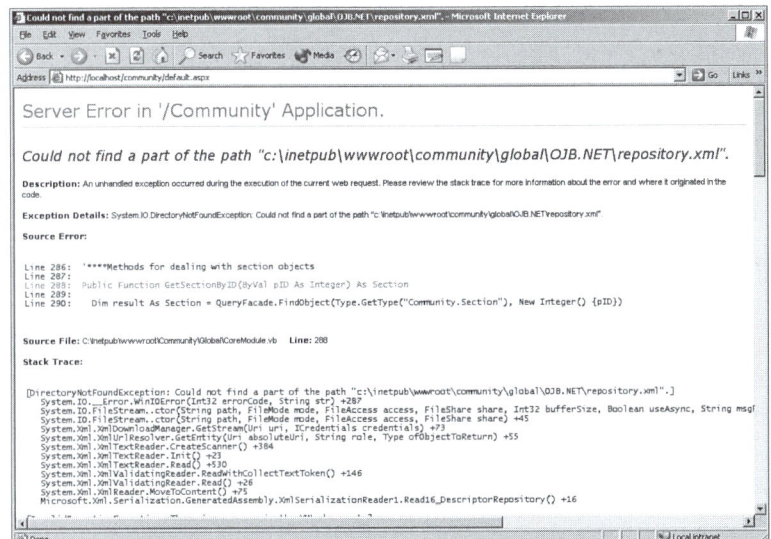

FIGURE 1.3
Could not find repository error.

We will solve this error along with the database error in the next section.

Setting Up the Database

The online community application relies on a database to store the information that its members add. This database is stored by SQL Server 2000 or MSDE.

In the `Starting_Point` folder, you will find a SQL script that you can use to set up the database tables. The script also adds some preliminary data that is required by the application along with some demo data so that you can see the application working in the next chapter.

If you browse to `http://localhost/community` again, you will find that you still get an error. The database is now installed, but the application still cannot find it because the application needs to be configured to access the database. That is our next move.

Checking the Application Configuration

In Visual Studio .NET, open the `repository.xml` file from the `Community/Global/Ojb.Net` folder. This is the configuration file for the persistence service that the application uses to interface with the database. (We will discuss the persistence service later in this book.)

Look for the line

```
ConnectionString="server=[your computer name];uid=community;
↪pwd=community;database=Community"
```

Replace [your computer name] with the name of your computer. (This can be found by right-clicking My Computer and selecting Properties > Computer Name.)

Check that the database setting is the same as the database name you selected and that the user ID and password match the database user who is set up to have access to the database.

Finally, make some changes to the main configuration file for the application. Open `Community/Web.config` and find the following two settings:

```
<add key="FileSystemRoot" value="c:\inetpub\wwwroot\community" />

<add key="RepositoryFilePath"
 value="c:/inetpub/wwwroot/community/global/OJB.NET/repository.xml" />
```

Ensure that these two paths both point to the place where you installed the code for the application.

The first setting is used by the application to find its data files. There are "automatic" ways to find the application path in code, but some hosting services can cause problems for them. It is therefore recommended that you use a configuration setting instead.

The second setting is used by the persistence service to find its repository file (the file to which we just made a change).

While we are editing the `Web.config` file, you should change the setting

```
<add key="SmtpServer" value="smtp.easynet.co.uk" />
```

so that it contains the correct address of your outgoing SMTP mail server. (You can find this by checking the settings of your email software.) The application will use this server when it needs to send email.

Copying the WebControl Client Script Files

The online community application makes use of one of the additional WebControls that Microsoft has made available for ASP.NET to provide a responsive tab strip on the Member Settings page. To work properly, the tab strip requires some client-side files to be installed on the Web server. (They are automatically downloaded to the client when required.)

Copy the `webctrl_client` folder from the `Starting_Point` folder on the CD-ROM to your `InetPub/wwwroot` folder.

Testing the Application

Finally, browsing to `http://localhost/community` should work! You should see the home page of the online community site. If you do see this, you are ready to proceed to Chapter 2 and explore the application.

If you see another error message, there is clearly a little more work required. Work back through the preceding steps and check that you have followed each of them. If you still have an error, try visiting the forum for this book and posting your problem—I check the forum daily (when I can) in order to give quick answers to problems.

Troubleshooting

Here are some errors that you might encounter, along with instructions for solving them.

Access Is Denied `Microsoft.Web.UI.WebControls`

We're not entirely sure why this error occurs, but don't worry—if you do encounter it, it is easy to fix.

The solution to this error is to stop and restart the indexing service on your machine.

Directory Not Found Exception for `C:\Inetpub\wwwroot\community\global\OJB.NET\repository.xml`

This error occurs if the application cannot find the configuration file that tells the persistence service how to link the objects that it stores to data in the database. (We will be looking at this in Chapter 3.)

If you see this error, you need to check that the Repository Path setting in the `Community/Web.config` file points to the correct path.

SQL Server Does Not Exist or Access Denied

This error occurs when the application cannot access SQL Server or MSDE.

Check the connection string setting in `community/Global/Ojb.Net/repository.xml` to ensure it is valid for your installation of SQL Server or MSDE.

Could Not Load Type

This error means that ASP.NET is trying to load a class that does not exist. It usually occurs because the code-behind class for an .aspx page or .ascx control has not been compiled.

The solution to this error is to ensure that the source code has been compiled.

Moving On

After working through this chapter, you should have a working installation of the online community application.

In the next chapter, we will take a tour of the application to see what it does.

The Online Community Application 2

In this chapter, we are going to take a quick tour of the online community application we installed and compiled in Chapter 1, "Getting Started."

We'll be making a lot of changes to this application as we move through the book. We'll add features and improve the ones that are there already. By the time we get to the end of the book, we will have a much more powerful application. You will also be able to customize the online community to your own needs—it doesn't have to look anything like our starting point!

Throughout the book, whenever I mention the *starting-point application*, I will be referring to the online community application as it is right now—before we have made any changes to it. There is also a *final application* included on the CD that contains all the modifications made in the book. The end of the book should not, however, be the end of the changes to the application—by then, you will know enough about how the application works to make many further customizations of your own.

In this chapter we will see

- ▶ How members' information is displayed in modules
- ▶ How global modules show information from all members
- ▶ How information is added to modules
- ▶ How members create, edit, and delete modules and pages
- ▶ How search helps users find information

What Does the Online Community Application Do?

The application we will be playing with in this book is designed to enable its members to stay in contact and share information with people of a like mind.

The sample application is set up as a site about artistic events in and around Birmingham, UK. However, the application is very easily adapted to cater to all sorts of communities, from groups of friends to departments of a corporation.

The online community system uses a number of modules to enable members to post information of different kinds to the community. The starting-point application includes modules for posting news, images, and short *Web log (blog)* entries. It also includes a module for storing and displaying short pieces of text, such as "thoughts of the day" or jokes at random, and a module that enables visitors to the site to send messages to members of the community. We will be adding more modules to the system later, and by the time you have finished working through this book, you should be able to add your own modules, allowing your members to post all kinds of different information.

Let's go ahead and take a look at what the starting-point application looks like. If you followed the instructions in Chapter 1, you will be able to browse to `http://localhost/community` and see the online community home page. You should see something like Figure 2.1.

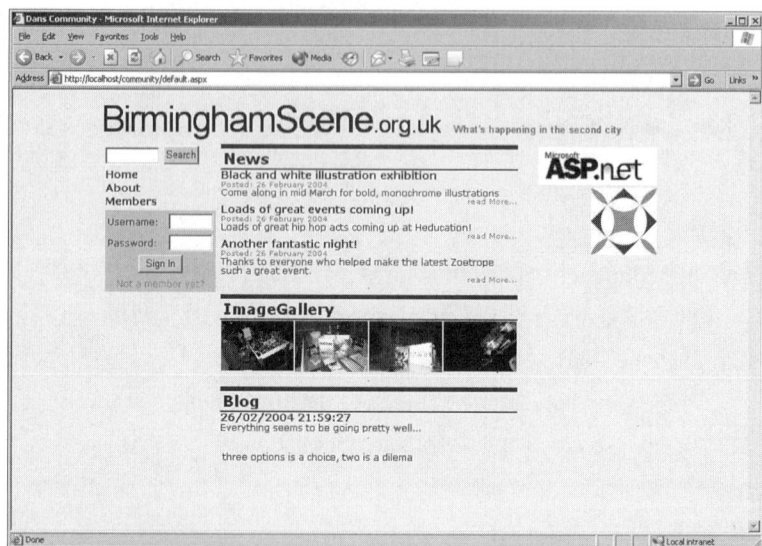

FIGURE 2.1
The home page of the community.

On the home page, you can see some of the modules. These include a set of news items, some image thumbnails, a blog entry, and a random text item. These items on the home page are called *global modules* because they include information from all of the members (well, all members who have chosen for their information to be shared globally, at least). The News module shows the latest news articles posted by members, the ImageGallery module shows thumbnails of the newest four images posted, the Blog module shows the latest blog entry, and the RandomText module shows single pieces of random text chosen from all of those that have been entered.

Global modules are important because they enable members and visitors to the community to see the newest information that has been posted by members without having to browse around the application to each member's own page. In fact, the global modules make the community what it is—without them, the site would really just be a collection of separate sites.

Members

Speaking of members' pages, let's take a look at one. First, we need to click on the Members link in the navigation tool on the left side of the page. That will take us to the Members page, as shown in Figure 2.2.

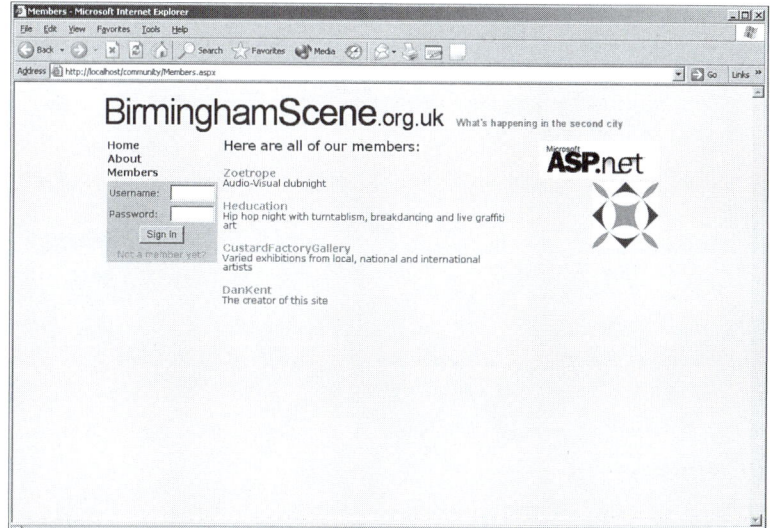

FIGURE 2.2
The Members page.

The Members page is a simple list of all the members of the community (although, as we will see later, some special members are invisible and are not shown on this list).

If you click on one of the members, you will be taken to her own page. Each member on the site has at least one page of her own that she can use for showing information to other members and visitors. A typical member's page is shown in Figure 2.3.

On this page, you can see two of the same modules (RandomText and News) that we saw on the home page, but this time they only display information for a single member. Each member is free to have one or more instance of each of the modules and to display "views" of them across multiple pages. This member has chosen to put views of her News and RandomText modules on her Member page and has put a view of her ImageGallery module on another page called, appropriately enough, Images.

Modules

FIGURE 2.3
A single member's own page.

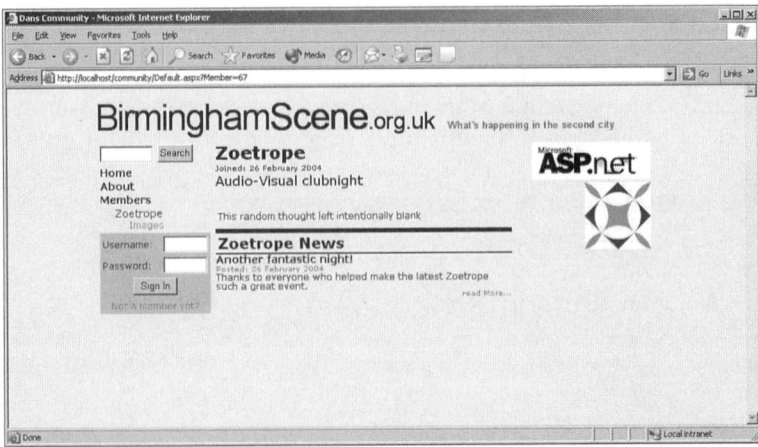

Notice how the navigation tool on the left has adapted to the fact that we are looking at Zoetrope's Member page. Under Members, it now shows that Zoetrope is selected and shows her pages.

Modules

If you click Zoetrope's Images page in the navigation tool, you will see her ImageGallery page, as shown in Figure 2.4.

FIGURE 2.4
Zoetrope's ImageGallery page.

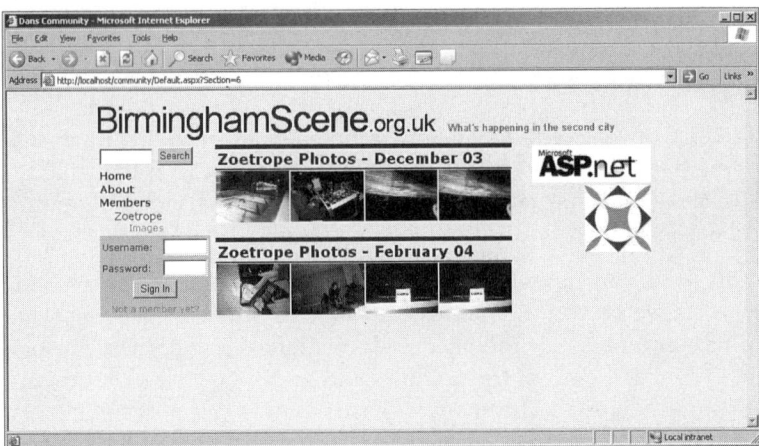

On this page, we can see views of two instances of the ImageGallery module. Zoetrope has created two instances in order to categorize her images. If you click on the heading of either instance or on one of the thumbnails, you will be shown the full gallery for that instance, as shown in Figure 2.5.

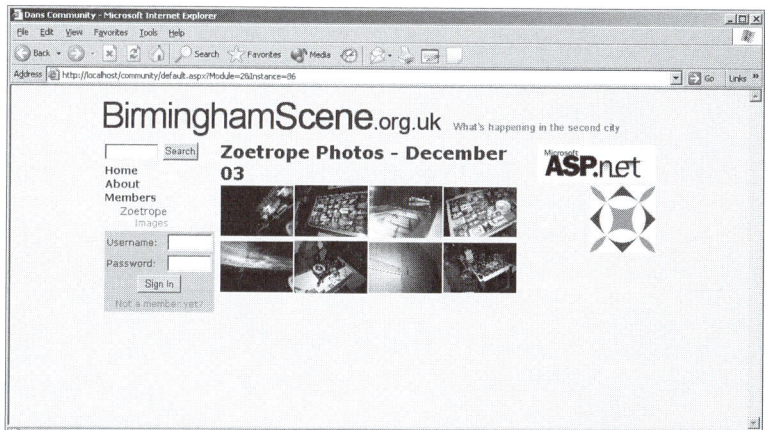

FIGURE 2.5

One of Zoetrope's image galleries.

This page shows all the images for the selected module instance. Clicking on one of the thumbnails will pop up the full image in a new window. Let's navigate back to Zoetrope's Member page and have a look at some other elements. This time, click one of the Read More links on Zoetrope's news items to see an individual news article, as shown in Figure 2.6.

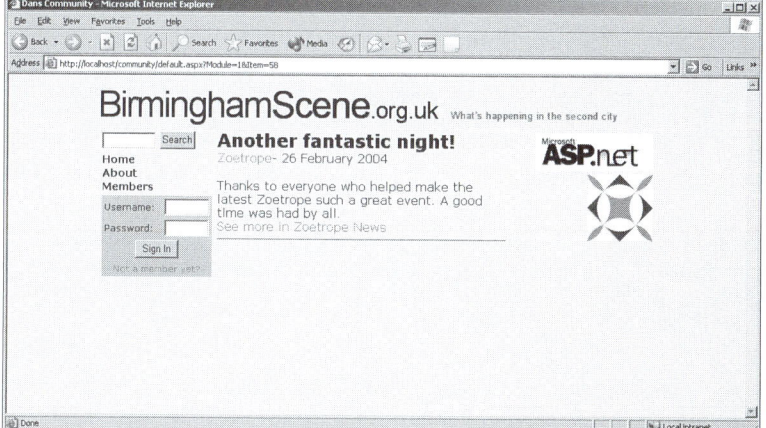

FIGURE 2.6

One of Zoetrope's news items.

Global Module Instances

The page now shows the news item we clicked, plus a link to all of Zoetrope's news. If you click that link, you will be taken to summaries of all of the news Zoetrope has posted in her News module instance (in fact, there is only one at the moment!). On that page, you will see a link to All News. This will take you to the global instance of the News module.

Global Module Instances

Each module has a global instance, which pulls together information from the module instances created by members. In many ways, it is this feature that makes the community application work. Each member can add his own information to his own module instances, but all of the information is aggregated to create the global instance of each module.

The global instance of the News module is shown in Figure 2.7.

FIGURE 2.7

The global News module.

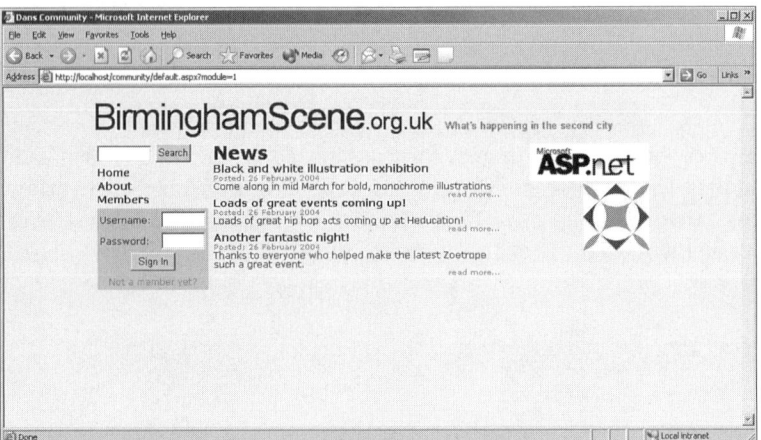

We can now see a list of all of the news items posted in instances of the News module, no matter which member posted them. (In fact, it is possible for members to elect for their modules to not be included in the global module, but no members currently have module instances set up like this.)

This list of news articles could get rather unwieldy if a lot of articles were posted. Imagine how big this page would be after a few hundred news articles were posted; it would take a long time to load and would be difficult to browse. That is definitely something we should improve—we could add a *paging* facility so that users can view the news in manageable batches. Let's take a look at the other global modules. Navigate back to the home page and click the Blog link. You should see something like Figure 2.8.

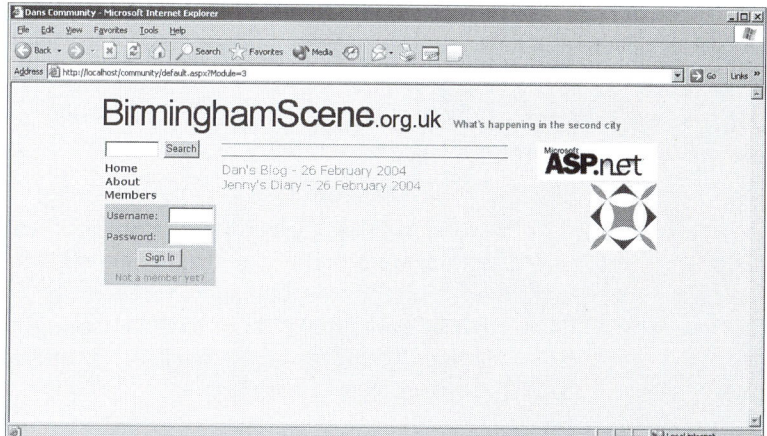

FIGURE 2.8
The global Blog module.

Rather than showing a list of all the individual blog entries that members have made, the global Blog module shows links to the most recently updated blogs in the community. Each module can behave differently, so we can choose the behavior that best suits each module that we build for the community.

The final global module is the ImageGallery. Navigate back to the home page and click the ImageGallery link or one of the thumbnails to the see the global ImageGallery module, as shown in Figure 2.9.

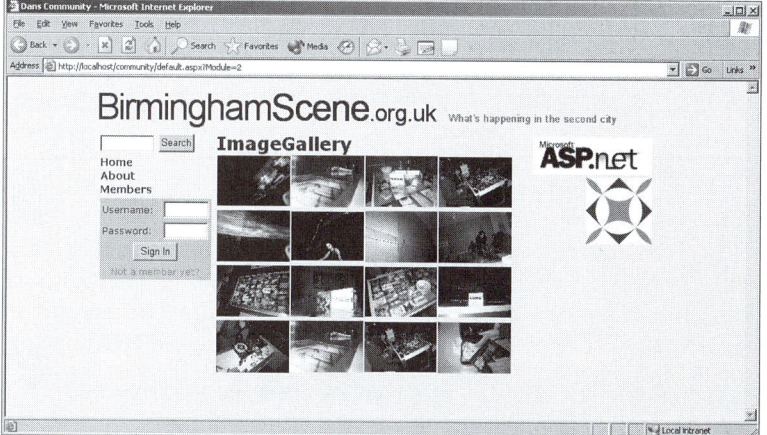

FIGURE 2.9
The global ImageGallery module.

The global ImageGallery module displays all the images in the same way that the global News module displays all the news, regardless of which member it comes from. However, whereas the News module displays the articles sorted by when they were posted, the ImageGallery module does not order the images by date.

Another difference in the global News module is that clicking one of the thumbnails will take us to the ImageGallery module that the thumbnail is taken from, rather than showing a single image.

Like the global News module, the global ImageGallery module could become cumbersome if a lot of images were posted. The problem is actually much worse for the ImageGallery module. The thumbnails are actually the complete images that members have uploaded, scaled down by the browser. Even with a small set of images, a lot of data has to be downloaded in order to view this page. It would be much better if "real" thumbnails were generated from uploaded images.

Adding Information to Module Instances

I'm sure you have been wondering how the members add information to their modules. The key to this lies in the login control underneath the navigation. After a user has logged in, he can add information to his modules, create new modules, and modify those that are already there.

Let's borrow Zoetrope's account (I'm sure she won't mind) to have a look at how this works.

Enter `Zoetrope` for the username and `movingpictures` for the password. (Zoetrope is almost asking for someone to use her account by setting such a weak password.) Click the Sign In button and we will be logged in as Zoetrope.

The login control now changes. Rather than showing the username and password boxes, it now shows Zoetrope's username and some options. Click the Member Page option to navigate to Zoetrope's page, which we have already seen (refer to Figure 2.3).

The Member page looks the same as it did before (aside from the login control). We only see a difference when we look at one of Zoetrope's modules. Navigate to Zoetrope's ImageGallery page and click on one of the ImageGallery modules. We saw one of these modules earlier (refer to Figure 2.5), but it now looks different, as shown in Figure 2.10.

There is now a set of controls that enables Zoetrope (or anyone, such as us, who has access to her login details) to add new images. Each image also has a Delete link.

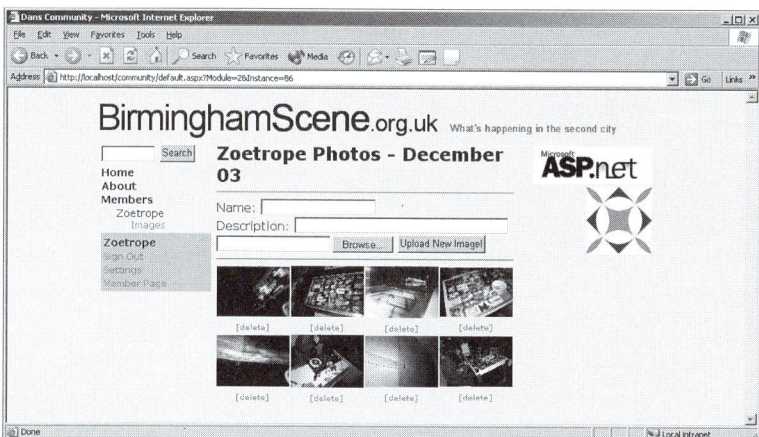

FIGURE 2.10
One of Zoetrope's image galleries as she sees it.

If you browse to Zoetrope's other modules, you will see that the interface she sees when looking at her own modules is different from what other members and visitors see. In each case, options to add and edit the items in appropriate ways are displayed.

Member Settings

So, we have seen how members add and edit information in their module instances; they simply log in and use the options that are presented. But how do members create module instances and pages in the first place, and how do they decide which module is shown on which page?

If you click Zoetrope's Settings link (in the login control), you will be taken to the Member Settings page for Zoetrope. This page has tabs for various kinds of settings. For example, the My Details tab, as shown in Figure 2.11, enables the member to set her password and email address.

This stuff is all pretty basic. Things get interesting on the My Modules and My Pages tabs. The My Modules tab is shown in Figure 2.12.

Here we can see a list of all of Zoetrope's module instances. She has a News module, two ImageGallery modules, and a RandomText module. Zoetrope can add more module instances by selecting a module type from the drop-down list and clicking the Create a New Module button.

Existing module instances can be edited by clicking the Edit button for the relevant module. Doing this will show something like Figure 2.13.

Member Settings

FIGURE 2.11
The My Details tab of the Member Settings page.

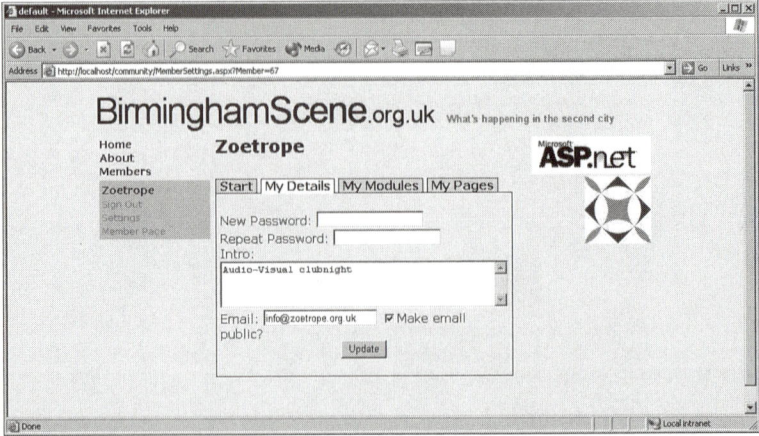

FIGURE 2.12
The My Modules tab of the Member Settings page.

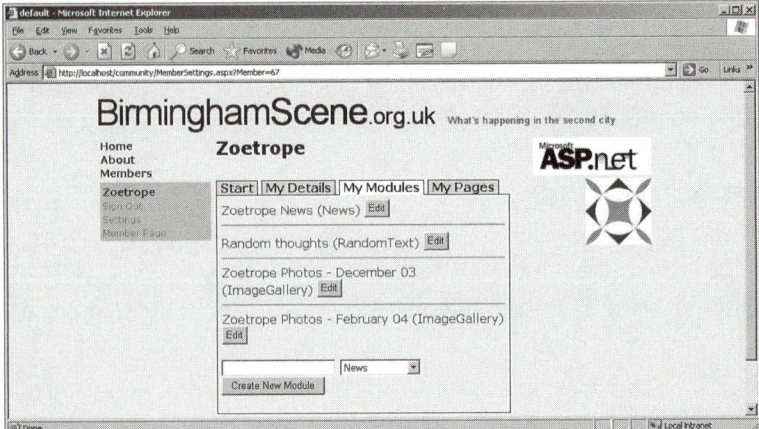

FIGURE 2.13
The My Modules tab with a module instance selected for editing.

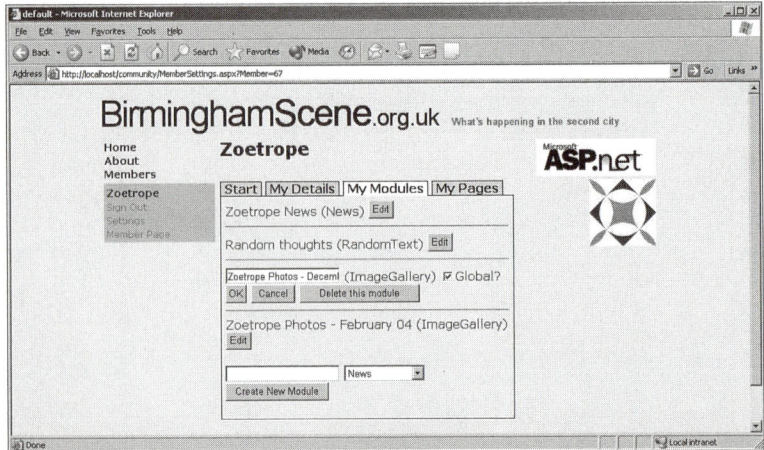

The module in the list is now replaced by a set of controls that enable us to rename the module, delete it, or set whether it should be included in the global version of the module.

So, members use the My Modules tab to create instances of the available modules. After they have their modules, they need to specify how they are displayed in the community. This is done with the My Pages tab, which is shown in Figure 2.14.

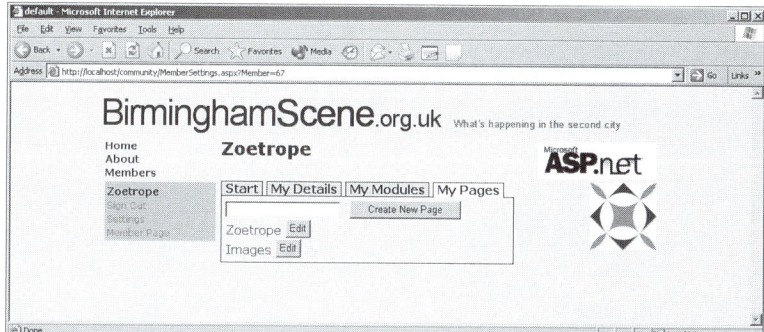

FIGURE 2.14

The My Pages tab of the Member Settings page.

This tab shows a list of the pages that the member has created, along with an option to create a new page and buttons for editing existing pages. Clicking one of the Edit buttons replaces the page name with controls for editing the page, as shown in Figure 2.15.

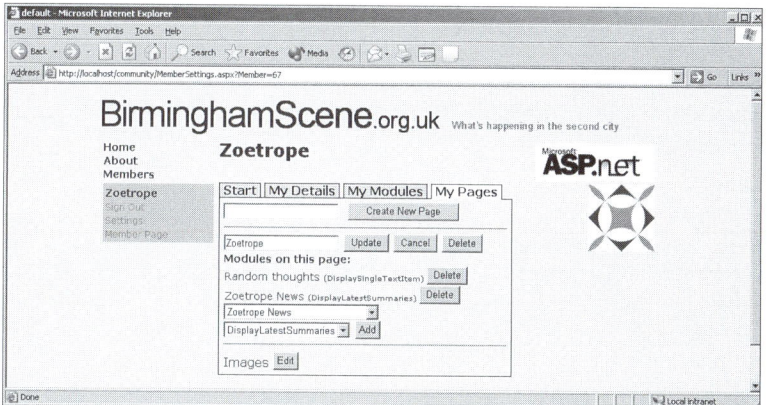

FIGURE 2.15

The My Pages tab with a page selected for editing.

The member is now given an option to rename the page, along with a list of modules that are included on that page. Each module instance can be included on several pages or several times on the same page if the member wishes. When a page is selected for editing, the member can add new views of modules to the page by selecting the module instance and the view type from the drop-down lists at the bottom of the page. Each module can provide a number of different views, meaning that members can decide how they want their information to be displayed.

Before we move on, we should look at the one module that we have not seen so far. Select the Members link in the navigation tool and select DanKent. You should now see my Member page, as shown in Figure 2.16.

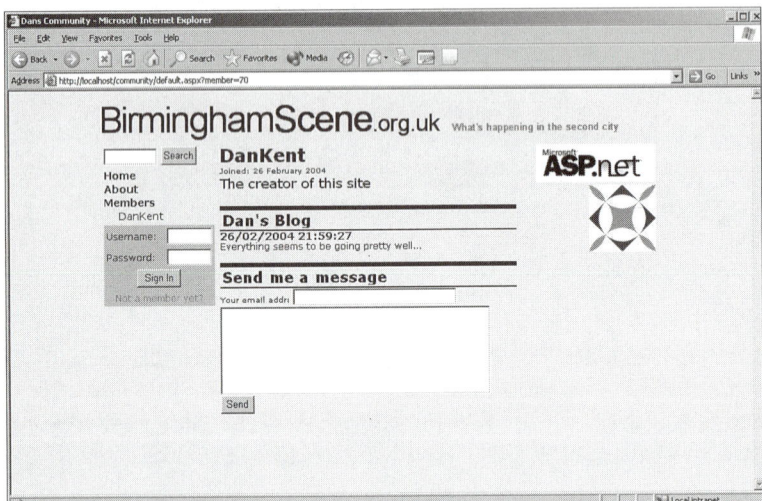

FIGURE 2.16
The Member page of DanKent.

Here you can see the final module—the Send Message module. This module provides a way for visitors to the site to send an email message to a member of the site, without the member having to publish his email address in public.

Search

Another feature of the online community application is Search. The sample community has only a few members with a few module instances between them, so browsing the information on the site is not very difficult. When a community has more members, however, Search becomes very important.

You can try out the Search system by browsing back to the home page and entering something in the Search Terms box at the top left of the page. Because there is not much data in the community at present, try something really general, such as "the." You should see a Search Results page like that shown in Figure 2.17.

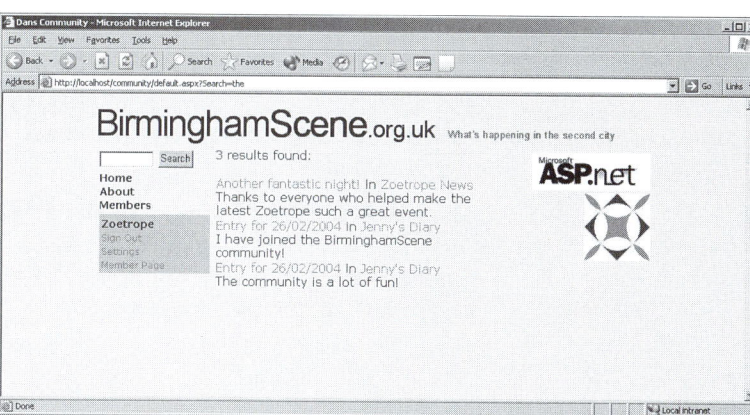

FIGURE 2.17
Search results.

Note that the search results include results from more than one module (in this case, the News and Blog modules). The search system collects results from the different modules and combines them into a single Results page.

There is one element of the online community that we have not seen—the administration system. In fact, there is not much of an administration system in the online community application as it stands. Like most Web applications, the administration system has been the last thing to be developed. We will be adding more features to the administration system in later chapters, but for now, all we can do with it is specify what modules should be shown on the home page.

If you are logged in as a member, sign out. Now sign in as the member admin. (The password is also *admin*—an even worse password than Zoetrope chose!) Then click the new Admin link that is shown in the login control.

You should see a very simple menu. (It has only one option.) Click Admin Global Sections and you should see a page that works very much like the My Pages tab of the Member Settings page that we looked at earlier. We can add new global sections, delete existing global sections (aside from the home page section), and set which global module views should be displayed on each global section.

Moving On

We have now seen what the online community application does. We have seen that it enables its members to add information to module instances and gathers this information together into global modules that show all members' information.

We have also seen that each member can select her own modules from those that are available and that she can create multiple pages, which she can use for displaying views of her modules.

Now that we have seen the application at work, it is time to start digging into the code to see how it works. In Chapter 3, "Exploring the Code," we will look at the most important bits of code in the application, along with some that are not particularly crucial, but are interesting for one reason or another.

Exploring the Code 3

In this chapter, we are going to pick apart the code of the online community application, seeing how it works. We will not be covering every last code file in this chapter (it would be a very long chapter indeed if we did). However, we will cover all the fundamentals here and will return to the other code in later chapters.

We will look at

- Terminology that is used to refer to parts of the application
- The overall structure of the application and its code
- How the application uses a persistence service to make data access simpler and more efficient
- The basic code that executes with each page request to the application
- How the application provides a flexible search system
- An overview of how security is handled

Terminology

Before we get started with the code, it is worth defining some terms that are used throughout the code and this book:

- **User**—Any human who is viewing the online community.
- **Member**—A user who is logged in as a member of the community.
- **Visitor**—A user who is not logged in.
- **Administrator**—A member who has permission to access administration options.
- **Module**—A collection of controls and database tables that provides a feature of the site. The modules in the starting-point application are Blog, ImageGallery, and News. Modules are key features of the application. It is the modular approach that makes the application easy to extend. Using modules also enables us to offer members choices about what features they use.
- **Module instance**—A particular example of a module, created by a member. Each member can have many module instances, even more than one of the same module. For example, I might have an ImageGallery and a News module, whereas you might have two ImageGalleries. All the instances of a particular module will share the same basic functionality but will have their own data.

- **Global instance**—A module that is being displayed without a specific instance. Data is collected from all instances of that module that are marked for inclusion in the global module. The global instance of each module enables the community application to collate the information that all the members have added. Therefore, the information from my News module might be combined with all the other news that members have added to create a set of headlines for the home page.

- **Module view**—A way of displaying a module. For example, the News module includes views for Latest Headlines and Latest Summaries, and the ImageGallery includes views for Latest Images and Random Images. Module views enable us to offer options to members about how their information is displayed.

- **Section**—An area of the community, created by a member. (The term *section*, rather than *page*, was used to avoid confusion with ASP.NET pages.) Each member can have a number of sections. Each section can contain a number of section items.

- **Section item**—A combination of a module instance and a module view, placed in a section. The module instance defines which data to display, whereas the module view defines how it should be displayed. A section item without a module instance will display the global instance of the module the view is for.

Don't worry if you are not totally clear about all of these terms right now; we will look at each of these things in more detail later in this chapter.

Why Was the Online Community Built the Way It Was?

Every application can be built in a lot of different ways; there are always a lot of options that lead to different advantages and disadvantages. The online community application covered in this book was built with the following aims in mind:

- Ease and flexibility of changing the look and feel
- Ease and flexibility of adding new modules and features
- Allowing members to decide how their content is displayed

As we move through this book, we will refer back to these aims, showing where the design decisions that resulted from the aims led to the code being written in a particular way.

The Overall Logical Structure

The structure of the application is shown in Figure 3.1.

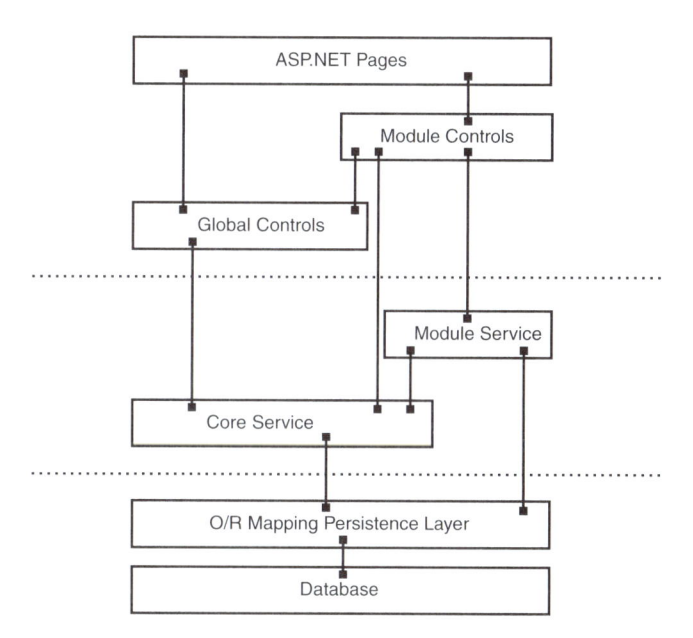

FIGURE 3.1

The overall structure of the online community application.

As you can see, the application is constructed in layers. Let's take a look at each of the layers in the application and briefly describe what they do.

ASP.NET Pages

At the top of the tree are the ASP.NET pages users request when viewing the site. There are actually very few of these; most of the users' requests go to `default.aspx`. Other pages have only been used when a different layout is required than that provided by `default.aspx`, or where it is thought that a different layout might be required in the future.

All the ASP.NET pages provide very little other than a basic layout. They simply act as containers for controls, which do the bulk of the work of displaying the online community.

Controls

Most of the work of actually displaying the community is done by ASP.NET user controls. User controls were used rather than server controls because they make it very easy to make changes to their appearance. (Their HTML code is separated from the code that provides their functionality.) This means that a Web developer who is not quite so good with code can make changes to the site appearance, whereas those with programming skills can concentrate on the features of the site.

Server controls are great for building highly reusable controls, but we want to get our community up quickly and also maintain as much flexibility as possible in how it looks.

There are a few different types of user controls in the online community. Some of the controls are standard user controls, whereas others are specialized to the community application. Where several controls need to provide the same features, base classes have been created. Each control inherits from the base class that defines the features it needs.

Inheritance was used to create sets of controls with common features:

- `ModuleControl`—Base class for all controls that display information from a module.
- `ModuleInstanceControl`—Base class for controls that display a complete module instance.
- `ModuleItemControl`—Base class for controls that display a particular item from a module (for example, a news story).
- `SectionItemControl`—Base class for module views.

The biggest potential causes of confusion here are `ModuleInstanceControl` and `SectionItemControl`. Controls that derive from `ModuleInstanceControl` provide the main display for a module. There will be one of these controls for each module in the application. Controls that derive from `SectionItemControl` are the views of the modules. There may be several of them per module, each selecting different data from the module and displaying it in a different way.

Business Services

The ASP.NET pages and controls get data to display by making requests to business service classes. There is one business service class that provides "core" services that are used by the whole application and one business service class for each module.

Persistent Objects

These objects are not shown in Figure 3.1. They are, however, very important. The persistent objects are used to carry information between the layers of the application. For example, when information about a member is required by a page or control, a `Member` persistent object is requested from the core business service class. The core business service class, in turn, requests the `Member` object from the persistence service, which handles data access. This process is shown in Figure 3.2.

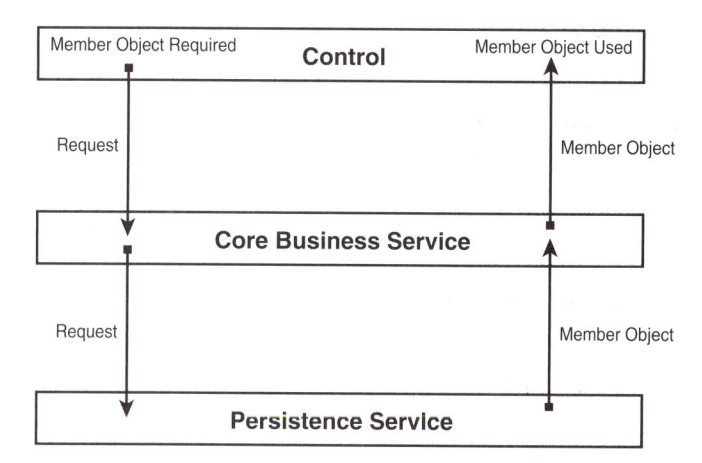

FIGURE 3.2
Requesting and passing a `Member` persistent object between layers.

The persistent objects have relationships between them, so after we have requested one object, we can access other related objects without having to make requests to other layers of the application. So, for example, after we have a `Member` object in the presentation layer, we can access all of the module instances created by that member directly. Doing this might involve further requests to the database to get the data we need, but this is handled transparently by the persistence service.

An important point to note is that the presentation layer pages and controls *never* directly make changes to persistent objects—they always make requests to the business service layer for changes to be made. We will discuss why this is important in the next section.

The core persistent objects and the relationships between them are shown in Figure 3.3.

Each persistent object class represents a particular entity within the online community application. You might want to refer to the "Terminology" section at the beginning of this chapter for explanations of the concepts that the persistent objects represent.

FIGURE 3.3

Relationships between the persistent objects.

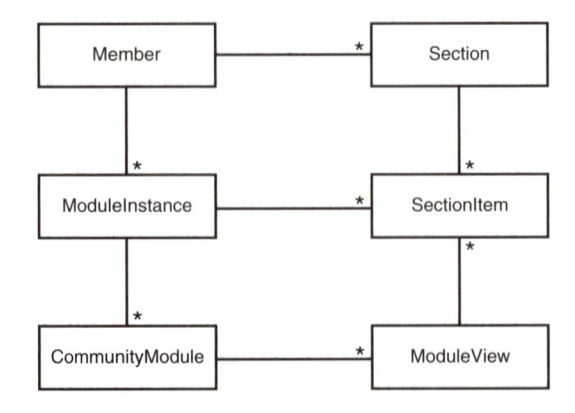

The stars on Figure 3.3 indicate the type of relationship that is involved. All of the relationships are one-to-many, with the stars indicating the "many" end of the relationship. For example, each member can have many sections. Each `ModuleInstance` object can be connected to many `SectionItem` objects, but each `SectionItem` object only links to a single `ModuleInstance`.

We will now look at each of the persistent objects and the properties they provide.

In addition to the properties shown for each persistent object, they each have a *primary key*. A primary key is a value that is unique for each instance of a particular persistent object. If you are familiar with relational databases, you know that primary keys are used to uniquely identify entities within the data. In fact, a primary key column is used in each database table that stores the data for a persistent object. The same primary key value is stored in the persistent objects themselves.

Member

The `Member` object holds data for a single member of the community. It has the following properties:

- **Username (String)**—The name the member uses to identify himself.

- **Password (Write-only String)**—The member's password. This is set to write-only because we don't intend for any code to have access to the member's password after it is set.

- **IntroText (String)**—Some text that is displayed on the member's personal page and also in the list of members.

- ▶ `DateJoined (DateTime)`—The date the member registered with the community.
- ▶ `LastAccess (DateTime)`—The last date and time the member used the community application.
- ▶ `Email (String)`—The member's email address.
- ▶ `PublicEmail (Boolean)`—A value that determines whether to display the member's email address to other users of the community.
- ▶ `MemberPageSection (Section)`—A `Section` object for the section that should be displayed when users view the member's personal page.
- ▶ `Sections (IList)`—A collection of `Section` objects for all the sections the member has created. This includes the section that is referred to by `MemberPageSection`.
- ▶ `NonMemberPageSections (IList)`—A collection containing all the member's sections except for her `MemberPageSection`.
- ▶ `ModuleInstances (IList)`—A collection containing all the module instances the member has created.

Note that some of the properties have type `IList`. This means they guarantee that they will return an object of a class that implements the `IList interface`, but they will not guarantee exactly which collection class that will be. Code that uses these properties must only use the features required by `IList` when using these objects.

Fortunately, the code can assume that the `IList` objects contain objects of a particular type (because the persistence service will fill the collections with appropriate objects), and `IList` provides the means to access those objects. In particular, `IList` enables us to use the `For Each` statement to loop through all of the objects in the collection.

CommunityModule

This persistent object holds information about modules that are used to add features to the application. Note that the persistent object does not provide the features itself—it simply holds information about the module the core community code needs to use it.

`ModuleView`

It has the following properties:

- ▶ `Name (String)`—The name of the module. The name is used as an identifier so that the code for a module can access its persistent object. It is also used as the name of the folder in which the module's code is kept.
- ▶ `Description (String)`—A text description of the module. It's not currently used for anything, but it's useful for documenting the modules.
- ▶ `AllowGlobal (Boolean)`—Specifies whether a global instance should be allowed for the module.
- ▶ `AllowMember (Boolean)`—Specifies whether members should be allowed to create instances of the module.
- ▶ `ModuleViews (IList)`—A collection of `ModuleView` objects for all of the views provided by the module.
- ▶ `ModuleInstances (IList)`—A collection of `ModuleInstance` objects for all of the instances that exist for this module.
- ▶ `ServiceClassName (String)`—The name of a class that inherits from `ModuleBase` that contains the business service functionality for the module. This class should be defined in a source code file in the `Module` folder.

It is worth noting that all of the properties of `CommunityModule` are read-only. When new modules are added to the system, their details are added directly to the database by an administrator, so there is no need to allow write access to the properties in code.

`ModuleView`

Each `ModuleView` object contains information about a view provided by a particular module. This system enables us to define a number of different ways in which the data held by module instances can be displayed to users.

As with `CommunityModule`, the `ModuleView` persistence object does not contain the implementation of the view it represents but rather holds the information the application needs to access the implementation.

`ModuleView` objects have the following properties:

- **`Name (String)`**—The name of the view.
- **`Description (String)`**—A text description of the view.
- **`AllowMember (Boolean)`**—Defines whether members are allowed to create views of this type. (We might want to reserve some views for use with global module instances.)
- **`ControlName (String)`**—The name of the ASP.NET user control that implements the view. When the view is displayed, this control will be found in the `Views` subfolder of the `Module` folder and will be loaded into the page.
- **`CommunityModule (CommunityModule)`**—The persistent object for the module to which this view belongs.
- **`SectionItems (IList)`**—A collection of all the `SectionItem` objects that use this view.

Like those of `CommunityModule`, the properties of `ModuleView` are all read-only.

`ModuleInstance`

This persistent object represents a particular instance of a module that has been created by a member. It has the following properties:

- **`Name (String)`**—The name the member has given the module instance.
- **`CommunityModule (CommunityModule)`**—The module in which the instance is an example.
- **`Member (Member)`**—The member who created the instance.
- **`SectionItems (IList)`**—A collection of all the section items that are based on this module instance.
- **`ShowInGlobal (Boolean)`**—Enables the member to define whether the data from this module instance should be included in the global instance of the module and in the community-wide search system.
- **`LastUpdated (DateTime)`**—The last time that any data was changed in the module instance.

SectionItem

The section items bring together module instances, sections, and module views to define which module instances should be displayed where, and how they should be displayed.

They have the following properties:

- `Section (Section)`—The section to which the section item belongs.
- `ModuleInstance (ModuleInstance)`—The module instance the section item should display. This property is set to `nothing` if the section item should display the global instance of a module.
- `ModuleView (ModuleView)`—The view that should be used to display the module instance.
- `IsGlobal (Boolean)`—Returns `true` if there is no `ModuleInstance` and thus the section item should display the global instance of the module to which its view belongs.

Section

`Section` objects are created by members to group together their information. Each section can contain a number of section items, each displaying different module instances.

`Section` objects have the following properties:

- `Member (Member)`—The member who created the section.
- `Name (String)`—The name the member has given to the section. This will be used in the navigation.
- `Description (String)`—A description of the section. (This is not currently used.)
- `LastUpdated (DateTime)`—The last time any of the module instances referred to by section items in the section were updated.
- `SectionItems (IList)`—A collection containing the section items in the section.
- `IsGlobal (Boolean)`—Returns `true` if there is no member defined for the section. Global sections are used for community-wide content (especially global module instances).

There are some other persistent objects in the application. These are specific to modules. For example, the News module has a `NewsItem` persistent object that represents a single article, whereas the ImageGallery module has a `GalleryImage` persistent object that represents a single image. These persistent objects typically have a one-way relationship with a `ModuleInstance` persistent object; each module-specific object knows to which `ModuleInstance` it belongs.

We will look at the module-specific persistent objects later in this book when we dig into the code for the modules.

The Persistence Service

So, we know that the persistent objects are used to carry information between different parts of the application. The big question is, where do the persistent objects come from?

The data behind the persistent objects is ultimately stored in the database, so when we were designing the application, we needed a way to get the data from the database (and also a way to change the data). We could have chosen to write our own data access code to extract the data from the database and then used it to create the objects. Instead, we opted to use a system that had already been created to do just this job.

The persistence service that was chosen for the application is called *OJB.NET*. OJB.NET is an object/relational mapping service. This means that it handles all the hard work of storing objects in a relational database, enabling us to simply request the objects we want and use them. The really great thing about OJB.NET is that it also handles the work of updating the database when we make changes to persistent objects. We just treat the objects as objects, and the database is updated automatically.

Later in this chapter, we will see just how much the use of a persistence service simplifies our data access. We will also look at how this approach can improve performance in some ways.

There is one very important point to bear in mind, though. Remember how, in the previous section, I said that we always have to use the business service layer rather than the presentation layer to make changes to persistent objects? Well, the reason for this is that any code that changes the persistent objects must be transactional.

By making changes to persistent objects in transactions, we know that our data will not become corrupted by part operations taking place and that multiple, simultaneous page requests will not cause clashes with each other.

TIP
If you want to learn more about OJB.NET directly, you can download the full source code for it from `http://Ojb-Net.Sourceforge.net/`. The code is not for the faint-hearted, but it is well worth looking at because it uses a wide variety of advanced .NET programming techniques.

TERMINOLOGY
Transactional means that sets of operations are carried out as transactions. Each transaction is treated as a single whole rather than a series of separate operations. After a transaction is defined, the whole set of operations will be completed without interference from other operations, or none of them will be completed.

The Persistence Service

All the business service classes are transactional (we will see how this is achieved later), so making changes to persistent objects within their code is safe. The presentation layer code is not transactional, so making changes to persistent objects there is not safe.

When our application makes a call to a business service class, a new transaction is created. No changes are persisted to the database until all of the operations of the business service class are completed. If anything fails, no changes are made to the database. If everything succeeds, OJB.NET makes the required changes.

Another feature of OJB.NET is that it caches persistent objects. This means that after a specific object has been retrieved from the database, it is stored in memory. If that same object is needed again, it can be used from memory rather than retrieving it from the database.

There are limits to the caching that OJB.NET provides. The main limitation is that caching only works when we retrieve a specific object by its primary key. If we use a query to retrieve a set of objects, we have to make a query to the database to determine which objects are selected in the query; queries use SQL so that the database does the work of the query. However, OJB.NET will only extract what it needs to from the database; if the objects exist in the cache, the full data of the object will come from there rather than from the database.

The final persistence service feature we will look at for now is *lazy loading*. This means that when we retrieve a persistent object that contains a collection of other persistent objects, we do not retrieve all of the other objects immediately. Instead, OJB.NET waits until we first access the collection and retrieves them at that stage. The great thing about the way this works is that it is totally transparent to us—we don't have to worry about it at all. We just access our objects and let OJB.NET do the work.

We will be looking in more detail at how we use OJB.NET, but for now it is enough to understand that it enables us to request, use, update, create, and delete persistent objects without having to worry about how it actually communicates with the database.

The Database

The final element of the application is the SQL Server database. This is the store for all the persistent objects the application uses.

In many Web applications, development starts with the database. In our case, the database is simply a store for persistent objects, so its structure was determined by the needs of the persistent objects. There is a table for each class of persistent objects, with a column for each data member. Each table row represents a specific object.

As mentioned earlier, each persistent object class provides a primary key field to enable each object to be uniquely identified. In the database, these fields are implemented as identity columns so that when new persistent objects are created, they will be assigned a unique primary key value.

The Modules

Each module must provide

- A set of module views that can be used either to display data from a single module instance or data taken from all instances that are included in the global instance
- A main module view that is used to display all the data from a particular instance or all data from all instances that are included in the global instance
- A module business service class that derives from `ModuleBase` and provides the required members (see "The `ModuleBase` Class") and any other methods that are required by the presentation code of the module

The module might also need other code to work properly. Some things that might be required are

- A display item control that displays a single item (for example, a news story); this control can be accessed through `default.aspx` but is used only if the module writer chooses to use it
- An edit item page that enables the member to edit an item (or enter the details of a new item)
- One or more persistent object classes to store the data for the module

The `ModuleBase` Class

The business service class for each module derives from the `ModuleBase` class. The core business service class also derives from this class.

The `ModuleBase` Class

`ModuleBase` exists to provide some standard features that all the business service classes require and also to define some features each class is required to provide.

The class provides one property, `ModuleInstance`, which contains the `ModuleInstance` persistent object for the module instance on which the business service class instance has been created to operate. This `ModuleInstance` is provided when the instance of the business service class is created. If no `ModuleInstance` is provided, the instance of the business service class will operate on the global instance (and thus all globally exposed data in the module).

`ModuleBase` also provides the `IsGlobal` property so that code can determine whether an instance of a business service class is currently operating on the global instance. This is typically used by the business service class code itself to decide which data to expose.

`ModuleBase` includes three members without implementations, which must be implemented by each business service class that derives from it:

- **`Name`**—A property that returns the name of the module to which the business service class belongs.

- **`PrepareForDeletion`**—A method that is called when a particular instance of the module is about to be deleted. This method should be used to clean up any remaining data. For example, the ImageGallery module uses this method to delete the image files that belong to it.

- **`GetSearchResults(String)`**—A method that is called to get search results from a module instance. This method is covered later in this chapter in the "Search" section.

How the Code Files Are Organized

We're going to start looking at the code very soon now! Just before we do, it is worth taking a look at the folder structure the application uses. This will help you find the files you want to read in more detail or the code you need to change to get a particular result.

The root `Community` folder should be in your `inetpub/wwwroot` folder (or wherever you installed it, if you chose to put it in a different location). In it, you will find the folder structure shown in Figure 3.4.

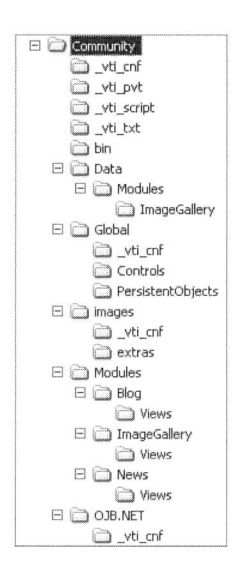

FIGURE 3.4

The online community application folder structure.

```
Community
    _vti_cnf
    _vti_pvt
    _vti_script
    _vti_txt
    bin
    Data
        Modules
            ImageGallery
    Global
        _vti_cnf
        Controls
        PersistentObjects
    images
        _vti_cnf
        extras
    Modules
        Blog
            Views
        ImageGallery
            Views
        News
            Views
    OJB.NET
        _vti_cnf
```

The `Bin` folder is where the compiled code that ASP.NET actually uses to run the site is stored. We don't need to mess with it directly, apart from when we install third-party add-ons to the community that come in compiled form. This folder already contains files for the community itself, the persistence service, and the additional Microsoft WebControls, one of which is used in the application.

The `Data` folder is where we store any data that might be transient. For example, the ImageGallery module uses it to store the image files for uploaded images. The `Data` folder has a subfolder for modules, which in turn has a subfolder for each module that needs to store data.

We could have stored the image data directly in the database as binary columns, but storing them in the `Data` folder makes linking to them much easier. (We can simply point the user's browser at them rather than extract each image from the database every time someone views it.)

The `Global` folder is where we keep the code that is not specific to a particular module. The `Global` folder itself contains the core business service class (`CoreModule.vb`), which is probably the most-used class in the entire application, along with some other classes we will look at later. The `Controls` folder contains ASP.NET controls that are used throughout the application, along with base classes that module-specific controls inherit from. The `PersistentObjects` folder contains the core persistent objects we discussed earlier. Finally, the `Search` subfolder contains two classes that are used for managing search results.

The Images folder contains image files that are used by the system itself (for example, the site logo). It is important to distinguish between the images stored in this folder and the transient images that are stored in the Data folder. This folder is for images that are used by the online community system itself, whereas the Data/Modules/ImageGallery folder contains images uploaded by members.

The Modules folder contains all of the code that implements the modules. Each module has its own subfolder, within which are some classes and controls. Each module also has a Views subfolder to store the controls that implement its views.

The OJB.NET folder contains the XML files that define how the object relational mapper should convert between objects and relational data and vice versa.

Now that we have taken an overview of the application from top to bottom, let's start digging into the code to see how it works.

CODE TOUR:
Default.aspx

It makes sense to start our exploration of the code with the file that is loaded when we first visit the application. This is default.aspx. As we will discover, this file actually handles most of the requests for the application, so understanding what it does is very important.

Start by opening the Community project in VS.NET. Double-click default.aspx in the Solution Explorer to see the design view for the file, as shown in Figure 3.5.

You can immediately see that the page consists of a simple table structure with user controls for standard page elements, such as the header, navigation, and so on. The other thing you have probably noticed is that there is a big gap in the center where the content should be. Clearly, the content is being added by the code.

If you click the HTML view for default.aspx, you will see what you would expect—a simple table structure with a sprinkling of user controls. Find the table cell that forms the content area in the center. It looks like this:

```
<td id="sectionItems" vAlign="top" width="400" runat="server">
</td>
```

CODE TOUR: `Default.aspx`

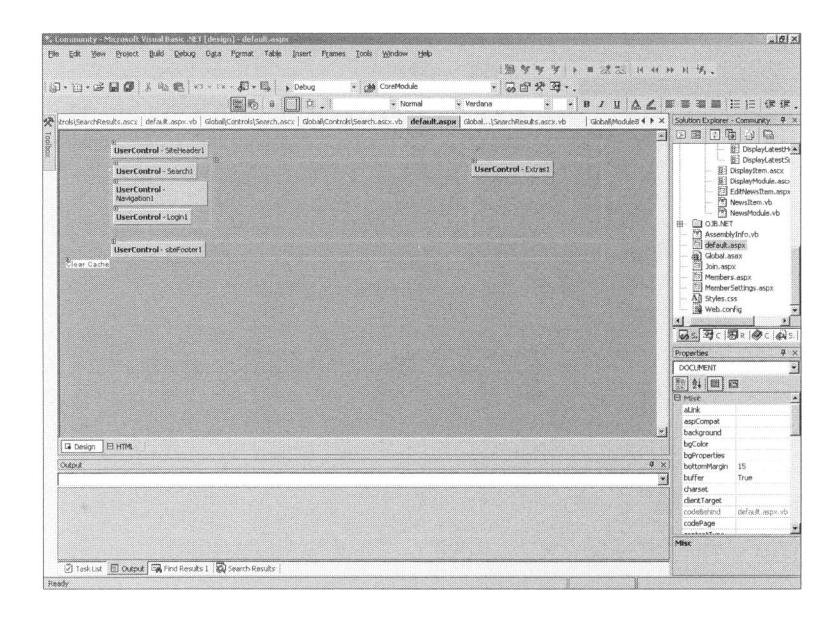

FIGURE 3.5
The design view of `default.aspx`.

The cell is, as expected, empty, but some things to note are that it has an ID (`"sectionItems"`) and it is set as a server-side control (`runat="server"`). This is a sure sign that it is being manipulated from the code-behind file (`default.aspx.vb`).

Let's open `default.aspx.vb` and see what it does.

There are nearly 200 lines of code in `default.aspx.vb`, so an overview of what it contains is shown in Figure 3.6.

`default.aspx.vb` has a pretty simple task—it analyzes the URL query string for the request and loads appropriate controls into the content area of the page. The key to this is the `Page_Load` event handler:

```
Private Sub Page_Load(ByVal sender As System.Object, _
                ByVal e As System.EventArgs) _
        Handles MyBase.Load
```

`Page_Load` does not actually do anything itself—after it has determined what needs to be done, it calls the appropriate method. The code from the methods could have simply been put within `Page_Load`, but it would be very difficult to make out what is going on.

So what is `Page_Load` doing?

How the Code Files Are Organized

CODE TOUR: **Default.aspx**

FIGURE 3.6
Code map: default.aspx.vb.

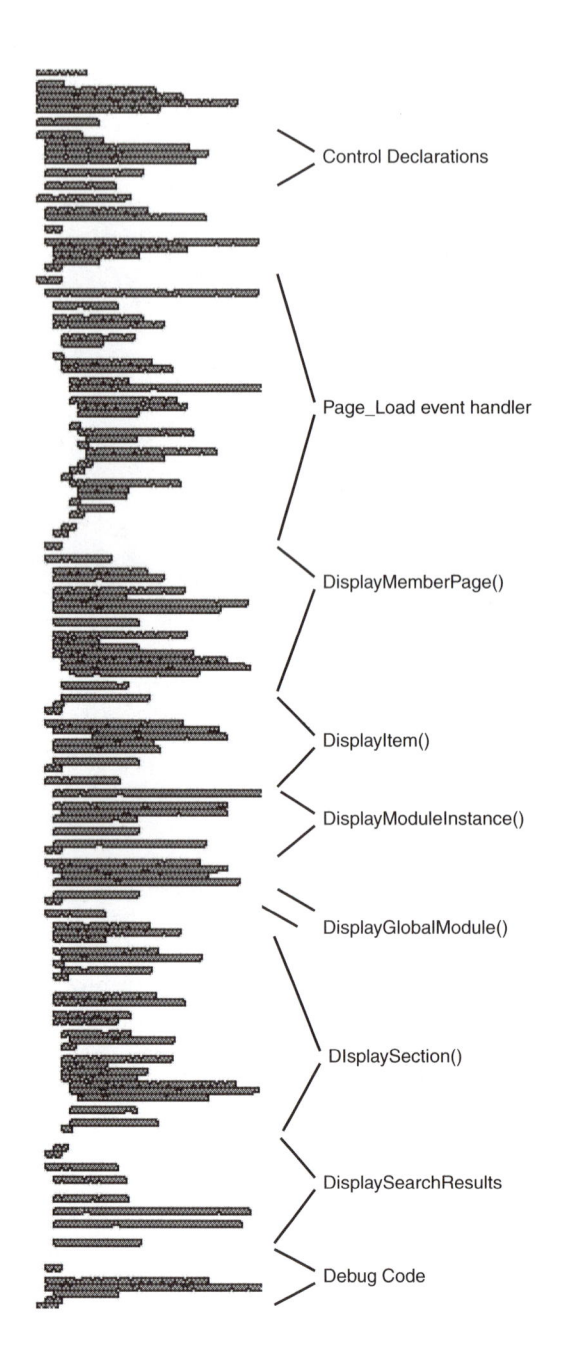

- Control Declarations
- Page_Load event handler
- DisplayMemberPage()
- DisplayItem()
- DisplayModuleInstance()
- DisplayGlobalModule()
- DIsplaySection()
- DisplaySearchResults
- Debug Code

CODE TOUR: `Default.aspx`

First, it creates an instance of the core business service module and stores it in a member of the class (`_coreModule`) so that it can be accessed by any of the other methods.

```
_coreModule = New CoreModule()
```

Next, it checks whether there is a `Member` parameter in the query string. If there is, a member ID has been specified, so the code to display a member's details is called.

```
'check whether a member has been specified
If Not Request.QueryString("Member") Is Nothing Then

    'we need to display a members page
    DisplayMemberPage()
```

> **TIP**
> Throughout the code for the online community application, private members of classes are prefixed with an underscore to identify them clearly.

If there was no member ID, we next check whether a module has been specified:

```
Else
    'check whether a module has been specified
    If Not Request.QueryString("Module") Is Nothing Then
```

If there is a module ID, we make a call to the core module service we created earlier to get a `CommunityModule` persistent object that represents the specified module:

```
'get the module from the ID
Dim moduleToDisplay As CommunityModule =
➥_CoreModule.GetModuleByID(Request.QueryString("Module"))
```

We now want to know whether we are displaying the global module, a particular module instance, or a single module item (such as a particular news report). We first check whether an item has been specified:

```
If Not Request.QueryString("Item") Is Nothing Then
    'an item has been specified so we should display it
    DisplayItem(moduleToDisplay)
```

If there is no item ID, we check for an instance ID:

```
Else
    If Not Request.QueryString("Instance") Is Nothing Then
        DisplayModuleInstance()
```

CODE TOUR: Default.aspx

If there was no item ID or instance ID, we assume that the user wants us to display the global instance:

```
Else
    'no instance specified so we should display the global module
    DisplayGlobalModule(moduleToDisplay)
    End If
End If
```

If there was no module ID, we check whether there are any search terms in the URL:

```
Else
    If Not Request.QueryString("Search") Is Nothing Then
        'display search results
        DisplaySearchResults()
```

Finally, if we have found nothing else, our default case is to display a section:

```
        Else
            DisplaySection()
        End If

    End If
End If

End Sub
```

In the case of the first request to the application, with no URL parameters, it is the `DisplaySection()` method that will be called. Let's follow the execution into that method and see what happens there:

```
Private Sub DisplaySection()
```

The first thing we want to do is determine whether a `sectionID` has been specified at all. If no ID was specified, we need to get the default home page section ID that is stored in the `Web.config`. (If you open `Web.config`, you will find the configuration setting in the `AppSettings` section.)

```
'check whether a sectionID has been specified
'otherwise, set sectionID to the configured homepage section
Dim sectionID As Integer
```

CODE TOUR: `Default.aspx`

```
If Request.QueryString("Section") Is Nothing Then
    sectionID = ConfigurationSettings.AppSettings("HomePageSectionID")
Else
    sectionID = Request.QueryString("Section")
End If
```

Now that we have a section ID, we want to get a `Section` persistent object, which will contain all of the details we need to display the section. This is done with a call to the core module service class:

```
'get the Section object for the selected section
Dim theSection As Section = _CoreModule.GetSectionByID(sectionID)
```

It is possible that this call will not return a section (if the ID does not match any sections), so we need to check whether we got a `Section` object back:

```
'check that we have a section object
If Not theSection Is Nothing Then
```

Next, we check whether the section belongs to a member by checking its `IsGlobal` property. If the section does belong to a member (that is, it is not global), we tell the navigation control the ID of the member in question (so that the navigation control can show the other sections owned by the member):

```
If theSection.IsGlobal = False Then
  Navigation1.MemberID = theSection.Member.PrimaryKey1
End If
```

This is the first real use of a persistent object we have seen. In fact, we are using two persistent objects here. First, we access the `IsGlobal` property of a `Section` object (`theSection`). Then, if it does belong to a member, we access the `Member` property, which is a `Member` object. We then take the value of the `PrimaryKey1` property from the `Member` object to pass to the navigation control. `PrimaryKey1` is the integer identifier for the member.

Each persistent object has a `PrimaryKey1` property, which is unique within that type of persistent object. This property is not provided by default by the persistence service, which uses an array of integers for the primary key to support multifield primary keys. However, because the online community application uses only a single primary key value, all of the persistence objects in it derive from `CommunityPO`, which was created to provide the `PrimaryKey1` property. The property simply accesses the primary key array and returns the first element.

CODE TOUR: Default.aspx

We didn't have to specifically tell the system to retrieve the member from the database—we simply accessed the `Member` property and the persistence service did the rest.

Now, we want to get down to the business of displaying the section on the page. This basically involves displaying each of the section items that are in the section. Therefore, we loop through all the `SectionItem` objects in the `SectionItems` collection of the `Section` object:

```
'loop through the SectionItems of the Section object
Dim si As SectionItem
Dim currentControl As SectionItemControl
For Each si In theSection.SectionItems
```

Again, notice how we do not explicitly request the `SectionItem` objects—we simply access the property, and the persistence service does the rest.

Now comes the complicated part. Each section item will relate to a specific module view that needs to be displayed on the page. The module views are user controls that are held within the `Views` folder of their modules. We can, therefore, access the correct module view control for each section item and load it with a call to `Page.LoadControl`:

```
'Create a control of the correct type for each SectionItem and add to
'the page
currentControl = CType(Page.LoadControl("Modules/" +
↪si.ModuleView.CommunityModule.Name _
    + "/views/" + si.ModuleView.Name + ".ascx"), SectionItemControl)
```

The module view control will not be able to do very much if it does not know which section item it is displaying, so we set its `SectionItem` property to the current section item:

```
currentControl.SectionItem = si
```

Finally, we add the control to the content area of the page. (Remember the table cell that has the ID `"sectionItems"` and was set to `"runat=server"`?)

```
    sectionItems.Controls.Add(currentControl)
Next
```

By looping through all the section items in the section, the code will add them all to the page, in the order in which they are stored in the `SectionItems` collection.

```
    End If
End Sub
```

The other `Display...` methods do very similar jobs to `DisplaySection`, so there seems little point in going through the code for all of them in detail. However, it would be worth taking some time at this point to have a read through the code. It is all commented with explanations of what is going on and, if you get stuck on anything, you can always ask me questions at this book's forum.

In the code we have looked at so far from `default.aspx.vb`, we saw several calls to the core business service class (`CoreModule`). Let's make that class our next stop. It's the foundation on which most of the application rests, so the earlier you understand what it does, the better.

CODE TOUR: CoreModule.vb

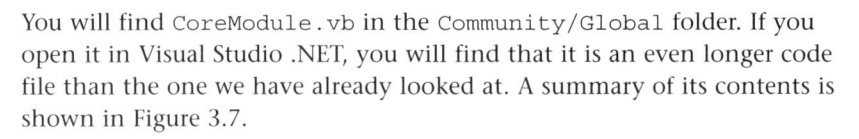

You will find `CoreModule.vb` in the `Community/Global` folder. If you open it in Visual Studio .NET, you will find that it is an even longer code file than the one we have already looked at. A summary of its contents is shown in Figure 3.7.

As you can see from the code map, the class consists mainly of methods for dealing with the various core persistent objects. There are different numbers of methods for different objects, depending on what operations are required for each. `CoreModule` also includes a method for retrieving search results and a property for returning its name ("Core").

Why does `CoreModule` need to provide the name property? Actually, it is not really required for the core module, but we have to include it because it is a requirement of the `ModuleBase` class, which `CoreModule` inherits from. The `Name` property is important for all of the other module classes because it provides the link between the code and the data about the module that is represented by a persistent object and ultimately stored in the database.

In our tour of `default.aspx.vb`, we saw several calls to an instance of `CoreModule`. One of these was to retrieve a particular `Section` object:

```
Dim theSection As Section = _CoreModule.GetSectionByID(sectionID)
```

How the Code Files Are Organized

CODE TOUR: `CoreModule.vb`

FIGURE 3.7
Code map:
`CoreModule.vb`.

- Name property
- GetSearchResults
- Methods for dealing with modules
- Methods for dealing with module instances
- Methods for dealing with members
- Methods for dealing with Section objects
- Methods for dealing with section items

CODE TOUR: **CoreModule.vb**

This is an example of one of the most common uses of `CoreModule`—retrieving a persistent object based on an ID. Let's scroll down to the `GetSectionByID` method and see how it achieves this:

```
Public Function GetSectionByID(ByVal pID As Integer) As Section

  Return QueryFacade.FindObject(Type.GetType("Community.Section"),
  ➥New Integer() {pID})

End Function
```

`QueryFacade` is the class we use to access the persistence service. It only provides static methods, so we do not create an instance of it.

In this case, we are using one of several overloads of the `FindObject` method. This one takes a `Type` object for the type of object we want to find and an array of integers that specifies the primary key of the object we want.

There are several other overloads of `FindObject`. All of them take a `Type` object as their first parameter, but they differ in their second parameter:

▶ **FindObject(Type, String())**—Used for string-based primary keys.

▶ **FindObject(Type, ArrayList)**—Enables us to use an array list, rather than an array, for the primary keys.

▶ **FindObject(Type, Criteria)**—Accepts an OJB.NET `Criteria` object that specifies how to select an object. We will be looking more at `Criteria` objects later in this chapter.

▶ **FindObject(Type, String)**—Accepts a SQL query, which should be used to select the object. We will use this later in the book.

Therefore, we specify the type we want (using the `Type.GetType` method to get a `Type` object for the class we want) and the primary key. The persistence service then retrieves the object so that we can return it. If the object was in the persistence service cache, no database access will be required to do this. If it is not in the cache, the persistence service will query the database to get the data for the object.

Let's now look at what we do when we want to get several objects from the persistence service. Scroll down to the `GetGlobalSections` method, which we use for getting all of the sections that are not owned by a

CODE TOUR: `CoreModule.vb`

member and are not the home page. (We use this in the navigation control.)

```
Public Function GetGlobalSections() As IList
  Dim crit As Criteria = New Criteria

  crit.AddEqualTo("_MemberID", 0)
  crit.AddNotEqualTo("_primaryKey", _
            ConfigurationSettings.AppSettings("HomePageSectionID"))

  Return QueryFacade.Find(SectionType, crit)

End Function
```

This is somewhat more complicated than the `GetSectionByID` method. Overall, what is happening is that we create a `Criteria` object to specify how we want to select objects and then we call `QueryFacade.Find` to run the query.

Let's step through line by line and look at what is being done.

First, we create a new `Criteria` object.

Next, we add two subcriteria to the `Criteria`. `Criteria` objects are like a tree composed of other `Criteria` objects. In this case, our main `Criteria` has two branches—one that specifies that the `_MemberID` of the selected objects must be 0 (sections that have no member have their `_MemberID` field set to 0) and one that specifies that selected objects must not have a primary key equal to the home page ID (which we retrieve from the configuration file).

Note that we specify the field names by the names of the private fields from the persistent object classes. (Open `Global/CoreObjects/Section.vb` if you want to see the private fields the `Section` persistent object has.) Remember that in this application, all private fields are prefixed by an underscore.

Our code does not have any information about the structure of the database (table names, column names, and so forth) in it—the persistence service repository, which we will be looking at later in this chapter, holds the information required to link persistent object classes with database tables.

After we have the `Criteria` object set up how we want it, we make a call to `QueryFacade.Find(Type, Criteria)`.

CODE TOUR: **CoreModule.vb**

The `Find` method is very similar to the `FindObject` method, except that it returns a list of objects rather than a single object.

There are only two overloads of `FindObject`—the one we are using here that takes a `Criteria` object as its second parameter and an overload that takes a SQL query string as its second parameter. It does not make sense to try to find groups of objects by a primary key.

We have seen how we find persistent objects that are stored by the persistence service, but how do they get there in the first place?

Scroll down to the `CreateSection` method:

```
Public Function CreateSection(ByRef pMember As Member, _
                    ByVal pName As String, _
                    ByVal pDescription As String) _
            As Section
  Return New Section(pMember, pName, pDescription)
End Function
```

This might look ridiculously simple considering that this is how new `Section` objects are persisted to the database. All we do is create a new `Section` object and return it! How does it get to the database?

This is another case of the persistence service doing a lot of work behind the scenes for us. As mentioned earlier, all calls to `CoreModule` methods take place in a transaction. When the end of the transaction is reached, the persistence service writes changes made to persistent objects to the database.

Therefore, when the `CreateSection` method completes and the `Section` object is returned, the transaction completes and the persistence service writes the new `Section` object to the database, using the same mapping as is used to retrieve data to link class fields to database columns.

Next, let's look at the method we use for making changes to an existing section:

```
Public Function UpdateSection(ByVal pID As Integer, _
                    ByVal pName As String, _
                    ByVal pDescription As String)
  Dim section As Section = GetSectionByID(pID)

  section.Name = pName
  section.Description = pDescription

End Function
```

CODE TOUR: `CoreModule.vb`

We first use the `GetSectionByID` method to get the section we want to update.

Then, we set the properties we want to change.

That's it. Again, the persistence service does the work for us. When the transaction completes, the changes to the `Section` object we have altered are persisted to the database.

The final kind of operation is the deletion of objects. Again, this is made very simple by the persistence service:

```
Public Function DeleteSection(ByVal pSection As Section)
  pSection.Delete()
End Function
```

All we have to do is call the `Delete` method of the persistent object to mark the object for deletion.

At this stage, it would be a good idea to browse through `CoreModule.vb` and take a look at the various methods it provides. None of them are very complicated, and they all have comments that explain what they do. They are used throughout the application, so it is very useful to have an idea of their functions.

Let's now take a look at the `Section` class itself to see what features it has that enable the persistence service to do its job.

Open `Global/CoreObjects/Section.vb` and take a look at the code.

The first thing to notice is that the class derives from the `CommunityPO` class. We use the `CommunityPO` class as a base for all of our persistent objects so that we can add extra facilities to what the persistence service provides in its standard base classes.

```
Imports Ojb.Net.facade.Persist


Public Class Section
  Inherits CommunityPO
```

Then, we have declarations of the private fields of the class:

```
Private _MemberID As Integer
Private _Name As String
Private _Description As String

Private _Member As Member = Nothing
Private _SectionItems As IList = Nothing
```

CODE TOUR: `CoreModule.vb`

Notice that there are two fields related to the member that owns the section—`MemberID`, which is an integer, and `_Member`, which is a `Member` object. The persistence service will automatically populate the `_Member` field with the correct `Member` object.

Next, there is a special constructor, which is called the reconstructor:

```
Public Sub New(ByVal ID As Integer, _
            ByVal pMemberID As Integer, _
            ByVal pName As String, _
            ByVal pDescription As String)

    MyBase.New(ID)

    _MemberID = pMemberID
    _Name = pName
    _Description = pDescription

End Sub
```

We should not use this constructor to create new instances of `Section`—it exists for the use of the persistence service only. The key feature here is the call to `MyBase.New(Integer)`. It is this call that ensures that the persistent object is retrieved from the persistence service rather than created as a new `Section`.

Notice that we do not populate the `_Member` field in this reconstructor—the persistence service will do that for us.

We also do not need to populate the `_SectionItems` property—the persistence service will retrieve the correct `SectionItem` objects when they are needed.

After the reconstructor comes the standard constructor:

```
Public Sub New(ByVal pMember As Member, _
            ByVal pName As String, _
            ByVal pDescription As String)

    _Member = pMember
    _Name = pName
    _Description = pDescription

    _SectionItems = New ArrayList

End Sub
```

This time, we do not make a call to the constructor of the base class and we populate the `_Member` field rather than the `_MemberID` field—the persistence service will populate the `_MemberID` field for us.

In this instance, we have to initialize the `_SectionItems` field to an empty `ArrayList`.

Next up is a `ReadOnly` property to provide code that uses the `Section` object with access to the member that owns the section:

```
Public ReadOnly Property Member() As Member
  Get
    Return _Member
  End Get
End Property
```

The `SectionItems` property, which is also read-only, is very similar.

The code for read/write properties is slightly different, though. Here is the property that enables us to get or set the name of the section:

```
<Mutator()> _
Public Property Name() As String
  Get
    Return _Name
  End Get
  Set(ByVal Value As String)
    _Name = Value
  End Set
End Property
```

This property (and all other properties and methods that make changes to the persistent object's data) are decorated with the `Mutator` attribute. It is this attribute that lets the persistence service know when it needs to update the object to the database. If we don't include it, changes will not be persisted at the end of the transaction.

Therefore, each persistent object is a class that represents a particular aspect of the application data that includes a reconstructor, a constructor, and mutator attributes on properties and methods that cause changes to the data of the object.

Before we took a diversion to look at the persistent object code, we were following the code that loads the section items for a particular section and draws them onto the page.

CODE TOUR: `DisplayLatestHeadlines.ascx`

The process we have seen is as follows:

1. `default.aspx` is loaded.
2. The `Page_Load` event determines that there are not URL parameters, pulls the home page section ID from the `Web.config`, and calls `DisplaySection()`.
3. `DisplaySection` calls `CoreModule.GetSectionByID` to get the `Section` object that represents the home page section.
4. `DisplaySection` loops through all the `SectionItem` objects in the section, creates an appropriate view control for each, and adds them to the page.

But what happens next? What do those view controls do?

It makes sense to take a look at an example of one of these view controls at this stage. We will use the `DisplayLatestHeadlines` view provided by the News module.

CODE TOUR:
`DisplayLatestHeadlines.ascx`

You will find the `DisplayLatestHeadlines.ascx` in the `Community/Modules/News/Views` folder. If you double-click it in the Solution Explorer, you will see that it has a very simple user interface.

It consists of three elements—a `SectionItemHeader` user control, a Repeater (shown as a series of "data-bound" text items), and a `SectionItemFooter` user control.

The two user controls provide standard headers and footers for module views, helping us maintain consistency across the community and also saving us the time of designing headers and footers for each view.

We could have implemented the header and footer by rendering the HTML for them at a higher level (most likely in `default.aspx.vb` when we added the view controls to the page), but that would force us to use the header and footer for every single view. It is possible that we might want to build a view that does not use the standard header and footer, so it is more flexible to allow each view to use the standard controls if we choose to.

The Repeater is what does the work of displaying the headlines. Let's switch to the HTML view and see what it does:

56　How the Code Files Are Organized

CODE TOUR:　`DisplayLatestHeadlines.ascx`

```
<asp:Repeater id="Repeater1" runat="server">
  <ItemTemplate>
    <div>
      <a class="SummaryItemText" href="default.aspx?Module=
➥<%#Container.DataItem.ModuleInstance.CommunityModule.PrimaryKey%>
➥&Item=<%#Container.DataItem.PrimaryKey%>">
                <%#Container.DataItem.Title%>
            </a>
        </div>
    </ItemTemplate>
</asp:Repeater>
```

You can see that the Repeater will create a set of `<div>` elements that each contain a link. Both the link itself and the text inside the link are created from the DataSource of the Repeater.

To fully understand what is happening, we need to know what that DataSource is, so let's take a look in the code-behind file (`DisplayLatestHeadlines.aspx.vb`).

Here, we find a single event handler, `Page_Load`:

```
Private Sub Page_Load(ByVal sender As System.Object, _
            ByVal e As System.EventArgs) _
        Handles MyBase.Load
```

The first thing it does is create an `IList` object and also an instance of `NewsModule`, the business service class for the News module.

```
Dim newsItems As IList
Dim newsMod As NewsModule
```

Next, it checks whether it is displaying a global module instance. It does this with the `IsGlobal` method it inherits from `SectionItemControl`.

If it is global, it calls `NewsModule.GetLatestGlobalNewsItems`. If it is not, it calls `newsMod.GetLatestNewsItems`. In either case, the results are stored in the `newsItems` object that was declared earlier.

```
If Me.IsGlobal = True Then
    newsItems = NewsModule.GetLatestGlobalNewsItems(10)
Else
    newsMod = New NewsModule(Me.SectionItem.ModuleInstance)
    newsItems = newsMod.GetLatestNewsItems(10)
End If
```

Finally, it makes the `newsItems` object the DataSource for the Repeater and `DataBinds` it.

```
    Repeater1.DataSource = newsItems
    Repeater1.DataBind()
End Sub
```

It seems likely, then, that the DataSource for the Repeater is a collection of objects that represents news items. To be sure, however, we need to follow the code into the News module business service class (`NewsModule.vb`).

CODE TOUR: NewsModule.vb

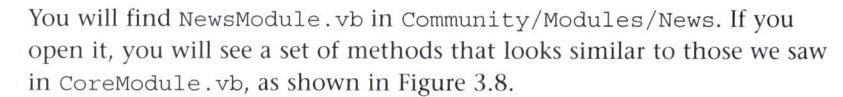

You will find `NewsModule.vb` in `Community/Modules/News`. If you open it, you will see a set of methods that looks similar to those we saw in `CoreModule.vb`, as shown in Figure 3.8.

`NewsModule` performs a very similar role to `CoreModule`, but it only deals with the requirements of the News module.

The methods we are interested in are `GetLatestGlobalNewsItems` and `GetLatestNewsItems`. They are similar, so let's look at `GetLatestGlobalNewsItems` because it is nearer the top of the file.

```
Public Shared Function GetLatestGlobalNewsItems(ByVal number As Integer)
➥As IList
```

The first part of the method should be familiar—it follows the standard sequence for requesting objects from the persistence service:

```
Dim crit As Criteria = New Criteria()

crit.addEqualTo("_ModuleInstance._ShowInGlobal", True)
crit.addOrderBy("_DatePosted", False)
```

We tell the criteria to accept only objects whose module instances are set to display globally. Also note that an `OrderBy` requirement was added to the criteria to instruct the persistence service to order the results by the `_DatePosted` field.

As expected, the next step is to request a set of objects from the persistence service:

```
Dim newsItems As IList =
➥QueryFacade.Find(Type.GetType("Community.NewsItem"), crit)
```

58 How the Code Files Are Organized

CODE TOUR: `NewsModule.vb`

FIGURE 3.8
Code map:
NewsModule.vb.

- name property
- PrepareForDeletion()
- GetSearchResults()
- Methods for dealing with global instance
- Methods for dealing with a specific instance

Here, we have the answer to our question about what type of object is returned—it is `Community.NewsItem`. This is a persistent object we have

CODE TOUR: **NewsModule.vb**

not seen yet. It represents a single news item and is used only by the News module.

The next part of the method creates a new collection (an `ArrayList` was chosen for its efficiency) and pulls off as many news items from the list returned by the broker as requested in the number parameter:

```
Dim trimmedNewsItems As ArrayList = New ArrayList()
Dim i As Integer = 0
While i < number And i < newsItems.Count
  trimmedNewsItems.Add(newsItems(i))
  i = i + 1
End While
```

The trimmed list of `NewsItem` objects is then returned:

```
  Return trimmedNewsItems
End Function
```

(If you are thinking that this is an inefficient way to go about getting a certain number of items from the database, well done! We will be looking at how we can improve this later in the book.)

Now we know that the News module returns a list of `NewsItem` objects to `DisplayLatestHeadlines.ascx.vb` and this is used as the DataSource for the Repeater that displays the headlines. Let's look again at the code for the Repeater:

```
<asp:Repeater id="Repeater1" runat="server">
  <ItemTemplate>
    <div>
```

First, it creates a link of the form

```
default.asx?Module=[moduleID]&Item=[ItemID]
<a class="SummaryItemText" href="default.aspx?Module=
➥<%#Container.DataItem.ModuleInstance.CommunityModule.PrimaryKey1%>
➥&Item=<%#Container.DataItem.PrimaryKey1%>">
```

The `moduleID` comes from

`Container.DataItem.ModuleInstance.CommunityModule.PrimaryKey1`

and the `ItemId` comes from

`Container.DataItem.PrimaryKey1`

CODE TOUR: `NewsModule.vb`

We know that `Container.DataItem` is going to refer to a `NewsItem` object (as the DataSource is a list of `NewsItem` objects), so what we are doing here is accessing properties of a `NewsItem` object.

We get the title of the news item in a similar way:

```
            <%#Container.DataItem.Title%>
        </a>
      </div>
    </ItemTemplate>
</asp:Repeater>
```

This shows that we can access the properties of our persistent objects directly from our data-binding definitions, provided we use a list of persistent objects of the same type as the DataSource for the data-bound control.

This is something that you will see throughout the online community application—we use a list of persistent objects as a DataSource and then access their properties in the data-binding definitions.

Search

The search system that is built into the starting point application is pretty simple. However, it does provide a foundation for a modular search system in which each module is responsible for providing a search service, but results are collated to provide a community-wide search. This means that as new modules are added, they can plug into the search system without the need to change the infrastructure code to include them.

Every module business service class includes a `GetSearchResults(String)` method. This is required by the `ModuleBase` base class from which they all inherit. This method returns a `SearchResultCollection` object. This is a custom collection that contains `SearchResult` objects.

Each `SearchResult` object has the following properties:

- **`name (String)`**—A few words that describe the result
- **`description (String)`**—A one-paragraph description
- **`relevance (Single)`**—A number between 0 and 1 that indicates how relevant the search result is to the search terms
- **`link (String)`**—The URL to which the user should be directed when she clicks on the search result

CoreModule, being derived from ModuleBase, also provides a GetSearchResults(String) method. It is ModuleBase.GetSearchResults that calls the SearchResults method for each installed module and collates the results.

The process for dealing with a search request is as follows:

1. The user enters search terms in the search control.
2. default.aspx is loaded, with the search URL parameter containing the search terms.
3. A new SearchResults user control is created.
4. The Results property of the control is set to the result of CoreModule.GetSearchResults.
5. CoreModule.GetSearchResults calls GetSearchResults for each installed module, passing the search terms.
6. Each module returns its search results.
7. CoreModule.GetSearchResults collates the results and returns them.
8. The results are displayed in the SearchResults control.

Each module can create its own set of search results in any way we like, so each module can work in the way that makes sense for its content.

Let's take a look at the GetSearchResults method for the News module. Open Modules/News/NewsModule.vb and find the method:

```
Public Overrides Function GetSearchResults(ByVal pSearchTerms As String) _
            As SearchResultCollection
  Dim results As New SearchResultCollection

  Dim crit1 As New Criteria

  crit1.AddLike("_Body", "%" & pSearchTerms & "%")

  Dim crit2 As New Criteria

  crit2.AddLike("_Title", "%" & pSearchTerms & "%")

  Dim crit3 As New Criteria
  crit3.AddLike("_Summary", "%" & pSearchTerms & "%")

  crit1.AddOrCriteria(crit2)
```

```
crit1.AddOrCriteria(crit3)

Dim crit4 As New Criteria

crit4.AddEqualTo("_ModuleInstanceID", Me.ModuleInstance.PrimaryKey1)

crit1.AddAndCriteria(crit4)

Dim newsItems As IList =
➥QueryFacade.Find(Type.GetType("Community.NewsItem"), crit1)

Dim ni As NewsItem

For Each ni In newsItems
    results.add(New SearchResult(ni.Title, ni.Summary, 0.5,
    ➥"default.aspx?Module=1&Item=" & ni.PrimaryKey1,
    ➥ni.ModuleInstance))
Next

Return results
End Function
```

First, we create a `SearchResultCollection` object. This is a custom collection class we will look at shortly.

We build a Criteria tree that will return a result if the search terms are found in the title, summary, or body of the news item. We also include a Criteria to require that the item is from the instance that is currently performing the search.

We then retrieve the items and create a `SearchResult` object for each of them in turn before returning the complete set of results.

The `SearchResult` class is a simple class, not a persistent object. We don't need to save `SearchResult` objects to the database, so they do not need to interact with the persistence service.

You can find the `SearchResult` class in `Global/Search/SearchResult.vb`. It is a simple combination of fields and properties to carry the data about the search result.

`SearchResultCollection`, found in `Global/Search/SearchResultCollection.vb`, is more complicated. Open that file now to take a look at it.

There are actually two classes in this file. To work properly, a custom collection class needs a matching custom enumerator class. Because they are so closely linked, we have put them in the same file.

The enumerator is important because, by providing an enumerator, our collection class can be used just like the standard collections. We can, therefore, use `For Each` loops and other standard looping techniques to access the members. The enumerator does the job of looping through the members of the collection.

Let's start at the top with `SearchResultEnumerator`.

It starts by stating that the class will implement the `IEnumerator` interface:

```
Public Class SearchResultEnumerator
  Implements IEnumerator
```

It is this interface that enables our custom enumerator to be treated as an enumerator by outside code. (We will see why this is important shortly.)

Next come the private fields:

```
Private _index As Integer = -1
Private _searchResultCollection As SearchResultCollection
```

We store the current index and the `SearchResultCollection` object to which the enumerator is attached.

Next, we provide a method to reset the enumerator back to the beginning of the collection:

```
Public Sub reset() Implements IEnumerator.Reset
  _index = -1
End Sub
```

In fact, we have to implement this method. As shown by the inclusion of the `Implements` statement, it is one of the methods that `IEnumerator` requires us to include.

`IEnumerator` also requires us to provide a method that returns the item to which the enumerator is currently pointing:

```
Public ReadOnly Property Current() As Object Implements
➥IEnumerator.Current
  Get
    If _index > -1 Then
      Return _searchResultCollection(_index)
```

```
    Else
      Return -1
    End If
  End Get
End Property
```

We check whether the current index is above −1. If it is, we return the relevant item from the collection. If it is not, we cannot return an item because the enumerator has not yet started enumerating the collection. We return -1 instead.

The final method we have to implement moves the enumerator to the next item in the collection:

```
Public Function MoveNext() As Boolean Implements IEnumerator.MoveNext
  _index = _index + 1
  If _index < _searchResultCollection.count Then
    Return True
  Else
    Return False
  End If
End Function
```

We move the index on and then check that we have not moved outside of the size of the collection. If we have, we return `False` to let the calling code know that the end of the collection has been reached.

So, we have seen the enumerator. Let's now look at the collection it enumerates.

We start by implementing the `IEnumerable` interface:

```
Public Class SearchResultCollection
  Implements IEnumerable
```

This is the key to a custom collection class—by implementing this interface, the calling code knows that it can get an enumerator to perform `For Each` loops and so on.

Then, we have a private field to hold the actual results:

```
Private results As ArrayList = New ArrayList
```

We provide a `this` property that will enable members of the collection to be accessed by their index:

```
Default Public Property this(ByVal index As Integer) As SearchResult
  Get
    Return CType(results(index), SearchResult)
  End Get
  Set(ByVal Value As SearchResult)
    results(index) = Value
  End Set
End Property
```

By including this property with the specific name `this`, we allow calling code to use standard indexed access syntax to access the members.

Then, we have a method to add items to the collection and a property to get the current length of the collection:

```
Public Sub add(ByVal item As SearchResult)
  results.Add(item)
End Sub

Public ReadOnly Property count() As Integer
  Get
    Return results.Count
  End Get
End Property
```

Finally, we have a method, required by `IEnumerable`, to get an enumerator for the collection:

```
Public Function GetEnumerator() As IEnumerator Implements
➥IEnumerable.GetEnumerator
  Return New SearchResultEnumerator(Me)
End Function
```

You might be wondering what the point of using a custom collection class is, as opposed to simply putting the search results into an `ArrayList` or similar.

By using our custom class, we guarantee that only `SearchResult` objects can be added to the collection (because the add method will only accept `SearchResult` objects) and we also get the opportunity to include custom logic if we want to. For example, we might decide to have the `SearchResultCollection` automatically sort the search results by priority. We might be able to do that more efficiently within the collection, as items are added, than calling code would be able to.

Security

The security infrastructure for the online community is actually very simple, but it provides a very easy-to-use system for members.

In later chapters, we will look at some ways in which the security system can be adjusted to give us different behaviors we might want to use.

The core online community security system takes responsibility for

- Authenticating members (that is, enabling them to log in)
- Controlling access to the Member Settings page (so only logged-in members can access it)
- Controlling access to the administration system (so only members who are marked as administrators can access it)
- Enabling modules to access the currently logged-in member

Each module is then responsible for controlling how users can read and write module-specific data. They do this by accessing the currently logged-in member's details and using them to make decisions about what should be shown to the current user.

This system allows maximum flexibility for modules. It means we can have modules that only allow the member who owns them to input data (for example, the News module) and also modules that allow any user to enter data (for example, a Visitors Book module). Reading and writing of data can be separately restricted to any of the following types of users:

- Anonymous users
- Logged-in members
- The member who owns the module

The other advantage to allowing modules to do their own security checks is that their user interface can adapt to different users. A good example is the News module. When no member is logged in, or when a member who does not own the News module being viewed is logged in, the module simply displays the news items. When the member who owns the module instance is logged in, the module displays the items, but with an Edit link for each. The member does not need to visit a special page to edit their news items—the option is right there where the items are displayed.

Moving On

You should now have a good overall idea of how the online community application works. From here on out, we are going to be doing more than passively looking at the application. We are going to get hands-on with it and change the way it looks and works.

In the next chapter, we will start experimenting with the code for the application, making some changes, and learning more about its inner workings.

Before moving on, you might want to try following some more execution paths in the code to see what the application does when it is displaying a member's personal page or a particular module. You should start from `default.aspx` in the same way as we did to find out what the application was doing to display the home page.

Experimenting with the Code 4

This is where things start getting fun! In this chapter, we will be playing with the code of the application and making all sorts of little changes to it. Some of them will be cosmetic; others will change the way the application works.

Some of the changes we make might even cause errors. This is not necessarily a bad thing. *Breaking* an application can be a great way to learn more about how the application works. It is also useful to understand error messages so that when we get one that we did not cause on purpose, we will know how to make it go away.

You will get the most out of this chapter if you do not limit yourself to following the instructions it contains. Play around with the code of the application. Make changes and see what happens. Try to understand how the code gives you the results that you see.

In this chapter, we will be

- Making big changes to how the application looks with just a few simple style sheet alterations
- Using debugging techniques to work out what the application is doing
- Beginning to add to the code of the application

Changing the Style of the Application

Let's start our tinkering by looking at some simple ways we can make pretty, sweeping changes to how the online community looks.

The online community application uses *cascading style sheets (CSS)* to make changing its appearance easy. The styles of the HTML elements that it renders are controlled from a single file, `styles.css`, so that a lot of changes can be made to the appearance without having to change code files.

EXPERIMENT:
Playing with the Style Sheet

Open the `styles.css` file from the `root` folder of the online community in Visual Studio .NET.

Here you can see a whole load of style classes, each controlling the style of a different type of element within the application.

Each class has a comment to explain what it controls, so you should be able to find the class for any specific element that you want to alter.

The classes are also grouped together depending on which section of the application or module they belong to.

Changing the Style of the Application

EXPERIMENT: **Playing with the Style Sheet**

> **DESIGN TIP**
>
> The separation of code, content, and appearance is often seen as an important aim when building Web applications. It is a good idea to keep the three elements as separated as possible—it makes the application easier to update—but there are limits to it. Like all rules, sometimes the best results require some bending.

It is perfectly safe to play around with these classes—the worst that will happen is that things will look weird or, in very extreme cases, unreadable. If you want to return to the default styles at any stage, you just need to copy the original `styles.css` file from the CD-ROM.

Here are some ideas for things to experiment with:

One role of the `SiteBody` class is to control the background of the community. At present, it defines the background color and the fact that the content is centered on the page:

```
.SiteBody
{
    background-color:#FBF19D;
    text-align:center;
    font-family: Verdana, Helvetica, sans-serif;
    color: #081162;
}
```

> **NOTE**
>
> CSS classes are different than the .NET classes that we build when developing ASP.NET applications. In CSS, the term *class* refers to a set of styles that many HTML elements can reference, rather than a software object that encapsulates data and behavior.

Note that the `SiteBody` class also sets the default font and text color settings for the community—because all other elements are within the `<body>` element, they will use these defaults if more specific settings are not made.

You can change the background color by changing the value of the `bgcolor` attribute. For example, to make the site have a red background, you would use

```
background-color:#FF0000
```

To utilize a background image, you would use

```
background-image: url(images/SiteHeader.png);
```

(You should copy whichever image you want to use as the background to the `images` folder of the community application.)

You might want to use some of the other background attributes to get the background exactly how you want it. For example

```
.SiteBody
{
    background-image: url(images/SiteHeader.png);
    background-attachment: fixed;
    text-align:center;
}
```

Changing the Style of the Application 71

EXPERIMENT: **Playing with the Style Sheet**

Play around with these attributes, along with

`background-repeat` and `background-position`

Using a background image in the `SiteBody` class will give a result that looks something like Figure 4.1.

A bit messy, I'm sure you will agree! Obviously, the problem here is exaggerated by using the site header image for the background—normally, we would use something more subtle. However, we usually want the content area of the site to have a plain background, even if we are using a background in the "spare" area around it.

If you want the page background to have a different background than the area of the page that actually shows the community, you need to modify the class that the main community HTML table uses. You can find out what this is by opening `default.aspx` and finding the corresponding `<table>` HTML tag. (Its comments state that it is the main community table.)

TIP
You can see which values each CSS attribute can take by typing the attribute and then waiting for Visual Studio .NET to provide a list of possibilities.
The Visual Studio .NET context help offers excellent information on the CSS properties and what they do.

FIGURE 4.1

The online community with a background image.

The tag is as follows:

`<table class="SiteTable" width="750" border="0">`

Therefore, the `SiteTable` CSS class defines the appearance of the table.

EXPERIMENT: Playing with the Style Sheet

If you return to `styles.css`, you will discover that the `SiteTable` class is used only to tell the browser that it uses fixed column widths. (This helps the table render faster and also ensures that long content is not allowed to distort the table layout.)

```
.SiteTable
{
    table-layout:fixed;
}
```

You can add the same attributes as were used with the `SiteBody` class. So, to make the background plain, we would do this:

```
.SiteTable
{
    table-layout: fixed;
    background-color:#FBF19D;
}
```

This makes things more readable, as shown in Figure 4.2.

FIGURE 4.2

The online community with a plain central table.

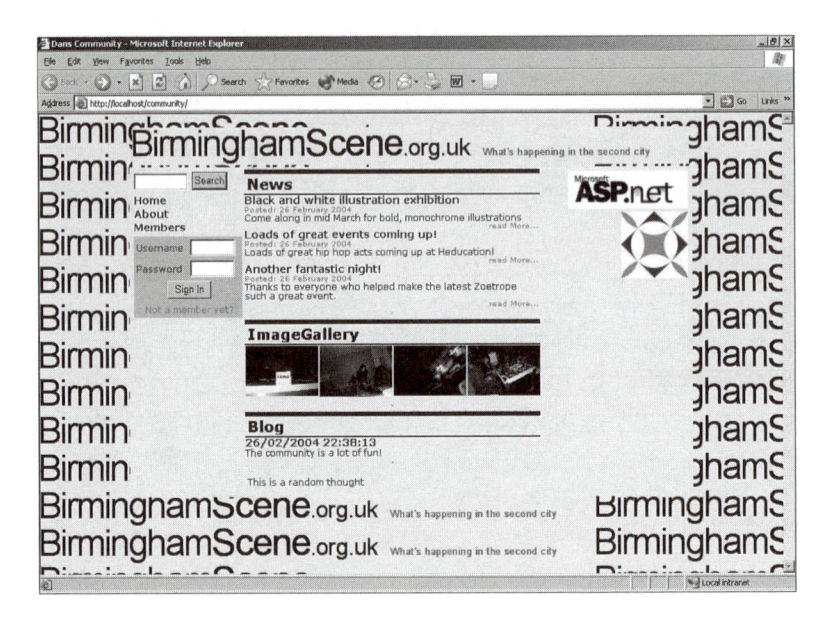

Because the `SiteTable` class is applied to a `<table>` element, you can also use some other CSS attributes that affect the display of tables. (In fact, you can use any attributes you like in any CSS class—only the ones that make sense will be used to format elements.)

EXPERIMENT: **Playing with the Style Sheet**

For example, you can put a border around the site table by adding a border attribute:

```
.SiteTable
{
    table-layout: fixed;
    background-color:#FBF19D;
border: #081162 medium dashed;
}
```

This will add a dashed border around the content area, using the same dark blue color that is used for the text of the community. The result is shown in Figure 4.3.

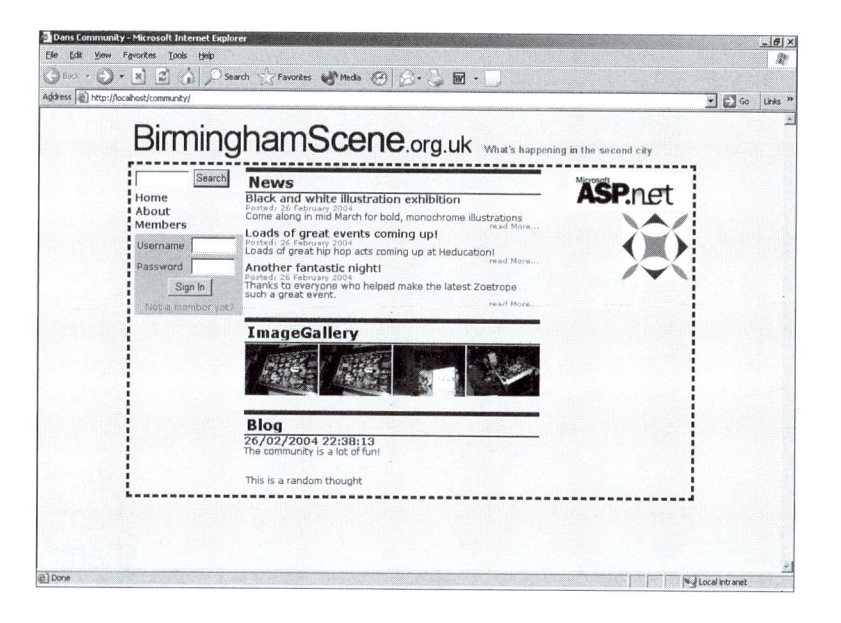

FIGURE 4.3
The online community with a border.

Notice that before taking the screenshot in Figure 4.3, I removed the code that added the background image. Feel free to undo any changes that you don't want to keep.

There are a lot of styles for different kinds of text in the community application—to allow maximum flexibility, plenty of classes were defined and used in text elements throughout the system.

For example, there are three classes for setting styles in the navigation: `A.NavigationItem`, `A.NavigationSubItem`, and `A.NavigationSubSubItem`. Each sets the style for a different level of navigation.

Changing the Style of the Application

EXPERIMENT: Playing with the Style Sheet

Notice that each of these classes starts with the letter *A*. This is because they are actually subclasses of the `Anchor` class (the class that sets the style for *anchors* or *links*).

The most important attributes for text are

- **Font**—Enables you to set the font to a specific one. (Bear in mind that the user browsing the site must have the font you name in order for him to see it.)

- **Font size**—Sets the size of the font (by default in points, but it is also possible to set it to standard sizes with the names that are shown in the VS.NET auto complete pop-up).

- **Font weight**—Enables you to set the font to be bold.

- **Font style**—Enables you to set the font to be italic.

- **Font family**—A more general way of setting the font, the user's browser will search for a font from the correct family. (This is the best approach to use for Web applications because it gives the user the best chance of seeing what we plan for her to see.)

- **Text indent**—Sets the indent.

- **Text decoration**—Enables you to set an underline.

- **Color**—Sets the color, using the same values as were used for the background color.

Play around with the navigation style classes and experiment with different styles.

Because the navigation items are links, you can also define what they should look like when the cursor is over them. To do this, define new subclasses. For example, to make the `Navigation Items` change to maroon when the cursor is over them, add

```
A.Navigation_Item:Hover
{
    color:#AA7C7C;
}
```

You can add `Visited` subclasses in the same way as `Hover` subclasses to define how the links should look when the user has already visited them. If you want the link to be the same color after being visited, you need to add a `Visited` subclass to specify this.

Try adding some extra `Hover` and `Visited` subclasses.

Changing the Style of the Application   75

EXPERIMENT: **Playing with the Style Sheet**

If you want to make all links on the site behave in a standard way, you need to add the following definitions to the `styles.css` style sheet:

```
A:link     {
    text-decoration:    none;
    color:     #AA7C7C;
    }

A:visited    {
    text-decoration:    none;
    color:     #AA7C7C;
    }

A:active   {
    text-decoration:    none;
    color:     #AA7C7C;
    }

A:hover    {
    text-decoration:    none;
    color:     #081162;
    }
```

This will color links in a maroon color and change the color to dark blue when the mouse pointer is over them.

These definitions are much more general than the classes we have seen so far. They will affect all links, not requiring a class to be referenced in the HTML.

If you make this change, you will notice that not all of the links take these settings. The `Navigation Item` links are still colored dark blue with a maroon mouse-over effect, rather than vice versa as the general definitions we just added would have it.

The reason for this is that the general definitions are overruled by the more specific classes—the settings in the class have precedence. This is really useful because it allows us to set a default that is then customized for specific situations.

At this stage, you might want to experiment with other classes in `styles.css`. There are some ideas for further changes to classes on this book's Web site.

We will continue to modify the navigation control now. Let's add graphical icons to the `Navigation Items`.

76   Changing the Style of the Application

EXPERIMENT: **Playing with the Style Sheet**

To do this, we are going to have to change more than the style sheet. We will need to edit the navigation control itself. This is, therefore, a good time to have a look at how the navigation control works.

Before we delve into the code, it might be useful to recap what the navigation control actually does. Its behavior is a little more complex than a fixed menu of navigation options.

The default state for the navigation control is to show a Home link, an About link, and a Members link, along with a link to each global section.

I mentioned global sections in Chapter 2, "The Online Community Application," when we toured the application. If you experimented with the rudimentary admin tool and created a global section, you will already know that they are displayed in the navigation control. If you didn't, play around with global sections now.

After adding a global section, you should see something like Figure 4.4.

> **TIP**
>
> I can't encourage you enough to play with the application, explore its code, and experiment with it. The way to get the best use out of this book and its sample application is through such activities.

FIGURE 4.4

Global section in the navigation.

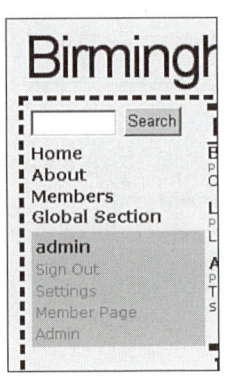

There is a different behavior when a Member page is being viewed or when any section created by a member is being viewed. Browse to one of the members or to one of their pages to see this. (Remember that a Member page is not an ASP.NET page at all, but rather a data-driven entity that we call a *section*.)

Now, the navigation shows the same links as before, but nested under the Members link is a link to the members' personal pages, and nested under that are links to all of their other sections. This is shown in Figure 4.5.

So, the navigation control behaves differently when sections related to a specific member are viewed. Let's move on to look at the code, where we will see how this is done.

FIGURE 4.5

The navigation control when a Member page is being viewed.

CODE TOUR: Navigation.ascx

You will find `navigation.ascx` in the `global/controls` folder of the community application.

If you open the control in VS.NET, you will see that it has three items (Home, About, and Members) that are fixed, one item (MemberNameLink) that is blank at design time (which we can tell because it shows just the name of the control in square brackets), and a set of data-bound items. Open `navigation.ascx.vb` and you'll see where the member name and the extra items come from.

It is very much like the code-behind for a normal user control—it has some subcontrol declarations and a `Page_Load` to initialize them. It does have a property, which is used to allow the community application to set which member's information is currently being viewed. The navigation control can then display the members' sections as subitems.

```
Public Property MemberID() As Integer
    Get
        Return _SelectedMember.PrimaryKey(0)
    End Get
    Set(ByVal Value As Integer)
        Dim coreModule As CoreModule = New CoreModule()
        _SelectedMember = coreModule.GetMemberByID(Value)
    End Set
End Property
```

You can see that the core module is called to convert the supplied numerical ID into a `Member` object before it is stored in the `_SelectedMember` field.

DESIGN TIP

This is an example of a property accessor being used to do a little more than just setting or returning a private field. It can be really useful to include some logic in property accessors, but as a rule, they should be kept small, sticking to code that handles the getting and setting of values.

CODE TOUR: **Navigation.ascx**

After the property has been set, `_SelectedMember` will be available to any of the other code of the control. Crucially, the property will be set before `Page_Load` runs, so we will be able to use it there.

How do we know that the property will be set before `Page_Load` runs? Apart from looking directly at the behavior of the application (quite a bad approach for verifying the specifics of how the application runs because many factors can affect the behavior), we can use ASP.NET Trace to see in what order things happen.

You might have encountered the Trace feature already. If not, it is something that is well worth getting accustomed to using—it is one of the best ways to find out what your applications are actually up to (and in what order).

Before we can use Trace, we need to activate it. Open the `Web.config` file and find the `<Trace>` element. Change the settings as follows:

```
<trace enabled="true" pageOutput="true" traceMode="SortByTime"
localOnly="true" />
```

We have activated tracing and have specified that we want to see the output in the Web browser, sorted by time, but only when we are browsing the site from the machine on which it is running.

Next, we need to add some calls to tell Trace which parts of the application we are interested in.

In `Navigation.ascx.vb`, add the following line to the `MemberID` property:

```
Public Property MemberID() As Integer
  Get
    Return _SelectedMember.PrimaryKey(0)
  End Get
  Set(ByVal Value As Integer)
    Trace.Write("Navigation member property set")
    Dim coreModule As CoreModule = New CoreModule
    _SelectedMember = coreModule.GetMemberByID(Value)
  End Set
End Property
```

CODE TOUR: `Navigation.ascx`

Scroll down to the `Page_Load` event and add a similar line to the start of it:

```
Private Sub Page_Load(ByVal sender As System.Object, _
                     ByVal e As System.EventArgs) _
    Handles MyBase.Load

  Trace.Write("Navigation Page_Load executing")
  Dim coreModule As CoreModule = New CoreModule
```

You should now see that browsing to the community home page shows some additional output below the community itself, as shown in Figure 4.6.

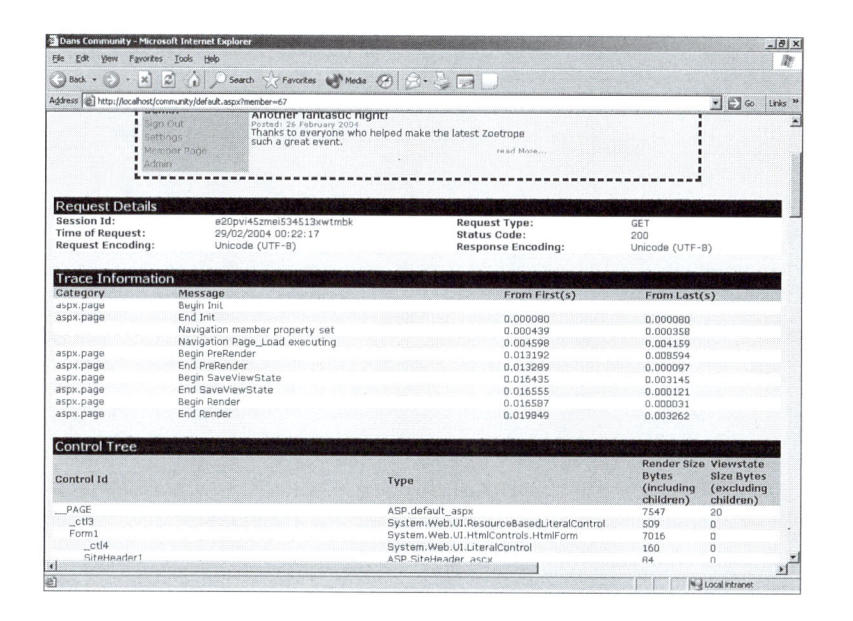

FIGURE 4.6

Trace output in the browser.

The additional output includes loads of really useful information, such as the complete control tree that the ASP.NET page has rendered (which is indispensable when debugging control-related issues) and details of the cookies and variables associated with the request. The part we are interested in right now, though, is the second section—Trace Information.

You should see the two messages that we added code for in the table. The Property Set message comes before the one we added to Page_Load, showing that the property is set before Page_Load runs.

CODE TOUR: **Navigation.ascx**

Trace shows us the order in which the two things happen, but it does not show us why they happen in this order. It is always useful to know why things happen, so we will use a slightly more brutal approach—breaking the application.

This might sound extreme, but purposely introducing an error into an application can often be a great way to find out how it works, provided we have some useful debug output as a result of the error.

Remove the Trace code that we added and add the following line to the `MemberID` property:

```
Public Property MemberID() As Integer
  Get
    Return _SelectedMember.PrimaryKey(0)
  End Get
  Set(ByVal Value As Integer)
    Throw New System.Exception
    Dim coreModule As CoreModule = New CoreModule
    _SelectedMember = coreModule.GetMemberByID(Value)
  End Set
End Property
```

We purposely throw an exception, causing an untrapped error that will result in an error message.

If you browse to the community now, you will see the message shown in Figure 4.7.

The Stack Trace section shows us a stack trace from the moment the exception was thrown. This is sort of like a summarized snapshot of what the application was doing when the error happened:

```
[Exception: Exception of type System.Exception was thrown.]
    Community.Navigation.set_MemberID(Int32 Value)
    ↪in C:\Inetpub\wwwroot\Community\
    ↪Global\Controls\Navigation.ascx.vb:34
    Community._default.DisplayMemberPage()
    ↪in C:\Inetpub\wwwroot\Community\default.aspx.vb:80
    Community._default.Page_Load(Object sender, EventArgs e)
    ↪in C:\Inetpub\wwwroot\Community\default.aspx.vb:43
    System.Web.UI.Control.OnLoad(EventArgs e) +67
    System.Web.UI.Control.LoadRecursive() +35
    System.Web.UI.Page.ProcessRequestMain() +720
```

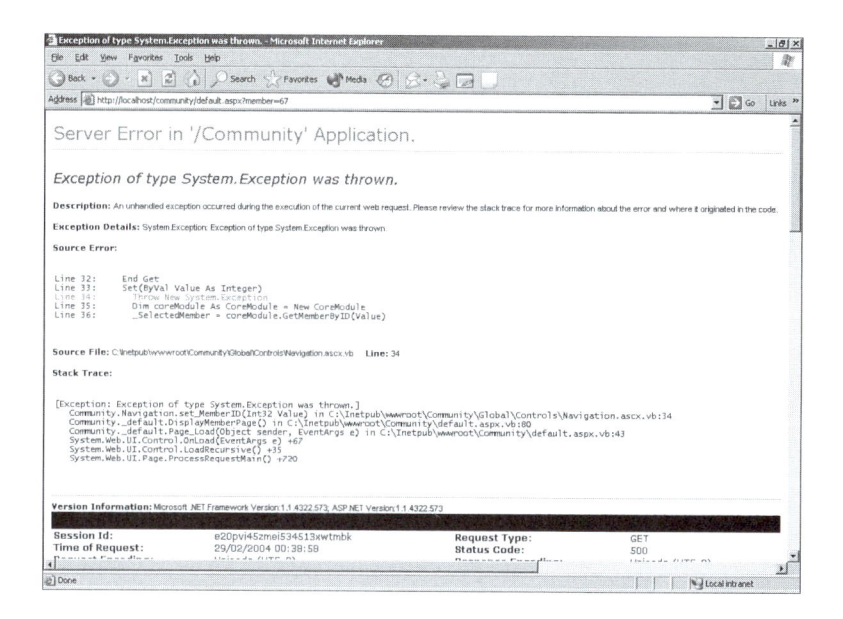

CODE TOUR: `Navigation.ascx`

FIGURE 4.7
The error message from the error we purposely caused.

The first item in the stack trace shows the `MemberID` set accessor where the exception was thrown. We can then follow the stack trace to see that the set accessor was called by `DisplayMemberPage()` in `default.aspx.vb`, which was in turn called by the `Page_Load` event handler in `default.aspx.vb`, which was in turn called the `OnLoad` event of a control (the `Default.aspx` page itself—pages are derived from control). The `OnLoad` event was fired by the `LoadRecursive` method, which was in turn called by the `ProcessRequestMain` method.

Now move the `throw` statement to the top of the `Page_Load` event handler in `navigation.ascx.vb`. The stack trace will now look like this:

```
[Exception: Exception of type System.Exception was thrown.]
    Community.Navigation.Page_Load(Object sender, EventArgs e) in
➥C:\Inetpub\wwwroot\Community\Global\Controls\Navigation.ascx.vb:40
    System.Web.UI.Control.OnLoad(EventArgs e) +67
    System.Web.UI.Control.LoadRecursive() +35
    System.Web.UI.Control.LoadRecursive() +98
    System.Web.UI.Control.LoadRecursive() +98
    System.Web.UI.Page.ProcessRequestMain() +720
```

So while the property accessor is executed through the `Load` event of the `default.aspx` `Page` object, the `Page_Load` event handler of the navigation control is executed through several calls to `Control.LoadRecursive`.

Changing the Style of the Application

CODE TOUR: `Navigation.ascx`

Presumably, the `LoadRecursive` methods for the controls in the control tree each call the `LoadRecursive` method of the subcontrols, down to the navigation control. Let's take a look at the control tree to find out whether this makes sense.

Remove the `throw` statement that we used to cause a purposeful error, recompile, and browse to the community. You should see the extra Trace output that we saw earlier. This time, concentrate on the Control Tree section, as shown in Figure 4.8.

FIGURE 4.8

The Control Tree in the Trace output.

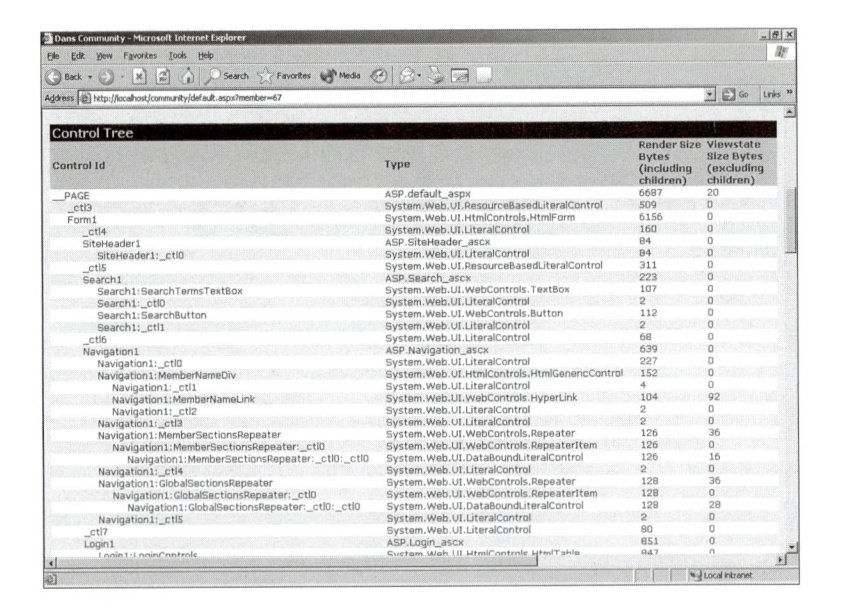

We can easily see that the navigation control is three levels down in the hierarchy. The top-level control has the ID page. The next control down is Form1. The navigation control falls directly under Form1. This makes sense—the `<form>` element in `default.aspx` has the `runat` property set to server, so it is server-side. The page as a whole must be server-side, but none of the other HTML elements that the navigation control is nested inside are set to run at the server.

We still don't know for sure why the nested calls to `LoadRecursive` happen after the call to the top-level Page_Load, though. To do that, we are going to have to dip into the .NET Framework itself, using the tool that Microsoft provides for peeking inside assemblies to see what they do.

CODE TOUR: `Navigation.ascx`

Open a Visual Studio .NET command prompt. (It is an option in the Visual Studio .NET Tools menu that should be under Visual Studio .NET in the Start menu.) Type `isdasm` and then press Enter to run the *ILDisASseMbler (ILDASM)*.

Use the File > Open menu option to open the file:

`C:\WINDOWS\Microsoft.NET\Framework\[latest version`
↪`number]\System.Web.Dll`

This is the assembly that contains the .NET Framework classes from all of the `System.Web.*` namespaces, including `System.Web.UI.Control`, which we are interested in.

You should now see something like Figure 4.9.

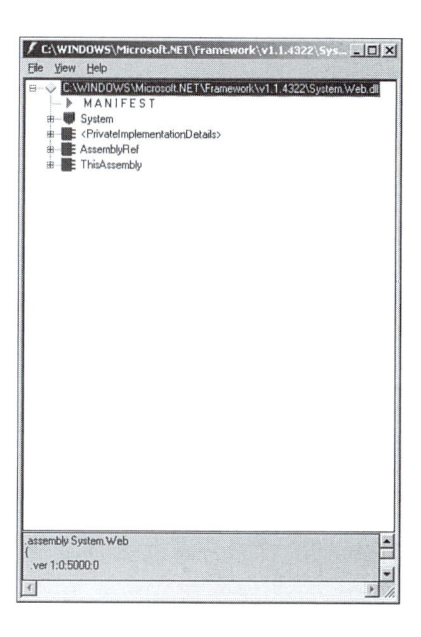

FIGURE 4.9

The Intermediate Language Dissassembler.

Expand the `System`, `System.Web`, and `System.Web.UI` branches of the tree control and finally expand the `Control` class.

Then, find the `LoadRecursive()` method of `Control` and double-click it. A new window should appear, containing *Intermediate Language (IL)* code. If you haven't looked at IL code before, this might look rather confusing. Don't worry, though—you don't need to understand what the codes mean to make use of IL.

CODE TOUR: Navigation.ascx

It is easy to find the code that triggers the `Load` event handler:

```
IL_0009:   ldarg.0
IL_000a:   ldsfld     class [mscorlib]System.EventArgs [mscorlib]
➥System.EventArgs::Empty
IL_000f:   callvirt   instance void System.Web.UI.Control::OnLoad
➥(class [mscorlib]System.EventArgs)
IL_0014:   ldarg.0
IL_0015:   ldfld      class System.Web.UI.ControlCollection
➥System.Web.UI.Control::_controls
IL_001a:   brfalse.s  IL_0063
```

And, a little further down, the code that calls `LoadRecursive`:

```
IL_003d:   ldarg.0
IL_003e:   ldfld      class System.Web.UI.ControlCollection
➥System.Web.UI.Control::_controls
IL_0043:   ldloc.2
IL_0044:   callvirt   instance class System.Web.UI.Control
➥System.Web.UI.ControlCollection::get_Item(int32)
IL_0049:   callvirt   instance void System.Web.UI.Control::
➥LoadRecursive()
IL_004e:   ldloc.2
IL_004f:   ldc.i4.1
```

So, we know that the `Page_Load` event handler will be executed before the calls to `LoadRecursive` for subcontrols. The property assignment that we do from the `Page_Load` event handler of `default.aspx` will therefore happen before the `Page_Load` event handler of the navigation control executes.

This might seem like a lot of effort to go to in order to find out something relatively simple, but the techniques of using Trace output, error messages, the control tree, and ILDASM together in this way are so useful that I just had to include an example.

Let's now move on to look at the `Page_Load` event handler in `Navigation.ascx.vb` in some more detail:

```
Private Sub Page_Load(ByVal sender As System.Object, _
                ByVal e As System.EventArgs) _
            Handles MyBase.Load
    Dim coreModule As CoreModule = New CoreModule
```

> **TIP**
>
> In case you are wondering whether Microsoft minds us poking around in its assemblies, be reassured that the documentation for `ISDASM.exe` mentions using it for just this purpose. So, Microsoft seems to expect us to do it.

```
'Set up data for the global sections
GlobalSectionsRepeater.DataSource = coreModule.GetGlobalSections
GlobalSectionsRepeater.DataBind()

If Not _SelectedMember Is Nothing Then
  'there is a member selected
  'display the navigation items for the selected member
  MemberNameDiv.Visible = True
  MemberNameLink.Text = _SelectedMember.Username
  MemberNameLink.NavigateUrl = "../../Default.aspx?Member=" _
                      & _SelectedMember.PrimaryKey1

  'set up the data for the members sections
  MemberSectionsRepeater.DataSource = _
            _SelectedMember.NonMemberPageSections
  MemberSectionsRepeater.DataBind()
Else
  'there is no member selected, so do not display the member name
  MemberNameDiv.Visible = False
End If


End Sub
```

`Page_Load` starts by creating an instance of the core module and then using the `GetGlobalSections` method to get all of the sections that are not owned by members. These are displayed directly in the navigation. (If you are not sure where, open `Navigation.ascx` in HTML mode and find the `GlobalSectionsRepeater` control.)

It then checks whether `_SelectedMember` has been set.

If it has, it makes the member's name visible, sets its text to the correct username, and sets its link to point to that member's page.

Then, it sets the datasource of the Repeater that renders the sub-subitems to the property of the `Member` object that returns the member's sections, apart from the section that is on her Member page.

If no member has been set, the `MemberNameDiv` is set to be invisible.

STEP-BY-STEP GUIDE: Adding Icons to the Navigation

STEP-BY-STEP GUIDE:
Adding Icons to the Navigation

We will now add some code to the navigation control to display an icon for each main navigation item. We will perform the following steps:

1. Create a folder and standard icons.
2. Add `<img>` tags to the navigation control for the standard items.
3. Add a `StyleSheet` class to format the images.
4. Create an image for each global section.
5. Add `<img>` tags for the data-bound global sections.
6. Add code to initialize the global section icons.

Create a folder and standard icons.

Create a new folder under `community/images/` called `NavIcons`. In this folder, create .png files for the following icons:

- Home
- About
- Members

There are some example icons on the CD-ROM for this book, which can be found under `Chapter05/NavIcons`.

Add `<img>` tags to the navigation control for the standard items.

Open `Global/Controls/Navigation.ascx` and find the HTML code that displays the links for Home, About, and Members.

Add `<img>` tags to the code that display the relevant image for each item. For example, here is the code for the Home icon:

```
<a class="Navigation_Item" href="default.aspx">
  <img src="images/navicons/home.png" class="Navigation_ItemIcon"
                         height="20" width="20" border="0" />
  Home
</a>
```

Note that we have included a style sheet class for the images so that we will be able to format them from the style sheet.

Add similar code for the About and Members items.

> **DESIGN TIP**
>
> Style sheets give a lot more control over elements, so it is a good idea to add style sheet classes to elements as they are created. Even if they are not needed immediately, it will make the elements easier to format later.

STEP-BY-STEP GUIDE: **Adding Icons to the Navigation**

Add a `StyleSheet` class to format the images.

If you check `styles.css`, you will discover that there is no `Navigation_ItemIcon` class. This does not do any harm (nonexistent classes do not stop the community from being rendered by browsers), but if we want to set the style of the icons, we will need to add a matching class to `styles.css`. Let's do that now:

```
IMG.Navigation_ItemIcon
{
    vertical-align: baseline;
}
```

Add this to `styles.css` (underneath the `NavigationItem_Item` class would be a good place) and add a comment to state what the class controls.

Note that we have actually added a subclass of the Image (IMG) definition—this is because the navigation icons are images. The class will not be used to format the images if we do not do this.

The `vertical-align` attribute will cause the bottom of the icons to be aligned with the baseline of the text for the navigation item. If you want a different alignment for your icons, change this attribute to one of the other possible values, such as middle or top. (You can use the intellisense or context help to find all the options.)

Create an image for each global section.

Things are a little more complex for global sections, as they are data-bound; we do not know in advance which global sections will be present or even how many there will be. We could simply show the same icon for each section. That would be easily accomplished, but it wouldn't be very eye-catching. It would be much better to allow a different icon to be specified for each global section.

There are a few different ways that we could go about this. We could add an extra property to the `Section persistent` object to store which image should be displayed for each section. We could have the system look for images named after the numerical ID of the section in question. What we decided to do was to have the system look for images named after the name of the section—this will make it easy to tell which image relates to which global section. It does mean we will have to be careful to ensure that we change the image name if a global section is renamed. Global sections will not be changed very often (and only by an administrator), so this won't be a big problem.

3 ▲

> **TIP**
>
> I have chosen to use the *Portable Network Graphic* (*.png*) format because it is an open standard that is widely supported by browsers and graphics-editing software and it is not encumbered with patent issues as the *Graphical Interchange Format* (*.gif*) format is. If you want to use .gif files, you simply need to change the .png references to .gif.

4 ▲

STEP-BY-STEP GUIDE: **Adding Icons to the Navigation**

We should keep these icons separate, so create a new folder under `image/navicons` called `globalSectionItems`.

Add an image called `[GlobalSectionName].png` for each global section to `images/NavIcons/globalSectionItems/`.

There are some example images on the CD-ROM for this book, which can be found under `Chapter04/NavIcons`.

5 ▲ **Add `<img>` tags for the data-bound global sections.**

Find the part of `Navigation.ascx` that displays each global section (inside the `<ItemTemplate>` of the Repeater). Add the following highlighted code:

```
<a class="Navigation_Item"
    href="Default.aspx?Section=<%#Container.DataItem.PrimaryKey1%>">
    <img src="images/NavIcons/globalSectionIcons/
➥<%#Container.DataItem.Name#%>.png"
class="Navigation_ItemIcon" height="20" width="20" border="0">
    <%#Container.DataItem.Name%>
</a>
```

The important part of what we have added is the `src` attribute of the `img` tag:

```
src="images/NavIcons/globalSectionIcons/
➥<%#Container.DataItem.Name#%>.png"
```

The folder and subfolder are specified, and then the filename is taken from the `Name` property of the `Section` object. (`Container.DataItem` points to a `Section` object because the Repeater that the code is within has a collection of `Sections` as its datasource.)

If you make the change and view the community, you should see that each global section now has an icon, as shown in Figure 4.10.

If there are any broken images, you need to ensure that each global section has a matching image in the `NavIcons` folder with the correct name.

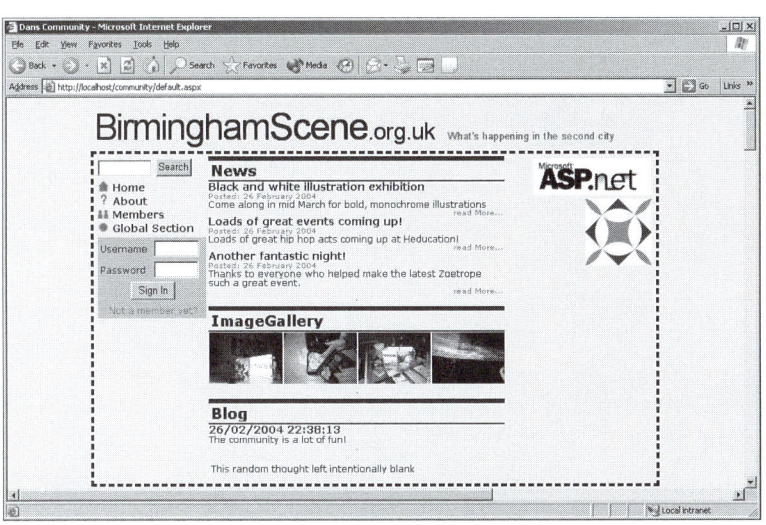

STEP-BY-STEP GUIDE: **Adding Icons to the Navigation**

FIGURE 4.10
Global sections with icons.

Moving On

In this chapter, we started to make some changes to the online community application. The changes we have made so far have been small changes, although we saw that making even small changes can have big results.

In the next chapter, we will continue to modify the user interface of the online community, but the changes we make will be bigger, requiring more additions to the source code.

Improving the User Interface 5

Up until now, we have been making small changes to the application by altering the code that is already there. In this chapter, we are going to go further by adding new code that will make the user interface of the online community more attractive and useful to its members. We will also be taking a closer look at the parts of the core community code that deal with the user interface by

- Having ImageGallery module instances show the number of images they contain
- Adding icons to the item headers to show which type of module is being displayed
- Adding a New icon to module instances that have been changed recently
- Adding icons to the navigation
- Adding New icons to the navigation to show which sections have been updated recently
- Displaying the newest member to join
- Allowing members to customize their Member pages with images of their choice

Section Items

We will start by looking at the standard user interface elements that are used when displaying module views in sections.

As we saw in Chapter 3, "Exploring the Code," each section item in the section is displayed in turn in the main part of the page. In order to give them a consistent look, there is a `SectionItemHeader` and a `SectionItemFooter` that module views should use. Views do not have to use the header and footer; for some modules, it might make sense to have views that do not have a header or footer at all. An example of this is the Random Text module, which is used to add text to the page and, therefore, works better without the standard header and footer.

`SectionItemHeader` is the more complex of the two controls, so we will look at that one in detail.

CODE TOUR:
`Global/Controls/SectionItemHeader.ascx`

If you open `SectionItemHeader` in the VS.NET Designer, you will see that it is very simple—a table layout with a hyperlink control in it.

The code-behind class includes two properties, as shown in Table 5.1.

Section Items

CODE TOUR: `Global/Controls/SectionItemHeader.ascx`

TABLE 5.1 Properties of `SectionItemHeader`

Property	Purpose
`LinkToModule`	Boolean value that indicates whether the header should be a link to the module or module instance
`Text`	The text to be displayed in the header

Both of these properties are set by the module view that includes the `SectionItemHeader`, so modules have quite a lot of control over the header.

The `Page_Load` event handler, shown in Listing 5.1, is used to initialize the header.

LISTING 5.1 `Page_Load` in `Global/Controls/SectionItemHeader.ascx.vb`

```
Private Sub Page_Load(ByVal sender As System.Object, ByVal e As System.EventArgs) _
        Handles MyBase.Load

    'get the section item object of the SectionItemControl that this control is attached to

    Dim sectionItem As SectionItem = CType(Me.Parent, SectionItemControl).SectionItem

    'check whether we are displaying a global instance
    If sectionItem.IsGlobal = True Then
      'create a link to the global instance of the module
      If _Text = Nothing Then
        'There is no text, so use the module name as the text
        HeaderLink.Text = sectionItem.ModuleView.CommunityModule.Name
      Else
        'there is some text, so use it
        HeaderLink.Text = _Text
      End If

      'check whether we should link to the module
      If _LinkToModule = True Then
        'we should link to the module, so set the URL
        HeaderLink.NavigateUrl = "../../default.aspx?Module=" + _
            sectionItem.ModuleView.CommunityModule.PrimaryKey1.ToString
      End If
    Else
      'we are not displaying a global instance
      If _Text = Nothing Then
        'no text defined, so use the name of the instance
```

▼ 1

▼ 2

▼ 3

CODE TOUR: Global/Controls/SectionItemHeader.ascx

LISTING 5.1 `Page_Load` in `Global/Controls/SectionItemHeader.ascx.vb` (continued)

```
      HeaderLink.Text = sectionItem.ModuleInstance.Name
    Else
      'text defined, so use it
      HeaderLink.Text = _Text
    End If

    'check whether we should link to the module instance
    If _LinkToModule = True Then
      'we should link to the instance, so set the URL
      HeaderLink.NavigateUrl = "../../default.aspx?Module=" + _
          sectionItem.ModuleView.CommunityModule.PrimaryKey1.ToString + _
          "&Instance=" + sectionItem.ModuleInstance.PrimaryKey1.ToString
    End If

  End If
End Sub
```

The first thing we do is to get the `SectionItem` object from the control that the `SectionItemHeader` is within. (We know that the control will be used by controls that derive from `SectionItemControl`, so we know its parent will have a `SectionItem` property.) **1**

Then we check whether the `SectionItem` object is global. **2**

If it is global, we use the module name as the default text in the header. If the `Text` property has been set, we use that instead.

If the `LinkToModule` property is set to true (the default value), we make the hyperlink point to the main module view for the module.

If the section item is not global, the code is very similar, but we use the module instance name as the default text and, if the `LinkToModule` property is set to true, we link to the main module view for the instance. **3**

Now that we know how the `SectionItemHeader` operates, let's put that knowledge to work by customizing the text that is displayed in it for one of the modules.

DESIGN TIP

It is a good idea to provide defaults like those in step 2 for properties in custom controls so that if we want the default behavior, we don't have to set the properties in the parent control. This reduces code and encourages consistency.

STEP-BY-STEP GUIDE: Adding the Number of Images to the Header of ImageGallery Module Instances

STEP-BY-STEP GUIDE:
Adding the Number of Images to the Header of ImageGallery Module Instances

At present, the two views for the ImageGallery module display a number of the images from the instance (if one is being displayed) or from all instances (if the global instance is being displayed). There is no indication of how many images are in the instance or module—there could be just the number that is displayed, or there could be many more.

We will add some code to have ImageGallery views that are displaying an instance include the number of images their instance contains in the `SectionItemHeader`. We will take the following steps:

1. Open `Modules/ImageGallery/Views/DisplayLatestImages.ascx.vb`.
2. Find the code in the `Page_Load` event handler that executes when the control is *not* displaying a global instance.
3. Add the code as highlighted in Listing 5.2.

LISTING 5.2 Addition to the `Page_Load` Event Handler in `Modules/ImageGallery/Views/DisplayLatestImages.ascx.vb`

```
Private Sub Page_Load(ByVal sender As System.Object, ByVal e As System.EventArgs) _
Handles MyBase.Load

    If Me.IsGlobal Then
        DataList1.DataSource = ImageGalleryModule.GetLatestGlobalImages(4)
    Else

        Dim galleryModule As ImageGalleryModule = New _
        ImageGalleryModule(Me.SectionItem.ModuleInstance)

        DataList1.DataSource = galleryModule.GetLatestImages(4)

        SectionItemHeader.Text = Me.SectionItem.ModuleInstance.Name & " (" & _
        galleryModule.GetAllImages.Count.ToString & " images)"

    End If

    DataList1.DataBind()

End Sub
```

IDEA: **Customizing the Header for Other Modules**

This code makes a call to the `GetAllImages` method of the ImageGallery module service class and then counts the results to get the number of images in the instance. This value is used when setting the `Text` property of the `SectionItemHeader` control.

4. Make the same addition in `Modules/ImageGallery/Views/DisplayRandomImages.ascx.vb`.

5. Recompile the project.

> **TIP**
> From now on, step-by-step instructions will not tell you to recompile the project after making each change. You will need to recompile after making changes to any .vb files.

When you view the community, you should be able to see the number of images in each instance of the ImageGallery module as in Figure 5.1.

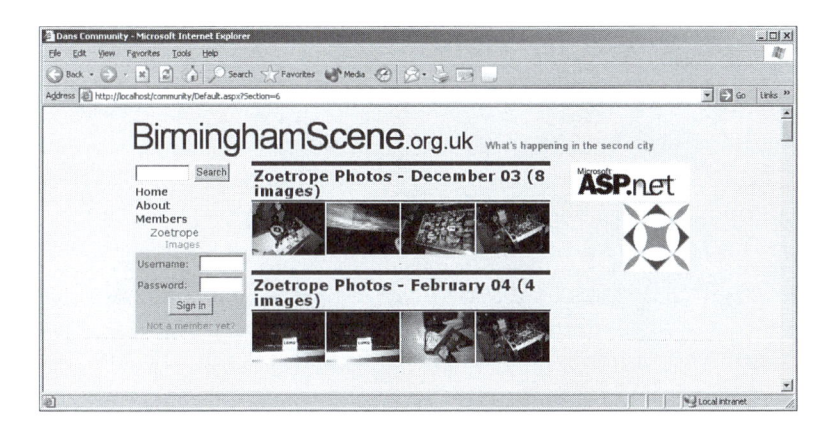

FIGURE 5.1
The ImageGallery module with the number of images displayed.

CHALLENGE:
Displaying the Number of Images for Global Instances

Try making a similar change to that covered in the previous "Step-By-Step Guide." This time, have the code work for the global instance and display the number of images in all instances of the ImageGallery module.

IDEA:
Customizing the Header for Other Modules

The `SectionItemHeader` text can be customized by any module. For example, you might want to display the number of news items that a News module instance contains or the number of posts in the last month made to a blog instance. These changes would all be very similar to those already shown for the ImageGallery module.

STEP-BY-STEP GUIDE: **Adding Icons to Module Headers**

STEP-BY-STEP GUIDE:
Adding Icons to Module Headers

Let's now make a change to the `SectionItemHeader` control that will affect all modules. We will insert code that will display an icon appropriate to the module to the left of the header text by following these steps:

1. Create a `ModuleIcons` folder under `/Images/`.

2. Create icons in the `ModuleIcons` folder with filenames of the form `[ModuleName].png`.

So, you will have files like

- `ImageGallery.png`
- `News.png`
- and so on

Some sample icons are included on the CD-ROM for this book in the `Chapters/Chapter5/ModuleIcons` folder.

3. Open `SectionItemHeader.ascx` in the Designer and drag a new image control to the layout. Just to the left of the header text is a sensible place to put it. Give it the ID `ModuleIcon`.

The HTML view for the control should now look like Listing 5.3.

LISTING 5.3 `Global/Controls/SectionItemHeader.ascx` After Adding an Image Control

```
<table border="0" width="400" class="SectionItemHeader_Table">
  <tr>
    <td>
      <asp:Image id="ModuleIcon" runat="server"></asp:Image>
      <asp:HyperLink CssClass="SectionItemHeader_Text" id="HeaderLink" runat="server">
      </asp:HyperLink>
    </td>
  </tr>
</table>
```

Section Items   97

STEP-BY-STEP GUIDE: **Adding Icons to Module Headers**

4. Open `SectionItemHeader.ascx`, find `Page_Load`, and add the code highlighted in Listing 5.4.

LISTING 5.4   Addition to `Global/Controls/SectionItemHeader.ascx.vb`

```
Private Sub Page_Load(ByVal sender As System.Object, ByVal e As System.EventArgs) _
Handles MyBase.Load

    'get the section item object of the SectionItemControl that this control is attached to
    Dim sectionItem As SectionItem = CType(Me.Parent, SectionItemControl).SectionItem

ModuleIcon.Height = New Unit(20)
ModuleIcon.Width = New Unit(20)
ModuleIcon.ImageUrl = "../../images/ModuleIcons/" & _
sectionItem.ModuleView.CommunityModule.Name & ".png"


    If sectionItem.IsGlobal = True Then
```

Note that we access the module name through `sectionItem.ModuleView.CommunityModule.Name`—this route will work whether it is an instance or a global instance that is being displayed (as all section items have a module view and all module views have a module).

You might want to change the height and width settings for the icons if your icons are different sizes. You might even want to remove these lines if your icons are not all the same size. Note that we don't just use numbers to set the height and width—we have to create Unit objects. (This is because the height and width of images are not always set in pixels.)

You should now see an icon in each section item header, as shown in Figure 5.2.

If you see any "broken" images, check that your .png files are named exactly the same as the modules.

5. Add code to display the module name as a tooltip.

As a final step, we will modify the code so that, when a user holds her mouse over one of the module icons, she will see a tooltip that shows which module it refers to (assuming she is using a browser that displays image `ALT` text in this way).

Section Items

STEP-BY-STEP GUIDE: **Adding Icons to Module Headers**

FIGURE 5.2
Module icons in the section item header controls.

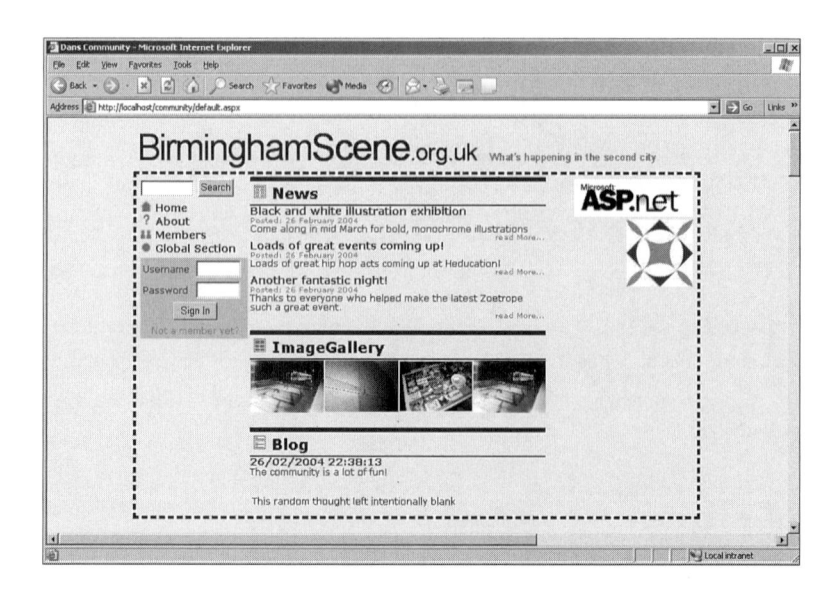

Open `SectionItemHeader.ascx.vb` and add the code highlighted in Listing 5.5.

LISTING 5.5 Addition to `Global/Controls/SectionItemHeader.ascx.vb`

```
Private Sub Page_Load(ByVal sender As System.Object, ByVal e As System.EventArgs) _
Handles MyBase.Load

  'get the section item object of the SectionItemControl that this control is attached to
  Dim sectionItem As SectionItem = CType(Me.Parent, SectionItemControl).SectionItem

  ModuleIcon.Height = New Unit(20)
  ModuleIcon.Width = New Unit(20)
  ModuleIcon.ImageUrl = "../../images/ModuleIcons/" & _
  sectionItem.ModuleView.CommunityModule.Name & ".png"
  ModuleIcon.AlternateText = sectionItem.ModuleView.CommunityModule.Name
```

You should now see tooltips when you hold the mouse over module icons.

`ALT` text is a great way to add information about what graphical icons mean.

STEP-BY-STEP GUIDE: Adding a New Icon to Module Instances That Have Been Updated in the Last Week

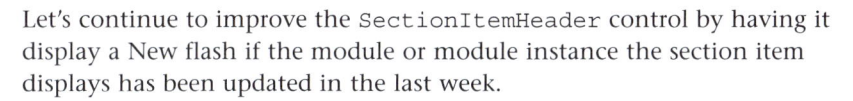

CHALLENGE:
Distinguishing Global Instances

It would be good to distinguish global module instances from specific module instances somehow. An obvious way to do this would be through the module icons because different icons could be used for global instances.

Add additional code to display an alternative icon for modules when the global instance is being displayed.

STEP-BY-STEP GUIDE:
Adding a New Icon to Module Instances That Have Been Updated in the Last Week

Let's continue to improve the `SectionItemHeader` control by having it display a New flash if the module or module instance the section item displays has been updated in the last week.

The steps we need to take are

1. Open `Global/CoreObjects/CommunityModule.vb` and add the following property at the end (but before the end class line):

```
Public ReadOnly Property LastUpdated() As DateTime
  Get
    Dim instance As ModuleInstance
    Dim result As DateTime = DateTime.Now.AddYears(-10)
    For Each instance In Me.ModuleInstances
      If instance.LastUpdated > result Then
        result = instance.LastUpdated
      End If
    Next
    Return result
  End Get
End Property
```

The property loops through each instance of the module and finds the one that was updated most recently. It then returns that date and time.

We need to add this because, at present, we have the ability to tell when a module instance was last updated (because the `ModuleInstance` object stores the date and time it was last updated), but in order to find when a module was updated, we need to check when each of its instances was updated. We could do this at each point where we need the information, but it is much easier to add the property to `ModuleInstance`.

100 Section Items

STEP-BY-STEP GUIDE: **Adding a New Icon to Module Instances That Have Been Updated in the Last Week**

2. Add a new image control to `SectionItemHeader`, to the right of the text. Give it the ID `NewIcon` and set the `ImageUrl` property to `../../images/NewIcon.png`.

   Although the image control will end up rendering to an `<IMG>` element in `default.aspx`, we give the path to the image file relative to the control in which we are currently coding. This is a good thing because it means that user controls that reference images will work, no matter where the page they are placed in is located in the application.

3. Open `Community/Web.config` and find the `<appSettings>` section. Add a new setting, as shown in the following highlighted code:

```
<appSettings>

<add key="CommunityName" value="Dan's Community" />
<add key="HomePageSectionID" value="64" />
<add key="NewIconDays" value="7" />
<add key="connectionString"
        value="Data Source=inspiron;Initial Catalog=community;
        ↪User Id=community;
        ↪Password=community;" />
```

> **DESIGN TIP**
>
> It is a good idea to try to keep values that might be changed in the `Web.config` file. That way, changing them does not require changes to source code files or a recompile of the project.

This will enable us to change the number of days that a module or instance remains new after being modified. We could have hard-coded this value into the code that we are going to add, but it would then be much harder to alter it later.

4. Open `SectionItemHeader.ascx.vb` and find the code that executes when a global instance is being displayed. Add the following highlighted code:

```
If sectionItem.IsGlobal = True Then
    'create a link to the global instance of the module
    If _Text = Nothing Then
        HeaderLink.Text =
        ↪sectionItem.ModuleView.CommunityModule.Name
    Else
        HeaderLink.Text = _Text
    End If

    If _LinkToModule = True Then
        HeaderLink.NavigateUrl = "../../default.aspx?Module=" + _
```

STEP-BY-STEP GUIDE: **Adding a New Icon to Module Instances That Have Been Updated in the Last Week**

```
sectionItem.ModuleView.CommunityModule.PrimaryKey1.ToString
    End If

  If sectionItem.ModuleView.CommunityModule.LastUpdated >
  ↪DateTime.Now.AddDays(0 -
  ↪ConfigurationSettings.AppSettings("NewIconDays")) Then
    NewIcon.Visible = True
    NewIcon.AlternateText = "Updated: " &
    ↪sectionItem.ModuleView.CommunityModule.LastUpdated.
    ↪ToShortDateString
  Else
    NewIcon.Visible = False
  End If
Else
```

You can see that we check the `LastUpdated` value for the module against the current date minus the number of days that we set up in the `Web.config`. If the `LastUpdated` value is greater (that is, later), we set the New icon to be visible and set its `ALT` text (which will appear when the user holds the cursor over the image) to the date the module was last updated.

   5. Add the following highlighted code to the code that executes when a module instance is being displayed:

```
If _LinkToModule = True Then
  HeaderLink.NavigateUrl = "../../default.aspx?Module=" + _
      sectionItem.ModuleView.CommunityModule.PrimaryKey1.ToString + _
      "&Instance=" + sectionItem.ModuleInstance.PrimaryKey1.ToString
End If

If sectionItem.ModuleInstance.LastUpdated > DateTime.Now.AddDays(0 -
↪ConfigurationSettings.AppSettings("NewIconDays")) Then
  NewIcon.Visible = True
  NewIcon.AlternateText = "Updated: " &
  ↪sectionItem.ModuleInstance.LastUpdated.ToShortDateString
Else
  NewIcon.Visible = False
```

This does the same thing as the previous code, but this time we are checking the `LastUpdated` property of the module instance, rather than the module.

Figure 5.3 shows the global Blog module with a new icon in the section item header.

STEP-BY-STEP GUIDE: **Adding a New Icon to Module Instances That Have Been Updated in the Last Week**

FIGURE 5.3
The global Blog module with a New icon.

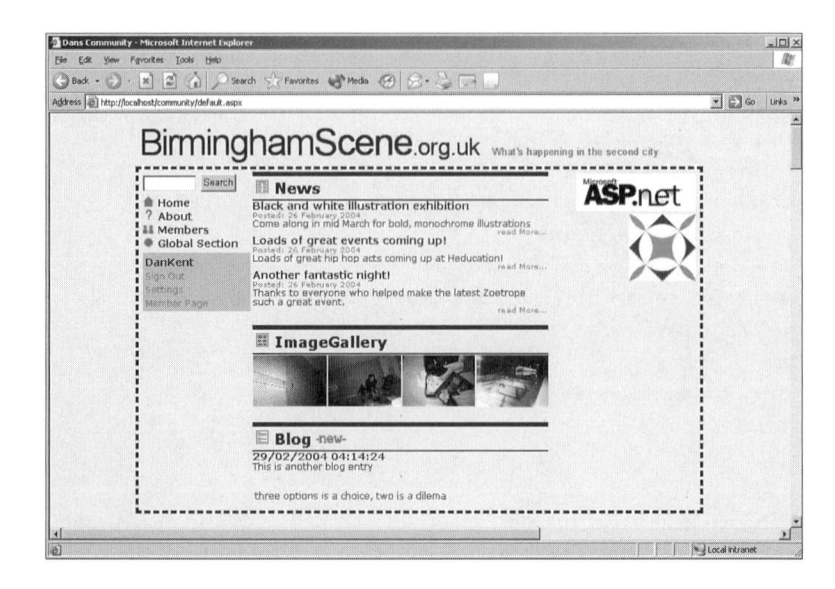

In this case, I added a new blog entry in order to check that the New icon was displayed for that module.

The icon is also displayed on the Blog module on my Member page, as shown in Figure 5.4.

FIGURE 5.4
An instance of the Blog module with a New icon.

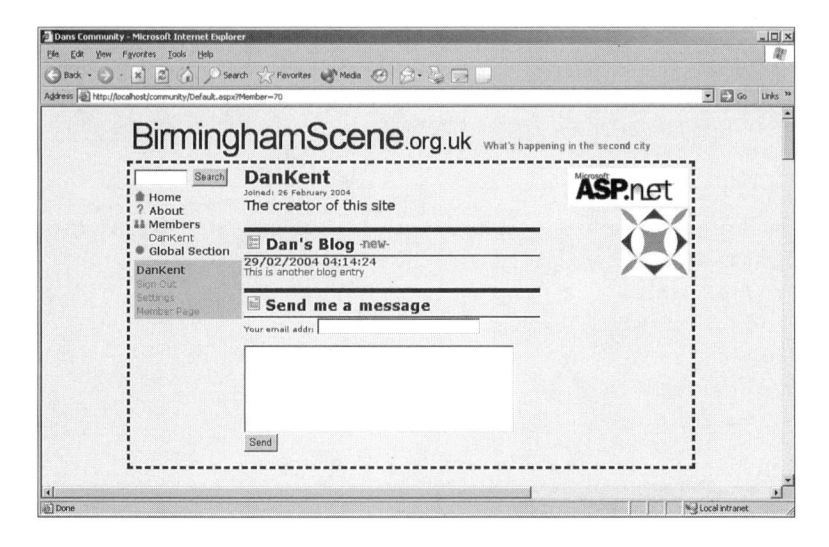

STEP-BY-STEP GUIDE: **Adding New Icons to the Navigation**

The New icon will not be displayed on other members' Blog modules (unless they have recently added an entry). Jenny's Member page, shown in Figure 5.5, does not show the icon.

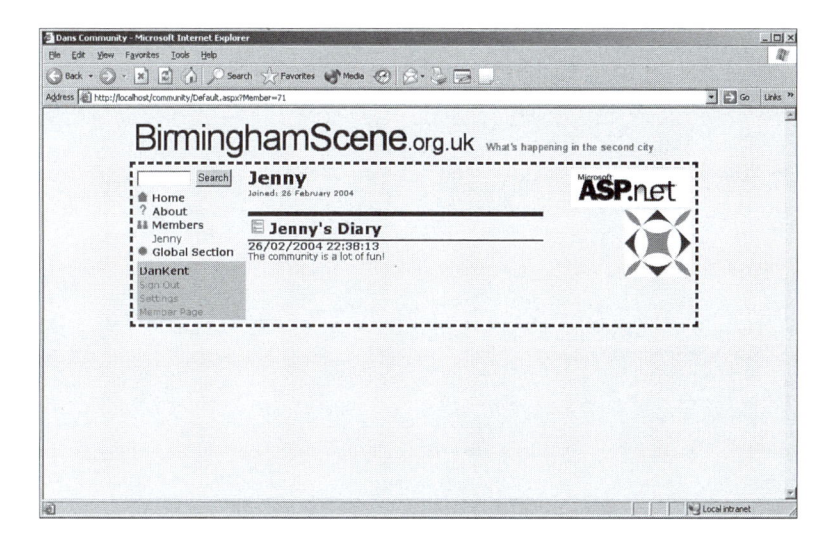

FIGURE 5.5

An instance of the Blog module that does not show a New icon.

STEP-BY-STEP GUIDE:
Adding New Icons to the Navigation

We have already added code that will tell users which modules and module instances have been updated recently. However, they will only see those icons if they view a section that contains a recently updated module or instance. It would be good to provide similar icons in the navigation to show which sections contain recently updated items.

We will now look at some changes that we can make to add a similar feature to the navigation control. We looked at how the navigation control works in detail in Chapter 4, "Experimenting with the Code."

Here are the steps we need to take to achieve this:

1. Add the `LastUpdated` property to the `Section` object.

The first problem we have is that there is currently no way of telling directly when a section was last updated. We could retrieve all of the `SectionItems` from each section, but it would be much better if the Section object had a `LastUpdated` property just like some of the other objects.

Open `Global/CoreObjects/Section.vb` and add the property shown in Listing 5.6.

STEP-BY-STEP GUIDE: Adding New Icons to the Navigation

LISTING 5.6 `LastUpdated` Property to Add to `Global/CoreObjects/Section.vb`

```
Public ReadOnly Property LastUpdated() As DateTime
  Get
    Dim sectionItem As SectionItem
    Dim result As DateTime = DateTime.Now.AddYears(-100)
    For Each sectionItem In Me.SectionItems
      If sectionItem.IsGlobal Then
        If sectionItem.ModuleView.CommunityModule.LastUpdated > result Then
          result = sectionItem.ModuleView.CommunityModule.LastUpdated
        End If
      Else
        If sectionItem.ModuleInstance.LastUpdated > result Then
          result = sectionItem.ModuleInstance.LastUpdated
        End If
      End If
    Next
    Return result
  End Get
End Property
```

First, we create a new `DateTime` object with a date of 100 years ago.

We loop through the section items contained in the section. If the section item is global, we get the `LastUpdated` value for the module it refers to and compare it to the local `DateTime` variable. If it is more recent, we update the variable with the newer value.

If the section item is not global, we get the `LastUpdated` value from the `ModuleInstance` of the section item and do the comparison in the same way.

When the loop is completed, we return the local `DateTime` variable.

Now that we can tell when a section was last updated, we can proceed with our modifications to the navigation control.

2. Add image controls to the navigation control.

Open `Navigation.ascx` in HTML mode and find the code that displays the global sections. Add the tag that is highlighted in Listing 5.7.

STEP-BY-STEP GUIDE: **Adding New Icons to the Navigation**

LISTING 5.7 `<IMG>` Tag Added to `Global/Controls/Navigation.ascx` for Global Sections

```
<div>
    <a class="Navigation_Item" href="Default.aspx?Section=
➥<%#Container.DataItem.PrimaryKey1%>">
        <img src="images/NavIcons/<%#Container.DataItem.Name%>.png">
        <%#Container.DataItem.Name%>
        <img src="images/NavNew.png" id="GlobalNewIcon" width="20" height="20"
➥runat="server">
    </a>
</div>
```

Next, find the code that loops through the selected member's sections and add the highlighted code shown in Listing 5.8.

LISTING 5.8 `<IMG>` Tag Added to `Global/Controls/Navigation.ascx` for the Selected Member's Sections

```
<asp:Repeater ID="MemberSectionsRepeater" Runat="server" onItemDataBound=
➥"MemberSectionsRepeater_ItemBound">
    <ItemTemplate>
        <div>
            <a class="Navigation_SubSubItem" href="Default.aspx?Section=
➥<%#Container.DataItem.PrimaryKey1%>">
                <%#Container.DataItem.Name%>
                <img src="images/NavNew.png" id="MemberNewIcon"
                    width="15" height="15" runat="server" border="0">
            </a>
        </div>
    </ItemTemplate>
</asp:Repeater>
```

   3. Add an event handler for when the global sections repeater is data-bound.

We need to decide whether the New icon is displayed for each section individually, as the Repeater is binding to the sections. We can use the `ItemBound` event of the repeater control to do this. Using this event, we can write code that will run as each item in the Repeater is data-bound.

Section Items

STEP-BY-STEP GUIDE: **Adding New Icons to the Navigation**

Open the code view for `Navigation.ascx` and add the method shown in Listing 5.9.

LISTING 5.9 `ItemBound` Event Handler to Be Added to `Global/Controls/Navigation.ascx.vb`

```
Protected Sub GlobalSectionsRepeater_ItemBound(ByVal sender As Object,
➥ByVal e As RepeaterItemEventArgs)
  Dim image As HtmlImage
  image = CType(e.Item.FindControl("GlobalNewIcon"), HtmlImage)

  Dim section As Section = CType(e.Item.DataItem, Section)

  If section.LastUpdated > DateTime.Now.AddDays(0 -
➥ConfigurationSettings.AppSettings("NewIconDays")) Then
    image.Visible = True
  Else
    image.Visible = False
  End If

End Sub
```

First, we declare a new `HtmlImage` variable. We need to make this point to the object created by the `<img>` tag that we added to `Navigation.ascx`, so we access the `RepeaterItem` through the `RepeaterItemEventArgs` parameter of the event arguments object (e) and use its `FindControl` method to locate the control we want. We have to use `CType` to cast it to the `HtmlImage` type because `FindControl` returns the control as a Control object.

We then use a similar approach to get the Section object that the Repeater item is bound to, through `e.Item.DataItem`.

After we have the image control and the Section object, the rest is easy. We compare the `LastUpdated` value of the section with the current date minus the number of days specified in the configuration. If it is new enough, we make the control visible. If it's not, we make it invisible.

4. Add the event handler to the Repeater object.

The event handler we have just added will not do anything unless it is linked to the correct event of the Repeater.

STEP-BY-STEP GUIDE: **Adding New Icons to the Navigation**

Open `Navigation.ascx` in HTML view and modify the global sections repeater to add the following highlighted attribute:

```
<asp:Repeater id="GlobalSectionsRepeater" runat="server"
➥OnItemDataBound="GlobalSectionsRepeater_ItemBound">
```

This will link the handler to the event.

5. Add an event handler for the member sections repeater.

We will use a very similar approach to add new icons to sections owned by members. Add the method shown in Listing 5.10 to the code-behind for the navigation control.

LISTING 5.10 `ItemBound` **Event Handler for the Member Sections Repeater to Be Added to** `Global/Controls/Navigation.ascx.vb`

```
Protected Sub MemberSectionsRepeater_ItemBound(ByVal sender As Object, _
                                              ByVal e As RepeaterItemEventArgs)
   Dim image As HtmlImage
   image = CType(e.Item.FindControl("MemberNewIcon"), HtmlImage)

   Dim section As Section = CType(e.Item.DataItem, Section)

   If section.LastUpdated > DateTime.Now.AddDays(0 - _
   ➥ConfigurationSettings.AppSettings("NewIconDays")) Then
      image.Visible = True
   Else
      image.Visible = False
   End If
End Sub
```

This works in the exact same way as the event handler for the global sections repeater.

6. Add the event handler to the Repeater object.

Again, we need to link the event handler to the repeater control. Open `Navigation.ascx` in HTML mode and find the Repeater that displays the sections owned by a member. Add the highlighted attribute:

```
<asp:Repeater ID="MemberSectionsRepeater" Runat="server"
         OnItemDataBound="MemberSectionsRepeater_ItemBound">
```

108   Section Items

STEP-BY-STEP GUIDE: Adding an Automated What's New? Page

If you now view the navigation control, you should see the New icons, as shown in Figure 5.6.

FIGURE 5.6
The New icons.

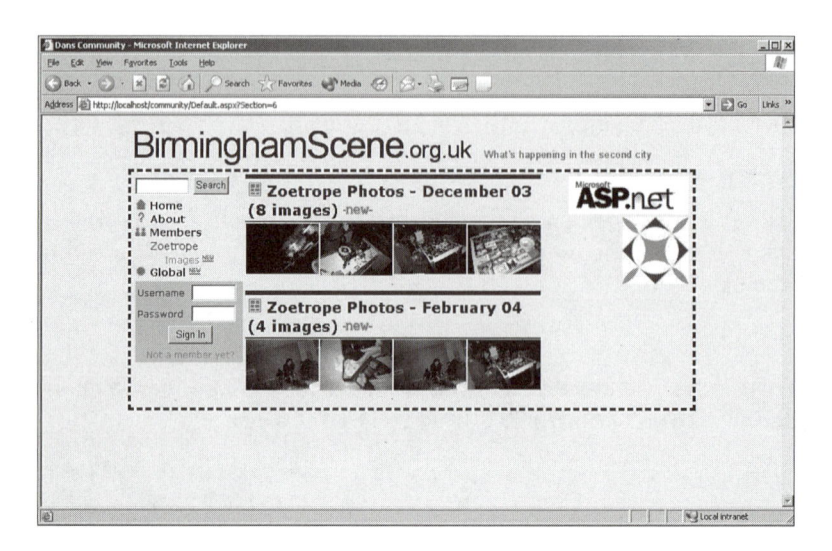

If you don't see icons at all, it might be that the `LastUpdated` dates for items in the community are not recent enough—make some changes or cheat and set the configuration value to a large number of days.

If you see broken-image icons, check that you have an icon with the right name in your `images/` folder.

Let's provide users with another way to see what has been recently updated on the site, by adding an automated What's New? page.

STEP-BY-STEP GUIDE:
Adding an Automated What's New? Page

A What's New? page is a great way for visitors to the site to see what has changed since their last visit.

Here are the steps we will need to take:

1. Create a new Web Form.

Use the Solution Explorer to add a new Web Form to the root folder of the application. Name it `whatsnew.aspx`.

Section Items 109

STEP-BY-STEP GUIDE: **Adding an Automated What's New? Page**

You will probably also want to change the `<title>` element in the HTML view to set the text that is displayed in the title bar.

2. Copy the `default.aspx` layout to `whatsnew.aspx`.

Open `default.aspx` in HTML view and copy everything apart from the opening page directive. Paste the code you have copied into `whatsnew.aspx`.

3. Add a `DataList` to the form.

In design view, drag a new `DataList` control into the central content area of the form. Use the Property Explorer to set the ID property to `UpdatedSectionsDataList`.

4. Add a method to `CoreModule.vb` to get the most recently updated sections.

Before we can display recently updated sections in the `DataList`, we need a way to get the sections. To do this, we will add a new method to `CoreModule.vb`.

Open `CoreModule.vb` and add the following method near the other methods dealing with sections, as shown in Listing 5.11.

TIP
We could have implemented `whatsnew` within `default.aspx`, but I decided that major pages such as the Members page and `whatsnew` should be on a Web Form of their own so that the page layout can be altered, if desired. For example, we might not want to display the extras column on some pages.

LISTING 5.11 Method to Add to `Global/CoreModule.vb`

```
Public Function GetRecentlyUpdatedSections(ByVal number As Integer) As IList

  Dim crit As New Criteria

  Dim allSections As IList = QueryFacade.Find(Type.GetType("Community.Section"), crit)      1 ▼

  Dim sortedSections As New SortedList
  Dim s As Section
  For Each s In allSections                                                                 2 ▼
      AddSectionToSortedList(sortedSections, s, s.LastUpdated)
  Next

  Dim results As New ArrayList
  Dim length As Integer = sortedSections.Keys.Count - 1
  Dim count As Integer = 0


  While count < number And count < length + 1                                               3 ▼
```

STEP-BY-STEP GUIDE: **Adding an Automated What's New? Page**

LISTING 5.11 Method to Add to `Global/CoreModule.vb` (continued)

```
    results.Add(sortedSections.GetByIndex(length - count))
    count = count + 1
  End While

  Return results

End Function
```

1▲ First, we make a call to the persistence service to get all of the sections in the community.

2▲ Then, we loop through the sections, calling a special method (more on this later) to add them to a `SortedList` collection. `SortedList` is one of the less commonly used collections. It stores a set of key/value pairs, sorted by the keys. We use the `LastUpdated` value of each section as the key and the section itself as the value.

3▲ Next, we use a while loop to grab sections from the end of the list and add them to an `ArrayList` until we have the specified number or we have used all of the sections. The `ArrayList` is then returned.

This method requires a "helper" method to do its work. Add the following method to `CoreModule.vb`, just below the previous method:

```
Private Sub AddSectionToSortedList(ByVal list As SortedList, _
                                   ByVal s As Section, _
                                   ByVal d As System.DateTime)
    If list.Contains(d) Then
      AddSectionToSortedList(list, s, d.AddMinutes(1))
    Else
      list.Add(d, s)
    End If
End Sub
```

The reason we need this is that `SortedList` requires each of the keys that are stored in it to be unique—if we try to add a key/value pair with a key that already exists in the collection, we will cause an exception to be thrown.

Therefore, we check whether the `LastUpdated` key is already in the `SortedList`. If it is, we make another call to

STEP-BY-STEP GUIDE: **Adding an Automated What's New? Page**

`AddSectionToSortedList` with a `DateTime` one minute later. New calls will be made until a `DateTime` is found that does not already exist in the collection.

If the `DateTime` is not found in the collection, the key/value pair is added to the `SortedList`.

5. Add code to populate the `DataList`.

Now that we have a method for getting the recently updated sections, we can add code to `whatsnew.aspx` to bind the `DataList` that we added to the sections.

Open `whatsnew.aspx.vb` and add the following code to the `Page_Load` event handler:

> **DESIGN TIP**
>
> Recursive methods like this are really useful, but we have to be very careful to ensure that there are no circumstances in which the method will go on calling itself forever and end up in an infinite loop—that will result in a stack overflow exception as the number of method calls gets too great.

```
Private Sub Page_Load(ByVal sender As System.Object, _
            ByVal e As System.EventArgs) _
     Handles MyBase.Load

  Dim coreMod As New CoreModule
  UpdatedSectionsDataList.DataSource = _
       coreMod.GetRecentlyUpdatedSections(20)
  UpdatedSectionsDataList.DataBind()

End Sub
```

This will bind the `DataList` to the 20 most recently updated sections (or all of the sections if there are 20 or fewer sections in the community).

6. Add a template to the `DataList` to display the sections.

The `DataList` will not do anything with the data unless we tell it to, so open `whatsnew.aspx` in HTML view and add the following template to the `DataList`:

```
<asp:DataList id="UpdatedSectionsDataList" runat="server">
  <ItemTemplate>
    <a href="default.aspx?Section=<%#Container.DataItem.PrimaryKey1%>">
      <%#Container.DataItem.Name%>
    </a>
  </ItemTemplate>
</asp:DataList>
```

We use the primary key of each section to create a link to display that section. We also use the name of the section for the text of the link.

The `whatsnew.aspx` page should now look something like Figure 5.7.

Section Items

STEP-BY-STEP GUIDE: Adding an Automated What's New? Page

FIGURE 5.7
The `whatsnew.aspx` page.

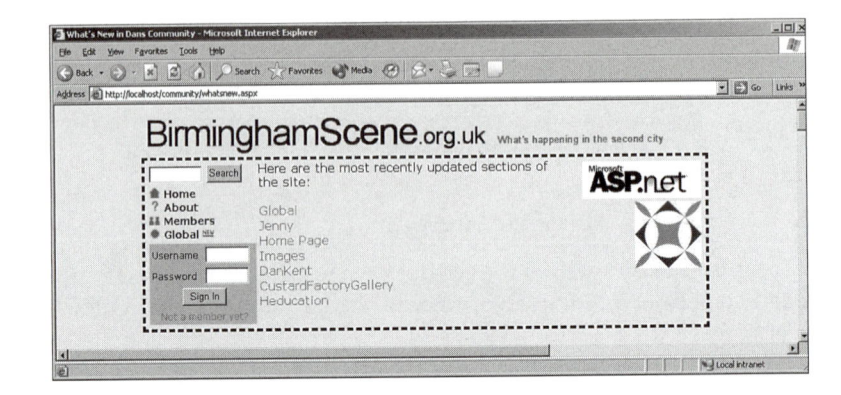

7. Add module icons to show what is in each section.

It would be nice if there was some way for users to see what types of content are included in each section. We can access the `SectionItem` objects that each section contains, and we already have icons for each module type, so this should be an easy addition.

In fact, we don't even have to modify the code-behind! Open `whatsnew.aspx.vb` in HTML view and find the `DataList` that displays the sections. Add the Repeater shown in Listing 5.12 to the item template.

LISTING 5.12 Repeater to Be Added to `whatsnew.aspx.vb`

```
<asp:DataList id="UpdatedSectionsDataList" runat="server">
 <ItemTemplate>
  <a href="default.aspx?Section=<%#Container.DataItem.PrimaryKey1%>">
   <%#Container.DataItem.Name%>
   <asp:Repeater ID="ModuleIconsRepeater"
      DataSource="<%#Container.DataItem.SectionItems%>" Runat="server">
    <ItemTemplate>
<img src="images/ModuleIcons/<%#Container.DataItem.ModuleView.CommunityModule.Name%>.png"
      border="0"
      alt="<%#Container.DataItem.ModuleView.CommunityModule.Name%>"/>
    </ItemTemplate>
   </asp:Repeater>
  </a>
 </ItemTemplate>
</asp:DataList>
```

STEP-BY-STEP GUIDE: **Adding an Automated What's New? Page**

Here, we are nesting one data-bound control inside another. One repeater control will be created for each item in the `DataList` control. The datasource of each Repeater is taken from the `SectionItems` property of the section to which the item in the `DataList` is bound. Therefore, the datasource is a collection of `SectionItem` objects.

Inside the Repeater, we create an `IMG` element, using the name of the module that the `SectionItem` displays. (We access it through `SectionItem.ModuleView.CommunityModule` rather than `SectionItem.ModuleInstance.CommunityModule` because using the oath through `ModuleView` will work whether the `SectionItem` is displaying a specific instance or the global instance of the module.)

We also set the `ALT` text of the `IMG` element to the name of the module so that users will get a tooltip when they hold the pointer over the icon.

This is a great example of how the persistence service enables us to add new features to the application very rapidly. Rather than having to write new data access code, we were able to simply bind the Repeater to a property of the objects that the `DataList` was displaying. All of the additional data access work to retrieve the `SectionItems`, `ModuleViews`, and module names that we need is done for us by the persistence service.

If you now view `whatsnew.aspx` in the browser, you should see that the icons have been added, as shown in Figure 5.8.

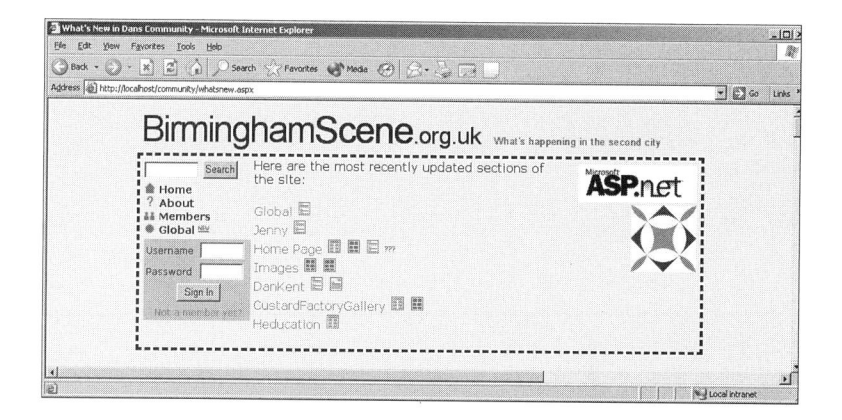

FIGURE 5.8
What's New? page with module icons.

   8. Add an automatic key of module icons.

Although users can use the module icon tooltips to see what the icons mean, it would be nice to provide a key on this page to explain the icons.

Section Items

STEP-BY-STEP GUIDE: **Adding an Automated What's New? Page**

This is very easily done. First, use the design view to drag a new `DataList` onto `whatsnew.aspx`, underneath the list of sections in the main body area. Use the Property Explorer to give it the ID `ModuleIconKeyDataList`. Then, open the HTML view and add a template to it as shown in Listing 5.13.

LISTING 5.13 `DataList` for the Automatic Key

```
<hr />
<asp:DataList id="ModuleIconKeyDataList" RepeatColumns="2" runat="server">
  <ItemTemplate>
    <img src="images/ModuleIcons/<%#Container.DataItem.Name%>.png"
         border="0"/>
    <%#Container.DataItem.Name%>
  </ItemTemplate>
</asp:DataList>
```

Note that I have also added an `<hr />` element to separate the key from the `DataList` of sections.

Also note that I have added the `RepeatColumns` attribute to the `DataList` in order to have it display with two columns.

You can see that this template will simply display the icon for each module in its datasource, followed by the module name.

All we need to do now is give this `DataList` a datasource. Open `whatsnew.aspx.vb` and add the following lines to the `Page_Load` event handler:

```
Private Sub Page_Load(ByVal sender As System.Object, _
                     ByVal e As System.EventArgs) _
           Handles MyBase.Load

   Dim coreMod As New CoreModule
   UpdatedSectionsDataList.DataSource = _
      coreMod.GetRecentlyUpdatedSections(20)
   UpdatedSectionsDataList.DataBind()

   ModuleIconKeyDataList.DataSource = coreMod.GetAllModules()
   ModuleIconKeyDataList.DataBind()

End Sub
```

STEP-BY-STEP GUIDE: **Displaying the Latest Member to Join**

We simply bind the `DataList` to the `GetAllModules` method of the core module business service class.

You should now see the key, as shown in Figure 5.9.

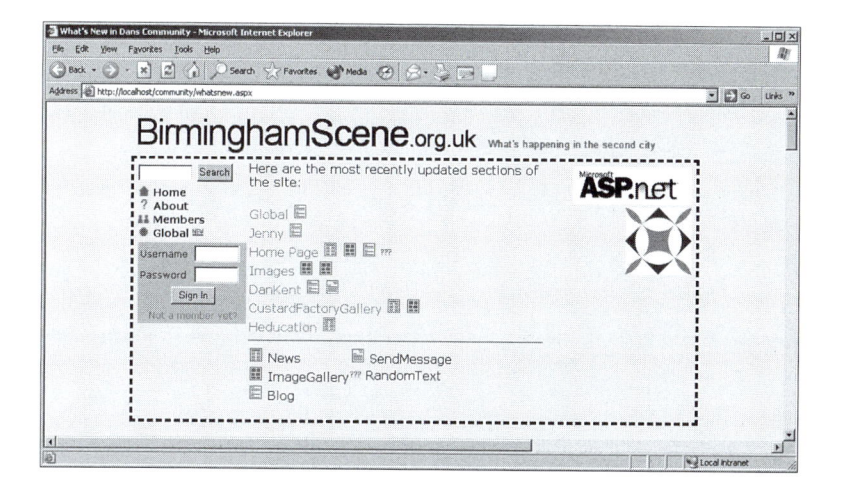

FIGURE 5.9
The automatic key of module icons.

CHALLENGE:
Showing Only Non-global Sections in What's New?

In many ways, it does not make sense to display global sections in `whats new.aspx`—global sections simply collect information from the sections that members add.

Make a change so that only nonglobal sections are displayed on `whats new.aspx`.

Hint: Only a small addition to `CoreModule.GetRecentlyUpdatedSections` is required.

STEP-BY-STEP GUIDE:
Displaying the Latest Member to Join

The nicest thing about many online communities is that when new members join, they bring new ideas and input. A common problem is that existing members are simply not aware when a new member has joined. A good solution to this is to display the newest member on the home page so that everyone can see that someone new has joined.

Section Items

STEP-BY-STEP GUIDE: **Displaying the Latest Member to Join**

One way of doing this would be to simply add code to `default.aspx` to display the member and a link to his Member page. This would work, but it would go against our aims of organizing our code logically and building reusable controls where possible. Instead, we will create a new control that will do the work of displaying the newest member.

Here are the steps we will take:

1. Create a method in `CoreModule.vb` to return the newest `Member` object.

> **DESIGN TIP**
>
> Where possible, the presentation layer should only receive the data that it needs to display. Having the presentation code do a lot of data processing breaks the separation-of-layers concept.

The first thing we have to do is provide a way to get the newest member. We could retrieve all members and search through for the newest, but it is much better to provide a method in the business service class that returns exactly what we want.

Because we want to retrieve a `Member` object, which is one of the core persistent objects, we need to add a method to the `CoreModule` class.

Open `Global/CoreModule.vb` and scroll to the part of the file that defines methods for dealing with `Member` objects.

Add the following method. (It does not matter exactly where it goes, provided you do not add it inside another method.)

```
Public Function GetNewestMember() As Member
    Dim crit As New Criteria
    crit.AddEqualTo("_Visible", True)
    crit.AddOrderBy("_DateJoined", True)

    Return QueryFacade.FindObject(Type.GetType("Community.Member"), crit)
End Function
```

This shows a useful technique for requesting an object from the persistence service that has the most extreme value for one of its attributes. We use a criterion to sort the query by the `_DateJoined` attribute, but request only a single object (by calling `FindObject` rather than `Find`).

2. Create a new user control.

Use the VS.NET Solution Explorer to add a new user control called `NewestMember.ascx` in the `Global/Controls` folder.

3. Add text and hyperlink controls.

Open the HTML view of the new user control and add the following code:

STEP-BY-STEP GUIDE: **Displaying the Latest Member to Join**

```
<div class="NewestMember_Text">
    Welcome to our newest Member:
</div>
<div class="NewestMember_Link">
    <asp:HyperLink id="MemberNameLink" runat="server" />
</div>
```

After adding this code, move to the design view and click the new control followed by the Save button. Doing this automatically creates a declaration of the new hyperlink control in the code-behind. This doesn't happen automatically from the HTML view, so we need to switch briefly to design view.

4. Add style sheet classes.

Create some new classes in `styles.css` for the elements we have just defined in the newest user control:

```
.NewestMember_Table
{
    background-color: #D3C765;
}

.NewestMember_Text
{
    font-size: 12;
    line-height: 1;
    text-align:center;
}

.NewestMember_Link
{
    font-size: 14;
    font-weight: bold;
    line-height: 1;
    text-align:center;
}
```

5. Add initialization code.

Open the code view for the `NewestMember.ascx` control that we just created. Add the code shown in Listing 5.14 to `Page_Load`.

STEP-BY-STEP GUIDE: **Displaying the Latest Member to Join**

LISTING 5.14 Initialization Code for the Newest Member Control

```
Private Sub Page_Load(ByVal sender As System.Object, _
                ByVal e As System.EventArgs) _
        Handles MyBase.Load

Dim coreModule As New CoreModule

Dim member As Member = CoreModule.GetNewestMember

If Not member Is Nothing Then
   MemberNameLink.Text = member.Username
MemberNameLink.NavigateUrl = "../../default.aspx?Member=" & member.PrimaryKey1
Else
   Me.Visible = False
End If
End Sub
```

Note that we check that `CoreModule.GetNewestMember` does actually return a `Member` object. If we do not, a community site with no visible members would return an error on the home page—not a good way to get a new community started!

> **DESIGN TIP**
>
> It is always a good idea to check for null results (results of nothing) when there is any possibility that they could occur.

If there is no `Member` object, we set the `NewestMember` control itself to be invisible—there's no point displaying the newest member control if there are no members.

6. Add the control to `default.aspx`.

Open `default.aspx` in HTML view and add the following directive at the top of the file, along with the other register directives:

```
<%@ Register tagprefix="community"
        tagname="NewestMember"
        src="global/controls/NewestMember.ascx" %>
```

Find the code that displays the right column. (There is a comment above it.) Add the following highlighted line:

```
<!--Right hand Column-->
<td vAlign="top" width="200">
  <community:NewestMember runat="server" />
  <community:Extras id="Extras1" runat="server" />
</td>
```

STEP-BY-STEP GUIDE: **Allowing Members to Have a Custom Image on Their Page**

This will add the control at the top of the right column, just under the site header. You can, of course, add the control wherever you like. You might want to experiment with different positions for it. In the position I have used, the result looks like Figure 5.10.

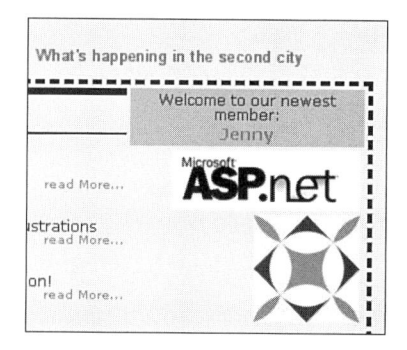

FIGURE 5.10
The newest member control in action.

STEP-BY-STEP GUIDE:
Allowing Members to Have a Custom Image on Their Page

The final modification we will make in this chapter is to allow members more control over their Member pages. They can already change their introductory text to whatever they like. We are now going to allow them to upload an image that will be displayed alongside their introductory text.

Here are the steps we need to take:

1. Create a `MemberImages` subfolder in `/data/`.

We create this folder in `/data/`, rather than in `images`, because users will be able to upload new images—all updatable data is kept in the `/data/` folder.

2. Add the image to the `MemberControl`.

Open `Global/Controls/MemberControl.ascx` in HTML view and change the code as shown in Listing 5.15 to include an image.

Section Items

STEP-BY-STEP GUIDE: Allowing Members to Have a Custom Image on Their Page

LISTING 5.15 Adding an Image for the Member's Personal Image in `Global/Controls/MemberControl.ascx`

```
<table width="100%">
    <tr>
        <td valign="top" width="10%">
            <asp:Image id="MemberImage" runat="server" Width="200px"></asp:Image>
        </td>
        <td valign="top">
            <div class="MemberPageName">
                <asp:Label id="NameLabel" runat="server"></asp:Label>
            </div>
            <div class="MemberPageDateJoined">
                Joined:
                <asp:Label id="DateJoinedLabel" runat="server"></asp:Label>
            </div>
            <div class="MemberPageIntroText">
                <asp:Label id="IntroTextLabel" runat="server"></asp:Label>
            </div>
        </td>
    </tr>
</table>
```

As previously, remember to step briefly into design view and click the new controls followed by the Save button to create declarations in the code-behind.

You can also see that a table has been added to lay out everything properly.

3. Add code to `Page_Load` to initialize the image.

Open the code-behind for `MemberControl.ascx` and add the code that is highlighted in Listing 5.16.

LISTING 5.16 Initialization Code to Display the Member's Personal Image in `Global/Controls/MemberControl.ascx.vb`

```
Private Sub Page_Load(ByVal sender As System.Object, _
                ByVal e As System.EventArgs) 
        Handles MyBase.Load
```

STEP-BY-STEP GUIDE: **Allowing Members to Have a Custom Image on Their Page**

LISTING 5.16 Initialization Code to Display the Member's Personal Image in `Global/Controls/MemberControl.ascx.vb` (continued)

```
  NameLabel.Text = _Member.Username
  IntroTextLabel.Text = _Member.IntroText
  DateJoinedLabel.Text = _Member.DateJoined.ToLongDateString

  If File.Exists(ConfigurationSettings.AppSettings("FileSystemRoot") & _
➥"/Data/MemberImages/" & _Member.PrimaryKey1.ToString & ".jpg") Then
    MemberImage.Visible = True
    MemberImage.ImageUrl = "../../data/MemberImages/" & _
      ➥_Member.PrimaryKey1.ToString & ".jpg"
  Else
    MemberImage.Visible = False
  End If
End Sub
```

You will also need to add the following `Imports` statement to the top of the file in order to be able to use the `File` class:

`Imports System.IO`

We check whether a file named `[MemberID].jpg` exists. If it does, we make the image visible and set its URL. If not, we make it invisible.

Note that we use a configuration setting to get the physical file system root for the application. We could use `Server.MapPath` to do this, but there can be problems with some Web hosts, so we opted to manually configure it.

The `MemberControl` will now display the member image if it exists. We now need to allow members to upload their member images.

4. Add the Upload Image option to `MemberSettings.aspx`.

Open `MemberSettings.aspx` in HTML view and find the part of the code that displays the My Details tab. Add the highlighted code in Listing 5.17.

Section Items

STEP-BY-STEP GUIDE: Allowing Members to Have a Custom Image on Their Page

LISTING 5.17 Adding Controls to Set the Member Image in `MemberSettings.aspx`

```
<mytab:PageView>
    <DIV> </DIV>
    <DIV>New Password:
        <asp:TextBox id="Password" runat="server" TextMode="Password">
        </asp:TextBox>
    </DIV>
    <DIV>Repeat Password:
        <asp:TextBox id="RepeatPassword" runat="server" TextMode="Password">
        </asp:TextBox>
    </DIV>
    <DIV>Intro:
    </DIV>
    <DIV>
        <asp:TextBox id="IntroText" runat="server" TextMode="MultiLine" Height="63px"
        ➥Width="389px"></asp:TextBox></DIV>
    <DIV>Email:
        <asp:TextBox id="Email" runat="server"></asp:TextBox>
        <asp:CheckBox id="PublicEmail" runat="server" Text="Make email public?">
        ➥</asp:CheckBox></DIV>
    <DIV align="center">
        <asp:Button id="UpdateDetails" onclick="UpdateDetails_Click" runat="server"
        ➥Text="Update"></asp:Button>
    </DIV>
    <DIV>
        <hr>
    </DIV>
    <div>
        <INPUT id="MemberImage" type="file" runat="server" NAME="MemberImage">
        <asp:Button id="UploadMemberImage_Button" runat="server" Text="New Member Image"
        ➥Width="129px"></asp:Button>
    </div>
    <div>
        <asp:Image id="MemberImagePreview" runat="server" Width="100px"></asp:Image>
    </div>
</mytab:PageView>
```

This time, we cannot simply click the controls in design view to add the declarations that we need to the code-behind. An unfortunate downside of the tabstrip WebControl is that it is not fully compatible with the Visual Studio .NET design view. Although we can view the controls that

STEP-BY-STEP GUIDE: Allowing Members to Have a Custom Image on Their Page

are inside the tabstrip, we cannot select them. We therefore have to add the declarations to the code-behind ourselves, as shown in Listing 5.18.

LISTING 5.18 Adding Declarations for the Controls to `MemberSettings.aspx.vb`

```
Protected WithEvents NewSectionButton As System.Web.UI.WebControls.Button
Protected WithEvents SectionsDataList As System.Web.UI.WebControls.DataList
Protected WithEvents SectionItemsDataList As System.Web.UI.WebControls.DataList
Protected WithEvents MemberImage As System.Web.UI.HtmlControls.HtmlInputFile
Protected WithEvents MemberImagePreview As System.Web.UI.WebControls.Image
Protected WithEvents UpdateDetails As System.Web.UI.WebControls.Button

Protected _Member As Member
```
---

5. Add code to `Page_Load` to initialize the preview.

Open the code-behind for `MemberSettings.aspx` and find the `Page_Load` event handler. Add the highlighted code in Listing 5.19.

LISTING 5.19 Adding Code to Initialize the Member Image in `MemberSettings.aspx.vb`

```
NewModuleDropDown.DataSource = coreModule.GetAllModulesForMembers
NewModuleDropDown.DataTextField = "Name"
NewModuleDropDown.DataValueField = "PrimaryKey1"
NewModuleDropDown.DataBind()

SectionsDataList.DataSource = _Member.Sections
SectionsDataList.DataBind()

If File.Exists(ConfigurationSettings.AppSettings("FileSystemRoot") & _
➥"/data/MemberImages/" & _Member.PrimaryKey1 & ".jpg") Then
    MemberImagePreview.Visible = True
    MemberImagePreview.ImageUrl = "data/MemberImages/" & _
        _Member.PrimaryKey1 & ".jpg"
  Else
    MemberImagePreview.Visible = False
  End If

End If
```

Section Items

STEP-BY-STEP GUIDE: **Allowing Members to Have a Custom Image on Their Page**

As with the `MemberControl` code, you will need to add the following `Imports` statement to the top of the file:

```
Imports System.IO
```

This does the same as the code we added to `MemberControl.ascx.vb`—it checks whether a member image exists for the member and if it does, it sets up the image control to display it.

6. Add code to handle the `Click` event of the Upload button.

Add the following event handler to `MemberSettings.aspx.vb` as shown in Listing 5.20.

LISTING 5.20 Event Handler to Allow Upload of New Member Image in `MemberSettings.aspx.vb`

```
Private Sub UploadMemberImage_Button_Click(ByVal sender As System.Object, _
                                    ByVal e As System.EventArgs) _
        Handles UploadMemberImage_Button.Click
    Dim file As HttpPostedFile = MemberImage.PostedFile

    If file.ContentType = "image/jpg" Or file.ContentType = _
            "image/jpeg" Or file.ContentType = "image/pjpeg" Then
        Dim path As String = ConfigurationSettings.AppSettings("FileSystemRoot") & _
➥"/data/MemberImages/" & _Member.PrimaryKey & ".jpg"

        Dim fileLength As Integer = file.ContentLength
        'create a byte array to put the file into
        Dim fileData() As Byte = New Byte(fileLength) {}

        'read the file into the byte array
        file.InputStream.Read(fileData, 0, fileLength)

        'create a filestream to write the file
        Dim fileStream As FileStream = New FileStream(path, FileMode.Create)

        'write the file
        fileStream.Write(fileData, 0, fileData.Length)

        'close the file stream
        fileStream.Close()
    End If
End Sub
```

STEP-BY-STEP GUIDE: **Allowing Members to Have a Custom Image on Their Page**

First, we check whether the file that is being uploaded is a jpeg file. (To keep things simple, we only allow members to have a jpeg file as their member image.) To do this, we need to check the content type of the file against the different MIME types that jpeg files can have. (MIME types are supposed to be standard, but there is a surprising, or perhaps not so surprising, amount of variation in them.)

Then, we create a string variable to hold the path we want to save the image to and set it up.

Next, we get the length of the file that is being uploaded. At this point, we could check whether the file is within size limits of our choice, to prevent members from uploading images that are too big. For now, we allow files of any size.

We need a space in memory to receive the uploaded file, so we create an array of bytes of the same size as the file. We then read the file into the array through the file's input stream.

To save the file, we create a `FileStream` that points at the correct path. We then write the file from the byte array to the file stream and close the stream.

7. Set the encoding type of the form.

There is one more change that we need to make. In order to accept binary data (such as a jpeg image), our Web Form needs to be set to use the correct encoding type. If you open `MemberSettings.aspx` in HTML mode and look at the `<form>` element, you will see that it has no special encoding set:

```
<form id="Form1" method="post" runat="server">
```

This will only accept text data, ignoring any jpeg images that are sent to it.

If you open `default.aspx`, you will see that it uses a different encoding:

```
<form id="Form1"
      method="post"
      runat="server"
      enctype="multipart/form-data">
```

This allows it to receive both text and binary data. (It needs to because the ImageGallery module, and potentially other future modules, sit inside it and need to upload binary data.)

STEP-BY-STEP GUIDE: Adding Configurable Module Names

Therefore, change the `<form>` element in `MemberSettings.aspx` so that it uses multipart/form data as its encoding type and the Member Settings page will be able to upload binary data.

CHALLENGE:
Imposing a Size Limit on Uploaded Images

In the last section, we mentioned that the image upload code could have imposed a restriction on the image size that can be uploaded.

See if you can add code that will impose such a limit.

STEP-BY-STEP GUIDE:
Adding Configurable Module Names

In the current system, the names of modules are fixed—because the name is used by the system to locate the files belonging to the module, we cannot change the module name without making a lot of other changes. It would be much better if the name used by the framework were separate from the name displayed to users of the community.

> **DESIGN TIP**
>
> It is usually a good idea to separate text that is used by the system from text that is displayed—it is a common requirement to change display text (such as when translating an application to another language), so keeping them separate makes life a lot easier.

We will now make changes to the application so that we can configure the display name of each module separately from the name used by the framework to locate the module files.

1. Add a Modules column to the database table.

The first thing we need to do is to change the database table that stores the modules so that it stores the display name for each module.

Open Enterprise Manager and the server; open the database and then Tables. Right-click the tbl_Module table and select Design.

You can also do this right from within Visual Studio .NET. Open the Server Explorer and open Sql Servers > [Your computer] > Community. Then, right-click Tables and select New Table.

Add the DisplayName column—make it of `VARCHAR` type and maxlength 50. Leave `AllowNulls` as true—it is possible that we might want to have a module with no name, and it won't do any harm because this is only the display value.

2. Add `DisplayName` data for the existing modules.

Right-click the tbl_Module table and select Open Table > Return All Rows. (In the VS.NET Server Explorer, double-click the table name.) Add a display name for each module.

STEP-BY-STEP GUIDE: **Adding Configurable Module Names**

3. Add a private member and property to the `CommunityModule` object.

Next, we need to update the persistent object that represents modules so that it includes the `DisplayName` field.

Open `Global/CoreObjects/CommunityModule.vb` and add a `_DisplayName` private member as shown:

```
Inherits CommunityPO

Private _Name As String
Private _DisplayName As String
Private _AllowMember As Boolean
Private _AllowGlobal As Boolean
Private _Description As String
Private _ServiceClassName As String


Private _ModuleInstances As IList
Private _ModuleViews As IList
```

We will also need a property so that code can access this private member. Add the following property to the class:

```
Public ReadOnly Property DisplayName() As String
   Get
      Return _DisplayName
   End Get
End Property
```

4. Update the reconstructor to include `DisplayName`.

In order for the `DisplayName` value to be included in `CommunityModule` objects when the persistence service creates them from the data in the database, we need to include it in the reconstructor. Remember, the reconstructor is a special constructor that we create purely for the use of the persistence service. It has to have an argument for each field that the persistence service persists.

```
Public Sub New(ByVal ID As Integer, _
               ByVal pName As String, _
               ByVal pDisplayName As String, _
               ByVal pAllowMember As Boolean, _
               ByVal pAllowGlobal As Boolean, _
```

Section Items

STEP-BY-STEP GUIDE: Adding Configurable Module Names

```
                    ByVal pDescription As String, _
                    ByVal pServiceClassName As String)

    MyBase.New(ID)

    _Name = pName
    _DisplayName = pDisplayName
    _AllowMember = pAllowMember
    _AllowGlobal = pAllowGlobal
    _Description = pDescription
    _ServiceClassName = pServiceClassName

End Sub
```

5. Add a field descriptor to the persistence service repository.

The persistence service has to know how to link the DisplayName column in the database to the _DisplayName field, so we need to add an additional field descriptor to the persistence service repository.

Open `Global/OJB.NET/repository.xml` and find the `<classdescriptor>` element that defines the mappings for the `CommunityModule` class. Add the new descriptor as shown in Listing 5.21.

LISTING 5.21 Adding a Field Descriptor to `Global/Ojb.Net/Repository.xml`

```xml
<ClassDescriptor TypeName="Community.CommunityModule" TableName="tbl_Module">
  <PrimaryKeyDescriptor IsAutoIncremented="true">
    <FieldDescriptor Id="Module1" FieldName="_primaryKey"
                     ColumnName="ID" DbType="Int32"/>
  </PrimaryKeyDescriptor>
  <FieldDescriptor Id="Module2" FieldName="_Name"
                   ColumnName="Name" DbType="String"/>
  <FieldDescriptor Id="Module2a" FieldName="_DisplayName"
                   ColumnName="DisplayName" DbType="String"/>
  <FieldDescriptor Id="Module3" FieldName="_AllowMember"
                   ColumnName="AllowMember" DbType="Boolean"/>
  <FieldDescriptor Id="Module4" FieldName="_AllowGlobal"
                   ColumnName="AllowGlobal" DbType="Boolean"/>
  <FieldDescriptor Id="Module5" FieldName="_Description"
                   ColumnName="Description" DbType="String"/>
  <FieldDescriptor Id="Module6" FieldName="_ServiceClassName"
                   ColumnName="ServiceClassName" DbType="String"/>
```

STEP-BY-STEP GUIDE: **Adding Configurable Module Names**

LISTING 5.21 Adding a Field Descriptor to `Global/Ojb.Net/Repository.xml` (continued)

```
  <CollectionDescriptor FieldName="_ModuleInstances"
                    RelatedClassName="Community.ModuleInstance">
    <InverseForeignKeyFieldId>ModuleInstance3</InverseForeignKeyFieldId>
  </CollectionDescriptor>
  <CollectionDescriptor FieldName="_ModuleViews"
                    RelatedClassName="Community.ModuleView">
    <InverseForeignKeyFieldId>ModuleView2</InverseForeignKeyFieldId>
  </CollectionDescriptor>
</ClassDescriptor>
```

It is important to add it in the correct location (between the `Name` and `AllowMember` field descriptors so that the ordering matches the order of the arguments to the reconstructor.

6. Change the `SectionItemHeader` to use the `DisplayName`.

Now that the `CommunityModule` object stores the display name, we can make use of the value.

Open `Global/Controls/SectionItemHeader.ascx.vb` and find the code that executes when a global section item is being displayed. Change the default text to use the `DisplayName` property rather than the `Name` property.

```
If sectionItem.IsGlobal = True Then
   'create a link to the global instance of the module
   If _Text = Nothing Then
     HeaderLink.Text = _
     sectionItem.ModuleView.CommunityModule.DisplayName
   Else
```

7. Amend the Member Settings page to use the display name.

Users of the community will now see the display names for modules, but members will see the original names when selecting modules in their settings. We will now change that as well.

Open `MemberSettings.aspx.vb` and locate the code that initializes the drop-down list of modules (it's in `Page_Load`) and change it to use the display name as shown:

STEP-BY-STEP GUIDE: **Adding Configurable Module Names**

```
If Not Page.IsPostBack Then

  MemberName.Text = _Member.Username

  IntroText.Text = _Member.IntroText
  Email.Text = _Member.Email
  PublicEmail.Checked = _Member.PublicEmail

  ModuleInstancesList.DataSource = _Member.ModuleInstances
  ModuleInstancesList.DataBind()

  NewModuleDropDown.DataSource = _
        coreModule.GetAllModulesForMembers
  NewModuleDropDown.DataTextField = "DisplayName"
  NewModuleDropDown.DataValueField = "PrimaryKey1"
  NewModuleDropDown.DataBind()

  SectionsDataList.DataSource = _Member.Sections
  SectionsDataList.DataBind()
```

We also need to change the list of the member's current modules to use the display name. Open `MemberSettings.aspx` in HTML mode and find the datalist that displays the current module instances. (You might want to search for `"ModuleInstancesList"`.) Make the change as shown:

```
<asp:DataList ID="ModuleInstancesList" Runat="server"
            OnItemDataBound="ModulesDataList_ItemDataBound"
            OnEditCommand="EditModule_Click"
            OnUpdateCommand="UpdateModule_Click"
            OnCancelCommand="CancelModule_Click"
            OnDeleteCommand="DeleteModule_Click">
  <ItemTemplate>
    <%# Container.DataItem.Name %>
    (<%# Container.DataItem.CommunityModule.DisplayName%>)
    <asp:Button CommandName="Edit" Text="Edit" Runat="server" />
  </ItemTemplate>
  <EditItemTemplate>
```

If you now check the Member Settings page for a logged-in user, you should see that the Modules drop-down list (on the Modules tab) displays the correct display names.

8. Update the Admin options to use the display name.

Section Items

STEP-BY-STEP GUIDE: **Adding Configurable Module Names**

The final place that the name of a module is used is in the admin settings. Open `Admin/AdminGlobalSections.aspx` in HTML view and find the code that displays the section items for a selected section. Make the change as shown in Listing 5.22.

LISTING 5.22 Changing `Admin/AdminGlobalSections.aspx` to Use the Display Name

```
<asp:DataList id=SectionItemsDataList
            OnDeleteCommand="DeleteSectionItem_Click"
            Runat="server"
            DataSource="<%#Container.DataItem.SectionItems %>"
            DataKeyField="PrimaryKey1">
  <ItemTemplate>
    <span class="Settings_ListItem">

    <%#Container.DataItem.ModuleView.CommunityModule.DisplayName %>
                                    </span>
      <span class="Settings_ListSubItem">
         (<%#Container.DataItem.ModuleView.name %>)
                                    </span>
                                    <asp:Button CommandName="Delete"
                                ➥Text="Delete" Runat="server" ID="Button1" />
                                    </ItemTemplate>
                                    </asp:DataList>
                                    <asp:DropDownList id="ModulesDropDown"
              runat="server"
              DataValueField="PrimaryKey1"
              DataTextField="DisplayName"
                                          OnSelectedIndexChanged="SelectedModuleChanged"
              AutoPostBack="true">
</asp:DropDownList>

<asp:DropDownList id="ModuleViewsDropDown" Runat="server" DataValueField="PrimaryKey1"
➥ DataTextField="Name"></asp:DropDownList>
                                    <asp:Button id="AddInstanceToSection"
      ➥onclick="AddInstanceToSection_Click" Text="Add" Runat="server"></asp:Button>
</DIV>
```

> **TIP**
> Changes to `.aspx` files do not require a recompile to take effect, whereas changes to code-behind or other classes do.

Notice that the admin options use a different approach than the member settings for setting the text in the drop-down list—`MemberSettings.aspx` left the field to be set in the code-behind, whereas the admin options declared it in the `.aspx` file itself.

Both approaches are valid. Declaring the field in the `.aspx` file is perhaps slightly better because it is then easier to change it (as we have done) without having to change the code-behind (and without the need to recompile the application).

CHALLENGE:
Display Names for Module Views

The same approach can be used to have module views use display names rather than the names they use internally.

Try making the changes required to do this.

Hint: The `ModuleView` name is only displayed on the Member Settings page and the Admin Options page, so you can skip the `SectionItemHeader` step.

STEP-BY-STEP GUIDE:
Solving a Problem with the Return Key

You might have already noticed a big problem with the user interface of the online community. When the user presses the Enter key after entering text in any of the `TextBox` controls, the application acts as if the Search button has been pressed, rather than the correct button.

For example, if you browse to the community site and enter a username and password in the login control, pressing Enter after the password, you would expect to be logged in. Instead, what happens is that search results are shown.

The reason for this problem is that all of the controls on the page are contained in a single HTML `<form>` element—this is a requirement of the ASP.NET Web Forms architecture. When the Enter key is pressed inside any text input control in the form, the default button of the form is activated. In the case of our application, this is the first button to be rendered—the Search button.

To solve this problem, we need to somehow ensure that each text input control is linked to the button that should be activated when the Enter key is pressed. Unfortunately, ASP.NET does not currently have a built-in

STEP-BY-STEP GUIDE: Solving a Problem with the Return Key

way to do this. Fortunately, this common problem has already been solved by other programmers, and a reusable solution is available to us.

The freely available `DefaultButtons` control provided by MetaBuilders (www.metabuilders.com) solves the problem in a very simple-to-use way. It also comes with full source code, so if you want to dig into how it works, you can.

Here are the steps we need to take to implement this solution to the problem:

1. Add the `DefaultButtons` assembly to the community.

Before we can use the control, we will need to ensure that the online community application can access the `DefaultButtons` code.

Copy the .dll file from `Chapter05/DefaultButtons/bin/Release/` on this book's CD-ROM to `Community/Bin`.

2. Add a reference to the assembly.

The assembly is now accessible to our project, but our application still does not know it is there. In order to make the control that it contains available to our code, we need to add a reference to it.

In the VS.NET Solution Explorer, right-click the References item and select Add Reference.

Click Browse and browse to the /bin folder; then select the `MetaBuilders.WebControls.DefaultButtons.dll` file.

Click OK to add the reference.

You can check that the reference has been added by expanding the References item in the Solution Explorer. Notice that, along with the standard system references, there is one for the Microsoft WebControls (used for the tab control on the Member Settings page) and one for the OJB.NET persistence service.

3. Add the control to the sign-in control.

The project now has a reference to the `DefaultButtons` assembly, so we can use the control in our code.

Open `Global/Controls/Login.ascx` in HTML mode and add the following `Register` directive to the top of the file:

```
<%@ Register tagprefix="mbdb" namespace="MetaBuilders.WebControls"
➥Assembly="MetaBuilders.WebControls.DefaultButtons" %>
```

> **REUSABILITY TIP**
> ASP.NET lends itself well to reusable code. Many common problems have already been solved, and reusable solutions have been made available for free. Before investing time and effort into creating a custom solution, it is well worth checking what is already available.

> **TIP**
> The `/bin` folder is where ASP.NET stores the assembly that is created when the project is compiled. It is also the best place to store any additional assemblies that are used.

CHALLENGE: Adding Default Buttons to Other Controls

As you can see, this is different than the register directives for the user controls in the application because it specifies an assembly rather than an .ascx file.

Now, add the control, just under the `Control` directive:

```
<mbdb:DefaultButtons runat="server" id="DefaultButtons">
  <mbdb:DefaultButtonSetting parent="UsernameTextBox"
  ➥button="LoginButton" />
  <mbdb:DefaultButtonSetting parent="PasswordTextBox"
  ➥button="LoginButton" />
</mbdb:DefaultButtons>
```

This configuration will cause both the username and password text boxes to activate the Login button when the Enter key is clicked.

If you now browse to the community site and enter login details followed by the Enter key, the search results will not be displayed. Instead, the Login button will be activated and (if the username and password are correct) the user will be logged in.

CHALLENGE:
Adding Default Buttons to Other Controls

A `DefaultButtons` control will need to be added to any other controls that use text boxes to avoid the search results being shown.

Try to find some text boxes that need to have the `DefaultButtons` control added and implement it in the same way as we have for the login control.

Also, remember that if you add controls to the application that use text boxes, you might need to use `DefaultButtons` to get the behavior that you want.

Moving On

So far, we have been working on the infrastructure of the application—the code that supports all of the modules. In Chapter 6, "Improving the Modules," we will be making changes to improve specific modules or adapt them to specific needs.

Improving the Modules 6

In this chapter, we will be looking at some of the many ways we can change the way the existing modules work. We will be changing their behavior in order to customize them to our own particular needs. At the same time, we will be looking at the inner workings of the modules much more closely than we have so far. You will gain the knowledge and confidence you need to customize these modules to your requirements by

- ▶ Requiring a valid email address in the Send Message module
- ▶ Reporting errors encountered when sending emails
- ▶ Creating a global `SendMessage` instance
- ▶ Improving the formatting of news items
- ▶ Checking the length of news item inputs
- ▶ Allowing members to use pseudo code markup
- ▶ Generating thumbnail images in the ImageGallery module

The Send Message Module

Currently, the simplest module is the Send Message module. It does not store any data in the database; it just provides a way for visitors of the site to send emails to members. It only has two files:

- ▶ `SendMessageModule.vb`—The business service class.
- ▶ `Views/SimpleSendMessageBox.ascx`—A simple form to submit messages.

If you open the tbl_Module table in the database and find the row for the Send Message module, you will notice that the AllowMember column is set to 1 (true), whereas the AllowGlobal column is set to 0 (false). This means that the Send Message module will be available to members to add to their sections, but it will not be offered as an option for administrators to add to global sections.

CODE TOUR:
SendMessageModule.vb

The `SendMessageModule` class really only provides one method—`SendMessage(string, string)`. It also includes all of the methods that are required by the `ModuleBase` base class, but they are all minimal implementations, as shown in Listing 6.1.

The Send Message Module

CODE TOUR: `SendMessageModule.vb`

LISTING 6.1 Part of `Modules/SendMessage/SendMessageModule.vb`

```vb
Public Class SendMessageModule
  Inherits ModuleBase

  Public Sub New()
    MyBase.New()
  End Sub

  Public Sub New(ByVal pModuleInstance As ModuleInstance)
    MyBase.New(pModuleInstance)
  End Sub

  Overrides ReadOnly Property Name() As String
    Get
      Return "SendMessage"
    End Get
  End Property

  Overrides Sub PrepareForDeletion()
  End Sub

  Overrides Function GetSearchResults(ByVal searchTerms As String) _
           As SearchResultCollection
    Return New SearchResultCollection()
  End Function
```

So really, the class only exists to provide the `SendMessage` method, which is shown in Listing 6.2.

LISTING 6.2 `SendMessage` in `Modules/SendMessage/SendMessageModule.vb`

```vb
Public Sub SendMessage(ByVal pFromEmail As String, ByVal pMessage As String)
  Dim message As MailMessage = New MailMessage()

  message.Subject = "Message sent through " & CoreModule.CommunityName
  message.To = Me.ModuleInstance.Member.Email
  message.Body = pMessage
  message.From = pFromEmail
```

CODE TOUR: `Modules/SendMessage/SimpleSendMessageBox.ascx`

LISTING 6.2 `SendMessage` in `Modules/SendMessage/SendMessageModule.vb` (continued)

```
  Try
    SmtpMail.SmtpServer = ConfigurationSettings.AppSettings("SmtpServer")
    SmtpMail.Send(message)
  Catch e As System.Web.HttpException

  End Try

End Sub
```

First, it creates a new `MailMessage` object. Note that the `MailMessage` class is from the `System.Web.Mail` namespace. We can refer to it directly because there is an `imports system.web.mail` line at the top of the file.

We then fill the properties of the `MailMessage` with appropriate values.

Next, we need to actually send the email. Because this may well involve an external server (the SMTP server), there is a chance of something beyond our control going wrong. Therefore, we enclose all of this code in a try/catch/end try block. The catch block is currently empty, meaning that any errors will simply be ignored.

There are two parts to sending the email: First, we configure SmtpMail (another `System.Web.Mail` class) to use the SMTP server configured in the Web.config appSettings section. Then, we use the `Send` method to send our message.

Note that we do not have to create an instance of SmtpMail to use it—the property and method that we use are both shared, so we simply access them through the class name.

> **DESIGN TIP**
>
> Try/catch blocks should always be used when we are relying on anything beyond our control—it is much better for any error to be dealt with in a way that we choose rather than for the user to get the exception error message.

CODE TOUR: `Modules/SendMessage/SimpleSendMessageBox.ascx`

The single view that the Send Message module provides is a very simple form that enables users to submit messages to be sent to members.

138   **The Send Message Module**

CODE TOUR: `Modules/SendMessage/SimpleSendMessageBox.ascx`

Open the control in VS.NET. You will see that it consists of

- The SectionItemHeader control
- A single-line text box for the user's email address
- A multiline text box for the message
- A Send button
- A server-side `DIV` element that contains a Thankyou message

If you now open the code-behind file, you will see the code that initializes the control, as shown in Listing 6.3.

LISTING 6.3   Initialization Code in `Modules/SendMessage/Views/SimpleSendMessageBox.ascx.vb`

```
Private Sub Page_Load(ByVal sender As System.Object, _
                ByVal e As System.EventArgs) _
        Handles MyBase.Load
  'Put user code to initialize the page here
  If Not Page.IsPostBack Then
    SendMessageControls.Visible = True
    ThankyouMessage.Visible = False

  End If
End Sub
```

`Page_Load` simply sets the SendMessage controls to visible and the Thankyou message to invisible, but only if the control is rendering a postback. (If it is a postback, we will display the Thankyou message.)

The only other member is the `Click` event handler for the Send button, which is shown in Listing 6.4.

LISTING 6.4   Code for Sending a Message in `Modules/SendMessage/Views/SimpleSendMessageBox.ascx.vb`

```
Private Sub SendButton_Click(ByVal sender As System.Object, ByVal e As System.EventArgs) _
      Handles SendButton.Click
```

STEP-BY-STEP GUIDE: **Requiring a Valid Email Address**

LISTING 6.4 Code for Sending a Message in `Modules/SendMessage/Views/SimpleSendMessageBox.ascx.vb` (continued)

```
  Dim messageModule As New SendMessageModule(Me.SectionItem.ModuleInstance)

  messageModule.SendMessage(EmailTextBox.Text, MessageTextBox.Text)

  SendMessageControls.Visible = False
  ThankyouMessage.InnerText = "Thankyou for your message, it is now being" _
                    & " delivered to " _
                    & Me.SectionItem.ModuleInstance.Member.Username _
                    & " by email."
  ThankyouMessage.Visible = True
End Sub
```

We create a new instance of the Send Message module business service class and call its `SendMessage` method.

Then, we make the message sending controls invisible, set the Thankyou message, and make it visible.

The module is very simple, but there are some improvements we can make to it, as follows:

- ▶ At present, users can enter anything for their email address. They might mistype their address, so it would be good to require valid addresses.

- ▶ We don't currently do anything about errors, so users might think their email has been sent when, in fact, it has not. It would be better to display a message saying that the email could not be sent.

- ▶ The module does not, at the moment, allow a global instance. It would be useful to have a way for users to send messages to the site administrators, so a global instance would make sense.

STEP-BY-STEP GUIDE:
Requiring a Valid Email Address

Requiring users to enter a valid email address is very easy, thanks to ASP.NET's validation controls. We will use a regular expression validator, which will enable us to ensure that the input fits the format we define with a regular expression.

The Send Message Module

STEP-BY-STEP GUIDE: Requiring a Valid Email Address

> **TIP**
> If you have not already learned about regular expressions, you really should—they provide a great way of matching, filtering, and processing string data.

1. Add a RegularExpressionValidator control to the form. (Find the control in the toolbox and drag it onto the form.)

   Add the control just after the email text box and give it the ID `EmailValidator`.

2. Set the `ControlToBeValidated` property.

   Make sure the RegularExpressionValidator control is selected and use the Property Explorer to set the `ControlToBeValidated` property to `EmailTextBox`.

3. Set the error message.

   Set the `ErrorMessage` property to `Please enter a valid email address` or something similar.

4. Set the regular expression to use.

   Set the `RegularExpression` property to the following value:

   `^[A-Za-z0-9](([_\.\-]?[a-zA-Z0-9]+)*)@([A-Za-z0-9]+)(([\.\-]?[a-zA-Z0-9]+)*)\.([A-Za-z]{2,})$`

   If you are not familiar with regular expressions, you will probably find this value a little confusing. Let's break it down to see what it means:

RegEx Part	Matches To
`^`	The beginning of the string.
`[A-Za-z0-9]`	A letter or digit.
`(([_\.\-]?[a-zA-Z0-9]+)*)`	An underscore, period, or dash, followed by one or more letters or digits. (The ? means that the underscore, period, or dash is optional, whereas the * means that this whole element can appear 0 or more times.)
	The square brackets are used to define sets of characters so that any of the characters specified can be used.
	The period and dash symbols are preceded by slashes because these symbols are used in regular expressions themselves. The slashes let the engine know that we want to specify the actual period and dash characters.
`@`	One @ sign.
`([A-Za-z0-9]+)`	One or more letters or digits.

STEP-BY-STEP GUIDE: **Requiring a Valid Email Address**

RegEx Part	Matches To
`(([\.\-]?[a-zA-Z0-9]+)*)`	A period or dash followed by one or more letters or digits. (Again, the `?` means that the period or dash is optional, whereas the `*` means that this whole element can appear 0 or more times.)
`\.`	A single period.
`([A-Za-z]{2,})`	At least two letters.
`$`	The end of the string.

So, what the regular expression means is:

Match a letter or digit followed by zero or more groups of letters and digits (optionally preceded by an underscore, period, or dash), followed by an @ sign, followed by one or more letters or digits, followed by any number of groups of letters and digits (each optionally followed by a period or dash), followed by a period, followed by at least two letters.

Simple, eh?

This should match any valid Internet email address. (The last thing we want to do is use a regular expression that is too strict and end up rejecting valid email addresses.)

If you now try using the Send Message module, you will find that it will only allow valid email addresses and will display the error message when an invalid email address is entered, as shown in Figure 6.1.

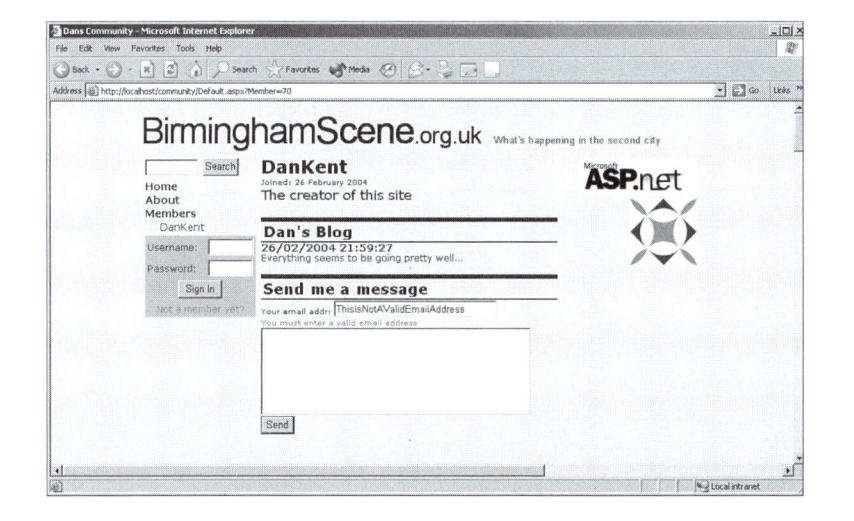

> **TIP**
>
> As with many common programming solutions, regular expressions for all sorts of situations are available online. There is a sizable database at `www.regexlib.com`, which contains freely usable, regular expressions for a wide variety of common (and not-so-common) purposes.

FIGURE 6.1

Error message for an invalid email address.

STEP-BY-STEP GUIDE: Dealing with Errors

CHALLENGE:
Requiring a Valid Email Address from New Members

The New Member Registration page does not currently require a valid email address. (It requires users to enter an email address but does not check that it is valid.)

Use the technique that we looked at in the previous section to require the new member's email address to be valid.

Hint: You will need to edit `Join.aspx` similar to how we edited `SimpleSendMessageBox.ascx`.

STEP-BY-STEP GUIDE:
Dealing with Errors

At the moment, we do nothing with error experiences when sending email, apart from hiding them from the user.

We will now change the Send Message module so that it displays a simple message to the user when an email cannot be sent.

Here are the steps we will take:

1. Change the `SendMessage` method to return a success value.

The first thing we need to do is have the business service class provide feedback to the presentation layer control on whether the email was successfully sent. We will do this by adding a Boolean return value to the `SendMessage` method, as shown in Listing 6.5.

LISTING 6.5 Change to the `SendMessage` Method in `Modules/SendMessage/SendMessageModule.vb`

```
Public Function SendMessage(ByVal pFromEmail As String, ByVal pMessage As String) _
      As Boolean
  Dim message As MailMessage = New MailMessage

  message.Subject = "Message sent through " & CoreModule.CommunityName
  message.To = Me.ModuleInstance.Member.Email
  message.Body = pMessage
  message.From = pFromEmail
```

STEP-BY-STEP GUIDE: **Dealing with Errors**

LISTING 6.5 Change to the `SendMessage` Method in `Modules/SendMessage/SendMessageModule.vb` (continued)

```
  Try
    SmtpMail.SmtpServer = ConfigurationSettings.AppSettings("SmtpServer")
    SmtpMail.Send(message)
  Catch e As System.Web.HttpException
    'there was an exception, so return false
    Return False
  End Try

  'no exception was raised, so return true
  Return True
End Function
```

We have changed the sub into a function and added the Boolean return value.

We have also added code to return false if an exception is caught.

If there was no exception and execution gets to the end of the method, we return true.

2. Change the control to display the error message.

Now we need to update the control so that it makes use of the returned value.

The updated `Click` event handler for the Send button is shown in Listing 6.6.

LISTING 6.6 Change to the `Click` Event Handler in `Modules/SendMessage/Views/SimpleSendMessageBox.ascx.vb`

```
Private Sub SendButton_Click(ByVal sender As System.Object, _
                             ByVal e As System.EventArgs) _
        Handles SendButton.Click

  Dim messageModule As New SendMessageModule(Me.SectionItem.ModuleInstance)
  Dim result As Boolean
  result = messageModule.SendMessage(EmailTextBox.Text, MessageTextBox.Text)
```

STEP-BY-STEP GUIDE: **Dealing with Errors**

LISTING 6.6 Change to the `Click` Event Handler in `Modules/SendMessage/Views/SimpleSendMessageBox.ascx.vb`
(continued)

```
    SendMessageControls.Visible = False

    If result = True Then
      ThankyouMessage.InnerText = "Thankyou for your message, it is now being" _
                          & " delivered to " _
                          & Me.SectionItem.ModuleInstance.Member.Username _
                          & " by email."
    Else
      ThankyouMessage.InnerText = "Sorry, we couldn't send the message - you could" _
                          & " try again later."
    End If

    ThankyouMessage.Visible = True
End Sub
```

We have made changes to extract the return value from the `SendMessage` method and then use that result to decide whether to display the Thankyou message or an error message.

You can test the new code by changing the `SmtpServer` setting in the `Web.config` to a nonexistent server (or one that cannot be accessed from your machine). You will then see the error message when you attempt to send a message, as shown in Figure 6.2.

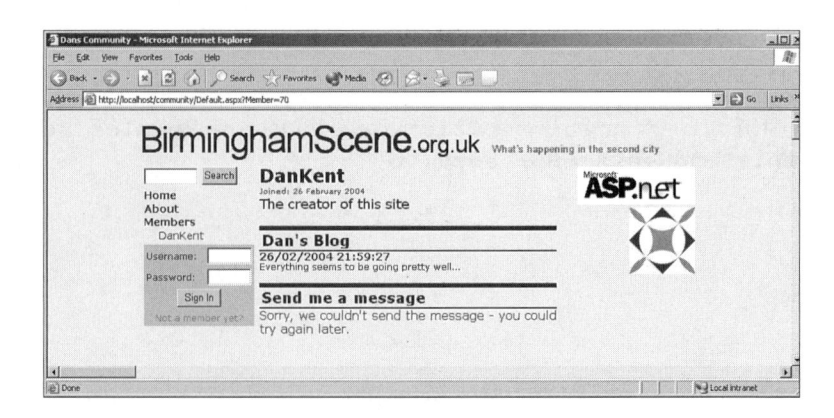

FIGURE 6.2
Error message shown when the application cannot send the email.

STEP-BY-STEP GUIDE: **Allowing a Global** `SendMessage` **Instance**

STEP-BY-STEP GUIDE:
Allowing a Global `SendMessage` Instance

We are now going to change the Send Message module so that it allows a global instance. This instance will send an email to all the site administrators rather than to an individual member.

Here are the steps we need to take to implement this:

1. Add a method to `CoreModule` to get all administrators.

We are going to need a way to access all of the administrators in order to email the message to them. Looking through the methods in `CoreModule` that retrieve members, we can see that there is currently not one that retrieves a list of the administrators. We will need to add one.

Add the following method to `CoreModule`, in the section that contains the methods for dealing with `Member` objects, as shown in Listing 6.7.

LISTING 6.7 Method to Add to `Global/CoreModule.vb`

```vb
Public Function GetAdministrators() As IList
  Dim crit As New Criteria
  crit.addEqualTo("_IsAdministrator", True)

     Return QueryFacade.FindObject(Type.GetType("Community.Member"), crit)
End Function
```

This is basic code for getting the objects from the persistence service, similar to that which we have seen many times already.

2. Add a global `SendMessage` method to `SendMessageModule`.

Next, we need to add a new method to `SendMessageModule.vb` to send a global instance method, as shown in Listing 6.8.

The Send Message Module

STEP-BY-STEP GUIDE: Allowing a Global `SendMessage` Instance

LISTING 6.8 Method to Add to `Modules/SendMessage/SendMessageModule.vb`

```
Public Shared Function SendGlobalMessage(ByVal pFromEmail As String, _
    ByVal pMessage As String)

  Dim message As MailMessage = New MailMessage
  message.Subject = "Message to admins from " & CoreModule.CommunityName
  message.Body = pMessage
  message.From = pFromEmail

  Dim coreMod As New CoreModule
  Dim admin As Member

  SmtpMail.SmtpServer = ConfigurationSettings.AppSettings("SmtpServer")

  Dim overallResult As Boolean = False
  Dim result As Boolean
  For Each admin In coreMod.GetAdministrators
    result = True
    message.To = admin.Email

    Try
      SmtpMail.Send(message)
    Catch ex As Exception
      result = False
    End Try
    If result = True Then
      overallResult = True
    End If
  Next

  Return overallResult

End Function
```

Loop through all the administrators returned by `CoreModule.GetAdministrators`.

For each administrator, store a temporary result, setting it to false if there was an error.

STEP-BY-STEP GUIDE: **Allowing a Global `SendMessage` Instance**

At the end of processing each administrator, check whether the temporary result is still true. If it is, set the overall result to true.

After processing all of the administrators, return the overall result value.

3. Update the `Click` event handler of the Send button.

We now need to add code to the module view that will call our global `SendMessage` method if the view is displaying the global instance. The changes are shown in Listing 6.9.

LISTING 6.9 Change to the `SendMessage` Method in `Modules/SendMessage/Views/SimpleSendMessageBox.vb`

```
Private Sub SendButton_Click(ByVal sender As System.Object, _
                             ByVal e As System.EventArgs) _
        Handles SendButton.Click

  Dim messageModule As New SendMessageModule(Me.SectionItem.ModuleInstance)
  Dim result As Boolean
  Dim recipientName As String

  If Me.SectionItem.IsGlobal Then
    result = messageModule.SendGlobalMessage(EmailTextBox.Text, MessageTextBox.Text)
    recipientName = "the site Administrators"
  Else
    result = messageModule.SendMessage(EmailTextBox.Text, MessageTextBox.Text)
    recipientName = Me.SectionItem.ModuleInstance.Member.Username
  End If

  SendMessageControls.Visible = False

  If result = True Then
    ThankyouMessage.InnerText = "Thankyou for your message, it is now being" _
                              & " delivered to " _
                              & recipientName _
                              & " by email."
  Else
    ThankyouMessage.InnerText = "Sorry, we couldn't send the message - you could" _
                              & " try again later."
  End If

  ThankyouMessage.Visible = True
End Sub
```

The method has been changed to use the global `SendMessage` method when a global instance is being displayed. We have also altered the code to use "the site Administrators" as the recipient name in the Thankyou message if the global instance is being displayed.

4. Update the database.

The final thing we need to do is configure the module to allow global instances.

Open the tbl_Module table in the database (using either SQL Server Enterprise Manager or the Server Explorer in Visual Studio .NET) and change the Allow Global module for the Send Message module to 1.

You should now be able to use the Admin page to add a global instance of the Send Message module to the community.

CHALLENGE:
User-Definable Subject Line

At present, thesubject line for emails sent through the Send Message module is fixed by the module.

See if you can alter the module so that users can enter their own subject line.

You might want to have the actual subject line of the email that is sent be a combination of the user's own subject line and the community name.

You might also want to have the community application add a footer to each email that is sent, with a link to the community site.

The News Module

We have already looked at some of the code for the News module, back in Chapter 3, "Exploring the Code," where we used it as an example of how modules fit into the community architecture. You might want to have a look back at that chapter for some information on the NewsModule business service class and the module views.

However, we did not see all the files, and there are some improvements we really need to make to the News module in order for it to work well.

CODE TOUR: `Modules/News/DisplayItem.ascx`

The `DisplayItem` control is used when the Item parameter is passed to `default.aspx` along with the Module parameter.

Not all the modules have `DisplayItem` controls. This is okay because the only links to them are within the modules themselves—if a module does not have a `DisplayItem` control, it should simply not provide a link to `default.aspx?Module=[moduleID]&Item=[ItemID]`.

The advantage of using a `DisplayItem` control is that users will be able to take the URL from an individual item and link it directly. For example, I can email the URL to an individual news item to a friend so that she can link straight to it.

The design view of `DisplayItem.ascx` shows that the control is in two parts. The first part provides labels for the heading, the date, and the body of the news item. It also provides hyperlinks for the name of the member who posted the item and a See More link.

The second part provides controls that enable the item to be edited. The `DisplayItem` control is multipurpose—it is used both to display and edit news items. Obviously, the edit controls should only be displayed when the correct member is viewing the item.

If you open the code-behind, you will find that there are three methods:

- `Page_Load`
- `UpdateButton_Click`
- `DeleteButton_Click`

We will look at the latter two methods later. For now, let's concentrate on `Page_Load`, which is shown in Listing 6.10.

LISTING 6.10 Initialization Code in `Modules/News/DisplayItem.ascx.vb`

```
Private Sub Page_Load(ByVal sender As System.Object, _
                ByVal e As System.EventArgs) _
        Handles MyBase.Load

  'default the edit controls to invisible
  EditControls.Visible = False
```

CODE TOUR: `Modules/News/DisplayItem.ascx`

LISTING 6.10 Initialization Code in `Modules/News/DisplayItem.ascx.vb` (continued)

```vb
    If Not Request.QueryString("Item") Is Nothing Then
      'all is good, so let's get the news item
      Dim newsMod As New NewsModule
      Dim item As NewsItem = newsMod.GetNewsItemByID(ItemID)

      If Not item Is Nothing Then
        HeadingLabel.Text = item.Title
        MemberLink.Text = item.ModuleInstance.Member.Username
        MemberLink.NavigateUrl = "../../default.aspx?Member=" + _
             item.ModuleInstance.Member.PrimaryKey(0).ToString

        DateLabel.Text = CType(item.DatePosted, DateTime).ToLongDateString
        BodyLabel.Text = item.Body

        SeeMoreLink.Text = "See more in " + " " + item.ModuleInstance.Name
        SeeMoreLink.NavigateUrl = "../../default.aspx?Module=" + _
            item.ModuleInstance.CommunityModule.PrimaryKey(0).ToString _
          + "&Instance=" + item.ModuleInstance.PrimaryKey(0).ToString

        'check whether the member who owns the item is logged in
        If Request.IsAuthenticated AndAlso _
                  CType(Context.User, CommunityPrincipal).Member.PrimaryKey1() = _
                    item.ModuleInstance.Member.PrimaryKey1 Then
          EditControls.Visible = True
          HeadingTextBox.Text = item.Title
          SummaryTextBox.Text = item.Summary
          BodyTextBox.Text = item.Body

          DeleteButton.Attributes.Add("onclick", "return confirm('Are You sure?');" )
        End If

      Else

        'there was a problem with getting the news item...

      End If

    End If

End Sub
```

CODE TOUR: Modules/News/DisplayItem.ascx

The first thing to do is to default the Edit Controls section of the control to be invisible. We want to make sure that the edit controls are only shown to the member who owns the news item, so we default them to invisible and only set them to visible for the right member.

Then, a check is made to ensure that the item parameter is present. If it is not, an error would be caused when we tried to access the value.

We then get the specified item from the News module business service class.

A further check is then performed. If a `NewsItem` result was not returned, we cannot proceed.

Assuming that a `NewsItem` was retrieved, its details are used to populate the labels and hyperlinks in the control.

After populating the "view" part of the control, we check whether the currently logged-in member is the owner of the news item, with the following line:

```
If Request.IsAuthenticated AndAlso _
    CType(Context.User, CommunityPrincipal).Member.PrimaryKey1() = _
    item.ModuleInstance.Member.PrimaryKey1 Then
```

Note the use of the `AndAlso` keyword. We need to check that a member is logged in and then check that the member owns the news item. By using `AndAlso`, we are saying that we only want to do the second part of the check if the first part succeeds. If we used a simple `And`, we would get an error when no member is logged in—the `Context.User` object would not be a `CommunityPrinciple`, so the `CType` would fail.

If the currently logged-in member does own the news item, we populate the edit controls with the current values from the news item and also use the following line to add a JavaScript confirmation pop-up to the Delete button:

```
DeleteButton.Attributes.Add("onclick", "return confirm('Are You sure?');")
```

This is a useful little bit of code for requiring confirmation of operations. The postback (and thus the server-side `OnClick` event of the button) will only fire if the user clicks OK.

We have to use this technique to add the JavaScript to the client-side `OnClick` event because the `OnClick` event on the control in the designer refers to the server-side event.

SECURITY TIP

When dealing with security issues, it is better to default to the most secure situation and allow specific cases, rather than defaulting to a less secure position and disallowing specific cases.

STEP-BY-STEP GUIDE: Formatting News Items Better

STEP-BY-STEP GUIDE:
Formatting News Items Better

There is a big problem with `DisplayItem.ascx`. Try adding a news item with multiple paragraphs of text. When you view the item, the paragraphs will be formatted as one very long paragraph, with no line breaks.

The reason for this is that our `DisplayItem` control simply dumps the body text of the item into a label control. This will end up being rendered as simple text in the HTML of the page. HTML does not add line breaks unless a tag tells it to do so, so the standard returns in the text will be ignored.

What we will do now is alter the `DisplayItem` control so that it formats the text into paragraphs.

Here are the steps we need to take:

1. Replace the body label with a server-side `DIV` element.

The first thing we need to do is to remove the label control that is used to display the body of news items and replace it with a `<div>` element. We have to do this because labels are rendered in HTML as `<span>` elements. `<span>`s cannot contain `<div>` elements, so we need to use a `<div>` (which can contain other `<div>` elements).

Delete the body label from `News/DisplayItem.ascx` and give the existing `<div>` element an ID and a `runat="server"` attribute, as shown in Listing 6.11.

LISTING 6.11 Adding a Server-Side `<DIV>` Element in `Modules/News/DisplayItem.ascx.vb`

```
<%@ Control Language="vb"
    AutoEventWireup="false"
    Codebehind="DisplayItem.ascx.vb"
    Inherits="Community.DisplayItem"
    TargetSchema="http://schemas.microsoft.com/intellisense/ie5" %>
<div class="ModuleItemHeading">
  <asp:label id="HeadingLabel" runat="server"></asp:label>
</div>
<div class="ModuleItemDateAndMember">
  <span class="ModuleMainMember">
    <asp:label id="MemberLabel" runat="server"></asp:label>
      <asp:hyperlink id="MemberLink" runat="server"></asp:hyperlink>
```

STEP-BY-STEP GUIDE: **Formatting News Items Better**

LISTING 6.11 Adding a Server-Side `<DIV>` Element in `Modules/News/DisplayItem.ascx.vb` (continued)

```
    </span>-
  <span class="ModuleMainDate">
    <asp:label id="DateLabel" runat="server"></asp:label>
  </span>
</div>
<p></p>
<div id="BodyDiv" class="ModuleItemBody" runat="server">
   
</div>
<div class="ModuleItemMore">
  <asp:HyperLink id="SeeMoreLink" runat="server">
    See more in
</asp:HyperLink>
</div>
<hr>
```

You will also need to add a declaration for this element in the code-behind:

```
Public MustInherit Class DisplayItem
    Inherits ModuleItemControl
Protected WithEvents BodyDiv _
        As System.Web.UI.HtmlControls.HtmlGenericControl
```

We now have a `<div>` element that we can access from the code-behind.

2. Create a method to do the formatting.

We now need to create the code that will actually do the formatting. It makes sense to put this code in a method of its own to organize the code. Furthermore, it is likely that we will have other modules that need to format text for display in items. It, therefore, makes sense to put the method in a place where all item display controls can access it.

The best way to do this is to put the method in the `ModuleItemControl` base class. All controls that display module items should inherit from this class, so they will all have access to the method.

Open `Global/Controls/ModuleItemControl.vb` and add the method shown in Listing 6.12.

The News Module

STEP-BY-STEP GUIDE: **Formatting News Items Better**

LISTING 6.12 Method to Add to `Global/Controls/ModuleItemControl.vb`

```
Public Shared Function FormatText(ByVal pText As String) As String
  Dim result As String
  Dim startRegEx As New Regex("^")

  result = startRegEx.Replace(pText, "<p class='ModuleItemBody'>")

  Dim returnRegEx As New Regex("\n")
  result = returnRegEx.Replace(result, "</p><p class='ModuleItemBody'>")

  Dim endRegEx As New Regex("$")
  result = endRegEx.Replace(result, "</p>")

  Return result

End Function
```

You will also need to add the following line to the top of the file:

`Imports System.Text.RegularExpressions`

The method is shared, so all controls that inherit from `ModuleItemControl` will share the same method.

In it, we create three regular expressions and use their `Replace` methods to replace the text that they match with HTML markup code.

The first regular expression, `"^"`, matches the start of the text. We use this to open a paragraph tag.

The second regular expression, `"\n"`, matches newlines. It ends the paragraph tag and starts a new one.

The final regular expression, `"$"`, matches the end of the file. It ends the paragraph tag.

The text, with the replacements made, is then returned.

3. Use the method to format the text.

Now that we have a method that will format the text, we can go back to `News/DisplayItem.ascx` and make use of it.

Open the code-behind for `DisplayItem.ascx` and make the change shown in Listing 6.13.

STEP-BY-STEP GUIDE: **Formatting News Items Better**

LISTING 6.13 Change to `Modules/News/DisplayItem.ascx.vb`

```
Else
  'all is good, so let's show the news item

  Dim item As NewsItem = NewsModule.GetNewsItemByID(ItemID)

  HeadingLabel.Text = item.Title
  MemberLink.Text = item.ModuleInstance.Member.Username
  MemberLink.NavigateUrl = "../../default.aspx?Member=" + .ModuleInstance.Member.
➥PrimaryKey(0).ToString

  DateLabel.Text = CType(item.DatePosted, DateTime).ToLongDateString
  BodyDiv.InnerHtml = FormatText(item.Body)

  SeeMoreLink.Text = SeeMoreLink.Text + " " + item.ModuleInstance.Name
  SeeMoreLink.NavigateUrl = "../../default.aspx?Module=" +
➥item.ModuleInstance.CommunityModule.PrimaryKey(0).ToString _
      + "&Instance=" + item.ModuleInstance.PrimaryKey(0).ToString
```

We simply set the inner HTML of the body `<div>` to the result of sending the news item body to the formatting method.

If you now browse to a news item that has multiple paragraphs in it, you should see that the text is formatted properly.

Entering and Editing News Items

Let's now look at the other side of the News module—entering and editing news items.

Entering new news items and editing existing ones are both handled by the `DisplayItem.ascx` control. We saw earlier that, when the correct member is logged in, the control displays subcontrols that allow editing of the item.

When a member clicks the Post New Item link, a new, empty news item is created and the `DisplayItem` control is displayed. You can see how this is done if you open the code-behind for `News/DisplayModule.ascx` and find the `click` event handler for the Post New Item link, which is shown in Listing 6.14.

LISTING 6.14 Event Handler for the Post New Item Link in `Modules/News/DisplayModule.ascx.vb`

```vb
Private Sub PostNewLink_Click(ByVal sender As System.Object, _
                              ByVal e As System.EventArgs) _
        Handles PostNewLink.Click

    'create a new item
    Dim newsMod As NewsModule = New NewsModule(Me.ModuleInstance)

    Dim item As NewsItem = newsMod.CreateNewsItem

    Response.Redirect("default.aspx?Module=" & item.ModuleInstance.CommunityModule.PrimaryKey1 _
              & "&Item=" & item.PrimaryKey1)

End Sub
```

First, the new item is created.

Then, the user is redirected back to the default page with the correct URL parameters to display the newly created, empty news item.

The code to deal with the member clicking an Edit link is very similar (aside from the fact that it doesn't create a new item, of course).

The two remaining methods from `Modules/News/DisplayItem.ascx` we have not seen already are responsible for actually making changes to an item or deleting one. They are very simple and very similar to each other.

`UpdateButton_Click` simply calls the `UpdateNewsItem` method of the News module business service class to do the update and then redirects the user back to the relevant module instance.

```vb
Private Sub UpdateButton_Click(ByVal sender As System.Object, _
                               ByVal e As System.EventArgs) _
        Handles UpdateButton.Click
    Dim newsMod As New NewsModule

    newsMod.UpdateNewsItem(Me.ItemID, HeadingTextBox.Text, _
                    SummaryTextBox.Text, _
                    BodyTextBox.Text)

    Response.Redirect(SeeMoreLink.NavigateUrl.TrimStart( _
                New Char() {"/", "."}))
End Sub
```

STEP-BY-STEP GUIDE: **Validating the Length of the Inputs**

Note the manipulation of the `NavigateUrl` in order to trim off leading slashes and periods. This is necessary because `Response.Redirect` works relative to the page it is used in, whereas the `NavigateUrl` property of the `LinkButton` control works relative to the control it is used in. The `DisplayItem` control is in the `Modules/News` folder, so the `NavigateUrl` property includes `../../` at the start, which we do not want in the `Response.Redirect` call.

STEP-BY-STEP GUIDE:
Validating the Length of the Inputs

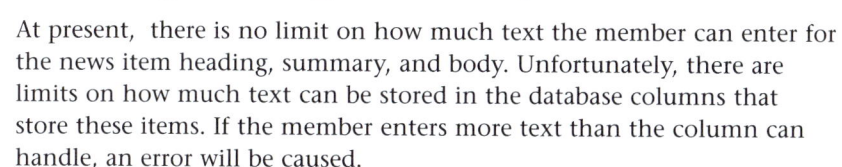

At present, there is no limit on how much text the member can enter for the news item heading, summary, and body. Unfortunately, there are limits on how much text can be stored in the database columns that store these items. If the member enters more text than the column can handle, an error will be caused.

We can prevent this from happening by using `CustomValidator` controls to check the lengths of the inputs before the news item is updated.

We need to perform two steps:

1. Add `CustomValidator` controls.

Add three `CustomValidator` controls to `Modules/News/DisplayItem.ascx`, one after each text box control. Give them the IDs `TitleLengthValidator`, `SummaryLengthValidator`, and `BodyLengthValidator`. Set their `ControlToValidate` properties to the IDs of the relevant controls.

2. Add validation methods.

We now need to add code to do the actual validation. Double-click the `TitleLengthValidator` control in design mode, and an empty validation method will be created in the code-behind. Add the following lines of code that are highlighted in Listing 6.15.

LISTING 6.15 Change to `Modules/News/DisplayModule.ascx.vb`

```
Private Sub TitleLengthValidator_ServerValidate(ByVal source As System.Object, _
        ByVal args As System.Web.UI.WebControls.ServerValidateEventArgs) _
        Handles HeadingLengthValidator.ServerValidate
    Dim length As Integer = args.Value.Length

    args.IsValid = (length <= 50)
End Sub
```

CHALLENGE: Automatic Summaries

Double-click each of the other validation controls and add similar code (changing the maximum allowed length to 200 for the summary and 2000 for the body).

Adding these controls does not in itself prevent the page from attempting to update the news item. We need to make the changes shown in Listing 6.16 to the `update click` handler.

LISTING 6.16 Change to `Modules/News/DisplayModule.ascx.vb`

```
Private Sub UpdateButton_Click(ByVal sender As System.Object, _
                    ByVal e As System.EventArgs) _
        Handles UpdateButton.Click

  If Page.IsValid Then
    NewsModule.UpdateNewsItem(Request.QueryString("item"), _
                    TitleTextBox.Text, _
                    SummaryTextBox.Text, _
                    BodyTextBox.Text)

    'close the window

    Dim closeWindowScript As String = _
      "<script language='javascript'>self.close();" & _
      "window.opener.__doPostBack('','');" & _
      "</script>"

    Page.RegisterStartupScript("CloseWindowScript", closeWindowScript)
  End If

End Sub
```

The item will now only be updated if all of the controls are valid.

CHALLENGE: Automatic Summaries

At the moment, if the member adds a news item with a body and no summary, a blank summary is used. It might be nice to generate a summary automatically, using the first 100 or so characters of the body (if there are 100 characters in it).

Change the code so that when the summary is blank, it is generated from the body.

STEP-BY-STEP GUIDE:
Allowing Markup Code

Thus far, we have not allowed members any ability to format their news items, aside from splitting them into paragraphs. ASP.NET will automatically prevent members from using HTML code, displaying an error message if a member attempts to do so. There are good reasons for this—allowing users to submit HTML freely can open up all sorts of security holes, so it is good to keep the protection enabled.

It would be nice, however, to allow members to use simple formatting, such as bold text.

A common solution to this dilemma is to use *pseudo code*. This means that we define a markup scheme of our own, limited to the formatting options we want to give members. We then convert the pseudo code to real HTML.

> **TIP**
>
> If you really do trust your members, you can configure ASP.NET not to check for HTML and script, but you will have to be careful to validate all inputs that anonymous users can get access to (the Search box, the Send Message module, and so on).

A commonly used format for pseudo code is to use a syntax that is very similar to HTML, but using [and] rather than < and >. When the text needs to be displayed, the application can substitute specific pseudo code elements with their HTML counterparts. For example, `[b]Bold Text[/b]` would become `<b>Bold Text</b>`, and `[hr]` would become `<hr>`.

The big advantage to this is that users who are familiar with HTML will have no problem understanding it (and it is simple enough for those without HTML experience to figure out).

We will now add code to allow such pseudo code in news items.

We don't need to make any changes to `EditItem.aspx`—it will already allow the text that makes up pseudo code to be entered. In fact, we don't need to change the News module at all—we only need to change the `FormatText` method that we added to `ModuleItemControl.vb`. If we have it do the conversion from pseudo code to HTML, the conversion will be used by the News module.

We need to take the following steps:

1. Add code to insert horizontal rules.

STEP-BY-STEP GUIDE: **Allowing Markup Code**

Insert the following code into the `FormatText` method in Core/Controls/ModuleItemControls.vb:

```
Dim endRegEx As New Regex("$")
result = endRegEx.Replace(result, "</p>")

Dim hrRegEx As New Regex("\[(h|H)(r|R)\]")
result = hrRegEx.Replace(result, "<HR>")



Return result
```

The regular expression will match to [hr], with the H and R in upper- or lowercase. Allowing upper- and lowercase will lessen the chances of members' pseudo code not working because of a typo.

Horizontal rules will now be inserted when members enter [hr] in the body of news items.

2. Add code to allow bold text.

To support bold formatting, we need two regular expressions—one for the opening tag and one for the closing tag:

```
Dim startboldRegEx As New Regex("\[(b|B)\]")
result = startboldRegEx.Replace(result, "<B>")

Dim endboldRegEx As New Regex("\[/(b|B)\]")
result = endboldRegEx.Replace(result, "</B>")
```

3. Add code to allow hyperlinks.

Allowing hyperlinks is a little more complicated. In order for a hyperlink to work, it needs to include the URL that it should point to.

We could allow very simple hyperlinks by simply having users surround the URL with [link] and [/link], but that wouldn't be as nice as allowing users to format text as a hyperlink, with a URL that is not actually displayed on the page.

What we will do is support hyperlinks that look like this:

```
[link url=http://www.sample.com]A sample link[/link]
```

The code that we need to add is shown in Listing 6.17.

STEP-BY-STEP GUIDE: **Allowing Markup Code**

LISTING 6.17 Code to Add to the `FormatText` Method

```
Dim linkRegEx _
  As New Regex("\[link url\=(\S*?)\]([\s\S]*?)\[/link\]", RegexOptions.IgnoreCase)

Dim match As Match = linkRegEx.Match(result)

While match.Success
  result = result.Remove(match.Index, match.Length)
  result = result.Insert(match.Index, "<A HREF=" + match.Groups(1).Value + ">" +
➥match.Groups(2).Value + "</A>")
  match = linkRegEx.Match(result)
End While
```

As you can see, the regular expression that we need is considerably more complex than those for horizontal rules and bold text. Let's break it down:

RegEx Part	Matches
\[link url\=	[link url=
(\S*?)	Any number of non-whitespace characters. The * means match any number, whereas the ? modifies it so that it will match the minimum number of characters it can. (This is important because it prevents the first match from matching everything from the first link to the last.) This is the URL; it will be stored as a *capture group* by the regular expression engine so that we can access it later.
\]	]
([\s\S]*?)	Any number of characters, whitespace or non-whitespace. This is the text within the link. Like the URL, it is stored as a group that we can access later.
\[/link\]	[/link]

We cannot do a simple replace operation this time because our `<a>` tags need to have the correct `href` attributes in them.

Instead, we create a `Match` object and load the first match of our regular expression into it. The `Match` object will enable us to access the position and length of the text that has matched our regular expression.

Entering and Editing News Items

CHALLENGE: Allowing Members to Upload an Image to Accompany Each News Item

We then loop until we no longer have a match. In each iteration, we replace the matching text with an `<a href="url">text</a>` element that we create. We access the two groups (for the URL and the text inside the link) through the `match.Groups` property.

After doing the replacement, we perform another match against the results string—if there are any more links, the first one will be loaded into match and the process will be repeated. If there are no more links, we exit the loop.

CHALLENGE:
Adding More Markup Options

There are plenty more markup options that could be implemented. Add some of your own, using the approaches we have already looked at. Most basic text-formatting options can be implemented using code similar to that we have already seen.

If you need more information on regular expressions, there is some great information in the VS.NET online help. It is a really good idea to become familiar with the regular expression syntax—it is a powerful and efficient way of searching and manipulating text of all kinds.

CHALLENGE:
Allowing Members to Upload an Image to Accompany Each News Item

Another great feature would be the ability for members to upload images to accompany their news items. Add some code to allow this.

Hint: You can use the same approach as we used to allow members to upload images to their Member pages.

Hint: You should create a new folder in `Data/Modules/News/` to store the images.

Hint: You could use the news item ID as the filename for the image. (Take a look at how the ImageGallery module does this.)

The ImageGallery Module

STEP-BY-STEP GUIDE:
Generating Thumbnails

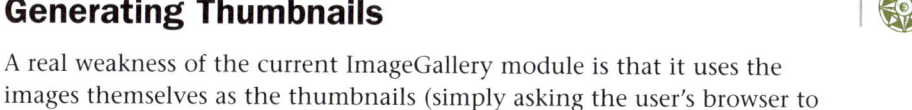

A real weakness of the current ImageGallery module is that it uses the images themselves as the thumbnails (simply asking the user's browser to scale them). If a gallery has even just a few large images in it, the page will take a long time to load.

It would be much better if we generated a smaller thumbnail for each image that is uploaded and used that on the gallery and views, saving the full file for when a user clicks on an image in the gallery. Fortunately for us, the graphics-processing capabilities of the .NET Framework make this a relatively easy task.

Here are the steps that we need to perform:

1. Add code to generate the thumbnails.

Our first task is to add code to the upload button event handler in `Modules/ImageGallery/DisplayModule.ascx.vb` that will generate and save the thumbnail.

We are going to need access to some of the graphics capabilities of the .NET Framework, so add the following two `Imports` statements to the top of the file:

```
Imports System.IO
Imports System.Drawing
Imports System.Drawing.Imaging
```

Then, find the code that uploads and saves the file and add the following highlighted code just after it, as shown in Listing 6.18.

LISTING 6.18 Code to Add to the File Upload Code in `Modules/ImageGallery/DisplayModule.ascx.vb`

```
'write the file
fileStream.Write(fileData, 0, fileData.Length)

'close the file stream
fileStream.Close()
```

164 The ImageGallery Module

STEP-BY-STEP GUIDE: **Generating Thumbnails**

LISTING 6.18 Code to Add to the File Upload Code in `Modules/ImageGallery/DisplayModule.ascx.vb` (continued)

```
'CREATE THUMBNAIL

file.InputStream.Position = 0
Dim bitmap As New Bitmap(file.InputStream)

Dim width As Integer = bitmap.Size.Width
Dim height As Integer = bitmap.Size.Height

Dim thumbnail As Image
If width > 98 Then

Dim myCallBack As Bitmap.GetThumbnailImageAbort =
➥New Image.GetThumbnailImageAbort(AddressOf ThumbnailCallback)
  thumbnail = bitmap.GetThumbnailImage(98, _
                                       height * (98 / width), _
                                       myCallBack, _
                                       IntPtr.Zero)
Else
  thumbnail = bitmap
End If

thumbnail.Save(Server.MapPath("Data/Modules/ImageGallery/" + _
       image.PrimaryKey1.ToString + "_thumb.jpg"), ImageFormat.Jpeg)

're-bind the images DataList in order to show the new image
ImagesDataList.DataSource = galleryModule.GetAllImages

ImagesDataList.DataBind()
```

We reset the input stream of the file upload to position 0 (the start) and then create a new bitmap object from it. We then get the width and the height of the image.

If the width is greater than 98 (the width of each image in our thumbnail display), we need to resize the image to create the thumbnail.

Fortunately for us, the `Image` class, which the `Bitmap` class derives from, includes a method specifically for generating thumbnails. In order to use it, we have to provide the address of a callback method for aborting the

STEP-BY-STEP GUIDE: Generating Thumbnails

operation. (We will not use this feature, but we have to provide the callback in any case.)

To have something for the delegate to point to, we need to add the following method to `DisplayModule.ascx.vb`:

```
Public Function ThumbnailCallback() As Boolean
  Return False
End Function
```

End Class

After we have the method and a local variable of type `Image.GetThumbnailImageAbort` that points to it, we can use the `Image.GetThumbnailImage` method.

We call the method, specifying the width of 98 and a height that is scaled to keep the proportions of the image correct.

If the image is not more than 98 pixels wide, we simply copy the original to the thumbnail.

After we have a thumbnail bitmap in memory, it is easy to save it to the `Data/Modules/ImageGallery/` folder by using the `Save` method of the bitmap. We specify a JPEG image format, so all images will be converted to JPEGs, no matter what their original format.

2. Adjust the main module display to use the thumbnails.

Now, we need to alter the display code so that the thumbnails will be used rather than the original images.

Open `Modules/ImageGallery/DisplayModule.ascx` and find the datalist that displays the images. Make the highlighted change as shown in Listing 6.19.

LISTING 6.19   Change to `Modules/ImageGallery/DisplayModule.ascx`

```
<asp:datalist id="ImagesDataList" DataKeyField="PrimaryKey1"
➥OnDeleteCommand="ImagesDataList_DeleteClick"
  runat="server" RepeatColumns="4" RepeatLayout="Table"
➥OnItemDataBound="ImagesDataList_ItemDataBound">
  <ItemTemplate>
    <asp:HyperLink ID="ImageLink" Runat="server">
      <img alt="<%#Container.DataItem.Description%>"
           src="data/modules/imagegallery/<%#Container.DataItem.PrimaryKey1%>_thumb.jpg"
           width="98" border="0" />
    </asp:HyperLink>
```

STEP-BY-STEP GUIDE: Generating Thumbnails

3. Adjust the two image gallery views to use the thumbnails.

We also need to change the display code in each of the two views that the ImageGallery module currently has. The change is the same in each case and is very similar to the change to the main module display, as shown in Listing 6.20.

LISTING 6.20 Change to the ImageGallery Module View .ascx Files

```
<asp:DataList id="DataList1" OnItemDataBound="DataList_ItemDataBound"
            runat="server" RepeatLayout="Table"
    RepeatColumns="4">
    <ItemTemplate>
        <asp:HyperLink ID="ImageLink" Runat="server">
            <img alt="<%#Container.DataItem.Name%>"
    src="data/modules/imagegallery/<%#Container.DataItem.PrimaryKey1%>_thumb.jpg"
    width="98" border="0" />
        </asp:HyperLink>
    </ItemTemplate>
</asp:DataList>
```

4. Update the `DeleteImage` method to delete the thumbnail.

The final thing we need to do is to update the `DeleteImage` method of the ImageGallery module business service class so that it deletes the thumbnail image as well as the main image.

Open `Modules/ImageGallery/ImageGalleryModule.vb` and find the `DeleteImage` method. Add the highlighted code shown in Listing 6.21.

LISTING 6.21 Change to the `DeleteImage` Method in `Modules/ImageGallery/ImageGalleryModule.vb`

```
Public Sub DeleteImage(ByVal pImage As GalleryImage)

    'get path to data files
    Dim root As String = ConfigurationSettings.AppSettings("FileSystemRoot")
    Dim path As String = root + "/Data/Modules/ImageGallery/"

    'delete data file
    File.Delete(path + pImage.Filename)
```

STEP-BY-STEP GUIDE: **Generating Thumbnails**

LISTING 6.21 Change to the `DeleteImage` Method in `Modules/ImageGallery/ImageGalleryModule.vb` (continued)

```
  'Delete the thumbnail
  File.Delete(path + pImage.PrimaryKey1.ToString + "_thumb.jpg")

  'delete persistent object
  Broker.Delete(pImage)
End Sub
```

The image gallery will now generate and use thumbnails.

Remember that this code will not generate thumbnails for any existing images, so you might see some broken image links if you already have some images in the image gallery.

Moving On

In this chapter, we have made several improvements to the modules that provide the features of the online community. In Chapter 7, "Managing Members," we will turn to the most important feature of all—the members. We will look at how we can make life as easy as possible for our members and how to deal with them when they become troublesome.

Managing Members 7

The most important part of any online community is its members—without them, the whole exercise has little point. Conversely, members can also be the biggest threat to an online community. Members have privileges that normal users browsing the site do not have—the main one being that they can post or alter information. These privileges mean that if a member decides to harm the community, she can often cause confusion or disruption unless she is stopped.

Given these things, it is obvious that a big weakness of our online community application is that it does not provide facilities for managing its members. We have no way to help members who, for example, have forgotten their passwords. We also have no way to deal with members who become troublesome.

In this chapter, we will add code to the application that will allow us to manage our members effectively. We will also look at some code we can add that will, to some extent, reduce the amount of "hands-on" management we have to do by helping members to help themselves.

We will look at

- Building a member administration system
- Helping users who forget their passwords
- Improving the registration system

Building a Member Administration System

From time to time, members will run into problems, so it is important that we can assist them. We can provide systems to help them to help themselves, but ultimately, we always end up needing direct control over member accounts.

Protecting the Administration System

All the pages in the `admin` folder are accessible only to administrators. To see how this is achieved, open the `Web.config` file and find the `<location>` element that refers to the `admin` folder. (It is near the top.)

```
<location path="admin">
<system.web>

    <authorization>
        <allow roles="administrator" />
```

Protecting the Administration System

```
            <deny users="*" />
        </authorization>

    </system.web>
</location>
```

This element specifies that special configuration settings should be used for the `admin` folder.

Inside it, we specify that users in the administrator role should be allowed access, whereas all other users (represented by * in the `<deny>` element) should be denied access.

If you open the code-behind for `global.asax`, you will find the event handler that ensures that administrators have the administrator role (see Listing 7.1).

LISTING 7.1 `AuthenticateRequest` Event Handler from `global.asax`

```
Sub Application_AuthenticateRequest(ByVal sender As Object, ByVal e As EventArgs)

    'check whether there is a logged in member
    If Request.IsAuthenticated Then
      'we want to attach a CommmunityPrincipal in place of the GenericPrincipal

      'get the member from the username that forms authentication has persisted
      Dim coreMod As CoreModule = New CoreModule
      Dim member As Member = coreMod.GetMemberByUserName(Context.User.Identity.Name)

      'create an empty roles array
      Dim roles As String() = {}

      'if the member is an administrator, add the administrator role to the roles array
      If member.IsAdmin Then
        ReDim roles(0)
        roles(0) = "administrator"
      End If

      'create a new principal object
      Dim principal As CommunityPrincipal = _
          New CommunityPrincipal(member, Context.User.Identity, roles)
```

CODE TOUR: Global/CommunityPrincipal.vb

LISTING 7.1 **AuthenticateRequest** Event Handler from **global.asax** (continued)

```
    'attach the principal to the context
    Context.User = principal

  End If
End Sub
```

We first check whether a user is logged in. **1▲**

If a user is logged in, we want to replace the `GenericPrincipal` (the object that represents the user and is stored in the `Context.User` property that we can access in our code) with a principal object of our own.

We retrieve the relevant user object from the persistence service. **2▲**

We then create an empty roles array and, if the user is an administrator (has `IsAdmin = true`), we add the administrator role to it. **3▲**

Finally, we create a new `CommunityPrincipal` object and place it in `Context.User`. **4▲**

So, when the user has his `IsAdmin` property set to true, the administrator role will be included in the `CommunityPrincipal` roles array. This will be picked up by the URL authorization module, which is activated by the section in the configuration file that we looked at earlier.

CODE TOUR: Global/CommunityPrincipal.vb

The `CommunityPrincipal` class represents a member who is making a particular page request. If a member is not logged in, a `GenericPrincipal` object is used, but when a member is logged in, we want to access that member's data, so we need a class of our own.

To be stored in `Context.User`, a class must implement the `IPrincipal` interface, so there are certain required things that we must include in our class. We could build a class from scratch that implements the interface, but it is much easier to create a subclass of the existing `GenericPrincipal` class.

If you open `CommunityPrincipal.vb`, you will see that the class is pretty simple:

TIP
It is worth looking for an existing class that can be subclassed before building a class from scratch. Most .NET Framework and ASP.NET classes can be subclassed.

Building a Member Administration System

STEP-BY-STEP GUIDE: Adding General Member Management Facilities

```
            Imports System.Web.Security
            Imports System.Security.Principal

            Public Class CommunityPrincipal
                Inherits GenericPrincipal
```
1 ▼
```
                Private _Member As Member
```
2 ▼
```
                Public Sub New(ByVal pMember As Member, _
                               ByVal pIdentity As IIdentity, _
                               ByVal pRoles() As String)
                    MyBase.New(pIdentity, pRoles)

                    _Member = pMember
                End Sub
```
3 ▼
```
                Public ReadOnly Property Member() As Member
                    Get
                        Return _Member
                    End Get
                End Property

            End Class
```

1 ▲ We create a private member to hold the `Member` object that is associated with the member.

2 ▲ We also provide a constructor that accepts a `Member` object, an `Identity` object (required by `GenericPrincipal`), and a set of roles. This constructor calls the constructor of its base class to set the identity and roles and then sets the private member to set the `Member` object.

3 ▲ Finally, we provide a read-only property so that our code can access the `Member` object.

So, we can access the member who is making a request through `Context.User.Member`. It is important that we do this after checking whether there is indeed a member logged in, or we will get an error (because the `GenericPrincipal` class does not have a `Member` property).

STEP-BY-STEP GUIDE:
Adding General Member Management Facilities

The first thing we will do is add some general member management facilities to the administration system.

STEP-BY-STEP GUIDE: **Adding General Member Management Facilities**

Here are the steps we will take:

1. Add a new Web Form to the `admin` subfolder.
2. Add a method to `CoreModule.vb` to get all members.
3. Add a utility class to convert the `IList` to a `DataTable`.
4. Add a `DataGrid` to display the members.
5. Initialize the `DataGrid` in `Page_Load`.
6. Define the columns we want to see.
7. Add check box columns for Boolean properties.
8. Add a link to the Member page.
9. Add the number of sections and module instances that each member owns.
10. Add sorting.
11. Enable editing.

This is a much longer series of steps than the activities in previous chapters, but don't worry—we will be able to check how we are doing along the way.

Add a new Web Form to the `admin` subfolder.

Create a new ASP.NET Web Form in the /admin subfolder. Name it `MemberAdmin.aspx` and set its `PageLayout` property to `FlowLayout`.

Add a method to `CoreModule.vb` to get all members.

We want the member admin system to show all members of the community, whether they are set to be visible or not. A quick look at `CoreModule.vb` shows that there is not currently a method for retrieving all members.

Add the following method to `CoreModule.vb`:

```
Public Function GetAllMembers() As IList
  Dim crit As New Criteria
  Return QueryFacade.Find(Type.GetType("Community.Member"), crit)
End Function
```

Add a utility class to convert the `IList` to a `DataTable`.

Our `GetAllMembers` list returns the members as a collection that implements `IList`. This is really convenient for access in our code—we can

STEP-BY-STEP GUIDE: **Adding General Member Management Facilities**

use for each loops and so on to access the members. However, it is not the ideal type to bind to an ASP.NET `DataGrid`. If we bind a `DataTable` object to the `DataView`, it will be much easier to code advanced functionalities, such as sorting and paging. `DataView` objects need to be based on a `DataTable`, so to do this we need to convert the list of members into a `DataTable`.

We could write some code that would take the list of members and build a `DataTable`; however, we would then have to write a new set of code the next time we wanted to convert a list to a table. Also, we would have to update it every time we made design changes to the objects (for example, if we added a new property). It would be much better to write a utility function that would convert any `IList` of objects into a `DataTable`.

We will now do just that.

Use the Solution Explorer to add a new folder under `/Global/`—call it `Utilities`.

Create a new class called `CollectionToDataTable` in the folder and add the following code to the new class (see Listing 7.2).

LISTING 7.2 Code to Add to `Global/Utilities/CollectionToDataTable.vb`

```
Imports System.Reflection

Public Class CollectionToDataTable

  'assumes that all objects in the collection are of same type as the first object
  'ignores objects of any other type
  Public Shared Function MakeDataTable(ByVal pCollection As IList) As DataTable

    If pCollection.Count > 0 Then

      Dim table As New DataTable

      Dim itemType As Type = pCollection.Item(0).GetType

      'build the columns from the properties of the first object
      Dim p As PropertyInfo
      For Each p In itemType.GetProperties
        table.Columns.Add(New DataColumn(p.Name, p.PropertyType))
      Next
```

STEP-BY-STEP GUIDE: **Adding General Member Management Facilities**

LISTING 7.2 Code to Add to `Global/Utilities/CollectionToDataTable.vb` (continued)

```
    Dim i As Object
    Dim r As DataRow
    For Each i In pCollection
      If i.GetType Is itemType Then
        r = table.NewRow

        For Each p In itemType.GetProperties
          If p.CanRead Then
            If p.GetValue(i, Nothing) Is Nothing Then
              r(p.Name) = DBNull.Value
            Else
              r(p.Name) = p.GetValue(i, Nothing)
            End If

          End If
        Next
        table.Rows.Add(r)
      End If
    Next
    Return table
  Else

    Return Nothing

  End If

  End Function
End Class
```

You can see that we have added a single, shared method to the class. The method will accept any object that implements `IList` and will return a `DataTable`. Also note that we have added an `Imports` statement to use the `System.Reflection` namespace. This is the namespace that contains classes that give us access to metadata about objects. We will be using it to get the list of properties that objects in the `IList` have. This will allow our code to work with objects with different properties.

We check whether the collection has any members before we do anything else. If there are no items in the collection, there is no point in

STEP-BY-STEP GUIDE: Adding General Member Management Facilities

doing anything else, and we return nothing. If there are items, we create an empty `DataTable`.

Next, we get the `Type` object from the first item in the collection. An instance of the `Type` class represents the .NET type of an object.

After we have the `Type`, we can loop through the properties it has. (They are represented as instances of the `PropertyInfo` class.) For each property, we add a column to the `DataTable` with the corresponding name.

We then want to loop through the items themselves. We don't know what type they are, so we have to treat them as being of Object type. (All .NET objects are of Object type.)

The first thing we do inside the loop is check that the current item is the same type as the first item. We need to do this because an `IList` can contain objects of different types. If we have passed an `IList` with different types in it, the properties might not match, and we won't be able to match them up to columns.

> **REUSABILITY TIP**
>
> This utility class can be copied to any project that needs to be able to convert collections that implement `IList` to `DataTable` objects. It can even be compiled into a standalone assembly for even easier reuse.

If the types match, we create a new `DataRow` object and loop through the properties of the current object, adding those we can read to the `DataRow`. If a property value is Nothing, we add a `DBNull` value to the `DataRow`. (`DataRows` cannot accept null values directly.)

If the types do not match, we simply ignore the object and move on to the next one in the collection. We might decide that we want to be strict and throw an exception when a nonmatching object is encountered but, for now at least, we are happy to ignore them.

After looping through all the properties, we add the row to the `DataTable`. After we have processed all the items, we return the completed `DataTable`.

4 ▲ **Add a `DataGrid` to display the members.**

Add a `DataGrid` control to the `MemberAdmin.aspx` page. Give it the ID `MembersDataGrid`.

5 ▲ **Initialize the `DataGrid` in `Page_Load`.**

Add the following members to the code-behind of `MemberAdmin.aspx`:

```
Public Class memberAdmin
  Inherits System.Web.UI.Page

  Protected _CoreModule As CoreModule
  Protected _MembersView As DataView
```

STEP-BY-STEP GUIDE: **Adding General Member Management Facilities**

Add the code in Listing 7.3 to the `Page_Load` method of `MemberAdmin.aspx.vb`.

LISTING 7.3 Code to Add to `Page_Load` in `Admin/MemberAdmin.aspx.vb`

```
Private Sub Page_Load(ByVal sender As System.Object, _
                     ByVal e As System.EventArgs) Handles MyBase.Load

  _CoreModule = New CoreModule

  If IsPostBack Then
    _MembersView = CType(Session("AdminMembersView"), DataView)
  Else

    Dim table As DataTable =
    ↪CollectionToDataTable.MakeDataTable(_CoreModule.GetAllMembers)


    Session("AdminMembersView") = New DataView(table)
    _MembersView = Session("AdminMembersView")

    MembersDataGrid.DataSource = _MembersView

    MembersDataGrid.DataBind()

  End If
End Sub
```

We need to persist the `DataView` object between page requests, as it is the `DataView` that will be storing the sort settings for the `DataGrid`. If we did not persist it in the `Session` object, it would continually "forget" which column the `DataGrid` was sorted on (and in which direction).

Therefore, if the page is a postback, we simply pull the `DataView` from the `Session` object.

If the page is not a postback, we get the members from the `CoreModule` and convert the `IList` to a `DataTable` using the utility class we added earlier. We then store it in the `Session` collection and databind the `DataGrid`.

178   Building a Member Administration System

STEP-BY-STEP GUIDE: **Adding General Member Management Facilities**

If you now browse to this page (remember, you need to be logged in as a member who is set as an administrator in the database), you will see the list of all members. However, as we can see in Figure 7.1, it is not formatted particularly well—the columns are not in an ideal order, and there are several columns that are not even from our `Member` object.

FIGURE 7.1
The default `DataGrid`.

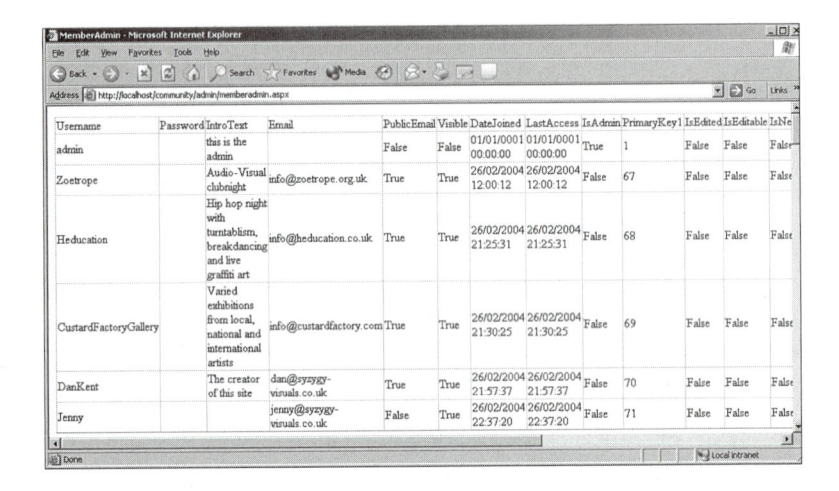

The extra columns are caused by the fact that the `Member` class inherits from `CommunityPO`, which in turn inherits from a base class provided by the persistence service. These columns correspond to the fields that the persistence service needs to do its job. The application does not know which fields we are interested in unless we specify them.

Before we move on to specify the columns we want, let's get the general formatting in line with our application standards. In order to do this, we need to add a link to the style sheet and set the class of the body element:

```
<meta name="vs_defaultClientScript" content="JavaScript">
<meta name="vs_targetSchema" content=
➥"http://schemas.microsoft.com/intellisense/ie5">
<LINK href="../styles.css" type="text/css" rel="stylesheet">
</HEAD>
<body class="SiteBody">
    <form id="Form1" method="post" runat="server">
```

We can also make the `DataGrid` look nicer very quickly by using the Visual Studio .NET Design View Autoformat and Property Builder

STEP-BY-STEP GUIDE: **Adding General Member Management Facilities**

options. Right-click the `DataGrid` and select AutoFormat to choose one of the predefined styles. Then select Property Builder to refine the look.

I set the autoformat to a colorful 5 and set the font size to smaller to get a grid as shown in Figure 7.2.

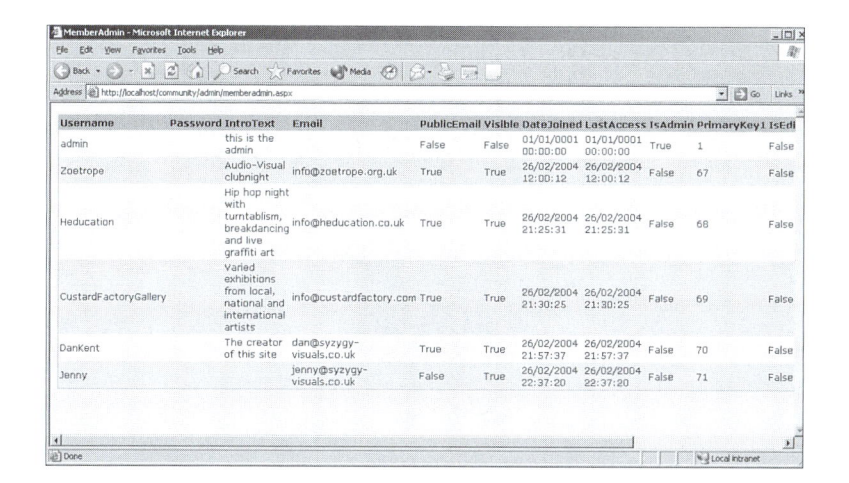

FIGURE 7.2
The autoformatted `DataGrid`.

Define the columns we want to see.

Open `MemberSettings.aspx` in design mode and select the `DataGrid`. Now click the Property Builder link at the bottom of the Properties panel.

Select Columns and uncheck the Auto Generate Columns check box.

Now that we have told ASP.NET not to simply use all of the available columns, we need to add each of the columns we want to see. Select Bound Column and click the arrow between the two selection boxes. A new column will be created. Set the header text to Username and the data field to Username. Check the read-only check box because we shouldn't change members' usernames.

If you save the file and view the page (remember, changes to aspx files do not require a recompile), you will see only the usernames of your members, as shown in Figure 7.3.

Add columns for Email, DateJoined, and LastAccess in the same way. The `DataGrid` should now look like that shown in Figure 7.4.

Let's change the two date columns so that they display only the date, not the time.

TIP

It is a very bad idea to allow changing of usernames in an online community. If members find out that they can get the administrator to change their usernames, they often want to change them frequently. Also, each member's username is his identity to other members, so allowing changes can cause confusion. In the very rare event that a username has to be changed, it can be altered in the database itself (but be careful not to have two members with the same username).

Building a Member Administration System

STEP-BY-STEP GUIDE: Adding General Member Management Facilities

FIGURE 7.3
The `DataGrid` showing only the Username column.

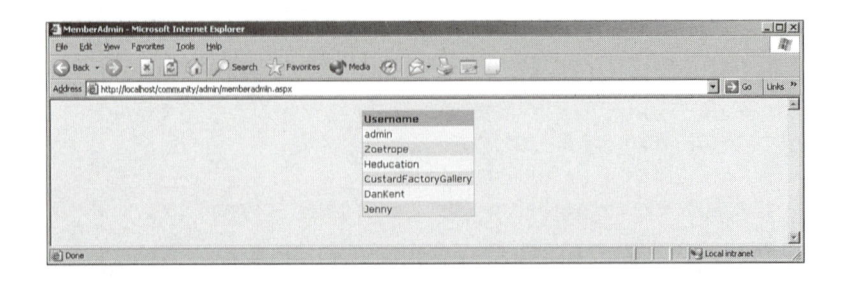

FIGURE 7.4
The `DataGrid` with some more columns.

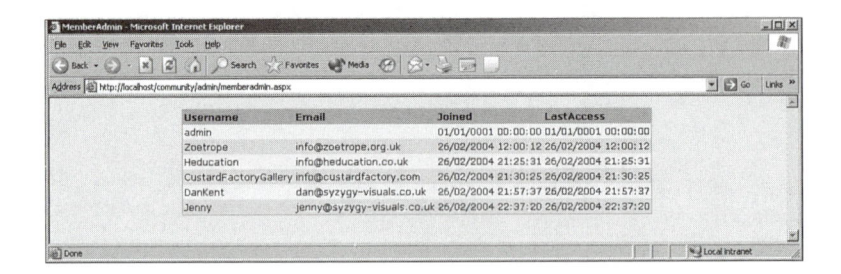

Open up the Property Builder for the `DataGrid` and select the Joined column. Set the Data Formatting Expression to

`{0:dd/MM/yy}`

This will display the date in UK format. (You are, of course, free to use your own preferred format.)

Do the same for the LastAccess column. The result is shown in Figure 7.5.

FIGURE 7.5
The `DataGrid` with date columns.

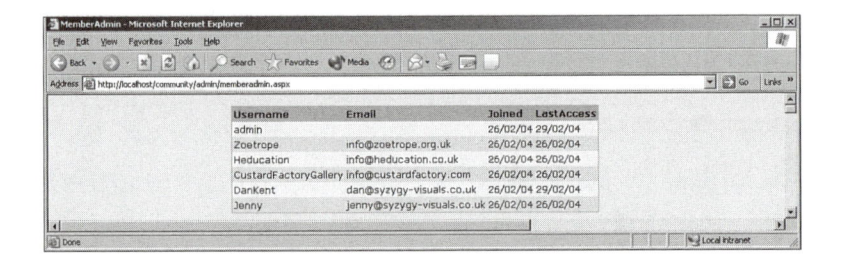

7 ▲ Add check box columns for Boolean properties.

`PublicEmail`, `Visible`, and `IsAdmin` are all Boolean properties, so the best way to represent them in the `DataGrid` is with check box controls. There is no default check box column in the `DataGrid`, so to add these,

STEP-BY-STEP GUIDE: **Adding General Member Management Facilities**

we will have to create template columns for them. Template columns enable us to specify whichever controls we would like to have displayed.

Go back to the Property Builder for the `DataGrid` and select Columns > Template Column > Right arrow. Give it the heading `PublicEmail` and click OK.

Now we need to add the check box control. Right-click the `DataGrid` and select Edit Template > PublicEmail. Click once inside the ItemTemplate box and drag a check box into it from the toolbox.

Select the check box control and select DataBinding in the Property Viewer. Click the ... box to bring up the DataBindings settings window.

Select the Checked property, then Custom Binding Expression, and add the following to the Binding Expression text box:

```
DataBinder.Eval(Container, "DataItem.PublicEmail")
```

This expression will use the `PublicEmail` property as the checked value of the check box.

At this stage, you should also set the `Enabled` property of the check box to False so that it will not be editable.

Now add another check box to the EditItemTemplate section in exactly the same way. This time, leave the `Enabled` property with the True value (because we will want to edit the value when we are in edit mode).

Follow the same process for the `Visible` and `IsAdmin` properties, adding a template column with text boxes for each. Remember to change the custom binding expression to point to the correct property in each case.

If you now view the page, you should see that the Boolean columns are shown with check boxes, as shown in Figure 7.6.

FIGURE 7.6
The `DataGrid` with check box columns.

STEP-BY-STEP GUIDE: **Adding General Member Management Facilities**

8 ▲ Add a link to the Member page.

It would be good to provide a link to the Member page of each member on this list. Use the Property Builder to add a Hyperlink column. Set the header to Page, the text to [link], the URL field to PrimaryKey1, and the URL format to ../default.aspx?member={0}.

We told the DataGrid to construct the correct URL with the member ID in it, to display the Member page. It is also a good idea to set the target to _blank so that the Member page will be displayed in a new window.

9 ▲ Add the number of sections and module instances that each member owns.

Another useful feature of this member list would be to list the number of sections or module instances that each member has created. This will allow us to see who the most active members are and which members have not actually added any information.

To do this, we will need to add some properties to the Member object that expose the number of sections and the number of module instances the member owns. We can access these values directly in code (as Member.Sections.Count and Member.ModuleInstances.Count), but the DataGrid will not access data that is not directly stored in a property of the objects it is bound to.

Add the following properties to Member.vb:

```
Public ReadOnly Property SectionsCount() As Integer
  Get
    Return Sections.Count
  End Get
End Property


Public ReadOnly Property InstancesCount() As Integer
  Get
    Return ModuleInstances.Count
  End Get
End Property
```

As you can see, we simply expose the two values so that the DataGrid will treat them as normal property values.

We can then add bound columns to the DataGrid that access these values the same way we did for other properties. The DataGrid should now look like Figure 7.7.

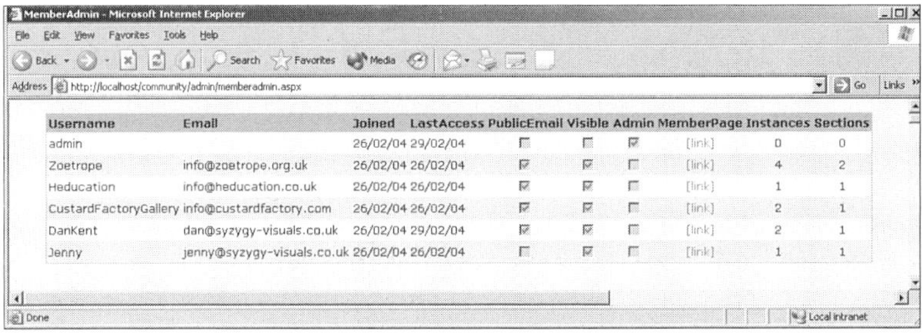

Building a Member Administration System 183

STEP-BY-STEP GUIDE: **Adding General Member Management Facilities**

FIGURE 7.7
The `DataGrid` with section and instance counts.

If you now view `MemberAdmin.aspx` in HTML view, it should look something like Listing 7.4.

LISTING 7.4 `MemberAdmin.aspx`

```
<asp:DataGrid id="MembersDataGrid" runat="server" BorderColor="Tan" BorderWidth="1px"
➥BackColor="LightGoldenrodYellow" CellPadding="2" GridLines="None" ForeColor="Black"
➥Font-Size="Smaller" AutoGenerateColumns="False" HorizontalAlign="Center">
  <SelectedItemStyle ForeColor="GhostWhite" BackColor="DarkSlateBlue">
  </SelectedItemStyle>
  <AlternatingItemStyle BackColor="PaleGoldenrod"></AlternatingItemStyle>
  <HeaderStyle Font-Bold="True" BackColor="Tan"></HeaderStyle>
  <FooterStyle BackColor="Tan"></FooterStyle>
  <Columns>
    <asp:BoundColumn DataField="Username" HeaderText="Username"></asp:BoundColumn>
    <asp:BoundColumn DataField="Email" HeaderText="Email"></asp:BoundColumn>
    <asp:BoundColumn DataField="DateJoined" HeaderText="Joined"
    ➥DataFormatString="{0:dd/MM/yy}"></asp:BoundColumn>
    <asp:BoundColumn DataField="LastAccess" HeaderText="LastAccess"
    ➥DataFormatString="{0:dd/MM/yy}"></asp:BoundColumn>
    <asp:TemplateColumn HeaderText="PublicEmail">
      <ItemStyle HorizontalAlign="Center"></ItemStyle>
      <ItemTemplate>
        <asp:CheckBox id=CheckBox1 runat="server" Checked='<%# DataBinder.Eval
        ➥(Container, DataItem.PublicEmail") %>' Enabled="False">
        </asp:CheckBox>
      </ItemTemplate>
      <EditItemTemplate>
        <asp:CheckBox id=CheckBox2 runat="server" Checked='<%# DataBinder.Eval
        ➥(Container, DataItem.PublicEmail") %>'>
        </asp:CheckBox>
      </EditItemTemplate>
        </asp:TemplateColumn>
    <asp:TemplateColumn HeaderText="Visible">
```

STEP-BY-STEP GUIDE: **Adding General Member Management Facilities**

LISTING 7.4 `MemberAdmin.aspx`
(continued)

```
          <ItemStyle HorizontalAlign="Center"></ItemStyle>
          <ItemTemplate>
            <asp:CheckBox id=CheckBox3 runat="server" Checked='<%# DataBinder.Eval
            ➥(Container, DataItem.Visible) %>' Enabled="False">
            </asp:CheckBox>
          </ItemTemplate>
          <EditItemTemplate>
            <asp:CheckBox id=CheckBox4 runat="server" Checked='<%# DataBinder.Eval
            ➥(Container, "DataItem.Visible") %>'>
            </asp:CheckBox>
          </EditItemTemplate>
        </asp:TemplateColumn>
        <asp:TemplateColumn HeaderText="Admin">
          <ItemStyle HorizontalAlign="Center"></ItemStyle>
          <ItemTemplate>
            <asp:CheckBox id=CheckBox5 runat="server" Checked='<%# DataBinder.Eval
            ➥(Container, DataItem.IsAdmin") %>' Enabled="False">
            </asp:CheckBox>
          </ItemTemplate>
          <EditItemTemplate>
            <asp:CheckBox id=CheckBox6 runat="server" Checked='<%# DataBinder.Eval
            ➥(Container, DataItem.IsAdmin") %>'>
            </asp:CheckBox>
          </EditItemTemplate>
        </asp:TemplateColumn>
        <asp:HyperLinkColumn Text="[link]" Target="_blank"
        ➥DataNavigateUrlField="PrimaryKey1"
        ➥DataNavigateUrlFormatString="../default.aspx?member={0}"
        ➥HeaderText="MemberPage">
          <ItemStyle HorizontalAlign="Center"></ItemStyle>
          </asp:HyperLinkColumn>
          <asp:BoundColumn DataField="InstancesCount" HeaderText="Instances">
            <ItemStyle HorizontalAlign="Center"></ItemStyle>
          </asp:BoundColumn>
          <asp:BoundColumn DataField="SectionsCount" HeaderText="Sections">
            <ItemStyle HorizontalAlign="Center"></ItemStyle>
          </asp:BoundColumn>
        </Columns>
        <PagerStyle HorizontalAlign="Center" ForeColor="DarkSlateBlue"
        ➥BackColor="PaleGoldenrod"></PagerStyle>
      </asp:DataGrid></P>
```

STEP-BY-STEP GUIDE: **Adding General Member Management Facilities**

You can see all the settings we have made, represented as elements and attributes.

Add sorting.

10 ▲

It would be useful to be able to sort the `DataGrid` by its various columns. Because we went to the effort of converting the list of members to a `DataView`, this is actually very easy.

First, we need to enable sorting in the `DataGrid`. Open the Property Builder and check the Allow Sorting check box.

We also need to set up sorting for the columns we want to sort. Open each column you would like to sort by in the Property Builder and enter a sort expression in the relevant box. In the case of our `DataGrid`, the sort expression will be the same as the property to which the column is bound, but we still have to enter it.

There is one more thing we need to do to enable sorting. Although the `DataView` object will do the sorting work for us, we need to add some code to tell it what to do.

Add the following method to `MemberAdmin.aspx.vb`:

```
Private Sub MembersDataGrid_SortCommand(ByVal source As Object, _
    ByVal e As System.Web.UI.WebControls.DataGridSortCommandEventArgs) _
    Handles MembersDataGrid.SortCommand

  MembersDataGrid.DataSource = _MembersView

  If CType(Session("AdminMembersView"), DataView).Sort =
  ➥e.SortExpression Then
    CType(Session("AdminMembersView"), DataView).Sort =
    ➥e.SortExpression & " DESC"
  Else
    CType(Session("AdminMembersView"), DataView).Sort = e.SortExpression
  End If
  MembersDataGrid.DataBind()
End Sub
```

This method will be called whenever the user clicks a column header in the `DataGrid`. We check whether the `DataView` is already sorted by the expression for the column that was clicked. If it is, we reverse the sort order by adding `DESC` to the expression. If it is not, we set it.

We then rebind the `DataGrid`.

STEP-BY-STEP GUIDE: **Adding General Member Management Facilities**

You will now be able to sort any of the columns for which you have set up sorting by clicking the column headers.

11 ▲ Enable editing.

One of the best features of the `DataGrid` is that it enables "in place" editing. We have already seen this feature in use with `DataLists` earlier in the book. We will now use the same technique with our members' `DataGrid`.

Open the Property Builder for the `DataList` and select Columns > Button > Edit Update Cancel and add the column. This will add a column to the `DataGrid` that will display an Edit link for each row (or Update and Cancel links when we are in edit mode).

The links will not do anything themselves; however, we have to add code to handle their events. Add the following event handler to the code-behind:

```
Private Sub MembersDataGrid_EditCommand(ByVal source As Object, _
ByVal e As System.Web.UI.WebControls.DataGridCommandEventArgs) _
Handles MembersDataGrid.EditCommand
   MembersDataGrid.DataSource = _MembersView
   MembersDataGrid.EditItemIndex = e.Item.ItemIndex
   MembersDataGrid.DataBind()
End Sub
```

This will enable the edit mode by setting the Edit Item Index to the index of the item that was clicked.

Add this event handler also:

```
    Private Sub MembersDataGrid_CancelCommand(ByVal source As Object, _
ByVal e As System.Web.UI.WebControls.DataGridCommandEventArgs) _
Handles MembersDataGrid.CancelCommand
       MembersDataGrid.DataSource = _MembersView
       MembersDataGrid.EditItemIndex = -1

       MembersDataGrid.DataBind()
    End Sub
```

This will cancel edit mode by setting the Edit Item Index to –1.

Before we can write the `Update` event handler, we need some code to call from it to actually update the persistent object that represents the member. Remember, we should not change the persistent objects directly

STEP-BY-STEP GUIDE: Adding General Member Management Facilities

from our presentation code, so we need to create a method in `CoreModule.vb` to do the update.

Add the following member to `CoreModule.vb`:

```
Public Function AdminUpdateMember(ByVal pID As Integer, _
            ByVal pEmail As String, _
            ByVal pPublicEmail As Boolean, _
            ByVal pVisible As Boolean, _
            ByVal pIsAdmin As Boolean)

  Dim mem As Member = GetMemberByID(pID)

  If Not mem Is Nothing Then
    mem.Email = pEmail
    mem.PublicEmail = pPublicEmail
    mem.Visible = pVisible
    mem.IsAdmin = pIsAdmin
  End If

End Function
```

Simple stuff—we just get the member from the ID and update the properties.

We can now write our `Update` event handler for `MemberAdmin.aspx` (see Listing 7.5).

LISTING 7.5 Update Event Handler in `Admin/MemberAdmin.aspx.vb`

```
Protected Sub MembersDataGrid_UpdateCommand(ByVal source As Object, _
ByVal e As System.Web.UI.WebControls.DataGridCommandEventArgs) _
Handles MembersDataGrid.UpdateCommand
    Dim email As TextBox = CType(e.Item.Cells(1).Controls(0), TextBox)
    Dim publicEmail As CheckBox = CType(e.Item.Cells(4).Controls(1), CheckBox)
    Dim visible As CheckBox = CType(e.Item.Cells(5).Controls(1), CheckBox)
    Dim IsAdmin As CheckBox = CType(e.Item.Cells(6).Controls(1), CheckBox)

    _CoreModule.AdminUpdateMember(MembersDataGrid.DataKeys(e.Item.ItemIndex) , _
                        email.Text, _
                        publicEmail.Checked, _
```

STEP-BY-STEP GUIDE: **Adding General Member Management Facilities**

LISTING 7.5 Update Event Handler in `Admin/MemberAdmin.aspx.vb` (continued)

```
                                    visible.Checked, _
                                    IsAdmin.Checked)

    Dim table As DataTable = _
            CollectionToDataTable.MakeDataTable(_CoreModule.GetAllMembers)


    Session("AdminMembersView") = New DataView(table)
    _MembersView = Session("AdminMembersView")

    MembersDataGrid.DataSource = _MembersView
    MembersDataGrid.EditItemIndex = -1
    MembersDataGrid.DataBind()
End Sub
```

Before this method will work, we need to make one further change to the properties of the `DataGrid`. Change the `DataKeyField` property to `PrimaryKey1`. This will cause each row of the table to have the primary key of the member it displays attached to it.

We get references to the controls that hold the data we want to update by using the `DataGridCommandEventArgs` object that is passed to the method. The `Item` property of `DataGridCommandEventArgs` is the row from the table we are editing, so we can access each of the columns through the `Cells` collection and thus access the controls we are interested in. This code uses numerical indexes, which aren't ideal (they are not as resilient to code changes as names).

Using the primary key we just configured, along with the values from the controls, we can call the method that we added to `CoreModule`.

After doing the update, we need to refresh the `DataTable` that holds our data so that the `DataGrid` will reflect the changes. We do this in the same way as we did when initializing the page.

You should now have a working `DataGrid` that will enable you to edit some of the member details.

Helping Users Who Forget Their Passwords

One of the most common problems members can run into is forgetting their password. Without their password, they will be unable to log in to the site and thus will not be able to actively participate.

There are several ways we can help these members. We could add a facility to our admin system so that we can find out members' passwords, or we can even reset the password to something different. However, that would mean work for the administrator and would also mean having passwords viewable in the admin system. We could use a *secret question* approach, in which the member is asked to answer a question she has previously entered the answer to. The problem with this is that really forgetful members will forget the answer to the secret questions as well as their passwords.

We could email the member's password to her, but that would mean sending out passwords over email—not an ideal solution by any means.

The solution we will implement is to email the member a special link that she can use to reset her password. The link will only be valid for a short time, to reduce the security implications. The link will allow the member access to a special page where she will be able to set a new password.

We will create the special link by using a cryptographic technique called *hashing*. Hashing is also called *one-way encryption* because it is a way of encrypting data in such a way that the original data cannot be recovered. You might wonder how unrecoverable encrypted data is of any use, so here is an explanation of the process.

When the user requests a password change, an email is sent to him with the special link. The link includes the date and time of the request, the user ID, and a hash. The hash is created by taking the date/time and member ID, along with a special password that is stored on the server, combining them, and passing the result through a hashing algorithm.

When the user clicks the link in the email, the server will use the date/time and member ID in the link, along with the password stored on the server, and create a new hash. This server-side hash is compared to the one being passed in the link. If they match, we can be confident that the member has clicked a genuine link. If they do not match, we should suspect that there is some funny business going on.

STEP-BY-STEP GUIDE: Automating Password Resetting

The system can then check that the date/time is within the allowed period before allowing the password to be changed.

This approach is secure (in the sense of the cryptography—it does not prevent someone with access to the member's email account from pretending to be him) because only someone with access to the password can create hashes that match a particular member ID/DateTime pair. Hashes made without the password will not match.

As an additional security precaution, this system will not work for any member who is an administrator. If he forgets his password, he will have to recover it from the database. We don't want access to an administrator account to be available to anyone who intercepts an email!

STEP-BY-STEP GUIDE:
Automating Password Resetting

We will now implement the system that was previously outlined.

1. Create a Forgot Password page.

Create a new Web Form in the /community/ folder. Name it `ForgotPassword.aspx` and change the `Layout` property to `Flow Layout`.

Add three server-side `DIV` elements:

- `ID RequestControls` for the controls that allow a member to request a password change
- `ID RequestMadeControls` for the message that is displayed after a request is made
- `ID ChangePasswordControls` for the controls that allow a user to actually change his password

Put a text box and a button inside the first `DIV`, a Thankyou message inside the second, and two text boxes and a button inside the third. The HTML view of the page should look like Listing 7.6.

LISTING 7.6 ForgotPassword.aspx

```
<%@ Page Language="vb" AutoEventWireup="false" Codebehind="ForgotPassword.aspx.vb"
➥inherits="Community.ForgotPassword"%>
<!DOCTYPE HTML PUBLIC "-//W3C//DTD HTML 4.0 Transitional//EN">
<HTML>
```

STEP-BY-STEP GUIDE: **Automating Password Resetting**

LISTING 7.6 ForgotPassword.aspx
(continued)

```
<HEAD>
  <title>ForgotPassword</title>
  <meta name="GENERATOR" content="Microsoft Visual Studio .NET 7.1">
  <meta name="CODE_LANGUAGE" content="Visual Basic .NET 7.1">
  <meta name="vs_defaultClientScript" content="JavaScript">
  <meta name="vs_targetSchema" content="http://schemas.microsoft.com/intellisense/ie5">
</HEAD>
<body>
  <form id="Form1" method="post" runat="server">
    <div id="RequestControls" runat="server">
      Enter your username to receive an email with instructions for changing your
      password
      <div>
       <asp:TextBox id="UsernameTextBox" runat="server"></asp:TextBox>
       <asp:Button id="RequestButton" runat="server" Text="Request a password change">
       </asp:Button>
      </div>
    </div>
    <div id="RequestMadeControls" runat="server">
      You will now receive an email with instructions for changing your password.
    </div>
    <div id="ChangePasswordControls" runat="server">
      <div>
        Enter a new password
        <asp:TextBox id="Password1TextBox" runat="server">
        </asp:TextBox>
      </div>
      <div>
        Enter the password again
        <asp:TextBox id="Password2TextBox" runat="server">
        </asp:TextBox>
      </div>
      <div>
       <asp:Button id="ChangePasswordButton" runat="server" Text="Change My Password">
       </asp:Button>
      </div>
    </div>
  </form>
</body>
</HTML>
```

STEP-BY-STEP GUIDE: **Automating Password Resetting**

We also need to add declarations to the code-behind so that we can access the controls we have added:

```
Protected WithEvents RequestControls As
➥System.Web.UI.HtmlControls.HtmlGenericControl
Protected WithEvents ChangePasswordControls As
➥System.Web.UI.HtmlControls
➥.HtmlGenericControl
Protected WithEvents RequestMadeControls As
➥System.Web.UI.HtmlControls.HtmlGenericControl
Protected WithEvents UsernameTextBox As
➥System.Web.UI.WebControls.TextBox
Protected WithEvents RequestButton As System.Web.UI.WebControls.Button
Protected WithEvents Password1TextBox As
➥System.Web.UI.WebControls.TextBox
Protected WithEvents Password2TextBox As
➥System.Web.UI.WebControls.TextBox
Protected WithEvents ChangePasswordButton As
➥System.Web.UI.WebControls.Button
```

2. Add code to initialize the page.

When a user first visits the page, only the first server-side DIV should be visible. If this is the case, the page will not be a postback and will not contain the special URL parameters that the link in the email contains.

Therefore, we can use the following Page_Load event handler to initialize the page:

```
Private Sub Page_Load(ByVal sender As System.Object, _
                     ByVal e As System.EventArgs) _
        Handles MyBase.Load
    If Not Page.IsPostBack Then
        If Request.QueryString("MemberID") Is Nothing Then
            RequestControls.Visible = True
            RequestMadeControls.Visible = False
            ChangePasswordControls.Visible = False
        End If
    End If
End Sub
```

3. Add a password configuration setting to the Web.config.

Helping Users Who Forget Their Passwords 193

STEP-BY-STEP GUIDE: **Automating Password Resetting**

Add the new setting that is highlighted in the following code to the `Web.config`:

```
<add key="SmtpServer" value="inspiron" />

<add key="AdminEmail" value="help@dansfriends.com" />

<add key="PasswordRequestHashPassword" value="hdagd54tfdg5t45tf4" />
```

This password will never have to be remembered by anyone, so there is no reason not to make it nice and long.

4. Add code to email the special link.

When the user clicks the button to make a password change request, we want to send him an email with a special link in it that includes his member ID, the date and time, and the hash that will validate his request.

Add the following event handler for the `click` event of the button (see Listing 7.7).

LISTING 7.7 Event Handler for the Request Button in `ForgotPassword.aspx.vb`

```
Private Sub RequestButton_Click(ByVal sender As System.Object, _
                                ByVal e As System.EventArgs) _
         Handles RequestButton.Click
  Dim coreMod As New CoreModule

  Dim member As Member = coreMod.GetMemberByUserName(UsernameTextBox.Text)

  If Not member Is Nothing Then

    Dim dateTimeTicks As Long = DateTime.Now.Ticks
    Dim stringToHash As String = member.PrimaryKey1.ToString & dateTimeTicks &
    ➥ ConfigurationSettings.AppSettings("PasswordRequestHashPassword")

    Dim hash As String = FormsAuthentication.HashPasswordForStoringInConfigFile
    ➥(stringToHash, "sha1")

    Dim email As New MailMessage
    email.To = member.Email
    email.From = ConfigurationSettings.AppSettings("AdminEmail")
    email.Subject = "Your password change request for " &
    ➥ConfigurationSettings.AppSettings("CommunityName")
```

STEP-BY-STEP GUIDE: **Automating Password Resetting**

LISTING 7.7 Event Handler for the Request Button in `ForgotPassword.aspx.vb` (continued)

```
    email.Body = "Navigate to the following link to change your password: "
    email.Body = email.Body & "http://" & Request.Url.Authority &
➥Request.Url.AbsolutePath _
            & "?MemberID=" & member.PrimaryKey1 & "&Date=" & dateTimeTicks _
            & "&Check=" & hash

    RequestMadeControls.InnerText =
➥"You will now receive an email with instructions for changing your password."
    RequestMadeControls.Visible = True
    RequestControls.Visible = False

    Try
      SmtpMail.SmtpServer = ConfigurationSettings.AppSettings("SMTPServer")
      SmtpMail.Send(email)
    Catch ex As Exception
      RequestMadeControls.InnerText =
➥"The email could not be sent - please contact the site admin"
    End Try

  Else
    RequestMadeControls.InnerText = "Username not recognized - did you mistype it?"
    RequestMadeControls.Visible = True
  End If
End Sub
```

First, we attempt to get a `Member` object that matches the username that has been entered. If we cannot find one, we put an error message in the `RequestMadeControls DIV` and display it.

If we did retrieve a `Member` object, we get the current date and time as a single *ticks* value. Ticks is a long integer that is the number of 100-nanosecond intervals there have been since 12:00 a.m., January 1, 0001. A ticks value is not very useful for outputting to users, but it is really useful for our purpose because a simple long integer value will be easy to include in a URL.

We then create a string that includes the ID from the `Member` object, the ticks value, and the password we stored in the configuration file.

STEP-BY-STEP GUIDE: **Automating Password Resetting**

After we have the string, we hash it using the `FormsAuthentication.HashPasswordForStoringInConfigFile` method. This method is a "helper" that is typically used for hashing users' passwords, but we can make use of it for our purposes. (See Chapter 9, "Improving the Code," for more on the other use for it.) We specify that we want to use the `SHA1` hashing algorithm.

We then have all the things we need to construct the email. We create a `MailMessage` object and fill the required properties. In the body, we build a URL that will point back to the `ForgotPassword.aspx` Web Form but with the member ID, ticks value, and hash in the relevant URL parameters. We also set the message `DIV` to a confirmation message.

Next, we attempt to send the email using the `SMTPMail` class. If there is an exception, we change the message `DIV` to tell the user that the email could not be sent.

If you try the system at this point, you should be able to send Change Password Request emails to an email account that you have configured in a member's settings.

5. Add code to accept the special URL.

We now need to deal with a member clicking the link in a Change Password Request email. Add the following new code to the `Page_Load` event handler (see Listing 7.8).

> **TIP**
>
> If you do not want to actually send emails to do the testing, you can set the SMTP server to `localhost` and see the emails in the `inetpub/mailroot/drop` folder. (This assumes that you have the SMTP service running and configured with the standard settings.)

LISTING 7.8 Code to Add to the `Page_Load` Method in `ForgotPassword.aspx.vb`

```
Private Sub Page_Load(ByVal sender As System.Object, _
                ByVal e As System.EventArgs) _
        Handles MyBase.Load
    If Not Page.IsPostBack Then

        If Request.QueryString("MemberID") Is Nothing Then
            RequestControls.Visible = True
            RequestMadeControls.Visible = False
            ChangePasswordControls.Visible = False
        Else
            Dim memberID As String = Request.QueryString("MemberID")
            Dim ticks As String = Request.QueryString("Date")
            Dim UrlHash As String = Request.QueryString("Check")
            Dim stringtohash As String = memberID & ticks & _
                ConfigurationSettings.AppSettings("PasswordRequestHashPassword")
```

1▼

2▼

STEP-BY-STEP GUIDE: Automating Password Resetting

LISTING 7.8 Code to Add to the `Page_Load` Method in `ForgotPassword.aspx.vb` (continued)

```
            Dim computedHash = _
                FormsAuthentication.HashPasswordForStoringInConfigFile(stringtohash, "sha1")

            If UrlHash = computedHash Then
                RequestControls.Visible = False
                RequestMadeControls.Visible = False
                ChangePasswordControls.Visible = True
            Else
                RequestControls.Visible = True
                RequestMadeControls.Visible = True
                ChangePasswordControls.Visible = False
                RequestMadeControls.InnerText = _
                    "There was a problem with your request, please request another email"

            End If
        End If
    End If
End Sub
```

1 ▲ If the `MemberID` query parameter is found, we extract the values for the member ID, date, and check parameters.

2 ▲ We then construct a new hash from the member ID and date (with the password from the config file) and compare it to the one in the URL parameter.

3 ▲ If the hashes match, this is a genuine password change request, and we display the password change controls.

4 ▲ If the hashes do not match, either there has been a problem (for example, the hash has been reformatted by email software or sloppy cutting and pasting) or someone is trying to use a false request. We display an error message and do not allow the password change to take place.

6. Add code to reset the password.

So, we now have a system that will only allow members with a valid Change Password email to access the Change Password controls. All we need to do now is add some code to deal with the `click` event of the Change Password button.

CHALLENGE: **One-Use-Only Change Password Emails**

Add the following event handler to the code-behind for
`ChangePassword.aspx` (see Listing 7.9).

LISTING 7.9 Event Handler for the Change Password Button in
`ForgotPassword.aspx.vb`

```
Private Sub ChangePasswordButton_Click(ByVal sender As System.Object, _
                                 ByVal e As System.EventArgs) _
        Handles ChangePasswordButton.Click
  If Password1TextBox.Text = Password2TextBox.Text Then
    Dim coreMod As New CoreModule

    Dim mem As Member = coreMod.GetMemberByID(CInt(Request.QueryString("MemberID")))

    If Not mem Is Nothing Then
      coreMod.UpdateMemberDetails(mem.PrimaryKey1, _
                             Password1TextBox.Text, _
                             mem.IntroText, _
                             mem.Email, _
                             mem.PublicEmail)
      RequestMadeControls.InnerHtml = "Your password has now been changed" _
             & "<a href='default.aspx'>Click here to return to the homepage"
      RequestMadeControls.Visible = True
      ChangePasswordControls.Visible = False
    End If
  End If
End Sub
```

We check whether the two password boxes are equal.

If they are, we attempt to get a `Member` object with the ID specified in
the query string.

If a member was retrieved, we update the member's details with the new
password and display a confirmation message.

CHALLENGE:
One-Use-Only Change Password Emails

Our system will currently refuse to accept a Change Password Request
email that is older than a configured number of hours. That is good, but

it still allows a Change Password email to be used any number of times within those hours. It would be better if each email could be used only once.

Change the code so that each Change Password email can only be used to change the password once.

Hint: If you include the user's current password in the hashed string, the hashes will not match after the password is changed.

Improving the Registration Process

The best place to control who becomes a member of the community is at the point where they join—the registration system. At the moment, the Registration page, `Join.aspx`, is a very simple form that will allow any user to create a New Member account. We will now look at some ways in which we can impose more restrictions on registrations.

STEP-BY-STEP GUIDE:
Requiring Approval for New User Registrations

If you do not expect (or wish) to have huge numbers of new members joining the community, one approach is to require the approval of an administrator before a member becomes active in the community.

To do this, we need to make a change to the `Member` class so that each `Member` object will store whether that member has been approved. We also need to persist this value in the database through the persistence service. After we have done this, we will be able to add code so that only approved members can sign in and so that administrators can approve new members.

Here are the steps we will take:

1. Add an Active field to the `Member` object.

We need the `Member` object to store a new field, so we know whether the member has been activated yet. Add the following highlighted code to `Member.vb`:

```
Public Class Member
    Inherits CommunityPO

    Private _Username As String
    Private _Password As String
```

STEP-BY-STEP GUIDE: **Requiring Approval for New User Registrations**

```
Private _IntroText As String
Private _DateJoined As DateTime
Private _LastAccess As DateTime
Private _Email As String
Private _PublicEmail As Boolean
Private _MemberPageSectionID As Integer = Nothing
Private _Visible As Boolean
Private _IsAdmin As Boolean
Private _IsActivated As Boolean

Private _Sections As IList
Private _ModuleInstances As IList
Private _MemberPageSection As Section = Nothing

'reconstructor for use by persistence service
Public Sub New(ByVal ID As Integer, _
               ByVal pUsername As String, _
               ByVal pPassword As String, _
               ByVal pIntroText As String, _
               ByVal pDateJoined As DateTime, _
               ByVal pLastAccess As DateTime, _
               ByVal pEmail As String, _
               ByVal pPublicEmail As Boolean, _
               ByVal pMemberPageSectionID As Integer, _
               ByVal pVisible As Boolean, _
               ByVal pIsAdmin As Boolean, _
               ByVal pIsActivated As Boolean)

  MyBase.New(ID)
  _Username = pUsername
  _Password = pPassword
  _IntroText = pIntroText
  _DateJoined = pDateJoined

  _LastAccess = pLastAccess
  _Email = pEmail
  _PublicEmail = pPublicEmail
  _MemberPageSectionID = pMemberPageSectionID
  _Visible = pVisible
  _IsAdmin = pIsAdmin
  _IsActivated = pIsActivated
```

STEP-BY-STEP GUIDE: **Requiring Approval for New User Registrations**

```
    End Sub

    'constructor for use when creating new members
    Public Sub New(ByVal pUsername As String, _
                   ByVal pPassword As String, _
                   ByVal pIntroText As String, _
                   ByVal pEmail As String, _
                   ByVal pPublicEmail As Boolean)

      _Username = pUsername
      _Password = pPassword
      _IntroText = pIntroText
      _Email = pEmail
      _PublicEmail = pPublicEmail
      _DateJoined = DateTime.Now
      _LastAccess = DateTime.Now
      _Visible = True
      _IsAdmin = False
      _IsActivated = False

      _MemberPageSection = Nothing
    End Sub
```

We add a private member to store whether the member has been activated. The field is added to the reconstructor so that the persistence service can populate it from the database.

We also add code to the constructor that will set the field to false for new members.

To be able to access the field, we need to add the following property:

```
<Mutator()> _
Public Property IsActivated() As Boolean
  Get
    Return _IsActivated
  End Get
  Set(ByVal Value As Boolean)
    _IsActivated = Value
  End Set
End Property
```

STEP-BY-STEP GUIDE: **Requiring Approval for New User Registrations**

Note that the property is decorated with the `Mutator` attribute to ensure that when the property is set, the persistence service will persist the change to the database.

2. Add the column to the database.

Add a new column to the `tbl_Member` table, called IsActivated, with a bit type. Remember, you can do this either with Enterprise Manager or through the Visual Studio .NET Server Explorer. (You can also do it through Query Analyzer if you know the SQL.)

At this stage, you should also open the table and set `IsActivated` to `1` for the existing members.

3. Add the field to the persistence service repository.

Open `Global/Ojb.Net/repository.xml` and add the following highlighted line to the `Member` descriptor (see Listing 7.10).

LISTING 7.10 Additions to `Global/Ojb.Net/repository.xml`

```
<ClassDescriptor TypeName="Community.Member" TableName="tbl_Member">
  <PrimaryKeyDescriptor IsAutoIncremented="true">
    <FieldDescriptor Id="Member1" FieldName="_primaryKey" ColumnName="ID"
    ➥DbType="Int32" />
  </PrimaryKeyDescriptor>
  <FieldDescriptor Id="Member2" FieldName="_Username" ColumnName="_UserName"
  ➥DbType="String" />
  <FieldDescriptor Id="Member3" FieldName="_Password" ColumnName="Password"
  ➥DbType="String" />
  <FieldDescriptor Id="Member4" FieldName="_IntroText" ColumnName="IntroText"
  ➥DbType="String" />
  <FieldDescriptor Id="Member5" FieldName="_DateJoined" ColumnName="DateJoined"
  ➥DbType="DateTime" />
  <FieldDescriptor Id="Member6" FieldName="_LastAccess" ColumnName="LastAccess"
  ➥DbType="DateTime" />
  <FieldDescriptor Id="Member7" FieldName="_Email" ColumnName="Email" DbType="String" />
  <FieldDescriptor Id="Member8" FieldName="_PublicEmail" ColumnName="PublicEmail"
  ➥DbType="Boolean" />
  <FieldDescriptor Id="Member9" FieldName="_MemberPageSectionID"
  ➥ColumnName="MemberPageSectionID" DbType="Int32" />
  <FieldDescriptor Id="Member10" FieldName="_Visible" ColumnName="Visible"
  ➥DbType="Boolean" />
  <FieldDescriptor Id="Member11" FieldName="_IsAdmin" ColumnName="IsAdmin"
  ➥DbType="Boolean" />
```

STEP-BY-STEP GUIDE: **Requiring Approval for New User Registrations**

LISTING 7.10 Additions to `Global/Ojb.Net/repository.xml` (continued)

```xml
<FieldDescriptor Id="Member11" FieldName="_IsActivated" ColumnName="IsActivated"
     DbType="Boolean"/>
<ReferenceDescriptor FieldName="_MemberPageSection"
     RelatedClassName="Community.Section">
  <ForeignKeyFieldId>Member9</ForeignKeyFieldId>
</ReferenceDescriptor>
<CollectionDescriptor FieldName="_ModuleInstances"
                     RelatedClassName="Community.ModuleInstance"
                     CascadeDelete="true">
  <InverseForeignKeyFieldId>ModuleInstance4</InverseForeignKeyFieldId>
</CollectionDescriptor>
<CollectionDescriptor FieldName="_Sections"
                     RelatedClassName="Community.Section"
                     CascadeDelete="true">
    <InverseForeignKeyFieldId>Section2</InverseForeignKeyFieldId>
</CollectionDescriptor>
</ClassDescriptor>
```

4. Add code so that only activated members can log in.

   We now persist whether each member is activated or not, so we can check this when they attempt to log in.

   Add the following code to the `AuthenticateMember` function in `CoreModule.vb` (see Listing 7.11).

LISTING 7.11 Addition to `AuthenticateMember` Function in `Global/CoreModule.vb`

```vb
Public Function AuthenticateMember(ByVal pUsername As String, _
                                   ByVal pPassword As String) As Boolean
  Dim crit As Criteria = New Criteria
  crit.AddEqualTo("_Username", pUsername)
  crit.AddEqualTo("_Password", pPassword)

  Dim member As Member = CType(QueryFacade.FindObject(Type.GetType("Community.Member"), _
                                               crit), Member)

  If member Is Nothing OrElse member.IsActivated = False Then
    Return False
```

STEP-BY-STEP GUIDE: **Requiring Approval for New User Registrations**

LISTING 7.11 Addition to `AuthenticateMember` Function in `Global/CoreModule.vb` (continued)

```
    Else
        member.Touch()
        Return True
    End If
End Function
```

You can see that this was very simple—we just added a check of the `IsActivated` property, treating it like a failed authentication if the member was not activated.

Note the use of the `OrElse` operator. This is really useful when we want to "short circuit" a logical expression. In this case, if the member is nothing, we don't want to bother evaluating `member.IsActivated`, so we use `OrElse`.

> **TIP**
>
> The other short-circuiting expression is `AndAlso`, which requires both parts to be true for a true result and will short circuit (returning `false`) if the first part is false.

5. Add the field to the Member admin system.

We have now changed the system so that members start off unactivated and require activation before they can log in. We now need to make it possible for administrators to activate members.

Open `Admin/MemberAdmin.aspx` and add a new column to the `DataGrid` with the header IsActivated. This column should be added in the same way as the IsAdmin column (see earlier in this chapter for instructions). Place the column at the top of the column list in the Property Builder, so it will be the first column that is displayed.

When you add the column to the `Update click` event handler, you will need to update the indexes of the other columns because they will have been moved along one (see Listing 7.12).

LISTING 7.12 Updated Index in the `Update` Command Handler in `Admin/MemberAdmin.aspx.vb`

```
Protected Sub MembersDataGrid_UpdateCommand(ByVal source As Object, _
        ByVal e As System.Web.UI.WebControls.DataGridCommandEventArgs) _
        Handles MembersDataGrid.UpdateCommand

    Dim IsActivated As CheckBox = CType(e.Item.Cells(0).Controls(1), CheckBox)
    Dim email As TextBox = CType(e.Item.Cells(2).Controls(0), TextBox)
```

STEP-BY-STEP GUIDE: **Requiring Approval for New User Registrations**

LISTING 7.12 Updated Index in the `Update` Command Handler in `Admin/MemberAdmin.aspx.vb` (continued)

```
Dim publicEmail As CheckBox = CType(e.Item.Cells(5).Controls(1), CheckBox)
Dim visible As CheckBox = CType(e.Item.Cells(7).Controls(1), CheckBox)
Dim IsAdmin As CheckBox = CType(e.Item.Cells(7).Controls(1), CheckBox)

CoreModule.AdminUpdateMember(MembersDataGrid.DataKeys(e.Item.ItemIndex), _
                email.Text, _
                publicEmail.Checked, _
                visible.Checked, _
                IsAdmin.Checked)

Dim table As DataTable = _
    CollectionToDataTable.MakeDataTable(_CoreModule.GetAllMembers)


Session("AdminMembersView") = New DataView(table)
_MembersView = Session("AdminMembersView")

MembersDataGrid.DataSource = _MembersView
MembersDataGrid.EditItemIndex = -1
MembersDataGrid.DataBind()
End Sub
```

You will also need to update the `AdminUpdateMember` function in `CoreModule.vb` to include the `IsActivated` value:

```
Public Function AdminUpdateMember(ByVal pID As Integer, _
            ByVal pEmail As String, _
            ByVal pPublicEmail As Boolean, _
            ByVal pVisible As Boolean, _
            ByVal pIsAdmin As Boolean, _
            ByVal pIsActivated As Boolean)

    Dim mem As Member = GetMemberByID(pID)

    If Not mem Is Nothing Then
        mem.Email = pEmail
        mem.PublicEmail = pPublicEmail
        mem.Visible = pVisible
```

IDEA: **Requiring Agreement to Terms and Conditions**

```
    mem.IsAdmin = pIsAdmin
    mem.IsActivated = pIsActivated
  End If

End Function
```

Admins can now activate (or deactivate) members by updating them in the Member admin system.

You can make the IsActivated column sortable by adding the `IsActivated` property as a sort expression to the column. This is useful because administrators can click to see all of the members that require activation.

CHALLENGE:
Email Reminders

It is important that administrators deal with new member requests quickly—there is nothing more likely to put a new member off than to leave her waiting for a long time.

Add code so that the administrators are emailed when a new member registers, reminding them to check and activate them.

Hint: We covered code for sending emails to all of the administrators in Chapter 6, "Improving the Modules."

CHALLENGE:
Requiring Email Confirmation for Registration

Rather than having admins manually approve each new registration, it might be enough to confirm that each member has signed up using a real email address that they own.

Add code so that members must click a special link in an email to activate their registration.

Hint: You can use the same technique as was used for the special password change email.

IDEA:
Requiring Agreement to Terms and Conditions

One of the best ways to dissuade members from behaving badly is to have a clear set of terms and conditions to which they must agree during

IDEA: **Requiring Agreement to Terms and Conditions**

registration. It is very easy to do this—just attach a page with the terms and conditions onto a link on the Registration page (with the target set to `_blank` so that it will open in a new window) and include a check box on the registration form. Do not accept the registration if the check box is not checked.

In fact, it isn't necessary to have the check box—just a statement that joining the site means agreeing to the terms and conditions is enough.

It would also be a good idea to include a link to the terms and conditions in the page footer (`Global/Controls/SiteFooter.ascx`).

Moving On

In this chapter, we have seen how to build a simple system that gives us some degree of control over the members of the community. We have also seen how to help the members help themselves to some extent.

In Chapter 8, "Keeping Members Under Control," we will add some more features that will help us manage the members and ensure that they do not get out of control.

Keeping Members Under Control 8

As mentioned in the previous chapter, members are the most important part of the community, but they are also its biggest threat.

In this chapter, we will look at some ways in which we can restrict the behavior of members in order to have some control over the way they use the application. We will also look at what we can do when a member becomes so much of a problem that we need to remove him from the community.

We will look at

- Setting a quota for the amount of data each member can upload
- Options for dealing with troublesome members
- Security configuration options

Managing Members' Resource Usage

Unfortunately, our community application will not have infinite resources. We might be hosting it on our own server and not have to worry too much about resource usage (although it would still be a good idea to have some control over it). On the other hand, we might be hosting it on a shared server, where we have a more tightly limited amount of disk space.

STEP-BY-STEP GUIDE:
Setting a Quota for Members' Data

We will now add code that will track the resources used by members so that we can prevent a member from adding more data when it would take his total above a certain amount.

We will add functions that will enable us to determine what resources are used by each module instance. We will then be able to add a function to calculate the total resources used by a member. We can then use that to check whether new data can be added.

This "Step-By-Step Guide" is the most complex so far—it involves changes to quite a few parts of the code. Follow the steps carefully and make sure that you complete them all!

Here are the steps we will take:

1. Add the resource usage function to `ModuleBase`. **1▼**
2. Override the `GetResourceUsage` function for the News module. **2▼**

STEP-BY-STEP GUIDE: Setting a Quota for Members' Data

3. Override the `GetResourceUsage` function for the RandomText module.

4. Override the `GetResourceUsage` function for the SendMessage module.

5. Override the `GetResourceUsage` function for the ImageGallery module.

6. Override the `GetResourceUsage` function for the Blog module.

7. Add the resource usage function to `ModuleInstance`.

8. Add the resource usage function to `Member`.

9. Check before adding new news items.

10. Check before adding new random text.

11. Check before adding new images.

Add the resource usage function to `ModuleBase`.

The resource usage for module instances will have to be calculated differently for each module. For example, the ImageGallery module will need to include the disk space used by the images, whereas the News module will only consider the database space consumed by the news items.

We therefore need to add a function to the module business service classes that will calculate the resource usage. Because we want to add the same function to all of the module business service classes, we should add it to their base class, `ModuleBase`.

Open `Global/ModuleBase.vb` and add the following function:

```
Public MustOverride Function GetResourceUsage() As Integer
```

Note that we use the `MustOverride` keyword and we do not provide a function body. We do this because we want to force module programmers to think about the resources their modules consume. By requiring them to implement a `GetResourceUsage` function, we will at least prompt them.

There is a downside to doing this—any existing modules will not compile until we add the `GetResourceUsage` function to them. By adding the function to the base class, we have "broken" the existing modules.

> **TIP**
> We could implement the function without breaking the module classes by using `Overrides` rather than `MustOverride` and providing a function body that returns 0. However, module programmers could then forget to override it.

STEP-BY-STEP GUIDE: Setting a Quota for Members' Data

Now open `CoreModule.vb` and add the following method to it:

```
Public Overrides Function GetResourceUsage() As Integer
  Return 0
End Function
```

Members will never have an instance of the core module, but we have to include the override because `CoreModule` inherits from `ModuleBase` just like the other module business service classes.

We will now "unbreak" the module business service classes by implementing the `GetResourceUsage` function in each of them.

Override the `GetResourceUsage` function for the News module.

Open `Modules/News/NewsModule.vb` and add the function shown in Listing 8.1.

LISTING 8.1 Function to Add to `Modules/News/NewsModule.vb`

```
Public Overrides Function GetResourceUsage() As Integer
  Dim crit As Criteria = New Criteria

  crit.addEqualTo("_ModuleInstanceID", _ModuleInstance.PrimaryKey(0))
  Dim newsItems As IList = QueryFacade.Find(Type.GetType("Community.NewsItem"),crit)

  Dim item As NewsItem
  Dim result As Integer = 0
  For Each item In newsItems
    result = result + item.Title.Length + item.Summary.Length + item.Body.Length
  Next
  Return result
End Function
```

We simply retrieve all the news items in the instance and add together the lengths of their titles, summaries, and bodies.

Override the `GetResourceUsage` function for the RandomText module.

Open `Modules/RandomText/RandomTextModule.vb` and add the function shown in Listing 8.2.

Managing Members' Resource Usage

STEP-BY-STEP GUIDE: **Setting a Quota for Members' Data**

LISTING 8.2 Function to Add to `Modules/RandomText/RandomTextModule.vb`

```
Public Overrides Function GetResourceUsage() As Integer
  Dim crit As New Criteria
  crit.addEqualTo("_ModuleInstanceID", Me.ModuleInstance.PrimaryKey1)

  Dim items As IList = QueryFacade.Find(Type.GetType("Community.RandomTextItem"), crit)
  Dim result As Integer = 0
  Dim item As RandomTextItem
  For Each item In items
    result = result + item.Text.Length
  Next
  Return result
End Function
```

This is similar to the function for the News module.

4 ▲ **Override the `GetResourceUsage` function for the SendMessage module.**

The SendMessage module does not consume any resources, so we simply have the `GetResourceUsage` function return 0. Open `Modules/SendMessage/SendMessageModule.vb` and add the following function:

```
Overrides Function GetResourceUsage() As Integer
  Return 0
End Function
```

5 ▲ **Override the `GetResourceUsage` function for the ImageGallery module.**

This is the most complex `GetResourceUsage` function to implement because we need to take the size of the image files into account.

We could access each file every time we want to check the resource usage to get its size, but that would be very inefficient. Instead, we will persist the size of each file in the `GalleryImage` object that relates to it.

First, open `Modules/ImageGallery/GalleryImage.vb` and add the following field:

```
Public Class GalleryImage
  Inherits CommunityPO
```

STEP-BY-STEP GUIDE: **Setting a Quota for Members' Data**

```
Private _Name As String
Private _ModuleInstanceID As Integer
Private _Description As String
Private _DatePosted As DateTime
Private _Extension As String
Private _Size As Integer
```

You will also need to add it to the reconstructor:

```
Public Sub New(ByVal ID As Integer, _
            ByVal pModuleInstanceID As Integer, _
            ByVal pName As String, _
            ByVal pDescription As String, _
            ByVal pDatePosted As DateTime, _
            ByVal pExtension As String, _
            ByVal pSize As Integer)
    MyBase.New(ID)

    _Name = pName

    _ModuleInstanceID = pModuleInstanceID
    _Description = pDescription
    _DatePosted = pDatePosted
    _Extension = pExtension
    _Size = pSize

End Sub
```

And the constructor:

```
Public Sub New(ByVal pModuleInstance As ModuleInstance, _
            ByVal pName As String, _
            ByVal pDescription As String, _
            ByVal pExtension As String, _
            ByVal pSize As Integer)
    _Name = pName
    _Description = pDescription
    _DatePosted = DateTime.Now
    _ModuleInstance = pModuleInstance
    _Extension = pExtension
    _Size = pSize

End Sub
```

212 Managing Members' Resource Usage

STEP-BY-STEP GUIDE: **Setting a Quota for Members' Data**

Also add a `ReadOnly` property to allow access to the value:

```
Public ReadOnly Property Size() As Integer
  Get
    Return _Size
  End Get
End Property
```

Next, open `Global/Ojb.Net/Repository.xml` and add a field descriptor for Size (see Listing 8.3).

LISTING 8.3 Adding a Field Descriptor to `Global/Ojb.Net/Repository.xml`

```
<ClassDescriptor TypeName="Community.GalleryImage" TableName="tbl_ImageGallery_Image">
  <PrimaryKeyDescriptor IsAutoIncremented="true">
    <FieldDescriptor Id="GalleryImage1" FieldName="_primaryKey" ColumnName="ID"
➥ DbType="Int32"/>
  </PrimaryKeyDescriptor>
  <FieldDescriptor Id="GalleryImage2" FieldName="_ModuleInstanceID"
➥ ColumnName="ModuleInstanceID" DbType="Int32"/>
  <FieldDescriptor Id="GalleryImage3" FieldName="_Name" ColumnName="Name"
➥ DbType="String"/>
  <FieldDescriptor Id="GalleryImage4" FieldName="_Description" ColumnName="Description"
➥ DbType="String"/>
  <FieldDescriptor Id="GalleryImage5" FieldName="_DatePosted" ColumnName="DatePosted"
➥ DbType="DateTime"/>
  <FieldDescriptor Id="GalleryImage6" FieldName="_Extension" ColumnName="Extension"
➥ DbType="String"/>
  <FieldDescriptor Id="GalleryImage7" FieldName="_Size" ColumnName="Size"
➥ DbType="Int32"/>
  <ReferenceDescriptor FieldName="_ModuleInstance"
➥RelatedClassName="Community.ModuleInstance">
    <ForeignKeyFieldId>GalleryImage2</ForeignKeyFieldId>
  </ReferenceDescriptor>
</ClassDescriptor>
```

Open the tbl_ImageGallery_Image table in the database and add the Size column (integer data type) to it. You will need to add values for the existing images.

In the process of adding the field, we have broken code that calls the `GalleryImage` constructor—the `CreateImage` function in

STEP-BY-STEP GUIDE: **Setting a Quota for Members' Data**

ImageGalleryModule. Open `ImageGalleryModule.vb` and alter the function to include the new field (see Listing 8.4).

LISTING 8.4 Alteration to `CreateImage` in `Modules/ImageGallery/ImageGalleryModule.vb`

```
Public Function CreateImage(ByVal pName As String, _
                            ByVal pDescription As String, _
                            ByVal pExtension As String, _
                            ByVal pSize As Integer) _
             As GalleryImage
  Dim image As GalleryImage = New GalleryImage(_ModuleInstance, _
                                        pName, _
                                        pDescription, _
                                        pExtension, _
                                        pSize)


  Return image
End Function
```

This change, in turn, will break the code that calls it—the `click` event of the Add Image button in `Modules/ImageGallery/DisplayModule.ascx.vb`. You will see that this is in the error message if you attempt to compile the application at this stage.

Open up that file and find the call to `CreateImage`. Change it as follows:

```
'create the persistent object for the image
Dim galleryModule As ImageGalleryModule = _
    New ImageGalleryModule(Me.ModuleInstance)

Dim image As GalleryImage = _
galleryModule.CreateImage(FileNameTextBox.Text, _
                FileDescriptionTextBox.Text, _
                extension, _
                file.ContentLength)

'get the path that we want to upload the file to
path = Server.MapPath("Data/Modules/ImageGallery/" + image.Filename)
```

STEP-BY-STEP GUIDE: Setting a Quota for Members' Data

Now we can add the `GetResourceUsage` function to `ImageGalleryModule` (see Listing 8.5).

LISTING 8.5 Function to Add to `Modules/ImageGallery/ImageGalleryModule.vb`

```
Public Overrides Function GetResourceUsage() As Integer
  Dim crit As Criteria = New Criteria
  crit.addEqualTo("_ModuleInstanceID", Me.ModuleInstance.PrimaryKey1)

  Dim images As IList = QueryFacade.Find(Type.GetType("Community.GalleryImage"), crit)

  Dim image As GalleryImage
  Dim result As Integer = 0
  For Each image In images
    result = result + image.Size
  Next
  Return result
End Function
```

As you can see, the function is not too complex in itself—we just had to do some extra work to make sure the data it needs is available.

6 ▲ Override the `GetResourceUsage` function for the Blog module.

The `GetResourceUsage` function for the Blog module is very similar to that for the News module:

```
Public Overrides Function GetResourceUsage() As Integer
  Dim crit As Criteria = New Criteria

  crit.addEqualTo("_ModuleInstanceID", _ModuleInstance.PrimaryKey(0))

  Dim newsItems As IList = _
      QueryFacade.Find(Type.GetType("Community.BlogEntry"),crit)

  Dim item As BlogEntry
  Dim result As Integer = 0
  For Each item In newsItems
    result = result + item.Text.Length
  Next
  Return result
End Function
```

Managing Members' Resource Usage

STEP-BY-STEP GUIDE: Setting a Quota for Members' Data

In fact, it is simpler because there is only the `Text` property to worry about.

Add the resource usage function to `ModuleInstance`.

Our next step is to add a function to the `ModuleInstance` persistent object that will call the `GetResourceUsage` function of the correct module business service class. This is the link between the core of the application and the module-specific code.

Open `Global/CoreObjects/ModuleInstance.vb` and add the function shown in Listing 8.6.

LISTING 8.6 Function to Add to `GlobalCoreObjects/ModuleInstance.vb`

```
Public Function GetResourceUsage() As Integer
  'create an instance of the module class
  'get module class name
  Dim moduleClassName As String = Me.CommunityModule.ServiceClassName

  'create an instance of the module service class
  Dim args() As Object = {CType(Me, Community.ModuleInstance)}

  Dim activationAttributes() As Object

  Dim typ As Type = Type.GetType(moduleClassName)

  Dim obj As Object = typ.Assembly.CreateInstance(typ.FullName, _
                        False, _
                        BindingFlags.CreateInstance, _
                        Nothing, _
                        args, _
                        Nothing, _
                        activationAttributes)

  Dim moduleClassInstance As ModuleBase = CType(obj, ModuleBase)

  'get the resource usage from the module class instance
  Return moduleClassInstance.GetResourceUsage
End Function
```

STEP-BY-STEP GUIDE: **Setting a Quota for Members' Data**

First, we get the name of the module from the `CommunityModule` persistent object associated with the instance:

```
Dim moduleClassName As String = Me.CommunityModule.ServiceClassName
```

We then create an arguments array with the current `ModuleInstance` in it. This will be the argument that is sent to the module business service class constructor:

```
Dim args() As Object = {CType(Me, Community.ModuleInstance)}
```

We create an empty activation `Attributes` array. We do not want to use any activation attributes, but we have to supply this when we create the instance of the module business service class.

```
Dim activationAttributes() As Object
```

The next part is the really important stuff. We create an instance of the class specified by the `CommunityModule`. This function call makes use of reflection, so we can create an instance of the dynamically chosen class. (Note the `Imports System.Reflection` statement at the top of the file, which is already there because this same technique is used when an instance is deleted.)

```
Dim typ As Type = Type.GetType(moduleClassName)

Dim obj As Object = typ.Assembly.CreateInstance(typ.FullName, _
                        False, _
                        BindingFlags.CreateInstance, _
                        Nothing, _
                        args, _
                        Nothing, _
                        activationAttributes)
```

After we have an object that is an instance of the module business service class, we cast it to `ModuleBase` so that we can call the `GetResourceUsage` function:

```
Dim moduleClassInstance As ModuleBase = CType(obj, ModuleBase)

'get the resource usage from the module class instance
Return moduleClassInstance.GetResourceUsage
```

Add the resource usage function to `Member`.

Open `Global/CoreObjects/Member.vb` and add the following function:

```
Public Function GetResourceUsage() As Integer
  Dim instance As ModuleInstance
  Dim result As Integer = 0
  For Each instance In _ModuleInstances
    result = result + instance.GetResourceUsage
  Next
  Return result
End Function
```

We simply loop through the module instances that `Member` owns, adding together the resource usage.

We will also add a function that will decide whether new data can be added by the member:

```
Public Function CanAddData(ByVal pDataLength As Integer) _
     As Boolean
  If Me.GetResourceUsage + pDataLength < _
    ConfigurationSettings.AppSettings("MaxDataPerUser") Then
    Return True
  Else
    Return False
  End If
End Function
```

We could do this comparison in each place we need to do the check, but that would split the same logic around different source files, meaning that if we decided to change the rules, we would have to update it in multiple places.

DESIGN TIP

Where possible, each piece of program logic should be kept in a single place and called from there rather than duplicated.

Check before adding new news items.

We now need to check when a member tries to add new data, to ensure that she will not exceed her quota.

The system we are using here relies on the modules being built to "play by the rules." It is possible for a module to ignore the member quota and add new data regardless. Unfortunately, this is very difficult to avoid—if we give modules the freedom to manage their own resources, we have to trust them to behave properly.

STEP-BY-STEP GUIDE: **Setting a Quota for Members' Data**

Open `Modules/News/DisplayItem.ascx.vb` and make changes to the `UpdateButton_Click` event handler (see Listing 8.7).

LISTING 8.7 Changes to `UpdateButton_Click` in `Modules/News/DisplayItem.ascx.vb`

```
Private Sub UpdateButton_Click(ByVal sender As System.Object, _
                               ByVal e As System.EventArgs) _
        Handles UpdateButton.Click
  If Page.IsValid Then
    Dim item As NewsItem = NewsModule.GetNewsItemByID(Request.QueryString("itemID"))

    Dim dataSize As Integer = TitleTextBox.Text.Length - item.Title.Length _
                            + SummaryTextBox.Text.Length - item.Summary.Length _
                            + BodyTextBox.Text.Length - item.Body.Length

    If item.ModuleInstance.Member.CanAddData(dataSize) Then

    Dim newsMod As New NewsModule

    newsMod.UpdateNewsItem(Me.ItemID, _
                           HeadingTextBox.Text, _
                           SummaryTextBox.Text, _
                           BodyTextBox.Text)

    Response.Redirect(SeeMoreLink.NavigateUrl.TrimStart(New Char() {"/", "."}))
    Else
      'the data could not be added, so display an error message
    End If

  End If

End Sub
```

We subtract the size of the existing item fields from the updated fields to get the change in data size that will take place. (The strings are stored in the database as VARCHAR columns, so one character is one byte.)

Note that this code does not currently display an error message—code to display an error message should be added where the appropriate comment is.

STEP-BY-STEP GUIDE: **Setting a Quota for Members' Data**

Check before adding new random text.

10 ▲

Open `Modules/RandomText/DisplayModule.ascx`. Add the following code to the `AddButton_Click` event handler (see Listing 8.8).

LISTING 8.8 Changes to `AddButton_Click` in `Modules/RandomText/DisplayModule.ascx.vb`

```
Private Sub AddButton_Click(ByVal sender As System.Object, _
                    ByVal e As System.EventArgs) _
        Handles AddButton.Click

  If Me.ModuleInstance.Member.CanAddData(NewItemTextBox.Text.Length) Then
    Dim randModule As New RandomTextModule(Me.ModuleInstance)

    randModule.AddRandomTextItem(NewItemTextBox.Text)

    NewItemTextBox.Text = ""

    ItemsDataList.DataSource = randModule.GetAllRandomTextItems
    ItemsDataList.DataBind()
  Else
    'quota exceeded so display error message
  End If

End Sub
```

Again, an error message should be displayed if the check fails.

Add the code in Listing 8.9 to `UpdateItem_Click`.

LISTING 8.9 Changes to `UpdateItem_Click` in `Modules/RandomText/DisplayModule.ascx.vb`

```
Protected Sub UpdateItem_Click(ByVal source As System.Object, _
      ByVal e As System.Web.UI.WebControls.DataListCommandEventArgs)
  Dim randModule As New RandomTextModule(Me.ModuleInstance)

  Dim text As String = CType(e.Item.FindControl("ItemTextBox"), TextBox).Text
  Dim id As Integer = CType(randModule.GetAllRandomTextItems.Item(e.Item.ItemIndex), _
                    RandomTextItem).PrimaryKey1
```

STEP-BY-STEP GUIDE: Setting a Quota for Members' Data

LISTING 8.9 Changes to `UpdateItem_Click` in `Modules/RandomText/DisplayModule.ascx.vb` (continued)

```
  Dim item As RandomTextItem = RandomTextModule.GetRandomTextItemByID(id)

  If Me.ModuleInstance.Member.CanAddData(text.Length - item.Text.Length) Then
    randModule.UpdateRandomTextItem(id, text)

    ItemsDataList.EditItemIndex = -1
    ItemsDataList.DataSource = randModule.GetAllRandomTextItems
    ItemsDataList.DataBind()
  Else
    'quota exceeded, so display error message
  End If
End Sub
```

This uses the same approach as we took with the News module—subtracting the old size from the new size to see what the change introduced by the update is.

11 ▲ Check before adding new images.

The final check we need to do is when a member attempts to add a new image to an instance of the ImageGallery module. Open `Modules/ImageGallery/DisplayModule.ascx` and add the following code (see Listing 8.10).

LISTING 8.10 Changes to `UploadButton_Click` in `Modules/ImageGallery/DisplayModule.ascx.vb`

```
Private Sub UploadButton_Click(ByVal sender As System.Object, _
                     ByVal e As System.EventArgs) _
         Handles UploadButton.Click

  If Not FileUpload.PostedFile Is Nothing Then
    Dim file As HttpPostedFile = FileUpload.PostedFile

    'check that the users quota allows the file to be uploaded
    If Me.ModuleInstance.Member.CanAddData(file.ContentLength) Then
```

LISTING 8.10 Changes to `UploadButton_Click` in `Modules/ImageGallery/DisplayModule.ascx.vb` (continued)

```
        Dim path As String

        Dim extension As String


        'check the content type against those we support and create the correct extension
        If file.ContentType = "image/gif" Then
          extension = ".gif"
        End If

        If file.ContentType = "image/jpeg" _
            Or file.ContentType = "image/jpg" Or file.ContentType = "image/pjpeg" Then
          extension = ".jpg"
        End If

        If file.ContentType = "image/png" Or file.ContentType = "image/x-png" Then
          extension = ".png"
        End If

        'if the file is of a supported content type, create a persistent object for it
        'and upload the file
        If Not extension Is Nothing Then

          'create the persistent object for the image
          Dim galleryModule As ImageGalleryModule = _
                New ImageGalleryModule(Me.ModuleInstance)

          Dim image As GalleryImage = _
                  galleryModule.CreateImage(FileNameTextBox.Text, _
                                            FileDescriptionTextBox.Text, _
                                            extension, _
                                            file.ContentLength)

          'get the path that we want to upload the file to
          path = Server.MapPath("Data/Modules/ImageGallery/" + image.Filename)

          'get the length of the uploaded file
          Dim fileLength As Integer = file.ContentLength
```

STEP-BY-STEP GUIDE: Setting a Quota for Members' Data

LISTING 8.10 Changes to `UploadButton_Click` in `Modules/ImageGallery/DisplayModule.ascx.vb` (continued)

```vb
        'create a byte array to put the file into
        Dim fileData() As Byte = New Byte(fileLength) {}

        'read the file into the byte array
        file.InputStream.Read(fileData, 0, fileLength)

        'create a filestream to write the file
        Dim fileStream As FileStream = New FileStream(path, FileMode.Create)

        'write the file
        fileStream.Write(fileData, 0, fileData.Length)

        'close the file stream
        fileStream.Close()

        'CREATE THUMBNAIL

        file.InputStream.Position = 0
        Dim bitmap As New Bitmap(file.InputStream)

        Dim width As Integer = bitmap.Size.Width
        Dim height As Integer = bitmap.Size.Height

        Dim thumbnail As Image

        If width > 98 Then
          Dim myCallBack As Bitmap.GetThumbnailImageAbort = _
              New Image.GetThumbnailImageAbort(AddressOf ThumbnailCallback)
          thumbnail = bitmap.GetThumbnailImage(98, _
                                               height * (98 / width), _
                                               myCallBack, _
                                               IntPtr.Zero)
        Else
          thumbnail = bitmap
        End If

        thumbnail.Save(Server.MapPath("Data/Modules/ImageGallery/" + _
                       image.PrimaryKey1.ToString + "_thumb.jpg"), _
                   ImageFormat.Jpeg)
```

LISTING 8.10 Changes to `UploadButton_Click` in `Modules/ImageGallery/DisplayModule.ascx.vb` (continued)

```
            're-bind the images DataList in order to show the new image
            ImagesDataList.DataSource = galleryModule.GetAllImages

            ImagesDataList.DataBind()


        Else
            'type was not recognized
            'we should show an error message here

        End If
    Else
        'file was too big to be added
        'we should show an error message here
    End If

  End If

End Sub
```

CHALLENGE:
Including the Member's Personal Page Image and Text in Her Resource Usage

At present, we do not include either the member's personal page image or her Member page intro text in the total of resources used.

Add code to include these resources in the total.

IDEA:
Personalized Resource Quotas

We might want to allow different members to have different quotas. For example, we might allow new members to have only a small amount of data, but after they have been in the community a while, we might want to increase their quota.

It would be quite easy to add a field for each member that would define his resource quota. It could be set to a default, configured value for new members.

Dealing with Troublesome Users

As we mentioned at the beginning of the chapter, members are the biggest asset of an online community, but they are also the biggest threat. Although it is important to look after the members, it is also essential to be able to control them if they misbehave.

> **STEP-BY-STEP GUIDE:**
> ### Temporarily Banning a Member

Sometimes there is just no other option for dealing with a "problem" member than to remove her access to the site.

This is actually a simple bit of functionality to add. Earlier, we saw how we can require new members to be activated before they can access the site. Members can be deactivated using the same system. That will prevent them from being able to log in.

There is one extra step we need to take. It is no good to deactivate a member if she is already logged in to the site and can simply continue to use the site with her current login session. We need to add some code that will take effect even if a member is logged in when she is deactivated.

Open `global.asax.vb` and change the `Application_AuthenticateRequest` event handler as shown in Listing 8.11.

LISTING 8.11 Changes to `Application_AuthenticateRequest` in `global.asax.vb`

```
Sub Application_AuthenticateRequest(ByVal sender As Object, ByVal e As EventArgs)

  If Request.IsAuthenticated Then
    'we want to attach a CommmunityPrincipal in place of the GenericPrincipal

    Dim coreMod As CoreModule = New CoreModule
```

STEP-BY-STEP GUIDE: **Temporarily Banning a Member**

LISTING 8.11 Changes to `Application_AuthenticateRequest` in `global.asax.vb` (continued)

```
    Dim member As Member = coreMod.GetMemberByUserName(Context.User.Identity.Name)

    If Not member.IsActivated Then
      'the member is not activated, so they should not be authenticated
      Dim id As New GenericIdentity("")
      Dim principal As New GenericPrincipal(id, New String() {})

      Context.User = principal
    Else

      Dim roles As String() = {}
      If member.IsAdmin Then
        ReDim roles(0)
        roles(0) = "administrator"
      End If


      Dim principal As CommunityPrincipal = _
          New CommunityPrincipal(member, Context.User.Identity, roles)

      Context.User = principal

    End If
  End If
End Sub
```

You will also need to add two `Imports` statements to the top of the file:

```
Imports System.Web.Security
Imports System.Security.Principal
```

After the usual check of whether the user is a logged-in member, we check whether the member is an inactive one.

If she is, we create a new `GenericIdentity` object with a blank username. This creates the same identity that nonauthenticated users have. We then use the identity to create a `GenericPrincipal` object—again, the same type of object that nonauthenticated users have.

STEP-BY-STEP GUIDE: **Hiding Deactivated Members' Data**

The `Context.User` property is then set to the `GenericPrincipal`. For the rest of the page request, the member will be treated in the same way as a nonauthenticated user.

Note that deactivating a member will prevent her from accessing the site as a member but will not prevent other members from seeing her data.

STEP-BY-STEP GUIDE:
Hiding Deactivated Members' Data

Often, when a member is barred from a community, it is because he has posted things he should not have posted. Posting offensive and even illegal content is the single biggest reason for members being banned.

We need to link the `ShowInGlobal` property of module instances to the `IsActivated` property of the member who owns each instance. We also need to link the `Visible` property of each member to her `IsActivated` property and check whether the member is activated when we display her Member page.

1. Make the `ShowInGlobal` property of module instances look at `IsActivated`.

Make the following change to the `ShowInGlobal` property in `Global/CoreObjects/ModuleInstance.vb`:

```
<Mutator()> _
Public Property ShowInGlobal() As Boolean
    Get
    If _Member.IsActivated = false then
        Return false
      Else
        Return _ShowInGlobal
      End If
    End Get
    Set(ByVal Value As Boolean)
       _ShowInGlobal = Value
    End Set
End Property
```

If the member is not activated, we return `false`, no matter what the member's setting for that module instance is.

2. Make the `Visible` property look at `IsActivated`.

STEP-BY-STEP GUIDE: **Hiding Deactivated Members' Data**

Make a similar change to the `Visible` property in
Global/CoreObjects/Member.vb:

```
<Mutator()> _
Public Property Visible() As Boolean
  Get
    If _IsActivated = false then
      Return false
    Else

      Return _Visible
    End If
  End Get
  Set(ByVal Value As Boolean)
    _Visible = Value
  End Set
End Property
```

3. Check that the member is activated in
`Default.aspx.DisplayMemberPage`.

The final thing we need to do is to deal with a user browsing to the Member page for a deactivated member, perhaps because he has a link saved as a bookmark.

Open `Default.aspx.vb` and find the method that executes when a member's page is displayed. Make the changes shown in Listing 8.12.

LISTING 8.12 Changes to `DisplayMemberPage` in `Default.aspx.vb`

```
Private Sub DisplayMemberPage()

    'select the member in the navigation control
    Navigation1.MemberID = Request.QueryString("Member")

    Dim mem As Member = _CoreModule.GetMemberByID(Request.QueryString("Member"))

    If mem.IsActivated = false Then
      Response.Redirect("Default.aspx")
    End If
    'first we display the membercontrol for the selected member...
    Dim memberControl As MemberControl
```

STEP-BY-STEP GUIDE: **Deleting a Member**

LISTING 8.12 Changes to `DisplayMemberPage` in `Default.aspx.vb` (continued)

```
    memberControl = CType(Page.LoadControl("global/controls/MemberControl.ascx"), _
                     MemberControl)
    memberControl.Member = mem

    sectionItems.Controls.Add(memberControl)

    'next, we display the SectionItems for the users member page...
    Dim si As SectionItem
    Dim currentControl As SectionItemControl
    For Each si In memberControl.Member.MemberPageSection.SectionItems
      'Create a control of the correct type for each SectionItem and add to the page
      currentControl = CType(Page.LoadControl("Modules/" _
         + si.ModuleView.CommunityModule.Name _
         + "/views/" + si.ModuleView.Name + ".ascx"), SectionItemControl)

      currentControl.SectionItem = si

      sectionItems.Controls.Add(currentControl)
    Next
  End Sub
```

We move the call to `CoreModule.GetMemberByID` up and output the result of it in a variable so that we can use it for the check of `Member.IsActivated` and also to populate the `MemberControl`. If the selected member is not activated, we redirect the user back to the community home page.

STEP-BY-STEP GUIDE: Deleting a Member

The ultimate course of action when dealing with a problem member is to delete her account. This course of action should not be taken lightly—only when we know for certain that the member will not be back should we delete her account and her data.

Deleting a member is not as simple as deleting the `Member` object that corresponds to her. If we did that, we would leave "orphan" data in the shape of the sections and module instances the member had created. It is important that we remove this data before deleting the member.

STEP-BY-STEP GUIDE: **Deleting a Member**

Fortunately for us, the persistence service offers a neat way to do this. We can simply tell it that we want it to *cascade* a delete from a member down to the objects associated with that member.

We need to change the persistence service repository in order to set up cascading deletion for `Member` objects. We then need to add a `DeleteMember` method to the code business service class. After we have that, we will be able to add the option to delete a member to the administration system.

Here are the steps that will achieve these things:

1. Change the persistence service repository.

Open `Global/Ojb.Net/Repository.xml` and find the class descriptor for `Member`. Make the additions shown in Listing 8.13.

LISTING 8.13 Changes to the `Member` Class Descriptor in `Global/Ojb.Net/Respository.xml`

```
<ClassDescriptor TypeName="Community.Member" TableName="tbl_Member">
  <PrimaryKeyDescriptor IsAutoIncremented="true">
    <FieldDescriptor Id="Member1" FieldName="_primaryKey" ColumnName="ID"
    ➥DbType="Int32" />
  </PrimaryKeyDescriptor>
  <FieldDescriptor Id="Member2" FieldName="_Username" ColumnName="_UserName"
  ➥DbType="String" />
  <FieldDescriptor Id="Member3" FieldName="_Password" ColumnName="Password"
  ➥DbType="String" />
  <FieldDescriptor Id="Member4" FieldName="_IntroText" ColumnName="IntroText"
  ➥DbType="String" />
  <FieldDescriptor Id="Member5" FieldName="_DateJoined" ColumnName="DateJoined"
  ➥DbType="DateTime" />
  <FieldDescriptor Id="Member6" FieldName="_LastAccess" ColumnName="LastAccess"
  ➥DbType="DateTime" />
  <FieldDescriptor Id="Member7" FieldName="_Email" ColumnName="Email" DbType="String" />
  <FieldDescriptor Id="Member8" FieldName="_PublicEmail" ColumnName="PublicEmail"
  ➥DbType="Boolean" />
  <FieldDescriptor Id="Member9" FieldName="_MemberPageSectionID"
  ➥ColumnName="MemberPageSectionID" DbType="Int32" />
  <FieldDescriptor Id="Member10" FieldName="_Visible" ColumnName="Visible"
  ➥DbType="Boolean" />
  <FieldDescriptor Id="Member11" FieldName="_IsAdmin" ColumnName="IsAdmin"
  ➥DbType="Boolean" />
```

STEP-BY-STEP GUIDE: **Deleting a Member**

LISTING 8.13 Changes to the `Member` Class Descriptor in `Global/Ojb.Net/Respository.xml` (continued)

```
<ReferenceDescriptor FieldName="_MemberPageSection"
➥RelatedClassName="Community.Section">
  <ForeignKeyFieldId>Member9</ForeignKeyFieldId>
</ReferenceDescriptor>
<CollectionDescriptor FieldName="_ModuleInstances"
                      RelatedClassName="Community.ModuleInstance"
                      CascadeDelete="true">
  <InverseForeignKeyFieldId>ModuleInstance4</InverseForeignKeyFieldId>
</CollectionDescriptor>
<CollectionDescriptor FieldName="_Sections"
                      RelatedClassName="Community.Section"
                      CascadeDelete="true">
  <InverseForeignKeyFieldId>Section2</InverseForeignKeyFieldId>
</CollectionDescriptor>
</ClassDescriptor>
```

Now, when a member is deleted, the sections and module instances that belong to her will also be deleted.

2. Add a `DeleteMember` method to the core module.

Open `Global/CoreModule.vb` and add the following new method:

```
Public Sub DeleteMember(ByVal pID As Integer)
  Dim mem As Member = Me.GetMemberByID(pID)

  mem.Delete()
End Sub
```

3. Add a Delete Member option to the member admin system.

Open `Admin/MemberAdmin.aspx` in design mode.

Use the Property Builder of the `DataGrid` to add a new Button column to the `DataGrid`. Select the Delete button.

4. Add code to do the delete.

Add the following event handler to the code-behind for `MemberAdmin.aspx` (see Listing 8.14).

STEP-BY-STEP GUIDE: **Deleting a Member**

LISTING 8.14 Event Handler to Add to `Admin/MemberAdmin.aspx.vb`

```
Protected Sub MembersDataGrid_DeleteCommand(ByVal source As Object, _
    ByVal e As System.Web.UI.WebControls.DataGridCommandEventArgs) _
    Handles MembersDataGrid.DeleteCommand

  Dim coreMod As New CoreModule

  coreMod.DeleteMember(MembersDataGrid.DataKeys(e.Item.ItemIndex))

  Dim table As DataTable = _
        CollectionToDataTable.MakeDataTable(_CoreModule.GetAllMembers)


  Session("AdminMembersView") = New DataView(table)
  _MembersView = Session("AdminMembersView")

  MembersDataGrid.DataSource = _MembersView
  MembersDataGrid.EditItemIndex = -1
  MembersDataGrid.DataBind()

End Sub
```

We simply call the method that we just added to the core module.

For this event handler to work, we need to add it to the definition of the `DataGrid` in `MemberAdmin.aspx`:

```
<asp:DataGrid id="MembersDataGrid"
              runat="server"
              AutoGenerateColumns="False"
              AllowSorting="True"
              Font-Size="Smaller"
              CellPadding="3"
              BackColor="White"
              BorderWidth="1px"
              BorderStyle="None"
              BorderColor="#CCCCCC"
              DataKeyField="PrimaryKey1"
              OnDeleteCommand="MembersDataGrid_DeleteCommand">
```

5. Add an 'Are You Sure?' requester.

STEP-BY-STEP GUIDE: Deleting a Member

It would be wise to require confirmation of such a drastic action. The best way to do this is to pop up a requester when the Delete link is clicked.

To do this, we need to attach some JavaScript to the Delete links. So that we can easily find the Delete control, we will convert the Delete column to a template column—that way, we can give the Delete link an ID.

Open the Property Builder and browse to the Delete button column. Click Convert to Template Column and enter `Delete` for the header.

If you now right-click the `DataGrid` and select Edit Templates, you will be able to select the Delete column. In the template, select the Delete link and change its ID to `DeleteLink`.

Add the event handler to the code-behind shown in Listing 8.15.

LISTING 8.15 Event Handler to Add to `Admin/MemberAdmin.aspx.vb`

```vb
Protected Sub MembersDataGrid_ItemDataBound(ByVal sender As Object, _
                                ByVal e As DataGridItemEventArgs)
    Dim control As Control
    Dim innerControl As Control
    For Each control In e.Item.Controls
        For Each innerControl In control.Controls
            If innerControl.ID = "DeleteLink" Then
                CType(innerControl, LinkButton).Attributes.Add("onclick", _
                "return confirm('Are You sure?');")
            End If
        Next
    Next
End Sub
```

You will also need to add the event to the definition of the `DataGrid`:

```
<asp:DataGrid id="MembersDataGrid"
     runat="server"
     AutoGenerateColumns="False"
     AllowSorting="True"
     Font-Size="Smaller"
     CellPadding="3"
     BackColor="White"
     BorderWidth="1px"
     BorderStyle="None"
```

```
BorderColor="#CCCCCC"
DataKeyField="PrimaryKey1"
OnDeleteCommand="MembersDataGrid_DeleteCommand"
         OnItemDataBound="MembersDataGrid_ItemDataBound">
```

We iterate through the controls in the `DataGrid` item until we find the Delete link. When we find it, we add some JavaScript to its client-side `onclick` event. (We have to do this the hard way because the `onclick` event in the `.aspx` file will refer to the server-side `click` event.)

We iterate through the controls rather than address the LinkButton directly because it proved troublesome to do so. Because the Admin page will be accessed relatively rarely, the minor overhead of the iteration does not cause any performance problems.

So, we now have a system for deleting a member and all of her data—use it wisely!

STEP-BY-STEP GUIDE:
Logging IP Addresses

If we suspect that there is any chance of foul play by any member, it is a wise precaution to log the IP address of the machine he uses to connect to the community site. It might then be possible to contact his ISP to report his misbehavior.

TIP

It would be a good idea to include a note in the community terms and conditions to state that IP addresses are logged.

We will add code to log the IP each member is using each time he logs in to the site.

Here are the steps we need to take:

1. Create an `IPAddress` persistent object.
2. Add the object to the persistence service repository.
3. Add a table to the database for the new object.
4. Add fields and a property to `Member`.
5. Update the persistence service repository entry for `Member`.
6. Add a method to `CoreModule`.
7. Add code to the login control.
8. Add code to view the `IPAddresses` in the member administration system.

STEP-BY-STEP GUIDE: Logging IP Addresses

1▲ Create an `IPAddress` persistent object.

Create a new class in `Global/CoreObjects/` and call it `IPAddress`. Add the following code to it:

```
Public Class IPAddress
  Inherits CommunityPO

  Private _MemberID As Integer
  Private _IP As String
  Private _Date As DateTime

  Private _Member As Member

  'reconstructor for use be persistence service
  Public Sub New(ByVal pID As Integer, _
              ByVal pMemberID As Integer, _
              ByVal pIP As String, _
              ByVal pDate As DateTime)
    MyBase.New(pID)

    _MemberID = pMemberID
    _IP = pIP
    _Date = pDate

  End Sub

  'constructor for creating new instances of IP
  Public Sub New(ByVal pMember As Member, _
              ByVal pIP As String)
    _Member = pMember
    _IP = pIP
    _Date = DateTime.Now
  End Sub

  Public ReadOnly Property Member() As Member
    Get
      Return _Member
    End Get
  End Property

  Public ReadOnly Property IP() As String
    Get
```

STEP-BY-STEP GUIDE: **Logging IP Addresses**

```
      Return _IP
    End Get
  End Property

  Public ReadOnly Property DateLogged() As DateTime
    Get
      Return _Date
    End Get
  End Property
End Class
```

You can see that this is a pretty simple persistent object—there are just a few fields and a reference to the member for whom the IP was logged.

Note that this class does not allow changes to be made after the object is created.

Add the object to the persistence service repository.   ▲2

Create a new class descriptor in `Global/Ojb.net/Respository.xml` as shown in Listing 8.16.

LISTING 8.16 Class Descriptor to Add to `Global/Ojb.Net/Repository.xml`

```xml
<ClassDescriptor TypeName="Community.IPAddress" TableName="tbl_IPAddress">
  <PrimaryKeyDescriptor IsAutoIncremented="true">
    <FieldDescriptor Id="IP1" FieldName="_primaryKey" ColumnName="ID" DbType="Int32"/>
  </PrimaryKeyDescriptor>
  <FieldDescriptor Id="IP2" FieldName="_MemberID" ColumnName="MemberID"
➥DbType="Int32"/>
  <FieldDescriptor Id="IP3" FieldName="_IP" ColumnName="IP" DbType="String" />
  <FieldDescriptor Id="IP4" FieldName="_Date" ColumnName="Date" DbType="DateTime"/>
  <ReferenceDescriptor FieldName="_Member" RelatedClassName="Community.Member">
    <ForeignKeyFieldId>IP2</ForeignKeyFieldId>
  </ReferenceDescriptor>
</ClassDescriptor>
```

Add a table to the database for the new object.   ▲3

Create a new database table called tbl_IPAddress. Add the following fields:

```
ID              integer         (Primary Key, Identity)
MemberID        integer
IP              VARCHAR
Date            DateTime
```

STEP-BY-STEP GUIDE: Logging IP Addresses

4▲ Add fields and a property to `Member`.

We want to be able to access the IP address logged for a particular member, so we need to make some additions to the `Member` class in `Global/CoreObjects/Member.vb`:

First, we add a private member for a collection of the IP addresses:

```
Public Class Member
  Inherits CommunityPO
  Implements IPersistenceBrokerAware


  Private _Username As String
  Private _Password As String
  Private _IntroText As String
  Private _DateJoined As DateTime
  Private _LastAccess As DateTime
  Private _Email As String
  Private _PublicEmail As Boolean
  Private _MemberPageSectionID As Integer = Nothing
  Private _Visible As Boolean
  Private _IsAdmin As Boolean
  Private _IsActivated As Boolean

  Private _Sections As IList
  Private _ModuleInstances As IList
  Private _MemberPageSection As Section = Nothing
  Private _IPAddresses As IList
```

Then, we add a property so that we can access the collection:

```
Public ReadOnly Property IPAddresses() As IList
  Get
    Return _IPAddresses
  End Get
End Property
```

5▲ Update the persistence service repository entry for `Member`.

We also need to update the persistence service repository so that the persistence service will initialize the `_IPAddresses` collection (see Listing 8.17).

LISTING 8.17 Adding a Collection Descriptor to `Global/Ojb.Net/Respository.xml`

```xml
<ClassDescriptor TypeName="Community.Member" TableName="tbl_Member">
  <PrimaryKeyDescriptor IsAutoIncremented="true">
    <FieldDescriptor Id="Member1" FieldName="_primaryKey" ColumnName="ID"
    ➥DbType="Int32" />
  </PrimaryKeyDescriptor>
  <FieldDescriptor Id="Member2" FieldName="_Username" ColumnName="_UserName"
  ➥DbType="String" />
  <FieldDescriptor Id="Member3" FieldName="_Password" ColumnName="Password"
  ➥DbType="String" />
  <FieldDescriptor Id="Member4" FieldName="_IntroText" ColumnName="IntroText"
  ➥DbType="String" />
  <FieldDescriptor Id="Member5" FieldName="_DateJoined" ColumnName="DateJoined"
  ➥DbType="DateTime" />
  <FieldDescriptor Id="Member6" FieldName="_LastAccess" ColumnName="LastAccess"
  ➥DbType="DateTime" />
  <FieldDescriptor Id="Member7" FieldName="_Email" ColumnName="Email"
  ➥DbType="String" />
  <FieldDescriptor Id="Member8" FieldName="_PublicEmail" ColumnName="PublicEmail"
  ➥DbType="Boolean" />
  <FieldDescriptor Id="Member9" FieldName="_MemberPageSectionID"
  ➥ColumnName="MemberPageSectionID" DbType="Int32" />
  <FieldDescriptor Id="Member10" FieldName="_Visible" ColumnName="Visible"
  ➥DbType="Boolean" />
  <FieldDescriptor Id="Member11" FieldName="_IsAdmin" ColumnName="IsAdmin"
  ➥DbType="Boolean" />
  <ReferenceDescriptor FieldName="_MemberPageSection"
  ➥RelatedClassName="Community.Section">
    <ForeignKeyFieldId>Member9</ForeignKeyFieldId>
  </ReferenceDescriptor>
  <CollectionDescriptor FieldName="_ModuleInstances"
                        RelatedClassName="Community.ModuleInstance"
                        CascadeDelete="true">
    <InverseForeignKeyFieldId>ModuleInstance4</InverseForeignKeyFieldId>
  </CollectionDescriptor>
  <CollectionDescriptor FieldName="_Sections"
                        RelatedClassName="Community.Section"
                        CascadeDelete="true">
    <InverseForeignKeyFieldId>Section2</InverseForeignKeyFieldId>
  </CollectionDescriptor>
```

STEP-BY-STEP GUIDE: Logging IP Addresses

LISTING 8.17 Adding a Collection Descriptor to `Global/Ojb.Net/Respository.xml`
(continued)

```
<CollectionDescriptor FieldName="_IPAddresses"
                     RelatedClassName="Community.IPAddress"
                     CascadeDelete="true">
  <InverseForeignKeyFieldId>IP2</InverseForeignKeyFieldId>
</CollectionDescriptor>

</ClassDescriptor>
```

The new `CollectionDescriptor` will populate the collection with all of the `IPAddresses` that reference the `Member`.

Note that we have included the `CascadeDelete` option to ensure that when a member is deleted, his logged IP addresses are cleaned up.

7 ▲ Add a method to `CoreModule`.

We need a method in `CoreModule.vb` to call each time we want to log an IP address. Add the following method to the `CoreModule` class:

```
Public Sub LogIP(ByVal pMember As Member, ByVal pIP As String)
   Dim existingIP As Boolean = False
   Dim i As IPAddress
   For Each i In pMember.IPAddresses
      If i.IP = pIP Then
         existingIP = True
      End If
   Next

   If existingIP = False Then
      Dim ip As New IPAddress(pMember, pIP)
   End If
End Sub
```

We loop through the member's existing IP logs to check whether the new IP has already been recorded. If it has, we do not bother adding it again.

6 ▲ Add code to the login control.

Open `Global/Controls/Login.ascx.vb` and make the addition shown in Listing 8.18.

STEP-BY-STEP GUIDE: **Logging IP Addresses**

LISTING 8.18 Change to `LoginButton_Click` in `Global/Controls/Login.ascx.vb`

```
Private Sub LoginButton_Click(ByVal sender As System.Object, _
                   ByVal e As System.EventArgs) _
       Handles LoginButton.Click
  Dim coreMod As CoreModule = New CoreModule
  If coreMod.AuthenticateMember(UsernameTextBox.Text, PasswordTextBox.Text) Then

    Dim mem As Member = coreMod.GetMemberByUserName(UsernameTextBox.Text)

    coreMod.LogIP(mem, Request.UserHostAddress)
    FormsAuthentication.SetAuthCookie(UsernameTextBox.Text, False)

    Response.Redirect(Request.Url.LocalPath)
  End If
End Sub
```

Therefore, every time a member successfully logs in, we will attempt to log his IP address, which we get through `Request.UserHostAddress`.

Add code to view the IP addresses in the member admin system.

The last piece of the puzzle is to make it easy for administrators to view the IP addresses of members.

Create a new .aspx page in the `admin` folder and call it `memberIPs.aspx`. Add a new `DataList` to the page:

```
<form id="Form1" method="post" runat="server">
  <asp:DataList id="DataList1" runat="server">
    <HeaderTemplate>
      IP Addresses for
      <%#_Member.Username%>
    </HeaderTemplate>
    <ItemTemplate>
      <%#Container.DataItem.IP%>
      -
      <%#Container.DataItem.DateLogged %>
    </ItemTemplate>
  </asp:DataList>
</form>
```

CHALLENGE: Updating the Date on Existing IP Addresses

You will also need to add a declaration for `DataList1` in the code-behind (or use the trick of opening design mode and clicking the `DataList` to add the declaration automatically). Then add code to the code-behind to initialize it:

```
Private Sub Page_Load(ByVal sender As System.Object, _
                ByVal e As System.EventArgs) _
           Handles MyBase.Load
  If Not Request.QueryString("MemberID") Is Nothing Then
     Dim coreMod As New CoreModule

    _Dim mem as Member = coreMod.GetMemberByID(Request.QueryString("MemberID"))

     DataList1.DataSource = _mem.IPAddresses
     DataList1.DataBind()

  End If

End Sub
```

All we need to do now is add a new Hyperlink column to the member admin `DataGrid`. You will need to set the URL field to `PrimaryKey1` and the URL format to `MemberIPs.aspx?MemberID={0}`. Make the target _blank so that a new window will be used to display the logged IPs.

If you are unsure about how to add the column, reread the earlier section in this chapter where we built the member admin `DataGrid`.

You should now be able to click and view the logged IP addresses for any member.

CHALLENGE:
Updating the Date on Existing IP Addresses

It would be nice if, when an existing IP address matches the one being logged, the date on the existing address were updated to the current date and time.

Change the code to do this.

Hint: Remember to use the `<Mutator()>` attribute when you make the `DateLogged` property write-enabled.

Security Configuration Options

There are a lot of ways in which we can change the behavior of the application toward members by changing the security configuration options.

Always be careful when changing security options—double-check everything to ensure you have not inadvertently opened any security holes.

STEP-BY-STEP GUIDE:
Changing the Timeout Period

At the moment, a member's login to the community will be automatically timed out after 30 minutes of inactivity (30 minutes without a page request). It is easy to change this to a different period of time.

Open `Web.Config` and find the `<authentication>` element:

```
<authentication mode="Forms">
    <forms name="Community"
        loginUrl="notRegistered.aspx"
        timeout="30"
        path="/"
        protection="All">
    </forms>
</authentication>
```

Changing the timeout attribute will change the timeout period (in minutes).

STEP-BY-STEP GUIDE:
Remembering Members Between Visits

As well as the timeout period, members' logins will be automatically ended if they close their Web browsers. If we want to, we can change the system so that their logins will be persisted in a cookie.

Open `Global/Controls/Login.ascx.vb` and make the change shown in Listing 8.19.

Security Configuration Options

STEP-BY-STEP GUIDE: **Remembering Members Between Visits**

LISTING 8.19 Change to `Global/Controls/Login.ascx.vb`

```vb
Private Sub LoginButton_Click(ByVal sender As System.Object, _
                              ByVal e As System.EventArgs) _
        Handles LoginButton.Click
  Dim coreMod As CoreModule = New CoreModule
  If coreMod.AuthenticateMember(UsernameTextBox.Text, PasswordTextBox.Text) Then

    Dim mem As Member = coreMod.GetMemberByUserName(UsernameTextBox.Text)

    coreMod.LogIP(mem, Request.UserHostAddress)
    FormsAuthentication.SetAuthCookie(UsernameTextBox.Text, True)

    Response.Redirect(Request.Url.LocalPath)
  End If
End Sub
```

By changing the second parameter of `SetAuthCookie` from `false` to `true`, we specify that we want a persistent login cookie to be created. Members' logins will now be persisted until they manually log out from the community by clicking the Sign Out link.

We can set up the system so that there will be a timeout, even on persistent cookies (see Listing 8.20).

LISTING 8.20 Change to `Global/Controls/Login.ascx.vb`

```vb
Private Sub LoginButton_Click(ByVal sender As System.Object, _
                              ByVal e As System.EventArgs) _
        Handles LoginButton.Click
  Dim coreMod As CoreModule = New CoreModule

  If coreMod.AuthenticateMember(UsernameTextBox.Text, PasswordTextBox.Text) Then

    Dim mem As Member = coreMod.GetMemberByUserName(UsernameTextBox.Text)

    coreMod.LogIP(mem, Request.UserHostAddress)
    Dim authenticationCookie As HttpCookie = _
            FormsAuthentication.GetAuthCookie(UsernameTextBox.Text, true)
```

STEP-BY-STEP GUIDE: **Building a Private Community**

LISTING 8.20 Change to `Global/Controls/Login.ascx.vb` (continued)

```
    authenticationCookie.Expires = _
        DateTime.Now.AddDays(ConfigurationSettings.AppSettings("LoginTimeOutDays"))

    Response.Cookies.Add(authenticationCookie)

    Response.Redirect(Request.Url.LocalPath)
  End If
End Sub
```

We get the cookie from the Forms authentication module and set the timeout for it ourselves. We then add it to the `HttpResponse`.

For this code to work, you will need to add the setting to the `Web.config`:

```
<add key="AdminEmail" value="help@dansfriends.com" />

<add key="MaxDataPerUser" value="10000" />

<add key="PasswordRequestHashPassword" value="hdagd5edfsf4tfdg5t45tf4" />
<add key="PasswordRequestTimeout" value = "6" />

<add key="LoginTimeOutDays" value="10" />
```

This will persist the cookie for 10 days from when the member logs in.

STEP-BY-STEP GUIDE:
Building a Private Community

A common scenario for online communities is to allow access only to members—for example, if we build a community for a club, society, or a group of friends.

The setting to deny access to all but members is easy—we simply change the `<authorization>` section of the `Web.config`:

```
<authorization>
    <deny users="?" />
     <allow users="*" />
</authorization>
```

However, we now have a problem—people who are not yet members will not be able to access the community to join it!

We need to allow access to the `Join.aspx` page so that new members can join. We can do this by adding a new `<location>` element to the `Web.config`:

```
<?xml version="1.0" encoding="utf-8" ?>
<configuration>
    <location path="admin">
    <system.web>

        <authorization>
            <allow roles="administrator" />
            <deny users="*" />
        </authorization>

    </system.web>
    </location>

    <location path="Join.aspx">
      <system.web>
        <authorization>
          <allow users="*" />
        </authorization>
      </system.web>
    </location>
```

We also need to move the login control to a page of its own, which members who are not logged in to can access. We can do this by setting the `LoginUrl` attribute of the `Forms` element in the `Web.config`:

```
<authentication mode="Forms">
    <forms name="Community"
        loginUrl="login.aspx"
        timeout="30"
        path="/"
        protection="All">
    </forms>
</authentication>
```

Users who try to access any part of the site while not logged in will be redirected to `Login.aspx`. ASP.NET automatically allows access to this page by all users.

STEP-BY-STEP GUIDE: **Building a Private Community**

The `Login.aspx` page is very simple to build—we simply use the `Login.ascx` control that we have already seen.

Create a new Web Form called `Login.aspx` and place the `Login.ascx` user control on it. (Remember to register the control at the top of the file.)

There is one complication: After the member has logged in, we want to take her back to the community site, specifically to the URL that she originally requested. Forms authentication helps us do this, by including the original URL request in the query string when it redirects the user to the login page.

We should, therefore, be able to redirect the member back to her original request by adding the following code to the code-behind for `Login.aspx`:

```
Private Sub Page_Load(ByVal sender As System.Object, _
                     ByVal e As System.EventArgs) _
        Handles MyBase.Load
  If Request.IsAuthenticated Then
    If Not Request.QueryString("ReturnUrl") Is Nothing Then
      Response.Redirect(Request.QueryString("ReturnUrl"))
    Else
      Response.Redirect("Default.aspx")
    End If
  End If
End Sub
```

However, if you try testing the login system, you will find that it always redirects the member back to the home page of the community, even if she requested some other page. Clearly, something is not doing what we expected.

In fact, it turns out that the problem is with the login control itself. Here is the `LoginButton_Click` event handler from `Global/Controls/Login.ascx.vb` (see Listing 8.21).

LISTING 8.21 `LoginButton_Click` from `Global/Controls/Login.ascx.vb`

```
Private Sub LoginButton_Click(ByVal sender As System.Object, _
                              ByVal e As System.EventArgs) _
        Handles LoginButton.Click
  Dim coreMod As CoreModule = New CoreModule
```

STEP-BY-STEP GUIDE: **Building a Private Community**

LISTING 8.21 `LoginButton_Click` from `Global/Controls/Login.ascx.vb` (continued)

```
    If coreMod.AuthenticateMember(UsernameTextBox.Text, PasswordTextBox.Text) Then

        Dim mem As Member = coreMod.GetMemberByUserName(UsernameTextBox.Text)

        coreMod.LogIP(mem, Request.UserHostAddress)
        Dim authenticationCookie As HttpCookie = _
            FormsAuthentication.GetAuthCookie(UsernameTextBox.Text, True)
        authenticationCookie.Expires = _
            DateTime.Now.AddDays(ConfigurationSettings.AppSettings("LoginTimeOutDays"))

        Response.Cookies.Add(authenticationCookie)

        Response.Redirect(Request.Url.LocalPath)
    End If
End Sub
```

Can you see the problem? After a successful login, the member is redirected back to the same URL, but the `Request.Url.LocalPath` property is used. Because this property does not include the query string, any query string parameters are omitted.

We can fix the problem by changing the line to

`Response.Redirect(Request.Url.PathAndQuery)`

The member will then be redirected to her original request, including any query string parameters.

Moving On

In the preceding chapters and this one, we have made a lot of changes to the way the application looks and behaves. It might surprise you to know that, in the next chapter, the changes we make will not have any immediately obvious effect on the application. Stay with me, though, because the changes will be valuable to us.

Improving the Code 9

In this chapter, we will not be offering any new features to members of the community, nor will we be changing the way the existing features behave. That might make the chapter sound like a bit of a waste of time, but please do read on—you will probably come to agree with me that time invested in the sort of activities it contains is paid back many fold.

Even after an application runs and does what it is supposed to do, there are all sorts of ways in which the code can be improved, and all sorts of advantages to be gained from doing so. Well-organized and structured code is easier to understand, maintain, and extend. Additionally, reviewing existing code will often present opportunities to improve the performance of the application or expose security flaws that must be addressed.

The process of revisiting existing code and looking for ways to improve it is often called *refactoring*. Frequently examining existing code to check for refactoring opportunities is a good habit to get into.

In this chapter, we will be looking at things we can do for our online community application, including

- Improving performance with caching
- Pruning the viewstate
- Improving text-handling performance with `StringBuilder`
- Eliminating magic numbers
- Reorganizing code
- Creating reusable code
- Improving file naming
- Improving data access

Improving Performance with Caching

The speed with which our online community responds to page requests from its members is obviously very important—if it is too sluggish, members will get frustrated and might stop using it. Performance is also important as new members join the community—the better our code performs, the more members we will be able to support without having to invest in a better server.

One of the best ways to improve the performance of a Web application is with appropriate use of *caching* (storing generated information so that we do not need to create it fresh from the raw data). Our online community application uses caching already, through the persistence service. As you might remember from Chapter 3, "Exploring the Code," the persistence service caches data internally, so it does not need to request data from the database it has recently retrieved. In fact, this automatic caching was one of the main reasons why the persistence service was chosen.

We can do some caching of our own, however, to further improve performance. ASP.NET provides some very rich features for caching, enabling us to cache everything from the output of particular controls right up to the entire page output.

We do have to be careful with how we implement caching, though. If we get caching wrong, we can end up showing users data that is not current or changing the behavior of the application. It should be our goal to improve performance without affecting the users' experience in the community.

STEP-BY-STEP GUIDE:
Caching Page Output

Perhaps the best option that is available to us is to cache the entire page output. By doing this, pages that have been generated already by ASP.NET can be returned to the user directly from the cache rather than having to generate them.

If our application consisted of simple pages, this would be a no-brainer. However, the community application dynamically generates pages based on the users' requests—we need to make sure that each user gets what he asked for.

In particular, the `default.aspx` page is used to respond to the vast majority of requests to the application and relies on a variety of parameters to do its job. It is not, therefore, a good candidate for page caching.

1. Add output caching to a simple page.

When looking for pages to cache, we need to identify pages that do not change a lot. One good example is the `Join.aspx` sign-up form. This will display the same page to all users and will not change often.

We can specify that we want ASP.NET to cache the output of the page by adding the following directive just under the page directive at the top of the file:

```
<%@ OutputCache Duration="500" VaryByParam="none"%>
```

ASP.NET will now cache requests for `Join.aspx` for 500 seconds, using the cached version if another request is made within that time.

2. Add output caching to a page with some dynamic controls.

STEP-BY-STEP GUIDE: **Caching Page Output**

We can add page output caching to pages that display dynamic data. The more dynamism there is, the less suitable for output caching a page is, but there are some pages in the community application that vary only a little and can use output caching with a little more configuration to ensure they display correctly.

The `Members.aspx` page that displays the members list changes in only a few ways:

- When a member is added to or removed from the application
- When a member changes her intro text
- When a member is logged in, depending on which member it is (the login controls will change)

The first two are not a problem—provided the cached version is updated periodically, changes to members will be reflected on the list. It is not vital for new members or changes to intro text to be shown immediately.

The third factor is more crucial—we don't want to display the login controls for a logged-in member when there is no member logged in, or the login controls for the wrong member.

Therefore, we need to specify that we want to store a different version of the page for each member (and one for when there is no member logged in).

We can do this by using the `VaryByCustom` parameter of the `OutputCache` directive:

```
<%@ OutputCache Duration="5000" VaryByParam="none"
➥VaryByCustom="Member"%>
```

In order for this to work, we need to tell ASP.NET how to deal with the `Member` value we have used.

Open `Global.asax.vb` and add the following function (see Listing 9.1).

LISTING 9.1 Function to Add to `Global.asax.vb`

```
Public Overrides Function GetVaryByCustomString(ByVal Context As HttpContext, _
                                                ByVal arg As String) As String

  If arg = "Member" Then
      Return Context.User.Identity.Name
  End If
End Function
```

STEP-BY-STEP GUIDE: **Partial-Page Caching**

We are overriding the `GetVaryByCustomString` function with a custom implementation of our own. (The default version allows the Browser option, which varies the cache by the browser and version.)

We return the member's username as the `VaryByCustom` string, so a newly cached version of the page will be created for each member.

If there is no member logged in, an empty string will be returned, so users who are not logged in will all get the same cached version of the page.

STEP-BY-STEP GUIDE:
Partial-Page Caching

We don't want to cache the whole of `default.aspx`, but we can still take advantage of the ASP.NET caching features. ASP.NET enables us to cache user controls individually. Because our page is constructed from user controls, we can selectively cache the parts of the page that do not vary much.

Open `Global/Controls/Extras.ascx` and add the `OutputCache` directive to it in the same way we did for `Join.aspx`.

The output of the extras control will now be cached. Note that if you later change this control (for example, to display random advertisements), it might no longer be suitable for caching.

Other controls that are suitable for simple caching are

- `Global/Controls/NewestMember.ascx` (although new members will not be reflected in it until the cache updates)
- `Global/Controls/Search.ascx`
- `Global/Controls/SiteFooter.ascx`

The module view controls are also candidates for caching—they only display data rather than allow direct editing, so their interface does not need to change rapidly.

Unfortunately, there are complications. The dynamic approach we use to add the controls to the page, which involves setting properties on the controls, means that caching their output will cause difficulties. In addition to that, we would need to cache a different version of each module view control for each module instance (and one for the global instance).

CHALLENGE:
Caching a Dynamic Control

Add caching to the `Login.ascx` control.

Hint: You can use the same technique we used on the `Members.aspx` page to ensure that each member gets a different cached version of the control.

Viewstate

As you might know, the viewstate is encrypted text that is added to the output of each page ASP.NET generates. It is posted back to the server to carry the values of the ASP.NET controls. This is really useful because it means that the server does not need to store these values but it can add some considerable weight to the pages ASP.NET sends to browsers.

If you browse to the home page of the community and select View > Source, you will find that the viewstate for the page is quite large:

```
<input type="hidden" name="__VIEWSTATE" value="
dDw4Njg4NjY2NTA7dDw7bDxpPDE+Oz47bDx0PDtsPGk8NT47aTw3PjtpPDk+
O2k8MTE+Oz47bDx0PDtsPGk8MT47aTw1Pjs+O2w8dDxwPGw8VmlzaWJsZTs+
O2w8bzxmPjs+Pjs7Pjt0PHA8bDxfIUl0ZW1Db3VudDs+O2w8aTwwPjs+Pjs7Pjs+
PjtOPDtsPGk8Mj47aTw0Pjs+O2w8dDxwPGw8VmlzaWJsZTs+O2w8bzxmPjs+
Pjs7Pjt0PDtsPGk8MD47PjtsPHQ8O2w8aTwwPjs+O2w8dDxwPGw8VmlzaWJsZTs+
O2w8bzxmPjs+Pjs7Pjt0PDtsPGk8MD47PjtsPHQ8cDxsPFRleHQ7PjtsPGFkbWluOz4+
Oz47Oz47dDxwPHA8bDxPYXZpZ2F0ZVVybDs+
O2w8Li4vLi4vTWVtVnyU2V0dGluZ3MuYXNweD9NZW1iZXJJZXMTMTs+Pjs+Ozs+
O3Q8cDxwPGw8TmF2aWdhdGVVcmw7PjtsPC4uLy4uL0RlZmF1bHQuYXNweD9NZW1iZXJJZXMTMTs
+Pjs+Ozs+O3Q8cDxwPGw8TmF2aWdhdGVVcmw7PjtsPC4uLy4uL1ZmlzaWJsZTs+
O2w8Li4vLi4vYWRtaW4vO288dD47Pjs7Pjs+Pjs+Pjs+
Pjt0PDtsPGk8MT47aTwyPjs7Pjs+O2w8Mz47PjtsPHQ8cDxsPFRleHQ7PjtsPGFkbWluOz4+
O2w8NT47PjtsPHQ8cDxwPGw8SGVpZ2h0O0O1dpZHRoO0OltYWdlVXJsOOFsdGVybmF0ZVRle
HQ7XyFTQjs+O2w8MTwyMHB4PjsxPDIwcHg+OjxPIwcHg+Oy4uLy4uL2ltYWdlcy9Nb2R1b
GVJY29uc29ZXhdzLnBuBzxOZXdzPjs+Ozs+O3Q8cDxwPGw8Pjs+Ozs+O3Q8O2w8Mzg0Zj47
PjtsPGk8Pjs7Pjs+O3Q8cDxwPGw8Pjs+Ozs+O3Q8cDxsPFRleHQ7PjtsPGFkbWluOz4+
DtOYXZpZ2F0ZVVybDs+O2w8bmV3cYsuOOuLi9rWZhdWx0LmFzcHg/TW9kdWxlSWQ/TW9kdWx
LzE7PjsrPjtsPHQ8cDxsPFRleHQ7PjtsPGFkbWluOz4+O2w8NT47PjtsPHQ8cDxwPGw8SHX
Ul0ZW1Db3VudDs+O2w8aTwwPjs7Pjs+O3Q8O2w8aTwxPjs+O2w8dDxwPHA8bDxIZWlnaHQ7V2l
dHhPZEXWFnZVVybDtBbHRlcm5hdGVUZXh0O1hTWjs+O2w8MTwyMHB4PjsxPDIwcHg+OjxP
Ul0ZW1Db3VudDs+O2w8aTwwPjs7Pjs+O3Q8cDxwPGw8VGV4dDs+OzE8MjA4MjZjNDE5Li4vLi4vaW1hZ2
VzL01v2ZHVsZU1jb25zL25lZ3MucG5nO05ld3M+O+O2w8MjwyMHB4PjsxPDIwcHg+
HVsZU1jbjZsLOltYWdlR2FsbGVyeS5wbmc7SWlhZ2VzLVhZXJ5OZ28wPjs+Ozs+
+O3Q8cDxwPGw8VGV4dDs+O2w8aW1hZ2VzOzE8MjA4MjZjNDE5Li4vLi4vUlZzbFBQHQu
```

STEP-BY-STEP GUIDE: **Pruning the Viewstate**

```
YXNweD9Nb2RlbGU9Mjs+Pjs+Ozs+O3Q8cDxwPGw8VmlzaWJsZTs+O2w8bzxmPjs+Pjs+
Ozs+Oz4+O3Q8QDA8cDxwPGw8RGF0YUtleXM7XyFJdGVtQ291bnQ7PjtsPGw8PjtpPDA+
Oz4+Oz47Ozs7Ozs7Oz47Oz47Pj47Pj47dDw7bDxpPDE+Oz47bDx0PHA8PHA8cFRleHQ7
TmF2aWdhdGVVcmw7PjtsPGNhY2hlVzdDsuLi8uLi9kZWZhdWx0Wx0LmFzcHg/TWV0YmVy
PTU4Oz4+Oz47Pj47Pj47Pj47PpZZ7uRg8V9+TKGeIL73/rgbKdut" />
```

In fact, this makes up nearly a fifth of the entire page source! (1,758 of 10,102 bytes). Your results will vary from mine depending on what you have displayed on your home page.

The viewstates for other parts of the application (for example, when displaying an ImageGallery) will be much larger because there are more controls being displayed.

Another way to see the amount of viewstate being generated is to set the `Trace` feature that we used in Chapter 5, "Improving the User Interface." If you activate the `Trace` option in the `Web.config`, you will see the trace information underneath the main output. The part we are interested in now is the control tree, which includes information about the size of the viewstate. The great thing about this is that we can not only see the total viewstate size, but the size of every control on the page. This is really useful for locating the controls that cause large viewstates.

Viewstate is useful for persisting values of controls between postbacks, but when we do not need to persist values, using viewstate just adds extra bulk to both requests and responses. Transferring more data impacts both performance and perhaps even the cost of hosting the community.

STEP-BY-STEP GUIDE:
Pruning the Viewstate

Let's see how much viewstate fat we can trim. Each of the following steps will use a different approach to cutting down the amount of viewstate that is sent to the client and is returned in subsequent requests.

1. Disable viewstate at the page level.

We can do away with viewstate completely by setting the `default.aspx` page not to use it. Open `default.aspx` in the VS.NET designer. Add an `EnableViewState="False"` attribute to the `Page` directive:

```
<%@ Page Language="vb"
    AutoEventWireup="false"
    Codebehind="default.aspx.vb"
    Inherits="Community._default"
    EnableViewState="False"%>
```

Now, when we browse to a page in the community (provided it is one that uses `default.aspx`), there will be no viewstate overhead.

Of course, disabling the viewstate at the page level means that viewstate can no longer be used by any of the controls that are displayed on the page. This is okay at the moment because none of our modules require viewstate to work. However, it does mean that, if we later want to use viewstate in a module control, we will have to re-enable viewstate for the whole page.

2. Disable viewstate at the control level.

An alternative to disabling viewstate for the whole page is to disable viewstate for the controls that do not use it. This gives us more flexibility should we want to use viewstate in a control in the future.

Re-enable viewstate for `default.aspx` and instead open the user control .ascx files individually, adding the `EnableViewState="False"` attribute to the `Control` directive of each one.

For example, here is the directive for the navigation control:

```
<%@ Control Language="vb"
    AutoEventWireup="false"
    Codebehind="Navigation.ascx.vb"
    Inherits="Community.Navigation"
    TargetSchema="http://schemas.microsoft.com/intellisense/ie5"
    EnableViewState="False"%>
```

The viewstate is now only very small—just the data for the page itself. This is acceptable, and it allows us the freedom to use viewstate wherever we might need to.

Improving Text-Handling Performance with `StringBuilder`

Many people will tell you that the `StringBuilder` class should always be used rather than concatenating strings directly with the `&` or `+` operator. This is because strings themselves are immutable—once created, they cannot be changed. When strings are concatenated, what is actually happening is that a whole new `String` object is created from the two strings. Creating a new `String` object has a performance overhead, which can be avoided by using a `StringBuilder`, which allows the addition of more strings without creating a new object.

In fact, `StringBuilder` should only be used when several strings are being concatenated together or the strings are very long. When only a small number (three strings or fewer) of short strings are being concatenated, the overhead of creating a `StringBuilder` is actually bigger than the overhead of concatenating the strings directly.

We can test this by creating a new Web Form with a simple table layout:

```
<%@ Page Language="vb" AutoEventWireup="false"
 Codebehind="sbTest.aspx.vb" Inherits="Community.sbTest"%>
<!DOCTYPE HTML PUBLIC "-//W3C//DTD HTML 4.0 Transitional//EN">
<HTML>
  <HEAD>
    <title>sbTest</title>
    <meta name="GENERATOR" content="Microsoft Visual Studio .NET 7.1">
    <meta name="CODE_LANGUAGE" content="Visual Basic .NET 7.1">
    <meta name="vs_defaultClientScript" content="JavaScript">
    <meta name="vs_targetSchema"
     content="http://schemas.microsoft.com/intellisense/ie5">
  </HEAD>
  <body>
    <form id="Form1" method="post" runat="server">
      <table>
        <tr>
          <td>Standard String append</td>
          <td id="nonSBResult" runat="server"></td>
        </tr>
        <tr>
          <td>StringBuilder append</td>
          <td id="SBResult" runat="server"></td>
        </tr>
      </table>
    </form>
  </body>
</HTML>
```

and placing the following code in the `Page_Load` event handler:

```
Private Sub Page_Load(ByVal sender As System.Object, _
                     ByVal e As System.EventArgs) _
             Handles MyBase.Load
    Dim iterations As Integer = 10000000
    Dim appends As Integer = 2
    Dim stringToAppend As String = "This is a test string"
```

```
  Dim nonSBStart As Long = DateTime.Now.Ticks
  Dim nonSBString As String
  For i As Integer = 0 To iterations
    nonSBString = ""
    For x As Integer = 0 To appends
      nonSBString = nonSBString & stringToAppend
    Next
  Next
  Dim nonSBEnd As Long = DateTime.Now.Ticks


  Dim SBStart As Long = DateTime.Now.Ticks
  Dim SB As StringBuilder
  For j As Integer = 0 To iterations
    SB = New StringBuilder
    For x As Integer = 0 To appends
      SB.Append(stringToAppend)
    Next

  Next
  Dim SBEnd As Long = DateTime.Now.Ticks


  Dim nonSBAv As Double = (nonSBEnd - nonSBStart) / iterations
  Dim SBAV As Double = (SBEnd - SBStart) / iterations

  nonSBResult.InnerText = nonSBAv
  SBResult.InnerText = SBAV
End Sub
```

You will also need to include an `Imports System.Text` line at the top of the code-behind and declarations for the `nonSBResult` and `SBResult` controls:

```
Protected WithEvents nonSBResult As _
          System.Web.UI.HtmlControls.HtmlTableCell
Protected WithEvents SBResult As _
          System.Web.UI.HtmlControls.HtmlTableCell
```

We run two separate tests, running each one for a certain number of iterations. Before each of them, we record the current time (in 100-nanosecond intervals since 12:00 a.m., January 1, 0001; provided by the `DateTime.Now.Ticks` property). We record the time after each test, allowing us to calculate the total time for the test and thus the average time for each iteration.

In the first test, we concatenate the test string the specified number of times using the standard & operator.

In the second test, we create a new `StringBuilder` for each iteration and then append the test string to it the specified number of times.

If you browse to the Web Form (because we are doing many tests, it will take a while to load), you will see that with three appends, the direct append method is actually faster than using a `StringBuilder`. The same is true of smaller numbers of appends.

If you change the number of appends to four and recompile, you should see that the results are very close to each other, with the direct method perhaps having an edge.

If you change the number of appends to five or more, you will see that the `StringBuilder` method is faster, with the difference getting greater as the number of appends increases.

The benefit of `StringBuilder` also increases if we make the test string longer. With a long string, the `StringBuilder` is faster at only three or four appends. With a very long string, `StringBuilder` is better even at only two appends.

> **NOTE**
> As with all performance tests, the results of this experiment will vary from machine to machine due to different hardware and software environments. You might find that your results differ from mine, but the overall pattern should be the same.

You might want to play with some different lengths of string and different numbers of appends to see what results you get.

We now want to find all the places in the code for the community where a number of strings are concatenated together so that we can decide whether to employ `StringBuilder` rather than the direct method.

We could go through the files manually to find these situations or perhaps rely on our memory of the code, but that could be very time-consuming and we may well miss some. Fortunately for us, Visual Studio .NET enables us to use regular expressions in its search tool. Select Edit > Find and Replace > Find in Files and check the relevant check box to enable regular expressions.

Now, enter the following regular expression in the Find box:

`&.*\n@.*&.*\n.*&`

This regular expression will look for

- An ampersand followed by
- Any number of non-newline characters (.*) followed by

- An option newline (\n@) followed by
- Any number of non-newline characters (.*) followed by
- Another ampersand followed by
- Any number of non-newline characters (.*) followed by
- An option newline (\n) followed by
- Any number of non-newline characters (.*) followed by
- A third ampersand

What it does is find groups of three ampersands that are not separated by more than one newline from each other. This will find lines of code that are doing concatenations of four or more strings.

We could broaden the search by shortening the regular expression:

`&.*\n@.*&`

This would find code that is concatenating three or more strings.

However, we will concentrate on the more specific search for now because this will find the places where there is the best chance we can improve things with `StringBuilder`.

Run the `Find` operation—you should see something like the following in the Search Results window (you might need to undock it to see it properly):

```
Find all "&.*\n@.*&.*\n.*&", Whole word, Regular expressions,
➥Subfolders, Find Results 1, Current Project:
➥http://localhost/Community_testing/Community.vbproj, "*.*"
C:\Inetpub\wwwroot\Community_testing\ForgotPassword.aspx.vb(89):
➥  email.Body = email.Body & "http://" & Request.Url.Authority
➥& Request.Url.AbsolutePath _
C:\Inetpub\wwwroot\Community_testing\ForgotPassword.aspx.vb(90):
➥& "?MemberID=" & member.PrimaryKey1 & "&Date=" & dateTimeTicks
C:\Inetpub\wwwroot\Community_testing\Modules\News\
➥DisplayModule.ascx.vb(82):
➥Dim popupScript As String = "<script language='javascript'>" &
C:\Inetpub\wwwroot\Community_testing\Modules\News\
➥DisplayModule.ascx.vb(83):
➥"window.open('modules/news/EditNewsItem.aspx?item=" & _
C:\Inetpub\wwwroot\Community_testing\Modules\News\
```

> **TIP**
>
> The regular expression `Find` option in VS.NET is a great way to find code that fits a certain pattern. It's another good reason to learn the regular expression syntax (but make sure to read the VS.NET help on the Find feature—its syntax is slightly different in some ways from standard regular expressions).

```
➥DisplayModule.ascx.vb(84):
➥item.PrimaryKey(0).ToString & _
C:\Inetpub\wwwroot\Community_testing\Modules\News\
➥DisplayModule.ascx.vb(95):
➥Dim popupScript As String = "<script language='javascript'>" & _
C:\Inetpub\wwwroot\Community_testing\Modules\News\
➥DisplayModule.ascx.vb(96):
➥"window.open('modules/news/EditNewsItem.aspx?item=" & _
C:\Inetpub\wwwroot\Community_testing\Modules\News\
➥DisplayModule.ascx.vb(97):    e.CommandArgument() & _
C:\Inetpub\wwwroot\Community_testing\Modules\SendMessage\Views\
➥Minimal.ascx.vb(57): & " delivered to " _
Total found: 9    Matching files: 3    Total files searched: 137
```

Therefore, it looks like there are four opportunities to put `StringBuilder` to use:

- In `ForgotPassword.aspx.vb` around line 89
- In `Modules/News/DisplayModule.ascx` twice, around lines 83 and 96
- In `Modules/SendMessage/Views/Minimal.ascx.vb` around line 57

Because the results in the News module will be code that is executed most often (the other two are probably in code that sends emails), let's look at those first.

Open `Modules/News/DisplayModule.ascx.vb` and find line 83. You will see it is in the `PostNewLink_Click` event:

```
Private Sub PostNewLink_Click(ByVal sender As System.Object, _
                    ByVal e As System.EventArgs) _
        Handles PostNewLink.Click

    'create a new item
    Dim newsMod As NewsModule = New NewsModule(Me.ModuleInstance)

    Dim item As NewsItem = newsMod.CreateNewsItem

    'now we need to pop up the edit news item page to
    'allow the user to edit their new item
    Dim popupScript As String = "<script language='javascript'>" & _
```

```
            "window.open('modules/news/EditNewsItem.aspx?item=" & _
            item.PrimaryKey(0).ToString & _
            "', 'CustomPopUp', " & _
            "'width=400, height=500, menubar=no resizable=yes')" & _
            "</script>"

        Page.RegisterStartupScript("PopupScript", popupScript)

End Sub
```

The concatenations are in code that creates JavaScript to open a new window.

Let's amend the code to use `StringBuilder`. First, add an `Imports System.Text` to the top of the file. Then, make the following changes (see Listing 9.2).

LISTING 9.2 Using `StringBuilder` in `Modules/News/DisplayModule.ascx.vb`

```
Private Sub PostNewLink_Click(ByVal sender As System.Object, _
                              ByVal e As System.EventArgs) _
        Handles PostNewLink.Click

    'create a new item
    Dim newsMod As NewsModule = New NewsModule(Me.ModuleInstance)

    Dim item As NewsItem = newsMod.CreateNewsItem

    'now we need to pop up the edit news item page to
    'allow the user to edit their new item
Dim popupScript As New StringBuilder("<script language='javascript'>")
popupScript.Append("window.open('modules/news/EditNewsItem.aspx?item=")
popupScript.Append(item.PrimaryKey(0).ToString)
popupScript.Append("', 'CustomPopUp', ")
popupScript.Append("'width=400, height=500, menubar=no resizable=yes')")
popupScript.Append("</script>")

Page.RegisterStartupScript("PopupScript", popupScript.ToString)

End Sub
```

> **TIP**
>
> We won't get a big performance gain from using `StringBuilder` because the community application doesn't do a lot of extended string concatenations, but it is worth looking out for situations in which using `StringBuilder` is better than direct appends—if only so that other programmers don't have a reason to criticize your code.

As you can see, using `StringBuilder` is very easy—we create a new `StringBuilder` object with an initial string, and then append additional strings with its `Append` method. When we want to use the resulting string, we use the `ToString` method of the `StringBuilder`.

Eliminating Magic Numbers

Magic numbers are constant values that are included in code in order to get it to behave in a certain way. Usually, it is better to move such values out of code into the configuration file.

It is not just numbers for which this can be true—strings are another common example of values that are often left in code when they really should be stored in a configuration file.

An example of a magic number can be found in `Modules/ImageGallery/Views/DisplayLatestImages.aspx.vb`. Open the file and find the method that loads the page. Can you see some values that would be better placed in the configuration file?

The values specify how many images should be displayed. At present, if we want to display a different number of images in this view, we need to change the code and recompile the application. If we move the value to the `Web.config`, all that will be required is a simple change to that file.

Make the changes in Listing 9.3 to the `Page_Load` event.

LISTING 9.3 Removing Magic Numbers from `Modules/ImageGallery/Views/DisplayLatestImages.ascx.vb`

```
Private Sub Page_Load(ByVal sender As System.Object, _
            ByVal e As System.EventArgs) _
      Handles MyBase.Load

   Dim numberOfImages As Integer = _
        ConfigurationSettings.AppSettings("ImageGallery_NumberOfImagesInViews")
   'check whether we are displaying a global instance
   If Me.IsGlobal Then
     'we are displaying a global instance,
     'so call the global method to get random images
     Dim galleryModule As New ImageGalleryModule
     DataList1.DataSource = galleryModule.GetRandomGlobalImages(numberOfImages)
   Else
```

LISTING 9.3 Removing Magic Numbers from `Modules/ImageGallery/Views/DisplayLatestImages.ascx.vb` (continued)

```vb
        'we are not displaying a global instance,
        ' so create an instance of the ImageGalleryModule
        Dim galleryModule As ImageGalleryModule = _
            New ImageGalleryModule(Me.SectionItem.ModuleInstance)

        'call the instance-specific method to get the random images
        DataList1.DataSource = galleryModule.GetRandomImages(numberOfImages)

        SectionItemHeader1.Text = Me.SectionItem.ModuleInstance.Name & " (" & _
                    galleryModule.GetAllImages.Count.ToString & " images)"
    End If

    DataList1.DataBind()

End Sub
```

You should also make similar changes to `Modules/ImageGallery/Views/DisplayRandomImages.vb`.

Now, add the key for the setting to the `Web.config`:

```
<add key="CommunityName" value="Dan's Community" />
<add key="HomePageSectionID" value="1" />

<add key="NewIconDays" value="7" />

<add key="SmtpServer" value="smtp.easynet.co.uk" />
<add key="FileSystemRoot" value="c:\inetpub\wwwroot\community" />

<add key="ImageGallery_NumberOfImagesInViews" value="8" />
```

You should now see eight images rather than four in the views of the ImageGallery module, as shown in Figure 9.1.

FIGURE 9.1

Eight images in an ImageGallery view.

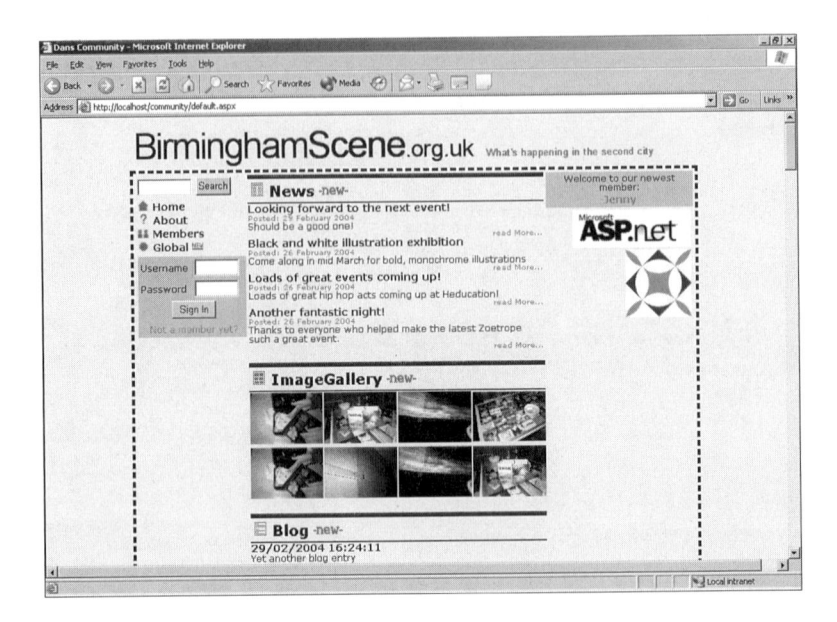

There is more that we can do to make the ImageGallery views more configurable. At present, the number of columns used to display the thumbnails is set by the .ascx files of the two views. This is not too bad because changing .ascx files does not require a recompile. However, it would be better to unify the settings between the two views and keep the setting in the same place as the number of images to display—in the `Web.config`.

The change we need to make to `Modules/ImageGallery/Views/DisplayRandomImages.ascx.vb` is shown in Listing 9.4.

LISTING 9.4 Adding Column Configuration to `Modules/ImageGallery/Views/DisplayRandomImages.ascx.vb`

```
Private Sub Page_Load(ByVal sender As System.Object, _
             ByVal e As System.EventArgs) _
     Handles MyBase.Load

  Dim numberOfImages As Integer = _
      ConfigurationSettings.AppSettings("ImageGallery_NumberOfImagesInViews")
  DataList1.RepeatColumns = _
```

Eliminating Magic Numbers

LISTING 9.4 Adding Column Configuration to `Modules/ImageGallery/Views/DisplayRandomImages.ascx.vb` (continued)

```
        ConfigurationSettings.AppSettings("ImageGallery_NumberOfColumnsInViews")
    'check whether we are displaying a global instance
    If Me.IsGlobal Then
      'we are displaying a global instance,
      ' so call the global method to get random images
      Dim galleryModule As New ImageGalleryModule
      DataList1.DataSource = galleryModule.GetRandomGlobalImages(numberOfImages)
    Else
      'we are not displaying a global instance,
      ' so create an instance of the ImageGalleryModule
      Dim galleryModule As ImageGalleryModule = _
          New ImageGalleryModule(Me.SectionItem.ModuleInstance)

      'call the instance-specific method to get the random images
      DataList1.DataSource = galleryModule.GetRandomImages(numberOfImages)

      SectionItemHeader1.Text = Me.SectionItem.ModuleInstance.Name & " (" & _
                  galleryModule.GetAllImages.Count.ToString & " images)"
    End If

    DataList1.DataBind()

End Sub
```

A similar change is required for `Modules/ImageGallery/Views/DisplayLatestImages.ascx.vb`.

We also need to add the configuration setting to the `Web.config`:

```
<add key="FileSystemRoot" value="c:\inetpub\wwwroot\community" />

<add key="ImageGallery_NumberOfImagesInViews" value="8" />
<add key="ImageGallery_NumberOfColumnsInViews" value="3" />
```

With this change, images will be displayed in three columns, as shown in Figure 9.2.

STEP-BY-STEP GUIDE: **Making the Thumbnail Width Configurable**

FIGURE 9.2

An ImageGallery view with three columns.

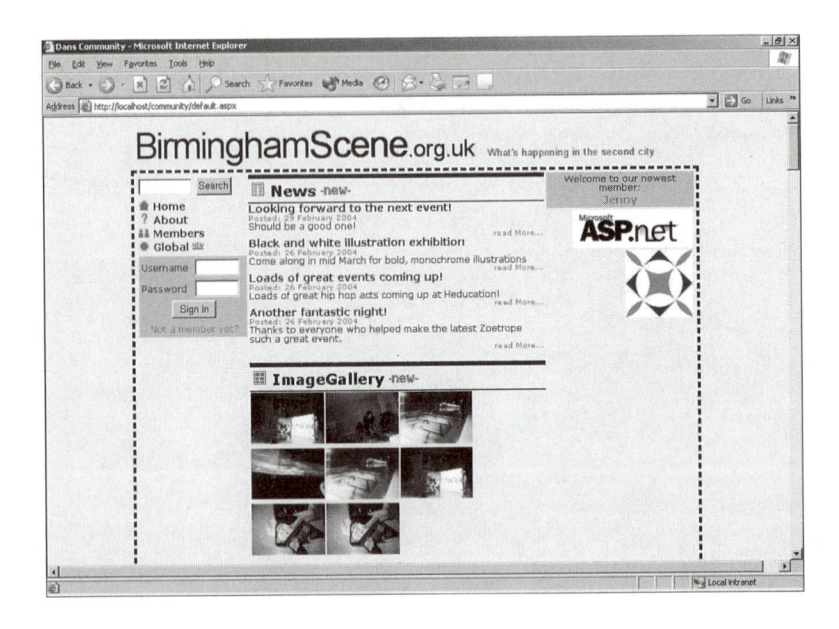

Notice that the thumbnails are still the same size as before. If we want to make the thumbnails fill the space, we will need even more control over the ImageGallery module.

Currently, the width of the thumbnails is fixed at 98. The code we added in Chapter 6, "Improving the Modules," generates thumbnails with a width of 98, and the `<IMG>` tag inside the datalist in the .ascx files for the two ImageGallery views is fixed to a width of 98. The `DisplayModule.ascx` file also uses the value.

This is a good example of a magic number. The figure of 98 is somewhat arbitrarily selected and is used in multiple source code files. Changing the value requires hunting it down in each file and then ensuring that all of them are changed. It would be far, far better to store the value in a single place.

STEP-BY-STEP GUIDE:
Making the Thumbnail Width Configurable

To make the image size configurable, we will have to add a new setting to the Web.config file, change the ImageGallery views and the main module control to use the configured width, and also change the code that generates the thumbnails so that they will be created at the right width.

1. Add the configuration option to `Web.config`.

STEP-BY-STEP GUIDE: **Making the Thumbnail Width Configurable**

Add the following setting to the `Web.config`:

```
<add key="ImageGallery_NumberOfImagesInViews" value="8" />
<add key="ImageGallery_NumberOfColumnsInViews" value="3" />
<add key="ImageGallery_ThumbnailWidth" value="130" />
```

The value of 130 was chosen because it will make the thumbnails fill the content area when arranged in the three columns we configured in the previous section.

2. Change the views to use the option.

There are a number of different approaches we can use to set the width of the thumbnail `<IMG>` elements the view controls generate.

The simplest is to add a new member to the code-behind classes. The addition to `Modules/ImageGallery/Views/DisplayRandomImages.ascx.vb` is shown in Listing 9.5.

LISTING 9.5 Adding a Thumbnail Width Member to `Modules/ImageGallery/Views/DisplayRandomImages.ascx.vb`

```
Public MustInherit Class DisplayRandomImages _
  Inherits SectionItemControl
  Protected WithEvents DataList1 As System.Web.UI.WebControls.DataList
  Protected WithEvents SectionItemHeader1 As SectionItemHeader

  Protected ThumbnailWidth As Integer = _
     ConfigurationSettings.AppSettings("ImageGallery_ThumbnailWidth")
```

Because the member is declared as protected and the class that `DisplayRandomImages.ascx` creates inherits from the code-behind class, this will be accessible in the .ascx file. (Remember that *protected* means accessible to this class and any classes that inherit from it.)

Therefore, we can now make the following change to `Modules/ImageGallery/Views/DisplayRandomImages.ascx`, as shown in Listing 9.6.

STEP-BY-STEP GUIDE: **Making the Thumbnail Width Configurable**

LISTING 9.6 Changing to `Modules/ImageGallery/Views/DisplayRandomImages.ascx` to Use the Configured Thumbnail Width

```
<Community:SectionItemHeader id="SectionItemHeader1" runat="server" />
<div>
  <asp:DataList id="DataList1" OnItemDataBound="DataList_ItemDataBound" runat="server"
➥RepeatLayout="Table"
    RepeatColumns="4">
    <ItemTemplate>
      <asp:HyperLink ID="ImageLink" Runat="server">
        <img alt="<%#Container.DataItem.Name%>"
             src="data/modules/imagegallery/<%#Container.DataItem.Filename%>"
             width="<%#ThumbnailWidth%>"
             border="0" />
      </asp:HyperLink>
    </ItemTemplate>
  </asp:DataList>
</div>
<Community:SectionItemFooter id="SectionItemFooter" runat="server" />
```

We insert the value of the member we just added in place of the magic number (98) that was hardcoded previously.

We will need to make the same changes for the other view as well.

3. Change `DisplayModule.ascx` to use the option.

The change for `DisplayModule.ascx` is very similar. First, we add a member to the code-behind class, `DisplayModule.ascx.vb`, as shown in Listing 9.7.

LISTING 9.7 Changing to `Modules/ImageGallery/DisplayModule.ascx.vb` to Support the Configured Thumbnail Width

```
Public MustInherit Class DisplayModule1
  Inherits ModuleInstanceControl
  Protected WithEvents UploadButton As System.Web.UI.WebControls.Button
  Protected WithEvents FileNameTextBox As System.Web.UI.WebControls.TextBox
  Protected WithEvents FileDescriptionTextBox As System.Web.UI.WebControls.TextBox
  Protected FileUpload As System.Web.UI.HtmlControls.HtmlInputFile
  Protected UploadControls As System.Web.UI.HtmlControls.HtmlGenericControl
```

STEP-BY-STEP GUIDE: **Making the Thumbnail Width Configurable**

LISTING 9.7 Changing to `Modules/ImageGallery/DisplayModule.ascx.vb` to Support the Configured Thumbnail Width (continued)

```
Protected Heading As System.Web.UI.HtmlControls.HtmlGenericControl
Protected WithEvents ImagesDataList As DataList

Protected ThumbnailWidth As Integer = _
    ConfigurationSettings.AppSettings("ImageGallery_ThumbnailWidth")
```

Then, we use the member in the .ascx file, as shown in Listing 9.8.

LISTING 9.8 Changing to `Modules/ImageGallery/DisplayModule.ascx` to Support the Configured Thumbnail Width

```
<asp:datalist id="ImagesDataList" DataKeyField="PrimaryKey1"
➥OnDeleteCommand="ImagesDataList_DeleteClick" runat="server" RepeatColumns="4"
➥RepeatLayout="Table" OnItemDataBound="ImagesDataList_ItemDataBound">
  <ItemTemplate>
    <asp:HyperLink ID="ImageLink" Runat="server">
      <img alt="<%#Container.DataItem.Description%>"
           src="data/modules/imagegallery/<%#Container.DataItem.Filename%>"
           width="<%#ThumbnailWidth%>" border="0" />
    </asp:HyperLink>
    <div class="ImageGallery_ImageTitle"><%#Container.DataItem.Name%></div>
    <div class="ImageGallery_DeleteLink">
      <div>
        <asp:LinkButton CommandName="Delete" CssClass="ImageGallery_DeleteLink"
        ➥ID="DeleteLink" Runat="server"
          Visible="False" />
      </div>
    </div>
  </ItemTemplate>
</asp:datalist>
```

4. Change the thumbnail generation code.

The final thing we need to do is to ensure that the thumbnails are generated at the configured size—there is no point generating them at one size and displaying them at another.

STEP-BY-STEP GUIDE: **Making the Thumbnail Width Configurable**

Note: You should have added the thumbnail generation code when you worked through Chapter 6.

Open the code-behind file for `Modules/ImageGallery/DisplayModule.ascx.vb` and find the method that deals with the Upload button being clicked. Make the changes shown in Listing 9.9.

LISTING 9.9 Changing to `Module/ImageGallery/DisplayModule.ascx.vb` to Generate Thumbnails Using the Configured Width

```
file.InputStream.Position = 0
Dim bitmap As New Bitmap(file.InputStream)

Dim width As Integer = bitmap.Size.Width
Dim height As Integer = bitmap.Size.Height

Dim thumbnail As Image

If width > ThumbnailWidth Then
  Dim myCallBack As Bitmap.GetThumbnailImageAbort = _
          New Image.GetThumbnailImageAbort(AddressOf ThumbnailCallback)
  thumbnail = bitmap.GetThumbnailImage(ThumbnailWidth, height * _
          (ThumbnailWidth / width), myCallBack, IntPtr.Zero)
Else
  thumbnail = bitmap
End If

thumbnail.Save(Server.MapPath("Data/Modules/ImageGallery/" + _
      image.PrimaryKey1.ToString + "_thumb.jpg"), ImageFormat.Jpeg)
```

This uses the same member we used to set the width of the images displayed by `DisplayModule.ascx`. The thumbnail generation code will now use the configured width.

So, now we can configure the width of the thumbnails from the `Web.config` file. There are plenty more values in the community application than would be worthwhile to make configurable. Have a look through the code, especially that for the modules, and choose some values to move to the `Web.config` file.

There is another type of magic number—values that we do not want to move out of code into the configuration file but that are nevertheless

STEP-BY-STEP GUIDE: **Removing the `Community.RandomTextItem` Duplication**

duplicated within code. It makes sense to define these values once within the code and to reuse the value rather than duplicate it. To see what I mean, open `Modules/RandomText/RandomTextModule.vb`.

Throughout this file, there are calls to the persistence service. These calls are to either `QueryFacade.Find` (to get a set of objects) or `QueryFacade.FindObject` (to get a single object).

All these calls require a `Type` object that represents the type of object to retrieve. In the case of this file, all of the calls use a `Type` object that refers to the `Community.RandomTextItem` class. This is retrieved with calls to `Type.GetType("Community.RandomTextItem")`, as in the `GetRandomTextItemByID` method:

```
Public Function GetRandomTextItemByID(ByVal pID As Integer) _
            As RandomTextItem
  Return CType(QueryFacade.FindObject(Type.GetType(
➥"Community.RandomTextItem"), pID), _
            RandomTextItem)
End Function
```

Because the string `"Community.RandomTextItem"` is used throughout this file, it makes sense to define it once rather than multiple times. In fact, we can define the entire `Type` object once and reuse it. This makes the code more concise and easier to read. It will also make our life easier if we change the class name or namespace of the `RandomTextItem` class. It should provide a (very minor) performance gain as we will be reusing the value rather than creating it fresh each time it is used.

STEP-BY-STEP GUIDE:
Removing the `Community.RandomTextItem` Duplication

We need to do two things to implement the change discussed in the previous section. First, we need to define a member to hold the `RandomTextItem` class. Then, we need to use it.

 1. Add a new member to the `RandomTextModule` class.

Add the member shown in Listing 9.10 to `Modules/RandomText/RandomTextModule.vb`.

270 Eliminating Magic Numbers

CHALLENGE: **Removing the `Type.GetType` Duplication in All Module Classes**

LISTING 9.10 Member to Add to `Modules/RandomText/RandomTextModule.vb`

```
Imports Ojb.net.Facade.Query

Public Class RandomTextModule
  Inherits ModuleBase

  Protected Shared RandomTextItemType As Type = Type.GetType("Community.RandomTextItem")

  Public Sub New(ByVal pModuleInstance As ModuleInstance)
    MyBase.New(pModuleInstance)
  End Sub
```

Note that we have made the member `Protected`, so it will only be accessible from this class or classes that derive from it. We also made the member `Shared`—there will only be a single `RandomTextItemType` for all instances of `RandomTextModule`. This makes sense because all instances will share the same value, so there is no point creating multiple ones.

The member is initialized with a call to `Type.GetType`—this will happen when the first instance of `RandomTextModule` is created. The value will then be stored for use by other instances.

2. Use the member rather than the `Type.GetType` call.

Now that we have a member that holds the `Type` object, we can replace all the other calls to `Type.GetType` with `RandomTextItemType`. For example, here is the method we saw before, updated to use the new class member:

```
Public Function GetRandomTextItemByID(ByVal pID As Integer) _
        As RandomTextItem
  Return CType(QueryFacade.FindObject( _
    RandomTextItemType, pID), RandomTextItem)
End Function
```

CHALLENGE:
Removing the `Type.GetType` Duplication in All Module Classes

This same technique can be used in all the module business service classes. (I recommend using Search and Replace to save manually changing all the `Type.GetType` calls.) Implement the change in all the business service classes.

Hint: In `CoreModule.vb`, you will need to create more than one new class member because `CoreModule` deals with more than one persistent object type.

Reorganizing Code

Well-organized code is easier to read, easier to understand for programmers who have not seen it before, and also easier to update. After source files are completed, compiled, and tested, it is worth revisiting them to see whether the code could be organized better. (This is also a good opportunity for adding all those comments you didn't have time to write when you were getting the code working.)

For example, when it was first written, all the code in the code-behind of `default.aspx` was in one long `Page_Load` event handler, which grew and grew as new features were added. It was very confusing indeed for anyone who wanted to see what it did or make changes.

The code was improved by breaking out key sections into separate subroutines, which are called from the `Page_Load` (which now has just the code that decides which type of page is being displayed).

This makes it much easier to see the decision-making flow of the method and also easier to find the code that deals with each circumstance.

We have already done a little reorganization of code in the previous section, in which we moved duplicated calls to `Type.GetType` to a single location in each module business service class.

Let's now take a look at one of the more complex module business service classes, `NewsModule`, to see if we can identify some more code reorganization opportunities.

Open `Modules/News/NewsModule.vb` and take another look through it. Can you spot some duplicated code?

Here is a list of the methods in the class:

`PrepareForDeletion` (inherited from ModuleBase)

`GetSearchResults` (inherited from ModuleBase)

`GetLatestGlobalNewsItems`

`GetAllGlobalNewsItems`

`GetNewsItemByID`

Reorganizing Code

```
UpdateNewsItem
DeleteNewsItem
GetLatestNewsItems
GetAllNewsItems
CreateNewsItem
```

There are two sets of method names that should make us suspect there is some duplication of code going on:

- `GetLatestGlobalNewsItems` and `GetLatestNewsItems`
- `GetAllGlobalNewsItems` and `GetAllNewsItems`

Let's look at the first pair. `GetLatestGlobalNewsItems` is shown in Listing 9.11.

LISTING 9.11 `GetLatestGlobalNewsItems` from `Modules/News/NewsModule.vb`

```
Public Function GetLatestGlobalNewsItems(ByVal number As Integer) As IList
  Dim crit As Criteria = New Criteria

  crit.AddEqualTo("_ModuleInstance._ShowInGlobal", True)
  crit.AddOrderBy("_DatePosted", False)

  Dim newsItems As IList = QueryFacade.Find(Type.GetType("Community.NewsItem"), crit)

  Dim trimmedNewsItems As ArrayList = New ArrayList
  Dim i As Integer = 0
  While i < number And i < newsItems.Count
    trimmedNewsItems.Add(newsItems(i))
    i = i + 1
  End While

  Return trimmedNewsItems
End Function
```

It is immediately apparent that this method is very similar to `GetLatestNewsItems`, which is shown in Listing 9.12.

LISTING 9.12 `GetLatestNewsItems` from `Modules/News/NewsModule.vb`

```
Public Function GetLatestNewsItems(ByVal number As Integer) As IList
  Dim crit As Criteria = New Criteria

  crit.AddEqualTo("_ModuleInstanceID", _ModuleInstance.PrimaryKey(0))
  crit.AddOrderBy("_DatePosted", False)

  Dim newsItems As IList = QueryFacade.Find(Type.GetType("Community.NewsItem"), crit)

  Dim trimmedNewsItems As ArrayList = New ArrayList
  Dim i As Integer = 0
  While i < number And i < newsItems.Count
    trimmedNewsItems.Add(newsItems(i))
    i = i + 1
  End While

  Return trimmedNewsItems
End Function
```

They differ by only a single line. Where `GetLatestGlobalNewsItems` has the line

`crit.AddEqualTo("_ModuleInstance._ShowInGlobal", True)`

`GetLatestNewsItems` has the following line instead:

`crit.AddEqualTo("_ModuleInstanceID", _ModuleInstance.PrimaryKey(0))`

This makes perfect sense—these methods both do the same thing, except one needs to select data from all module instances that are configured to be displayed globally and one needs to select data from a single instance.

We can combine these two methods into a single method very easily. The method will need to detect whether the current instance of the business service class refers to the global instance or a specific instance. Fortunately, this is very easy—we can simply check the `IsGlobal` property the class inherits from `ModuleBase`.

It would make sense for the new method to have the name `GetLatestNewsItems`, so we will remove `GetLatestGlobalNewsItems` either by deleting it or, preferably, by commenting it out. (It is usually best to avoid burning bridges by deleting code outright.) We will then make the changes to `GetLatestNewsItems` that are shown in Listing 9.13.

Reorganizing Code

LISTING 9.13 Making `GetLatestNewsItems` Work for Global Instances in `Modules/News/NewsModule.vb`

```
Public Function GetLatestNewsItems(ByVal number As Integer) As IList
    Dim crit As Criteria = New Criteria

    If Me.IsGlobal Then
      crit.AddEqualTo("_ModuleInstance._ShowInGlobal", True)
    Else
      crit.AddEqualTo("_ModuleInstanceID", _ModuleInstance.PrimaryKey(0))
    End If

    crit.AddOrderBy("_DatePosted", False)

    Dim newsItems As IList = QueryFacade.Find(NewsItemType, crit)

    Dim trimmedNewsItems As ArrayList = New ArrayList
    Dim i As Integer = 0
    While i < number And i < newsItems.Count
      trimmedNewsItems.Add(newsItems(i))
      i = i + 1
    End While

    Return trimmedNewsItems
End Function
```

We simply decide which clause to add to the selection criteria based on whether the current instance of the business service class refers to the global instance or to a specific instance.

Note that this also includes the change to use a class member to store a shared `Type` object for the `Community.NewsItem` class, as covered in the previous section.

If you try to compile the application at this point, you will receive some errors:

```
------ Rebuild All started: Project: Community, Configuration:
➥Release .NET ------

Preparing resources...
Updating references...
Performing main compilation...
```

Reorganizing Code

```
C:\Inetpub\wwwroot\Community\Modules\News\Views\
➥DisplayLatestHeadlines.ascx.vb(28) : error BC30456:
➥'GetLatestGlobalNewsItems' is not a member of
➥'Community.NewsModule'.
C:\Inetpub\wwwroot\Community\Modules\News\Views\
➥DisplayLatestSummaries.ascx.vb(31) : error BC30456:
➥'GetLatestGlobalNewsItems' is not a member of
➥'Community.NewsModule'.
Building satellite assemblies...
```

The `GetLatestGlobalNewsItems` method that we deleted was used in two places. If you click on these errors in the task list, you will be taken directly to the code that calls `GetLatestGlobalNewsItems`. We simply need to change the call to a call to `DisplayLatestNewsItems`. For example, here is the change to `DisplayLatestSummaries.ascx.vb`:

```
  Private Sub Page_Load(ByVal sender As System.Object, _
                   ByVal e As System.EventArgs) _
             Handles MyBase.Load

    Dim newsItems As IList
    Dim newsMod As New NewsModule
    If Me.IsGlobal = True Then
      newsItems = newsMod.GetLatestNewsItems(5)
    Else
      newsMod = New NewsModule(Me.SectionItem.ModuleInstance)

      newsItems = newsMod.GetLatestNewsItems(5)
    End If

    Repeater1.DataSource = newsItems
    Repeater1.DataBind()

  End Sub
```

If the control is displaying the global instance, the business service class is instantiated with no module instance and, therefore, will be global. Otherwise, it is instantiated with a module instance, and the call to `GetLatestNewsItems` will return items from that instance.

Actually, while we are looking at this method, can you see a way to organize the code just a little bit better?

Reorganizing Code

Take a look at this new version of the method:

```
Private Sub Page_Load(ByVal sender As System.Object, _
                      ByVal e As System.EventArgs) _
            Handles MyBase.Load

  Dim newsItems As IList
  Dim newsMod As NewsModule
  If Me.IsGlobal = True Then
    newsMod = New NewsModule
  Else
    newsMod = New NewsModule(Me.SectionItem.ModuleInstance)
  End If

  newsItems = newsMod.GetLatestNewsItems(5)

  Repeater1.DataSource = newsItems
  Repeater1.DataBind()

End Sub
```

There is now only a single call to `GetLatestNewsItems`, and a new `NewsModule` instance is only created once. (In the old version, a `NewsModule` was created and then a new one was created over the top of it when a specific instance was displayed.)

This is only a minor change, but it is good to get into the habit of being strict about code organization—badly organized code is easily the biggest cause of wasted programming time.

Okay, now back to what we were doing. We need to do the same work on `GetAllGlobalNewsItems` and `GetAllNewsItems` as we did for the other pair of methods.

Here is the updated version of `GetAllNewsItems`:

```
Public Function GetAllNewsItems() As IList
  Dim crit As Criteria = New Criteria

  If Me.IsGlobal Then
    crit.AddEqualTo("_ModuleInstance._ShowInGlobal", True)
  Else
```

Reorganizing Code

```
    crit.AddEqualTo("_ModuleInstanceID", _
                _ModuleInstance.PrimaryKey(0))
  End If

  crit.AddOrderBy("_DatePosted", False)

  Return QueryFacade.Find(NewsItemType, crit)
End Function
```

Remember to delete or comment out `GetAllGlobalNewsItems`.

This time, compiling the code only gives a single error—`GetAllGlobalNewsItems` is only used in a single place—`Modules/News/DisplayModule.ascx.vb`.

The changes we need to make are shown in Listing 9.14.

LISTING 9.14 Changing to `Modules/News/DisplayModule.ascx.vb`

```
Private Sub Page_Load(ByVal sender As System.Object, _
                ByVal e As System.EventArgs) _
        Handles MyBase.Load

  Dim newsItems As IList
  'check whether this is an instance or the global module
  Dim newsMod As NewsModule
  If Me.IsGlobal Then
    'this is global
    'get all relevant news items
    newsMod = New NewsModule
    newsItems = newsMod.GetAllNewsItems
    HeadingLabel.Text = Me.CommunityModule.Name
  Else
    'this is an instance
    'get the news items for the instance
    newsMod = New NewsModule(Me.ModuleInstance)
    newsItems = newsMod.GetAllNewsItems
    HeadingLabel.Text = Me.ModuleInstance.Name
    MoreLink.Text = "See all news"
    MoreLink.NavigateUrl = "../../default.aspx?module=" + _
            Me.CommunityModule.PrimaryKey(0).ToString

    'check whether the current user is the owner of the module instance
    'if they are, display the 'post new item' link
```

STEP-BY-STEP: Breaking Out Databinding Code into a Databinding Subroutine

LISTING 9.14 Changing to `Modules/News/DisplayModule.ascx.vb` (continued)

```
    PostNewLink.Visible = False
    If Request.IsAuthenticated Then
      If Me.ModuleInstance.Member.PrimaryKey(0) = _
          CType(Context.User, CommunityPrincipal).Member.PrimaryKey(0) Then
        PostNewLink.Visible = True
      End If
    End If
  End If

  NewsItemsRepeater.DataSource = newsItems
  NewsItemsRepeater.DataBind()

End Sub
```

Therefore, we have "refactored out" two methods from the `NewsModule` class, simplifying the class and avoiding some code duplication.

If you look through the other module business service classes, you will discover that similar changes can be made to all of them—they all have similar sets of pairs of methods to deal with the global instance and specific instances. All of these pairs of methods share the majority of their logic.

The same is not true of `CoreModule`—because it only deals with the `Core` objects, it does not have different behaviors for the global and specific instances.

STEP-BY-STEP:
Breaking Out Databinding Code into a Databinding Subroutine

One feature that is common in ASP.NET code is for there to be multiple event handlers within a file that all include the same databinding code. It is neater and easier to read and update if the databinding code is included in a single subroutine in the file that is called from the event handlers.

For example, pretty much all of the event handlers in `Admin/MemberAdmin.aspx` include the following code to rebind the `MembersDataGrid`:

```
MembersDataGrid.DataSource = _MembersView
MembersDataGrid.DataBind()
```

We can put this code in a subroutine of its own:

```
Private Sub BindDataGrid()
  MembersDataGrid.DataSource = _MembersView
  MembersDataGrid.DataBind()
End Sub
```

And then call the subroutine from the other event handlers:

```
Private Sub MembersDataGrid_CancelCommand(
➥ByVal source As Object, _
➥ByVal e As DataGridCommandEventArgs) _
Handles MembersDataGrid.CancelCommand
    MembersDataGrid.EditItemIndex = -1

    BindDataGrid()
End Sub
```

This is a simple example, but sometimes databinding code can be much more complex. This is especially true for situations in which multiple associated controls have to be refreshed.

CHALLENGE:
Breaking Out Databinding Code

Find some other files in which databinding code is duplicated between event handlers. Break it out into separate subroutines.

Creating Reusable Code

Sometimes there is code that is duplicated between code files. It makes sense to build this code in a reusable way from the start, like we did with the collection-to-data table converter, but if the code is embedded in the application, it makes sense to break it out to make it reusable.

An example of this is the code for sending an email to the community administrators. We created this code in Chapter 6 for the global instance of the Send Message module. You might also have used the same code if you took the challenge in the previous chapter of sending an email to the administrators when a new member joins.

In any case, sending an email to the administrators is a common enough scenario that it would be worthwhile to implement the code somewhere it can be used from all over our application.

Let's put the code in a function in `CoreModule.vb`. Open `Modules/SendMessage/SendMessageModule.vb` and find the code that sent the email. Copy it to the clipboard.

Create a new function in `CoreModule.vb`, make it shared, and give it parameters for the `FromEmail` address and the message itself. Paste the code into it, as shown in Listing 9.15.

LISTING 9.15 Function to Add to `Global/CoreModule.vb`

```
Public Shared Function SendEmailToAdministrators(ByVal pFromEmail As String, _
                                                 ByVal pMessage As String)

    Dim message As MailMessage = New MailMessage
    message.Subject = "Message to admins from " & CoreModule.CommunityName
    message.Body = pMessage
    message.From = pFromEmail

    Dim coreMod As New CoreModule
    Dim admin As Member

    SmtpMail.SmtpServer = ConfigurationSettings.AppSettings("SmtpServer")

    Dim overallResult As Boolean = False
    Dim result As Boolean
    For Each admin In coreMod.GetAdministrators
      result = True
      message.To = admin.Email

      Try
         SmtpMail.Send(message)
      Catch ex As Exception
         result = False
      End Try
```

LISTING 9.15 Function to Add to `Global/CoreModule.vb` (continued)

```
    If result = True Then
      overallResult = True
    End If
  Next

  Return overallResult
End Function
```

We can then replace the original code in `Modules/SendMessage/SendMessageModule.vb` with a call to the global function:

```
Public Shared Function SendGlobalMessage( _
➥ByVal pFromEmail As String, ByVal pMessage As String)
  Return CoreModule.SendEmailToAdministrators(pFromEmail, _
                                              pMessage)
End Function
```

We now have a function that we can use from anywhere in the application to attempt to send an email to the administrators.

It will not always be this easy to separate the reusable code out—sometimes the code is "entangled" with code specific to the file it is from, and some work is required to make it work on its own.

More Efficient Data Access

In general, using the OJB.NET persistence service is great—we get to use a nice object-oriented syntax for navigating our data, a lot of things are done automatically for us, and it also caches objects for efficiency.

The downside to using a persistence service is that sometimes it does not do things in the way we would like it to. For example, take a look at the method from `Modules/News/NewsModule.vb` that is shown in Listing 9.16.

LISTING 9.16 `GetLatestNewsItems` from `Modules/News/NewsModule.vb`

```vb
Public Function GetLatestNewsItems(ByVal number As Integer) As IList
  Dim crit As Criteria = New Criteria

  If Me.IsGlobal Then
    crit.AddEqualTo("_ModuleInstance._ShowInGlobal", True)
  Else
    crit.AddEqualTo("_ModuleInstanceID", _ModuleInstance.PrimaryKey(0))
  End If

  crit.AddOrderBy("_DatePosted", False)

  Dim newsItems As IList = QueryFacade.Find(NewsItemType, crit)

  Dim trimmedNewsItems As ArrayList = New ArrayList
  Dim i As Integer = 0
  While i < number And i < newsItems.Count
    trimmedNewsItems.Add(newsItems(i) )
    i = i + 1
  End While

  Return trimmedNewsItems
End Function
```

Can you see why I have a problem with this method? What will this method do when there are several hundred news items in the database? That's right—it will extract all the news items from the database and then take however many items we want to display from the result set. We have to get the whole set of news items just to display five!

At the time of writing, OJB.NET does not have the built-in facility to specify how many results to extract from the database. Fortunately, however, the author of OJB.NET did allow for the possibility that we might want to do things in a different way than the standard. We can, therefore, use a SQL query of our own choice to select the news items we want, rather than have OJB.NET create the SQL for us.

This gives us the best of both worlds in some ways—we can continue to use intuitive objected-oriented code to manipulate the data objects, but we can have full control over how the objects are retrieved from the database.

STEP-BY-STEP GUIDE: **Using Custom SQL to Get Recent News Items**

There is a downside to this approach. We will be hardcoding the SQL into our code. Changes to the database might need to be reflected in the SQL code. We lose some of the strengths of the persistence service for insulating us from code changes. In this case, though, it is definitely worth it to make a much more efficient query.

STEP-BY-STEP GUIDE:
Using Custom SQL to Get Recent News Items

We will change the `GetRecentNewsItems` method to use some custom SQL code to query the database so that we can select the news items we want.

We will need to figure out the SQL queries we will use (one for the global instance and one for specific instances) and then implement these queries in `GetRecentNewsItems`.

1. Figure out the SQL query for the global instance.

Before creating queries in code, where they will probably need to include some dynamic parameters, it is a good idea to develop and test the SQL in Query Analyzer or any other application that lets you enter SQL queries directly.

Here is a SQL query that will select the five latest global news items:

```
SELECT TOP 5 tbl_News_NewsItem.*
FROM tbl_News_NewsItem, tbl_ModuleInstance
WHERE tbl_News_NewsItem.ModuleInstanceID
  = tbl_ModuleInstance.ID
AND tbl_ModuleInstance.ShowInGlobal = 1
ORDER BY tbl_News_NewsItem.DatePosted DESC
```

We use the `TOP` keyword to specify how many results we want. We then specify that we want all of the columns from `tbl_News_NewsItem` and that we will be selecting from the `tbl_News_NewsItem` and `tbl_ModuleInstance` tables.

We need to include the `tbl_ModuleInstance` table because we need to check whether the module instance that each news item belongs to is set to show its news items in the global instance.

We then specify that the ID of the module instance must be the `ModuleInstanceID` specified in the news item and that we are only interested in the item if its matching module instance has `ShowInGlobal = 1`. (1 equates to `true`; we are using a `BIT` column to store the Boolean value.)

STEP-BY-STEP GUIDE: **Using Custom SQL to Get Recent News Items**

Finally, we order the items by the date they were posted, in descending order.

2. Figure out the SQL query for specific instances.

Here is a similar query that will select the five latest news items for a specific instance:

```
SELECT TOP 5 tbl_News_NewsItem.*
FROM tbl_News_NewsItem, tbl_ModuleInstance
WHERE tbl_News_NewsItem.ModuleInstanceID = 84
ORDER BY tbl_News_NewsItem.DatePosted DESC
```

This query is much simpler—we simply specify the `ModuleInstanceID` that we require. We specify the number of results and the ordering in the same way as before.

3. Implement the queries.

Now, we need to implement these queries to replace the inefficient logic in `NewsModule.GetLatestNewsItems` (see Listing 9.17).

LISTING 9.17 Changing `GetLastestNewsItems` to Use Custom SQL Queries in `Modules/News/NewsModule.vb`

```vb
Public Function GetLatestNewsItems(ByVal number As Integer) As IList
  Dim sqlQuery As New StringBuilder
  sqlQuery.Append("SELECT TOP ")
  sqlQuery.Append(number.ToString())
  sqlQuery.Append(" tbl_News_NewsItem.* ")
  sqlQuery.Append("FROM tbl_News_NewsItem ")

  If Me.IsGlobal Then
    sqlQuery.Append(", tbl_ModuleInstance ")
    sqlQuery.Append("WHERE tbl_ModuleInstance.ID = tbl_News_NewsItem.ModuleInstanceID ")
    sqlQuery.Append("AND tbl_ModuleInstance.ShowInGlobal = 1 ")
  Else
    sqlQuery.Append("WHERE tbl_News_NewsItem.ModuleInstanceID = ")
    sqlQuery.Append(Me.ModuleInstance.PrimaryKey1)
  End If
  sqlQuery.Append("ORDER BY tbl_News_NewsItem.DatePosted DESC")

  Return QueryFacade.Find(NewsItemType, sqlQuery.ToString())
End Function
```

STEP-BY-STEP GUIDE: **Using Custom SQL to Get Recent News Items**

Replace the old code with this code and also ensure that there is an `Imports System.Text` statement at the top of the file. (Because we are doing so many string concatenations, it makes sense to use a `StringBuilder` here.)

The first four appends to the `StringBuilder` are performed whether the global instance or a specific instance is being dealt with. These set up the `SELECT` query and specify the number of results. Then we have the three appends that are done for the global instance. These simply duplicate the code from the query we looked at earlier. Then come the two appends that are done in the case of a specific instance. We add the `WHERE` clause and then add the ID of the current module instance.

We then add the `ORDER BY` clause for both global and specific instances. Finally, we use an overload of `QueryFacade.Find` that we have not used before. This one takes the type of object we want and a custom SQL string that holds the query we want to perform.

The persistence service will now use our news items exactly as it did before, apart from using our custom SQL to select them from the database rather than the default-generated SQL.

We could actually go a stage further here and put the logic for selecting the news items into a stored procedure and then call that using the custom SQL option of `QueryFacade.Find`.

Retrieving Less Data with Summary Objects

Another way in which the persistence service sometimes does things we would not do ourselves is that it always retrieves all of the data for an object. As I mentioned in Chapter 3, it does perform "lazy loading" of collections associated with objects—only loading the collection items as required—but will always retrieve all of the data fields of each object it retrieves.

For example, when a news item is retrieved by the persistence service, we get the full news item with all of the fields, even if we only want to use the heading.

There are times when we know we do not need to use all the fields, and we want to avoid the inefficiency of retrieving all of them.

What we need to do in these cases is create a *summary class*. A summary class is a lot like the class that it summarizes, apart from

- A summary class will not contain all the fields the main class does.
- A summary class is read-only—persistent objects created from it cannot be changed or deleted, and we cannot create new persistent objects using the summary class. This is important in order to avoid conflicts with the main persistent object.

This means that summary classes are ideal for use when we are retrieving data for display.

For example, when we are retrieving news items for display in the views in the News module, we do not need the body text of the items. Because the body text is likely to be the bulkiest field in the NewsItem object, it makes sense to create a NewsItemSummary class that will contain all of the data of the NewsItem class, except for the body text.

STEP-BY-STEP GUIDE:
Using a NewsItemSummary Class

We will now create and use the NewsItemSummary class. Because this is the first summary object we have created, we will need to create a base class for all of our summary objects to derive from. We will then be able to implement NewsItemSummary. After we have done that, we will need to add an entry for it to the persistence service repository file. After we have a working summary object, we will add support for it to the News module business service class and to the module views.

1. Implement a CommunitySummaryPO base class.

Our first step is to implement a base class for our NewsItemSummary class and any future summary classes we create to derive from. Recall that all of the standard persistent objects in the community application derive from CommunityPO, which we use to add some extra code to the EditablePersistentObject base class provided by the persistence service.

We should not use CommunityPO as a base class for our summary classes—because it derives from EditablePersistenceObject, persistent objects based on it are editable, which is not the behavior we want for our summary classes.

Right-click the Global/CoreObjects folder in the Solution Explorer and select Add New Class. Give the new class the name CommunitySummaryPO and click OK.

STEP-BY-STEP GUIDE: **Using a `NewsItemSummary` Class**

Add the following code to the class:

```
Public Class CommunitySummaryPO
  Inherits Ojb.Net.Facade.Po.ReadOnlyObject

  'constructor required by persistence service
  Public Sub New(ByVal ID As Integer)
    MyBase.New(ID)
  End Sub

  'property to return the first primary key
  '(we only use the first primary key,
  ' and some ASP.NET databinding
  'cannot index into the primary key array)
  Public ReadOnly Property PrimaryKey1() As Integer
    Get
      Return Me.PrimaryKey(0)
    End Get
  End Property

End Class
```

If you compare this to `CommunityPO`, you will find that they are similar. Only the base class that they derive from is different.

As with `CommunityPO`, we pass on calls to the constructor to the base class. Also, as with `CommunityPO`, we provide a property to directly access the first element of the primary key array, which we need to do because some ASP.NET databinding expressions will not allow us to access the members of the primary key array directly.

   2. Implement the `NewsItemSummary` class.

Right-click the `Modules/News` folder and select Add New Class. Give the new class the name `NewsItemSummary`. Add the following code:

```
Imports Ojb.Net.Facade.Persist


Public Class NewsItemSummary
  Inherits CommunitySummaryPO

  Private _ModuleInstanceID As Integer
  Private _Title As String
```

Retrieving Less Data with Summary Objects

STEP-BY-STEP GUIDE: **Using a `NewsItemSummary` Class**

```
Private _Summary As String
Private _DatePosted As DateTime


Private _ModuleInstance As ModuleInstance

'reconstructor for use by the persistence service
Public Sub New(ByVal ID As Integer, _
               ByVal pModuleInstanceID As Integer, _
               ByVal pTitle As String, _
               ByVal pSummary As String, _
               ByVal pDatePosted As DateTime)

  MyBase.New(ID)

  _ModuleInstanceID = pModuleInstanceID
  _Title = pTitle
  _Summary = pSummary
  _DatePosted = pDatePosted
End Sub

Public ReadOnly Property ModuleInstance() As ModuleInstance
  Get
    Return _ModuleInstance
  End Get
End Property

Public ReadOnly Property Title() As String
  Get
    Return _Title
  End Get
End Property

Public ReadOnly Property Summary() As String
  Get
    Return _Summary
  End Get
End Property

Public ReadOnly Property DatePosted()
  Get
    Return _DatePosted
```

STEP-BY-STEP GUIDE: **Using a `NewsItemSummary` Class**

```
    End Get
  End Property

End Class
```

If you compare this to the code in `NewsItem.vb`, you will see that we have simply removed the constructor (we cannot create new instances of `NewsItemSummary` in any case) and also all parts of the code that deal with the `Body` field.

The reconstructor is required because we want the persistence service to create instances of this class. We have removed the body argument because the summary object does not include the body.

We have also made all the properties read-only and removed the set accessors that some properties had.

3. Add the `NewsItemSummary` persistent object to the repository.

Open `Global/Ojb.Net/Repository.xml` and add the following XML just after the end of the class descriptor for `NewsItem`:

```xml
<ClassDescriptor TypeName="Community.NewsItemSummary"
➥TableName="tbl_News_NewsItem">
    <PrimaryKeyDescriptor IsAutoIncremented="true">
      <FieldDescriptor Id="NewsItemSummary1"
      ➥FieldName="_primaryKey" ColumnName="ID" DbType="Int32" />
    </PrimaryKeyDescriptor>
    <FieldDescriptor Id="NewsItemSummary2" FieldName="_ModuleInstanceID"
    ➥ColumnName="ModuleInstanceID" DbType="Int32" />
    <FieldDescriptor Id="NewsItemSummary3" FieldName="_
    ➥Title" ColumnName="Title" DbType="String" />
    <FieldDescriptor Id="NewsItemSummary4" FieldName="_Summary"
    ➥ColumnName="Summary" DbType="String" />
    <FieldDescriptor Id="NewsItemSummary6" FieldName="_DatePosted"
    ➥ColumnName="DatePosted" DbType="DateTime"/>
    <ReferenceDescriptor FieldName="_ModuleInstance"
    ➥RelatedClassName="Community.ModuleInstance">
      <ForeignKeyFieldId>NewsItemSummary2</ForeignKeyFieldId>
    </ReferenceDescriptor>
  </ClassDescriptor>
```

Again, this is very similar to the descriptor for `NewsItem`—the class name has changed, and there is no field descriptor for `Body`. Note that the field descriptors are in the same order as the parameters in the reconstructor—this is important because the persistence service needs to know which

STEP-BY-STEP GUIDE: **Using a `NewsItemSummary` Class**

order to use when it calls the reconstructor to create instances of `NewsItemSummary`.

4. Create a method in `NewsModule` to retrieve the latest summaries.

We should now have a working `NewsItemSummary` persistent object, so we need to provide a way for display code to use it.

Open `Modules/News/NewsModule.vb` and add the following new declaration:

```
Public Class NewsModule
    Inherits ModuleBase

    Protected Shared NewsItemType _
        As Type = Type.GetType("Community.NewsItem")
    Protected Shared NewsItemSummaryType _
        As Type = Type.GetType("Community.NewsItemSummary")
```

Now, add the method shown in Listing 9.18.

LISTING 9.18 Method to Add to `Modules/News/NewsModule.vb`

```
Public Function GetLatestNewsItemSummaries(ByVal number As Integer) As IList
    Dim sqlQuery As New StringBuilder
    sqlQuery.Append("SELECT TOP ")
    sqlQuery.Append(number.ToString())
    sqlQuery.Append(" tbl_News_NewsItem.ID, ")
    sqlQuery.Append(" tbl_News_NewsItem.ModuleInstanceID, ")
    sqlQuery.Append(" tbl_News_NewsItem.Title, ")
    sqlQuery.Append(" tbl_News_NewsItem.Summary, ")
    sqlQuery.Append(" tbl_News_NewsItem.DatePosted ")
    sqlQuery.Append("FROM tbl_News_NewsItem ")

    If Me.IsGlobal Then
     sqlQuery.Append(", tbl_ModuleInstance ")
     sqlQuery.Append("WHERE tbl_ModuleInstance.ID = tbl_News_NewsItem.ModuleInstanceID ")
     sqlQuery.Append("AND tbl_ModuleInstance.ShowInGlobal = 1 ")
    Else
      sqlQuery.Append("WHERE tbl_News_NewsItem.ModuleInstanceID = ")
      sqlQuery.Append(Me.ModuleInstance.PrimaryKey1)
    End If
    sqlQuery.Append("ORDER BY tbl_News_NewsItem.DatePosted DESC")

    Return QueryFacade.Find(NewsItemSummaryType, sqlQuery.ToString())
  End Function
```

CHALLENGE: **Implementing Another Summary Class**

This is based on the same SQL queries as the updated version of `GetLatestNewsItems` we created in the previous section. This time, however, we explicitly specify the columns we want (excluding `Body`).

5. Use the new method in the views.

The final step is to actually use the `GetLatestNewsItemSummaries` rather than `GetLatestNewsItems` in the views of the module.

Open `Modules/News/Views/DisplayLatestSummaries.ascx.vb` and make the following change to the `Page_Load` method:

```
Private Sub Page_Load(ByVal sender As System.Object, _
                ByVal e As System.EventArgs) _
        Handles MyBase.Load

  Dim newsItems As IList
  Dim newsMod As NewsModule
  If Me.IsGlobal = True Then
    newsMod = New NewsModule
  Else
    newsMod = New NewsModule(Me.SectionItem.ModuleInstance)
  End If

  newsItems = newsMod.GetLatestNewsItemSummaries(5)

  Repeater1.DataSource = newsItems
  Repeater1.DataBind()

End Sub
```

This view will now use `NewsItemSummary` objects rather than full `NewsItem` objects. You should make a similar change to `Modules/News/Views/DisplayLatestHeadlines.ascx.vb`.

CHALLENGE:
Implementing Another Summary Class

The Blog module could also benefit from the use of a summary class. The text easily will be the biggest part of each `BlogEntry` object, and the text is only required when the month the entry is in is being displayed.

Implement a `BlogEntrySummary` class in the same way we implemented `NewsItemSummary`.

Improving File Naming

Something you might have noticed is that there are several user controls in the community application that share the same name. Several modules have `DisplayModule.ascx` controls.

In some ways, this is a bad idea—it makes the different controls harder to distinguish, and it also means that the code-behind classes for the controls have to have names like `DisplayModule2`.

We can eliminate this duplication of names relatively easily by including the module name of each module in the names of their user controls. Therefore, the News module would have `DisplayNewsModule.ascx`, and the ImageGallery module would have `DisplayImageGalleryModule.ascx`.

Let's implement that change now:

1. Change the News module `DisplayModule` control.

Right-click `Modules/News/DisplayModule.ascx` and select Rename. Rename it to `DisplayNewsModule.ascx`.

Then, open the control in HTML view and change the Control directive as follows:

```
<%@ Control Language="vb" AutoEventWireup="false"
➥Codebehind="DisplayNewsModule.ascx.vb"
➥Inherits="Community.DisplayNewsModule"
➥TargetSchema="http://schemas.microsoft.com/intellisense/ie5" %>
```

Then, open the code-behind and change the class name to match:

```
Public MustInherit Class DisplayNewsModule
    Inherits ModuleInstanceControl
    Protected WithEvents HeadingLabel
    ➥As System.Web.UI.WebControls.Label
    Protected WithEvents MoreLink
    ➥As System.Web.UI.WebControls.HyperLink
    Protected WithEvents PostNewLink
    ➥As System.Web.UI.WebControls.LinkButton
```

2. Change the other `DisplayModule` controls.

Perform the same changes for each `DisplayModule.ascx` control, making sure to name the control `Display[module name]Module.ascx` and the code-behind class `Display[module name]Module`.

3. Update `default.aspx` to use the new naming.

If you try to view the application at this stage and browse to either a global module or a specific module instance, you will get an error as `default.aspx` tries to locate the display module control with the old name.

Open `default.aspx.vb` and make the change to the `DisplayModuleInstance` method shown in Listing 9.19.

LISTING 9.19 Changing to `DisplayModuleInstance` in `default.aspx`

```
Private Sub DisplayModuleInstance()

  Dim instance As ModuleInstance = _
  _  CoreModule.GetModuleInstanceByID(Request.QueryString("Instance"))
  Dim moduleControl As ModuleInstanceControl = CType(Page.LoadControl("Modules/" + _
      instance.CommunityModule.Name + "/Display" + instance.CommunityModule.Name + _
      "Module.ascx"), ModuleInstanceControl)

  moduleControl.ModuleInstance = instance

  sectionItems.Controls.Add(moduleControl)

  Navigation1.MemberID = moduleControl.ModuleInstance.Member.PrimaryKey(0)
End Sub
```

We simply insert the module name into the filename that should be used. Make a similar change to `DisplayGlobalModule`, as shown in Listing 9.20.

LISTING 9.20 Changing to `DisplayGlobalModule` in `default.aspx`

```
Private Sub DisplayGlobalModule(ByVal moduleToDisplay As CommunityModule)
  Dim moduleControl As ModuleInstanceControl = CType(Page.LoadControl("Modules/" + _
```

LISTING 9.20 Changing to `DisplayGlobalModule` in `default.aspx` (continued)

```
        moduleToDisplay.Name + "/Display" + moduleToDisplay.Name + "Module.ascx"), _
        ModuleInstanceControl)

    moduleControl.CommunityModule = _CoreModule.GetModuleByID(Request.QueryString("Module"))

    sectionItems.Controls.Add(moduleControl)
End Sub
```

The application should now work just as it did before, but with a different name for each display module control.

If you still get errors, check that the naming of each of your controls and classes matches the appropriate module name exactly.

Moving On

In this chapter, we have looked at a lot of different ways in which we can improve the quality of the application code. Hopefully, you have seen that a bit of reorganization is easy to do and can make the code much more readable and maintainable.

In Chapter 10, "Extending the Application," we will be making the biggest changes yet to our application by adding completely new features to it.

Extending the Application 10

Up until now, we have been tweaking, modifying, and improving on the existing application code. In this, the final chapter, we will look at adding some completely new features to the application.

We will begin by making a relatively simple addition—a new view for the ImageGallery module. You will see how easy it is to create new views to display module data in different ways.

We will then add a whole new module to the system, giving the community members the ability to share key event dates. Because the community uses a standardized module system, after you have built the events module, you will be able to add further modules of your own—adding whatever functionality you think your members will appreciate. We will also see how we can integrate a separate application with the community. We will add a forums system to the community by using the ASP.NET Forums code.

We will see

- How to add a new view to an existing module
- How to build a new module
- How to integrate ASP.NET Forums with the online community application

Adding a New View

The first completely new thing we are going to add to the application is a new view for the ImageGallery module. This view will be quite simple—it will display a single, random image. However, after you have followed through this process, you should be able to add whatever additional views you like to the system.

Here are the steps we need to take:

1. Create the user control.   `1▼`
2. Inherit from `SectionItemControl`.   `2▼`
3. Add an image control.   `3▼`
4. Add code to initialize the image.   `4▼`
5. Add a database entry for the view.   `5▼`
6. Use the view on the community to test it.   `6▼`

Adding a New View

1. **Create the user control.**

Right-click the `Modules/ImageGallery/Views` folder and select Add New User Control. Give the new control the name `DisplaySingleImage.ascx`.

2. **Inherit from `SectionItemControl`.**

Open the code-behind file for the new control and change the `Inherits` statement so that the control inherits from `SectionItemControl`:

```
Public Class DisplaySingleImage
  Inherits SectionItemControl
```

You might remember that all view controls inherit from `SectionItemControl`—it provides the standard functionality that is required to display them within sections.

3. **Add an image control.**

In design view, drag an image control onto the control. Use the property viewer to give it the ID `TheImage`.

4. **Add code to initialize the image.**

Add the following code to the `Page_Load` method of the control:

```
Private Sub Page_Load(ByVal sender As System.Object, _
                    ByVal e As System.EventArgs) _
            Handles MyBase.Load

Dim imageGalleryMod As ImageGalleryModule
Dim image As GalleryImage

If Me.IsGlobal Then
  imageGalleryMod = New ImageGalleryModule
  image = CType(imageGalleryMod.GetRandomGlobalImages(1)(0), _
              GalleryImage)
Else
  imageGalleryMod = _
      New ImageGalleryModule(Me.SectionItem.ModuleInstance)
  image = CType(imageGalleryMod.GetRandomImages(1)(0), _
              GalleryImage)
End If
```

```
TheImage.Width = New Unit(400)
TheImage.ImageUrl = "../../../Data/Modules/ImageGallery/" _
                    + image.Filename

End Sub
```

Note that this code assumes you have not yet refactored the ImageGallery module to use a single method for getting both global and specific instance random images. If you have done the refactoring, give yourself a pat on the back and change the code here to use your refactored method.

Add a database entry for the view.

Use Enterprise Manager or the VS.NET Server Explorer to add a new entry to the tbl_ModuleView table, as shown in Figure 10.1.

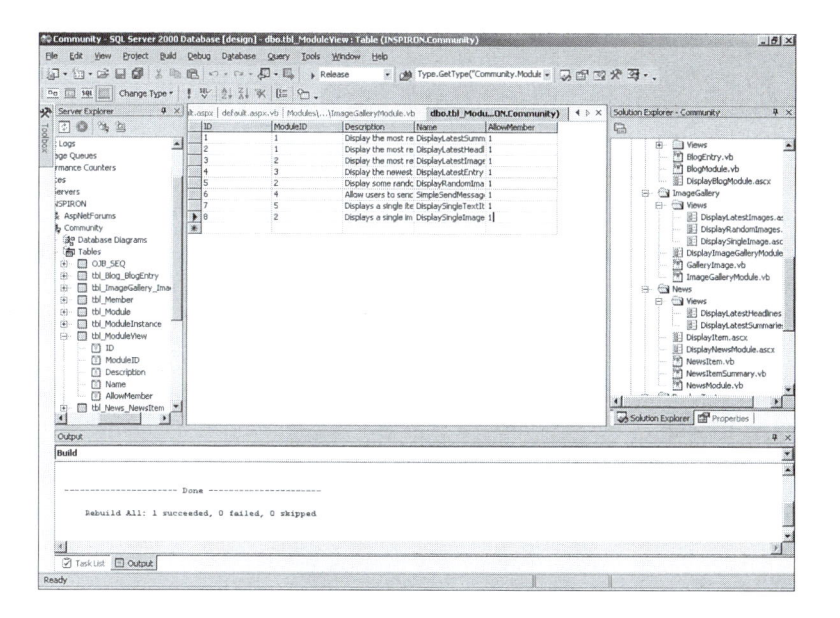

FIGURE 10.1

Adding a new entry to the tbl_ModuleView table.

Use the view on the community to test it.

Log in as one of the members who has an ImageGallery module. (You can use the user Zoetrope, who has the password `movingpictures`.)

Click the settings option, and then select the My Pages tab.

Edit one of the pages and then select the ImageGallery module followed by the DisplaySingleImage view, as shown in Figure 10.2.

FIGURE 10.2

Adding the `DisplaySingleImage` view to a section.

If you now browse to the section to which you added the view, you should see the single image view (in addition to any other views on the section). An example is shown in Figure 10.3.

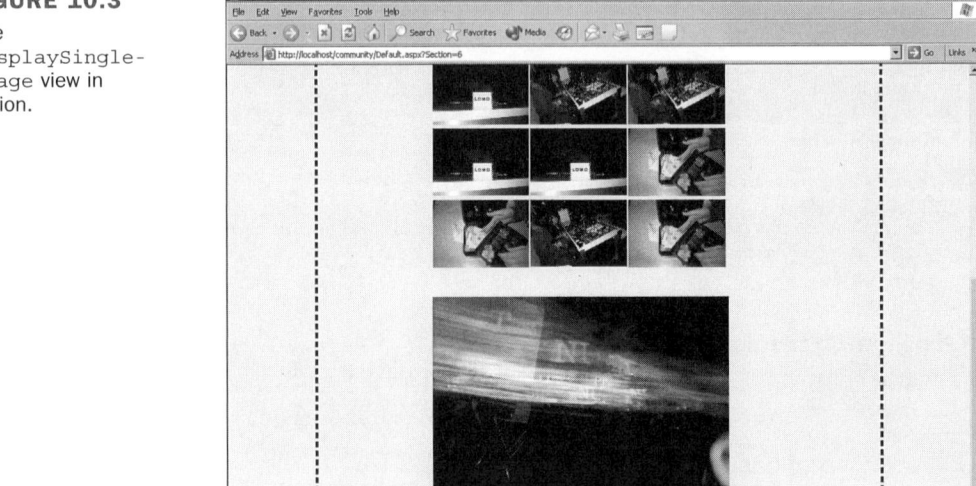

FIGURE 10.3

The `DisplaySingleImage` view in action.

Adding a new module view is that simple—just inherit from `SectionItemControl`, create your view, include the correct database entry, and you are ready to go.

CHALLENGE:
Improving the `DisplaySingleImage` View

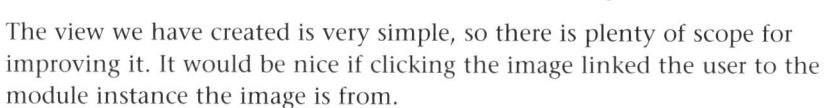

The view we have created is very simple, so there is plenty of scope for improving it. It would be nice if clicking the image linked the user to the module instance the image is from.

Implement this feature.

Hint: You can see how this is done by looking at the other ImageGallery views.

Adding a New Module

Next, we are going to go a step further and add an entire new module. This is easily the most complicated process we have covered, so it has been split up into a number of linked step-by-step activities. Follow the steps carefully and make sure you implement all the required code at each stage.

The module system works by specifying certain requirements that modules must provide, along with some optional things modules can take advantage of. There are also some recommendations to which it is best for modules to adhere.

We have seen all these things in the modules to which we have been making changes, but we will review them now so that we can see what we will need to do when building our own module.

Required Items

There are certain things each module is required to provide in order to work with the online community infrastructure. We have touched on these things throughout this book, but we will bring them together in one list here because we will soon need to implement them all for our new module:

- **Module views**—User controls that inherit from `SectionItemControl` and are in the `Views/` folder of the module folder.

STEP-BY-STEP GUIDE: Implementing the Persistent Object

- **Main module display**—User control in the file `DisplayCalendarModule.ascx` that inherits from `ModuleControl`. (Note that in Chapter 9, "Improving the Code," we changed the application code to include the module name in the name of this control. If you have not implemented this change, you will need to alter the name of this control accordingly.)

- **Database entry**—A row in the tbl_Module table.

- **Database entries for view**—A row in the tbl_ModuleView table for each view.

- **Business service class**—A class that inherits from `ModuleBase`.

Optional Items

In addition to the items that modules are required to implement, there are some extra features of the infrastructure that modules can take advantage of:

- A user control called `DisplayItem.ascx` and inheriting from the `ModuleItemControl` class that will be used when `default.aspx?Module=[moduleID]&Item=[ItemID]` is opened. (Note: You might have implemented code to have this control include the name of the module in its name. If you have, use the name, including the module name.)

- Additional persistent objects that inherit from `CommunityPO`.

- A folder in `Data/Modules` for module-specific data that members upload.

Our Calendar module will provide all these things, except for the data folder—the calendar does not need to store any data outside the database.

> **DESIGN TIP**
>
> It is often a good idea to start the design of a new system with the data structures. This is especially true when working with an object persistence model because the persistence objects directly represent important aspects of the system.

STEP-BY-STEP GUIDE:
Implementing the Persistent Object

The first part of the new module we will build is the persistent object, which will be used to store each event.

The persistent object will need to store

- The `ModuleInstance` to which it belongs
- The name of the event

- A description of the event
- The date on which the event will happen
- The date on which the details were last updated

Here are the steps we will take to implement the persistent object:

1. Create the `CalendarEvent` class file.
2. Inherit from the `CommunityPO` base class.
3. Add private fields.
4. Add a reconstructor.
5. Add a constructor.
6. Add properties.
7. Add a database table for the persistent object.
8. Add an entry to the persistence service repository.

Create the `CalendarEvent` class file.

Create a new folder in `/Modules` called `Calendar`. In that folder, add a new class called `CalendarEvent`.

Inherit from the `CommunityPO` base class.

Add an `Imports` statement to use the `Ojb.Net.Facade.Persist` namespace and an `Inherits` statement to inherit from the `CommunityPO` class.

```
Imports Ojb.Net.Facade.Persist

Public Class CalendarEvent
  Inherits CommunityPO
```

We need to import the `Ojb.Net.Facade.Persist` namespace because we need to use the `<mutator()>` attribute, which lets us tell the persistence service which properties or methods of our class make changes to the persistent object.

302 Adding a New Module

STEP-BY-STEP GUIDE: **Implementing the Persistent Object**

3 ▲ Add private fields.

Add the following private fields to the class:

```
Private _ModuleInstanceID As Integer
Private _Name As String
Private _Description As String
Private _EventDate As DateTime
Private _LastUpdated As DateTime

Private _ModuleInstance As ModuleInstance
```

We include a field for the ID of the instance to which the event belongs, along with the name, description, date of the event, and the last time it was updated. These values will all be stored in the database.

We also add a field for the module instance itself—this field will be populated by the persistence service, based on the ID that is stored in the database.

4 ▲ Add a reconstructor.

Add the following reconstructor to the class:

```
'reconstructor for use by persistence service
Public Sub New(ByVal pID As Integer, _
               ByVal pModuleInstanceID As Integer, _
               ByVal pName As String, _
               ByVal pDescription As String, _
               ByVal pEventDate As DateTime, _
               ByVal pLastUpdated As DateTime)
    MyBase.New(pID)
    _ModuleInstanceID = pModuleInstanceID
    _Name = pName
    _Description = pDescription
    _EventDate = pEventDate
    _LastUpdated = pLastUpdated
End Sub
```

The *reconstructor* is a special constructor the persistence service uses when it retrieves a persistent object from the database.

The first thing we do in it is call the constructor of the base class that takes the ID of the object as its only parameter. This is very important—without doing this, the persistence service will think we are constructing a new object.

STEP-BY-STEP GUIDE: **Implementing the Persistent Object**

We then initialize the object with the parameter values. Note that we do not initialize the _ModuleInstance field—the persistence service will do that for us from the _ModuleInstanceID field.

Add a constructor.

Add the following constructor to the class:

```
Public Sub New(ByVal pModuleInstance As ModuleInstance, _
               ByVal pName As String, _
               ByVal pDescription As String, _
               ByVal pEventDate As DateTime)

  _ModuleInstance = pModuleInstance
  _Name = pName
  _Description = pDescription
  _EventDate = pEventDate
  _LastUpdated = DateTime.Now
End Sub
```

We now add a constructor we will use when we want to create a new event. Note that this constructor has fewer parameters than the reconstructor—we do not supply an ID (because we will not have one for the event until it is created), and we also do not supply the LastUpdated date—it is created from the current date in the constructor.

This constructor, unlike the reconstructor, initializes the _ModuleInstance field from the parameter, rather than the _ModuleInstanceID field. The persistence service will populate the _ModuleInstanceID field for us.

Add properties.

We now need to add properties so that our code can access the various fields:

```
Public ReadOnly Property ModuleInstance() As ModuleInstance
  Get
    Return _ModuleInstance
  End Get
End Property

<Mutator()> _
Public Property Name() As String
  Get
    Return _Name
```

Adding a New Module

STEP-BY-STEP GUIDE: **Implementing the Persistent Object**

```
    End Get
    Set(ByVal Value As String)
      _LastUpdated = DateTime.Now
      _Name = Value
    End Set
End Property

<Mutator()> _
Public Property Description() As String
    Get
      Return _Description
    End Get
    Set(ByVal Value As String)
      _LastUpdated = DateTime.Now
      _Description = Value
    End Set
End Property

<Mutator()> _
Public Property EventDate() As DateTime
    Get
      Return _EventDate
    End Get
    Set(ByVal Value As DateTime)
      _LastUpdated = DateTime.Now
      _EventDate = Value
    End Set
End Property

Public ReadOnly Property LastUpdated()
    Get
      Return _LastUpdated
    End Get
End Property
```

Note that all the properties that are not read-only are decorated with the `<Mutator()>` attribute. As was mentioned earlier, we use this to tell the persistence service which properties or methods will lead to a change in the persistent object. It is important for us to do this—if we don't, the persistence service will not pick up and persist any changes that are made.

STEP-BY-STEP GUIDE: **Implementing the Persistent Object**

Add a database table for the persistent object.

Each type of persistent object is stored in its own table in the database. Create a new table called tbl_Calendar_Event and add the following columns:

ID	Integer	PrimaryKey	Identity
ModuleInstance	Integer	(no nulls)	
Name	VarChar(50)	(allow nulls)	
Description	VarChar(500)	(allow nulls)	
EventDate	(DateTime)	(no nulls)	
LastUpdated	(DateTime)	(no nulls)	

Add an entry to the persistence service repository.

Add the following class descriptor to Global/Ojb.Net/Repository.xml:

```xml
<ClassDescriptor TypeName="Community.CalendarEvent"
 TableName="tbl_Calendar_CalendarEvent">
  <PrimaryKeyDescriptor IsAutoIncremented="true">
   <FieldDescriptor Id="CalendarEvent1" FieldName="_primaryKey"
    ColumnName="ID" DbType="Int32" />
  </PrimaryKeyDescriptor>
  <FieldDescriptor Id="CalendarEvent2"
 FieldName="_ModuleInstanceID"
 ColumnName="ModuleInstanceID" DbType="Int32" />
  <FieldDescriptor Id="CalendarEvent3" FieldName="_Name"
 ColumnName="Name" DbType="String" />
  <FieldDescriptor Id="CalendarEvent4"
 FieldName="_Description" ColumnName="Description"
 DbType="String" />
  <FieldDescriptor Id="CalendarEvent5" FieldName="_EventDate"
   ColumnName="EventDate" DbType="DateTime" />
  <FieldDescriptor Id="CalendarEvent6"
 FieldName="_LastUpdated" ColumnName="LastUpdated"
 DbType="DateTime"/>
  <ReferenceDescriptor FieldName="_ModuleInstance"
 RelatedClassName="Community.ModuleInstance">
    <ForeignKeyFieldId>CalendarEvent2</ForeignKeyFieldId>
  </ReferenceDescriptor>
</ClassDescriptor>
```

If you read though the descriptor line by line, it is pretty clear what is happening. We define the class the `CalendarEvent` object uses, along with the database table that stores it.

Then, we define the primary key of the class. We specify that the primary key will be automatically incremented by SQL Server. We then define each of the fields from the class, specifying which database column stores the field and what type it is. Finally, we use a reference descriptor to define the relationship between the `ModuleInstance` object and the `_ModuleInstanceID` field that stores the foreign key for the `ModuleInstance` the `CalendarEvent` references.

After we have the class, the database table, and the repository descriptor, we should have a working persistent object. We can now move on to start building the module that will use it.

STEP-BY-STEP GUIDE:
Creating a Business Service Class for the Module

Now that we have a persistent object to represent calendar events, we need some business layer code that will enable our display code to access, create, update, and delete events.

Here are the steps we will take:

1. Create the class.

2. Implement a constructor.

3. Implement the `GetResourceUsage` method.

4. Implement the `GetSearchResults` method.

5. Implement the `Name` property.

6. Implement the cleanup method.

7. Implement a method to add a new event.

8. Implement methods for dealing with individual events.

9. Implement methods to retrieve groups of events.

Create the class.

Create a new class in `Modules/Calendar` called `CalendarModule`.

Adding a New Module 307

STEP-BY-STEP GUIDE: **Creating a Business Service Class for the Module**

Add the following `Imports` and `Inherits` statements:

```
Imports Ojb.Net.Facade.Query

Public Class CalendarModule
  Inherits ModuleBase

  Protected shared CalendarEventType As Type = _
          Type.GetType("Community.CalendarEvent")
```

We need to inherit from the `ModuleBase` class so that the community framework will know that this class provides the required functionality of a module business service class.

Also, the `ModuleBase` class itself derives from the `ContextBoundObject` class and is decorated by the `Transaction` attribute. This is vital to the persistence service. By making our requests to the persistence service through a class that has these features, we ensure that they happen in the context of a transaction. (The importance of transactions was discussed in Chapter 3, "Exploring the Code.")

You will notice that as soon as you enter the `Inherits` statement, some methods are automatically added to the class. These are the methods the base class requires us to implement.

Also notice the protected, shared member that has been added to store the `Type` object for the `CalendarEvent` class for use later in the code.

Implement a constructor.

2 ▲

Add the following constructor to the class:

```
Public Sub New(ByVal pModuleInstance As ModuleInstance)
  Me._ModuleInstance = pModuleInstance
End Sub
```

If you are wondering where the `_ModuleInstance` field is, open `Global/ModuleBase.vb` and you will find it in there—it is provided by the base class, marked as protected so that it is only accessible to classes that inherit from the base class.

Implement the `GetResourceUsage` method.

3 ▲

Add the following code to the `GetResourceUsage` method:

```
Public Overrides Function GetResourceUsage() As Integer
  Dim crit As New Criteria
```

STEP-BY-STEP GUIDE: Creating a Business Service Class for the Module

```
            crit.addEqualTo("_ModuleInstanceID", _
                    Me.ModuleInstance.PrimaryKey1)

    Dim events As IList = _
            QueryFacade.Find(CalendarEventType, crit)

    Dim ev As CalendarEvent
    Dim result As Integer = 0
    For Each ev In events
      result = result + ev.Name.Length _
                    + ev.Description.Length
    Next
    Return result

End Function
```

We get all the events in the instance and add together the lengths of their names and descriptions to get the total resource usage.

4 ▲ Implement the `GetSearchResults` method.

Add the code shown in Listing 10.1 to the `GetSearchResults` method.

LISTING 10.1 `GetSearchResults` Method for `Modules/Calendar/CalendarModule.vb`

```
Public Overrides Function GetSearchResults(ByVal pSearchTerms As String) _
                    As SearchResultCollection
  Dim results As New SearchResultCollection

  Dim crit1 As New Criteria
  crit1.AddLike("_Name", "%" & pSearchTerms & "%")

  Dim crit2 As New Criteria
  crit2.AddLike("_Description", "%" & pSearchTerms & "%")
  crit1.AddOrCriteria(crit2)

  Dim crit3 As New Criteria
  crit3.AddEqualTo("_ModuleInstanceID", Me.ModuleInstance.PrimaryKey1)
  crit1.AddAndCriteria(crit3)

  Dim calendarItems As IList = QueryFacade.Find(CalendarEventType, crit1)
```

STEP-BY-STEP GUIDE: **Creating a Business Service Class for the Module**

LISTING 10.1 `GetSearchResults` Method for `Modules/Calendar/CalendarModule.vb` (continued)

```
  Dim ev As CalendarEvent
  For Each ev In calendarItems
    results.add(New SearchResult(ev.Name, _
                       ev.Description, _
                       0.5, _
                       "default.aspx?Module=6&Instance=" _
                         & Me.ModuleInstance.PrimaryKey1, _
                       Me.ModuleInstance))
  Next

  Return results
End Function
```

We set up the criteria so that the search terms can be matched in either name or description. We do this by creating them in separate criteria objects and adding one to the other with `addOrCriteria`.

We then specify a new criteria that requires the matching `CalendarEvents` to be from the appropriate module instance. We add this criteria to the original one with `addAndCriteria`.

After running the query, we loop through the results, adding a `SearchResult` object to our `SearchResultCollection` object for each one.

Implement the `Name` property.

Add the following property to the class:

```
Public Overrides ReadOnly Property Name() As String
  Get
    Return "Calendar"
  End Get
End Property
```

This property is important if we need to link the module class back to the persistent object that represents the module to the community infrastructure. Not all modules need to use it, but some do.

310 Adding a New Module

STEP-BY-STEP GUIDE: **Creating a Business Service Class for the Module**

6 ▲ **Implement the cleanup method.**

Add the following code to the `PrepareForDeletion` method:

```
Public Overrides Sub PrepareForDeletion()
  Dim crit As New Criteria
  crit.AddEqualTo("_ModuleInstanceID", _
              Me.ModuleInstance.PrimaryKey1)

  Dim events As IList = _
            QueryFacade.Find(CalendarEventType, crit)

  Dim ev As CalendarEvent
  For Each ev In events
    ev.Delete()
  Next
End Sub
```

We simply get all the `CalendarEvent` objects that are in this instance and then delete them.

7 ▲ **Implement a method to add a new event.**

```
Public Function AddEvent(ByVal pName As String, _
                    ByVal pDescription As String, _
                    ByVal pEventDate As DateTime)
  Dim ev As New CalendarEvent(Me.ModuleInstance, _
                    pName, _
                    pDescription, _
                    pEventDate)
  Me.ModuleInstance.Touch()
  Return ev
End Function
```

8 ▲ **Implement methods for dealing with individual events.**

Add the following methods to the class (see Listing 10.2).

LISTING 10.2 Methods to Add to `Modules/Calendar/CalendarModule.vb`

```
Public Function GetEventByID(ByVal pID As Integer) As CalendarEvent

  Return CType(QueryFacade.FindObject(CalendarEventType, pID), CalendarEvent)
End Function
```

STEP-BY-STEP GUIDE: **Creating a Business Service Class for the Module**

LISTING 10.2 Methods to Add to `Modules/Calendar/CalendarModule.vb` (continued)

```
Public Function UpdateEvent(ByVal pID As Integer, _
                           ByVal pName As String, _
                           ByVal pDescription As String, _
                           ByVal pEventDate As DateTime) As CalendarEvent
    Dim ev As CalendarEvent = _
        CType(QueryFacade.FindObject(CalendarEventType, pID), CalendarEvent)

    ev.Name = pName
    ev.Description = pDescription
    ev.EventDate = pEventDate
    ev.ModuleInstance.Touch()

    Return ev
End Function

Public Sub DeleteEvent(ByVal pID As Integer)

    Dim ev As CalendarEvent = QueryFacade.FindObject(CalendarEventType, pID)

    ev.Delete()
End Sub
```

These provide us with the standard facilities to add, update, and delete events.

Implement methods to retrieve groups of events.   9▲

Add the following methods to the class. This method gets a specified number of upcoming events, starting with the one that will occur first:

```
Public Function GetUpcomingEvents(ByVal pNumber As Integer) _
                         As IList
    Dim crit As New Criteria

    If Me.IsGlobal Then
      crit.AddEqualTo("_ModuleInstance._ShowInGlobal", True)
    Else
      crit.AddEqualTo("_ModuleInstanceID", _
                     Me.ModuleInstance.PrimaryKey1)
    End If
```

Adding a New Module

STEP-BY-STEP GUIDE: Creating a Business Service Class for the Module

```
      crit.AddOrderBy("_EventDate", True)
      crit.AddGreaterOrEqualThan("_EventDate", DateTime.Now)

      Dim events As IList = QueryFacade.Find(CalendarEventType, _
                                              crit)

      Dim trimmedEvents As ArrayList = New ArrayList
      Dim i As Integer = 0
      While i < pNumber And i < events.Count
        trimmedEvents.Add(events(i))
        i = i + 1
      End While

      Return trimmedEvents
   End Function
```

This method returns all upcoming events:

```
Public Function GetUpcomingEvents() As IList
   Dim crit As New Criteria

   If Me.IsGlobal Then
     crit.AddEqualTo("_ModuleInstance._ShowInGlobal", True)
   Else
     crit.AddEqualTo("_ModuleInstanceID", _
                     Me.ModuleInstance.PrimaryKey1)
   End If

   crit.AddOrderBy("_EventDate", True)
   crit.AddGreaterOrEqualThan("_EventDate", DateTime.Now)

   Return QueryFacade.Find(CalendarEventType, crit)

End Function
```

This method gets all events for a specific day:

```
Public Function GetEventsForDay(ByVal pDate As DateTime)
   Dim startofday As New DateTime(pDate.Year, _
                                  pDate.Month, _
                                  pDate.Day)
   Dim endofday As DateTime = startofday.AddDays(1)

   Dim crit As New Criteria
```

STEP-BY-STEP GUIDE: **Creating a Business Service Class for the Module**

```
  If Me.IsGlobal Then
    crit.AddEqualTo("_ModuleInstance._ShowInGlobal", True)
  Else
    crit.AddEqualTo("_ModuleInstanceID", _
                    Me.ModuleInstance.PrimaryKey1)
  End If

  crit.AddGreaterOrEqualThan("_EventDate", startofday)
  crit.AddLessOrEqualThan("_EventDate", endofday)

  Return QueryFacade.Find(CalendarEventType, crit)
End Function
```

This method gets all events for a specific month:

```
Public Function GetEventsForMonth(ByVal pDate As DateTime)
  Dim year As Integer = pDate.Year
  Dim month As Integer = pDate.Month

  Dim startOfMonth As New DateTime(year, month, 1, 0, 0, 0)
  Dim endOfMonth As New DateTime(year, _
                                 month, _
                                 DateTime.DaysInMonth(year, month), _
                                 23, 59, 59)

  Dim crit As New Criteria

  If Me.IsGlobal Then
    crit.AddEqualTo("_ModuleInstance._ShowInGlobal", True)
  Else
    crit.AddEqualTo("_ModuleInstanceID", _
                    Me.ModuleInstance.PrimaryKey1)
  End If

  crit.AddGreaterOrEqualThan("_EventDate", startOfMonth)
  crit.AddLessOrEqualThan("_EventDate", endOfMonth)
  crit.AddOrderBy("_EventDate", True)

  Return QueryFacade.Find(CalendarEventType, crit)
End Function
```

STEP-BY-STEP GUIDE: Implementing the Display Module Control

This method gets all events:

```
Public Function GetAllEvents() As IList
  Dim crit As New Criteria

  If Me.IsGlobal Then
    crit.AddEqualTo("_ModuleInstance._ShowInGlobal", True)
  Else
    crit.AddEqualTo("_ModuleInstanceID", _
                    Me.ModuleInstance.PrimaryKey1)
  End If

  crit.AddOrderBy("_EventDate", True)

  Return QueryFacade.Find(CalendarEventType, crit)
End Function
```

All these methods detect whether they are being run from the global instance or a specific instance and behave appropriately.

STEP-BY-STEP GUIDE:
Implementing the Display Module Control

Our next move is to start implementing the presentation code of the module. We will start with the main module display, which will display upcoming events (if the viewer is not the owner of the module instance being viewed) or all events (if the viewer is the owner).

Implementing the main module will involve creating only one control—we will use the business service class foundation we built in the previous activity to do most of the work.

1. Create the control.

Create a new user control called `DisplayCalendarModule.ascx` in the `Modules/Calendar` folder (assuming you followed the activity in Chapter 8 where we renamed the display module controls).

Open its code-behind and have it inherit from the `ModuleInstanceControl` class:

```
Public Class DisplayCalendarModule
  Inherits ModuleInstanceControl
```

2. Add controls.

Add controls, as shown in Listing 10.3.

STEP-BY-STEP GUIDE: **Implementing the Display Module Control**

LISTING 10.3 Controls in `Modules/Calendar/DisplayCalendarModule.ascx`

```
<div class="ModuleItemHeading">
  <asp:Label id="HeadingLabel" runat="server"></asp:Label>
</div>
<div class="ModuleItemMore">
  <asp:HyperLink id="MoreLink" runat="server"></asp:HyperLink>
  <asp:LinkButton id="PostNewLink" runat="server" Visible="False">
      Post a new event
  </asp:LinkButton>
</div>
<div> </div>
<asp:DataList id="EventsDataList" runat="server">
  <ItemTemplate>
    <div class="SummaryItemHeading"><%#DataBinder.Eval
➥(Container.DataItem,"EventDate", "{0:D}")%>
      -
      <%#Container.DataItem.Name%>
    </div>
    <div class="SummaryItemDate">Last Updated:
      <%# DataBinder.Eval(Container.DataItem,"LastUpdated", "{0:D}") %>
    </div>
    <div class="SummaryItemReadMoreLink">
<a href="default.aspx?Module=<%#Container.DataItem.ModuleInstance.
➥CommunityModule.PrimaryKey(0)%>&Item=<%#Container.DataItem.PrimaryKey(0)%>">
      read more...</a>
    </div>
    <div> 
    </div>
  </ItemTemplate>
</asp:DataList>
```

The design view for the control is shown in Figure 10.4.

3. Add code to initialize the page.

If you used HTML view to add the controls, you will need to add declarations for the controls we added, or use the trick of opening the design view and clicking the controls.

Adding a New Module

STEP-BY-STEP GUIDE: **Implementing the Display Module Control**

FIGURE 10.4
Design view for `Display-Calendar-Module.ascx`.

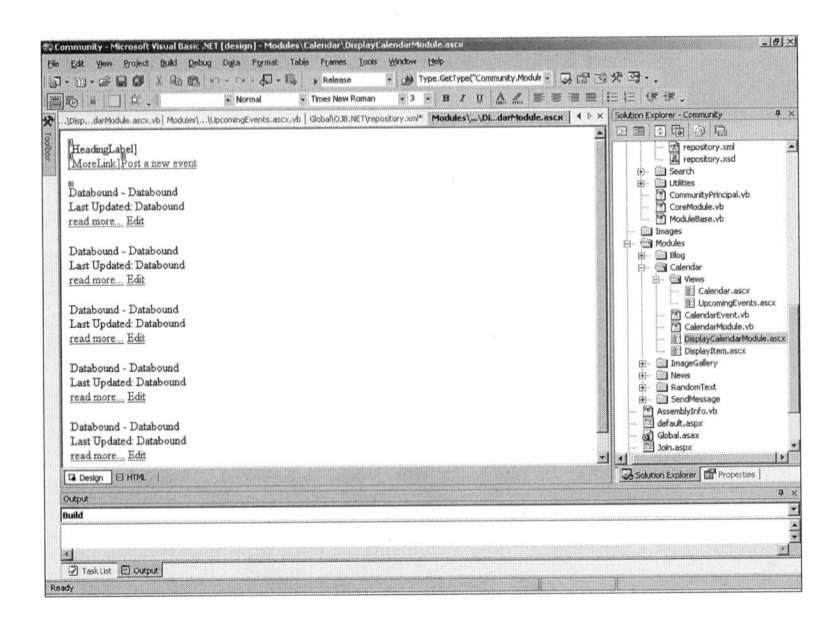

```
Private Sub Page_Load(ByVal sender As System.Object, _
                     ByVal e As System.EventArgs) _
                     Handles MyBase.Load


    Dim events As IList
    If Me.IsGlobal Then
       HeadingLabel.Text = Me.CommunityModule.Name
       events = CalendarModule.GetUpComingGlobalEvents
    Else
       HeadingLabel.Text = Me.ModuleInstance.Name
       Dim calMod As New CalendarModule(Me.ModuleInstance)

       If DisplayEditLinks() Then
          events = calMod.GetAllEvents
          PostNewLink.Visible = True
       Else
          events = calMod.GetUpcomingEvents

       End If
    End If
```

STEP-BY-STEP GUIDE: **Implementing the Display Module Control**

```
  EventsDataList.DataSource = events
  EventsDataList.DataBind()

End Sub
```

This code uses a call to another method to decide whether to display the Add New Event option:

```
Protected Function DisplayEditLinks() As Boolean
  If Me.IsGlobal Then
    Return False
  End If
  If Request.IsAuthenticated Then
    If Me.ModuleInstance.Member.PrimaryKey(0) =
    ⮕CType(Context.User, CommunityPrincipal).
    ⮕Member.PrimaryKey(0) Then
      Return True
    Else
      Return False
    End If
  Else
    Return False
  End If
End Function
```

We do a simple check of whether the currently logged-in member is the owner of the instance. We also need to provide a method to deal with the Add New Event link being clicked:

```
Private Sub PostNewLink_Click(ByVal sender As System.Object, _
                    ByVal e As System.EventArgs) _
                  Handles PostNewLink.Click
  Dim calMod As New CalendarModule(Me.ModuleInstance)
  Dim ev As CalendarEvent = calMod.AddEvent("", "", DateTime.Now)

  Response.Redirect("default.aspx?Module=" & _
              Me.CommunityModule.PrimaryKey1 & _
              "&Item=" & _
              ev.PrimaryKey1)
End Sub
```

We create a new event through the `CalendarModule` and then redirect the member to the Display Item page for that item. (We will create the `DisplayItem` control later.)

STEP-BY-STEP GUIDE: Implementing a View to Display Upcoming Events

STEP-BY-STEP GUIDE:
Implementing a View to Display Upcoming Events

The first view we will implement is fairly basic—it simply displays a list of upcoming events with each event name linking to more details of the event. Because we have already implemented an infrastructure for the module, we do not have to do much to implement a view—we just need to create an appropriate control in the `Views` folder.

1. Create the user control.

Create a `Views` folder in `Modules/Calendar` and create a user control called `UpcomingEvents.ascx`.

Open the code-behind and have the control inherit from the `SectionItemControl` class:

```
Public Class UpcomingEvents
    Inherits SectionItemControl
```

2. Add controls (see Listing 10.4).

LISTING 10.4 `Modules/Calendar/Views/UpcomingEvents.ascx`

```
<%@ Control Language="vb" AutoEventWireup="false" Codebehind="UpcomingEvents.ascx.vb"
➥Inherits="Community.UpcomingEvents"
➥TargetSchema="http://schemas.microsoft.com/intellisense/ie5" %>
<%@ Register Tagprefix="Community" Tagname="SectionItemFooter"
➥src="../../../Global/Controls/SectionItemFooter.ascx" %>
<%@ Register Tagprefix="Community" Tagname="SectionItemHeader"
➥src="../../../Global/Controls/SectionItemHeader.ascx" %>
<div>
  <Community:SectionItemHeader id="SectionItemHeader" runat="server" />
</div>
<div>
  <asp:Repeater id="EventsRepeater" runat="server">
    <ItemTemplate>
      <div>
        <a class="SummaryItemText" href="default.aspx?Module=
➥<%#Container.DataItem.ModuleInstance.CommunityModule.PrimaryKey1%>
➥&Item=<%#Container.DataItem.PrimaryKey1%>">
          <%#Container.DataItem.EventDate.ToLongDateString %>
➥ - <%#Container.DataItem.Name%>
```

STEP-BY-STEP GUIDE: **Implementing a View to Display Upcoming Events**

LISTING 10.4 `Modules/Calendar/Views/UpcomingEvents.ascx`
(continued)

```
      </a>
    </div>
  </ItemTemplate>
</asp:Repeater>
</div>
<div>
  <Community:SectionItemFooter id="SectionItemFooter" runat="server" />
  <P></P>
</div>
```

The design view for this control is shown in Figure 10.5.

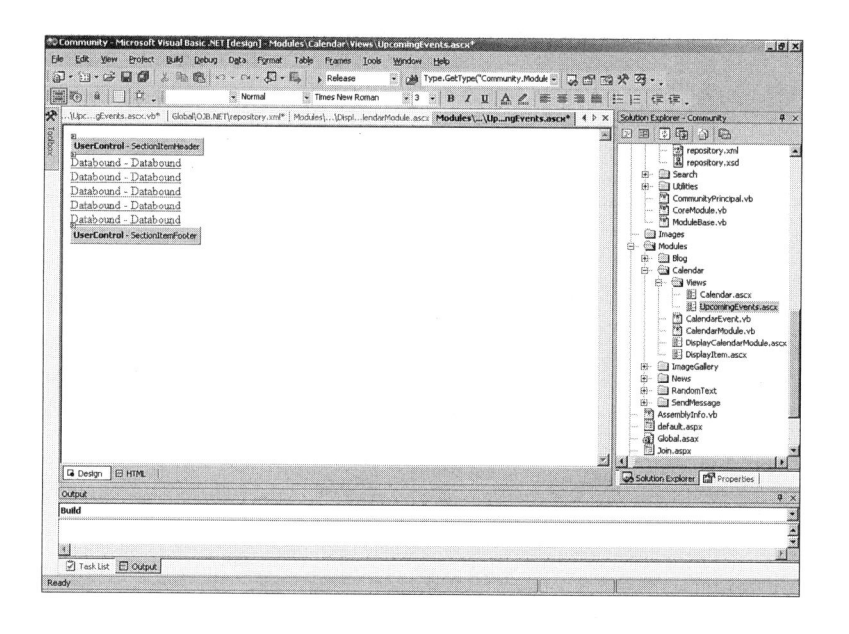

FIGURE 10.5
Design view for `Upcoming-Events.ascx`.

3. Add code to initialize the control.

Open the code-behind and add the following code to the `Page_Load` event handler:

320 Adding a New Module

STEP-BY-STEP GUIDE: **Adding a View to Display a Graphical Calendar**

```
Private Sub Page_Load(ByVal sender As System.Object, _
                     ByVal e As System.EventArgs) _
            Handles MyBase.Load

  Dim calMod As CalendarModule
  If Me.IsGlobal Then
    calMod = New CalendarModule
    EventsRepeater.DataSource = calMod.GetUpcomingEvents(5)
  Else
    calMod = New CalendarModule(Me.SectionItem.ModuleInstance)
    EventsRepeater.DataSource = calMod.GetUpcomingEvents(5)
  End If

  EventsRepeater.DataBind()

End Sub
```

STEP-BY-STEP GUIDE:
Adding a View to Display a Graphical Calendar

The first view we implemented wasn't particularly exciting. We will now make use of the excellent `Calendar` control that is included with ASP.NET to create a more graphical way for users of the community to see what is coming up.

As with the `DisplayUpcomingEvents` control, we only need to implement a single user control because we will be using the functionality we provided in the `CalendarModule` class to do most of the work.

1. Create the control.

Create a new user control in `Modules/Calendar/Views/`. Name it `Calendar.ascx`.

Open the code-behind and have the control inherit from the `SectionItemControl` class:

```
Public Class Calendar
   Inherits SectionItemControl
```

2. Add controls.

Add controls as shown in Listing 10.5.

STEP-BY-STEP GUIDE: **Adding a View to Display a Graphical Calendar**

LISTING 10.5 Modules/Calendar/Views/Calendar.ascx

```
<%@ Register Tagprefix="Community" Tagname="SectionItemHeader"
➥src="../../../Global/Controls/SectionItemHeader.ascx" %>
<%@ Register Tagprefix="Community" Tagname="SectionItemFooter"
➥src="../../../Global/Controls/SectionItemFooter.ascx" %>
<%@ Control Language="vb" AutoEventWireup="false"
➥Codebehind="Calendar.ascx.vb" Inherits="Community.Calendar"
➥TargetSchema="http://schemas.microsoft.com/intellisense/ie5" %>
<div>
  <Community:SectionItemHeader id="SectionItemHeader" runat="server" />
</div>
<div>
  <table>
    <tr>
      <td>
        <asp:Calendar id="Calendar1" runat="server" Width="184px" BorderWidth="1px"
        ➥NextPrevFormat="FullMonth"
          BackColor="Transparent" ForeColor="Black" Height="190px" Font-Size="9pt"
          ➥Font-Names="Verdana"
          BorderColor="Transparent">
          <TodayDayStyle BackColor="#CCCCCC"></TodayDayStyle>
          <NextPrevStyle Font-Size="8pt" Font-Bold="True" ForeColor="#333333"
          ➥VerticalAlign="Bottom"></NextPrevStyle>
          <DayHeaderStyle Font-Size="8pt" Font-Bold="True"></DayHeaderStyle>
          <SelectedDayStyle ForeColor="White" BackColor="#333399"></SelectedDayStyle>
          <TitleStyle Font-Size="12pt" Font-Bold="True" BorderWidth="4px"
          ➥ForeColor="#333399" BorderColor="Black"
            BackColor="White"></TitleStyle>
          <OtherMonthDayStyle ForeColor="#999999"></OtherMonthDayStyle>
        </asp:Calendar>
      </td>
      <td valign="top">
        <asp:DataList id="EventsDataList" runat="server">
          <ItemTemplate>
            <div>
              <a class="SummaryItemText" href="default.aspx?Module=
              ➥<%#Container.DataItem.ModuleInstance.CommunityModule.PrimaryKey1%>
              ➥&Item=<%#Container.DataItem.PrimaryKey1%>">
                <%#Container.DataItem.Name%>
              </a>
            </div>
          </ItemTemplate>
```

322 Adding a New Module

STEP-BY-STEP GUIDE: **Adding a View to Display a Graphical Calendar**

LISTING 10.5 `Modules/Calendar/Views/Calendar.ascx` (continued)

```
      </asp:DataList>
    </td>
  </tr>
</table>
<div>
  <Community:SectionItemFooter id="SectionItemFooter" runat="server" />
  <P></P>
</div>
</div>
```

The design view for the control is shown in Figure 10.6.

FIGURE 10.6
Design view for
Modules/Views/
Calendar.ascx.

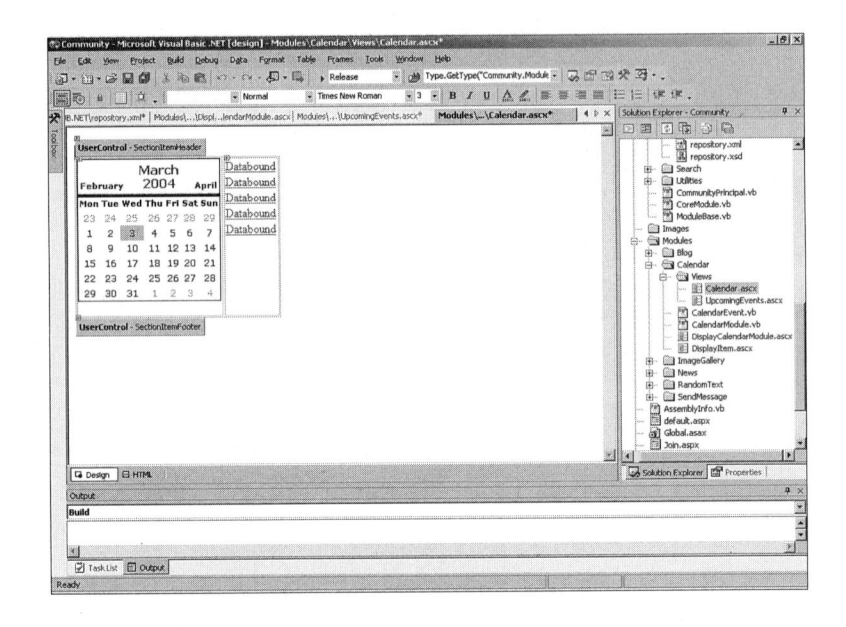

3. Add a method to bind the data.

Add the following method to the `Modules/Views/Calendar.ascx.vb`:

```
Private Sub BindData()

    Dim selectedDate As DateTime
    Dim selectedMonth As DateTime
```

STEP-BY-STEP GUIDE: **Adding a View to Display a Graphical Calendar**

```
    If Calendar1.SelectedDate = Nothing Then                            1 ▼
        selectedDate = DateTime.Now
    Else
        selectedDate = Calendar1.SelectedDate
    End If


    If Calendar1.VisibleDate = DateTime.MinValue Then                   2 ▼
        selectedMonth = DateTime.Now
    Else
        selectedMonth = Calendar1.VisibleDate
    End If


    Dim monthEvents As IList

    Dim calMod As CalendarModule
    If Me.IsGlobal Then                                                 3 ▼
        calMod = New CalendarModule
        monthEvents = calMod.GetEventsForMonth(selectedMonth)
    Else
        calMod = New CalendarModule(Me.SectionItem.ModuleInstance)
        monthEvents = calMod.GetEventsForMonth(selectedMonth)
    End If


    _DaysWithEvents = New ArrayList

    Dim todaysEvents As New ArrayList
    Dim ev As CalendarEvent
    For Each ev In monthEvents                                          4 ▼
        'if the event is on the selected
        'day then add it to todays events
        If ev.EventDate.Date = selectedDate.Date Then
            todaysEvents.Add(ev)
        End If
        _DaysWithEvents.Add(ev.EventDate.Date)
    Next

    EventsDataList.DataSource = todaysEvents                            5 ▼
    EventsDataList.DataBind()

End Sub
```

324 Adding a New Module

STEP-BY-STEP GUIDE: Adding a View to Display a Graphical Calendar

Note that a field of the class, `_DaysWithEvents`, is used to store an array of the dates in the current month that have events. Therefore, we need to add this field to the class:

```
Public Class Calendar
   Inherits SectionItemControl

   Private _DaysWithEvents As ArrayList
```

1▲ If the `Calendar` control has no date selected, we set our temporary selected date to the current date and time. If there is a date selected, we use it. The temporary selected date variable will be used to select the events that should be displayed in the list to the side of the calendar.

2▲ We do a similar thing for the selected month. We check whether the `Calendar` control has a month specified. In this case, if a month is not selected, its selected month will be set to `DateTime.MinValue`—the earliest possible date for a `DateTime`. If there is a month selected, we use it; if not, we use the current date (and thus the current month).

3▲ If we are displaying the global instance, we simply create an instance of the Calendar module business service class and get the events for the selected month. If we are displaying a specific instance, we create the business service class with the module instance and then get the events.

4▲ We then loop through the events and their dates to a private `ArrayList` class member (`_DaysWithEvents`), so we know which days to highlight in the `Calendar` control. If they happen on the selected day, we also add the events to the `ArrayList`, so we can display their details to the right of the `Calendar` control.

5▲ Finally, we set the data source of the `DataList` control to be today's events, and databind it.

4. Add event handlers.

We need to add several event handlers to the control.

First, add some code to `Page_Load` to do the initial databinding when the page is not processing a postback.

```
Private Sub Page_Load(ByVal sender As System.Object, _
                     ByVal e As System.EventArgs) _
        Handles MyBase.Load
   If Not Page.IsPostBack Then
      BindData()
   End If
End Sub
```

STEP-BY-STEP GUIDE: **Adding a View to Display a Graphical Calendar**

Then, add code to run when the selected day in the calendar is changed:

```
Private Sub Calendar1_SelectionChanged(ByVal sender As System.Object, _
                                ByVal e As System.EventArgs) _
          Handles Calendar1.SelectionChanged
  BindData()
End Sub
```

And code to run when the month shown in the calendar control is changed:

```
Private Sub Calendar1_VisibleMonthChanged(ByVal sender As Object, _
                                ByVal e As MonthChangedEventArgs) _
                 Handles Calendar1.VisibleMonthChanged
  BindData()
End Sub
```

5. Customize the way the days are displayed.

The calendar control gives us a large amount of control over how it is displayed. We will do something relatively simple—we will change the color of days that have events on them to red.

```
Private Sub Calendar1_DayRender(ByVal sender As Object, _
        ByVal e As System.Web.UI.WebControls.DayRenderEventArgs) _
    Handles Calendar1.DayRender
  If Not _DaysWithEvents Is Nothing Then
    If _DaysWithEvents.BinarySearch(e.Day.Date) < 0 Then
      e.Day.IsSelectable = False
    Else
      e.Cell.BorderColor = Color.Red
      e.Cell.BorderWidth = Unit.Pixel(2)
    End If
  End If

End Sub
```

We check that the `_DaysWithEvents DataList` has been populated. If it has, we use the `BinarySearch` method to check whether the current day is in the `ArrayList`. If it is not, we make it so it cannot be selected. If it is, we color it red and give it a border.

There are plenty of other formatting ideas that could be implemented in a similar way.

> **TIP**
> Binary search is a very efficient search algorithm. Using it is much faster than `ArrayList.Contains`, which will simply loop through the collection and compare each element to the value. When a binary search method is available, it is usually best to use it rather than `Contains`.

STEP-BY-STEP GUIDE: Implementing the View Item Control

Both of the module views we have implemented provide links to view specific events in more detail. We therefore need to implement the control that will display a single event.

The views use the `default.aspx?Module=[moduleID]&Item][itemID]` URL to display the events. This makes use of a feature of the community infrastructure that will look for a `DisplayItem.ascx` (or `Display[moduleName]Item`, if you implemented the name change suggested in the previous chapter) control in the module folder. Therefore, we need to implement `Modules/Calendar/DisplayCalendarItem.ascx`.

1. Create the user control.

Create a new user control in `Modules/Calendar` called `DisplayItem.ascx` (or `DisplayCalendarItem.ascx`, if you changed the code to include the module name in `DisplayItem` control names).

Open the code-behind and have the class inherit from the `ModuleItemControl` class:

```
Public Class DisplayItem1
    Inherits ModuleItemControl
```

2. Add controls (see Listing 10.6).

LISTING 10.6 Modules/Calendar/DisplayCalendarItem.ascx

```
<%@ Control Language="vb" AutoEventWireup="false" Codebehind="DisplayItem.ascx.vb"
➥Inherits="Community.DisplayItem1"
➥TargetSchema="http://schemas.microsoft.com/intellisense/ie5" %>
<div class="ModuleItemHeading">
  <asp:label id="HeadingLabel" runat="server"></asp:label>
</div>
<div class="ModuleItemDateAndMember">
  <span class="ModuleMainMember"><asp:label id="MemberLabel" runat="server"></asp:label>
    <asp:hyperlink id="MemberLink" runat="server"></asp:hyperlink>
  </span>
  -
  <span class="ModuleMainDate">
    <asp:label id="DateLabel" runat="server"></asp:label>
  </span>
```

STEP-BY-STEP GUIDE: **Implementing the View Item Control**

LISTING 10.6 `Modules/Calendar/DisplayCalendarItem.ascx` (continued)

```
</div>
<p></p>
<div class="ModuleItemBody" id="BodyDiv" runat="server"> </div>
<div class="ModuleItemMore">
  <asp:hyperlink id="SeeMoreLink" runat="server">
    See more in
  </asp:hyperlink>
</div>
<hr>
<div id="EditControls" runat="server">
  <div>Edit this item:</div>
  <table>
    <tr>
      <td style="WIDTH: 245px" vAlign="top">
        <asp:calendar id="EditCalendar" runat="server" Height="190px" Width="240px"
➥BorderWidth="1px" NextPrevFormat="FullMonth" BackColor="Transparent"
➥ForeColor="Black" Font-Size="9pt" Font-Names="Verdana" BorderColor="White">
          <TodayDayStyle BackColor="#CCCCCC"></TodayDayStyle>
          <NextPrevStyle Font-Size="8pt" Font-Bold="True" ForeColor="#333333"
          ➥VerticalAlign="Bottom">
          </NextPrevStyle>
          <DayHeaderStyle Font-Size="8pt" Font-Bold="True"></DayHeaderStyle>
          <SelectedDayStyle ForeColor="White" BackColor="#333399"></SelectedDayStyle>
          <TitleStyle Font-Size="12pt" Font-Bold="True" BorderWidth="4px"
          ➥ForeColor="#333399" BorderColor="Black" BackColor="White"></TitleStyle>
          <OtherMonthDayStyle ForeColor="#999999"></OtherMonthDayStyle>
        </asp:calendar></td>
      <td vAlign="top">
        <div>
          <asp:textbox id="NameTextbox" runat="server">
          </asp:textbox>
        </div>
        <div>
          <asp:textbox id="DescriptionTextBox" runat="server" Height="168px">
          </asp:textbox>
        </div>
      </td>
    </tr>
    <tr>
```

STEP-BY-STEP GUIDE: Implementing the View Item Control

LISTING 10.6 `Modules/Calendar/DisplayCalendarItem.ascx` (continued)

```
      <td align="center" colSpan="2">
        <asp:button id="UpdateButton" runat="server" Text="Update The Event"
➥Width="141px">
        </asp:button>
      </td>
    </tr>
  </table>
</div>
```

The design view for this control is shown in Figure 10.7.

FIGURE 10.7
Design view for Modules/Calendar/DisplayItem.ascx.

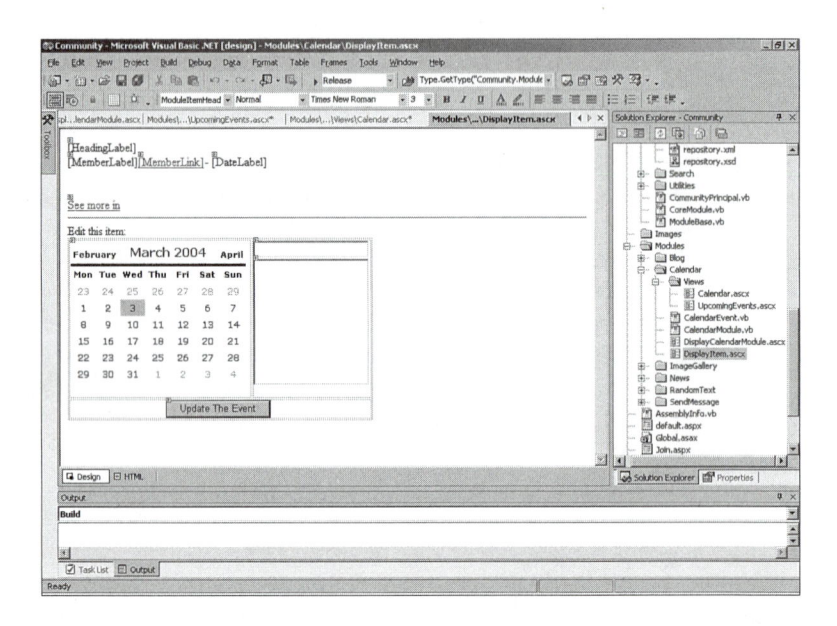

As previously, you will need to ensure that all of the controls have declarations in the code-behind, either by using the design view or by adding them manually.

3. Add code to initialize the control (see Listing 10.7).

STEP-BY-STEP GUIDE: **Implementing the View Item Control**

LISTING 10.7 Page_Load for Modules/Calendar/DisplayItem.ascx.vb

```
Private Sub Page_Load(ByVal sender As System.Object, _
                ByVal e As System.EventArgs) _
        Handles MyBase.Load

  If Request.QueryString("Item") = Nothing Then                              ①▼

    'show an error message here

  Else
    'all is good, so let's show the news item
    Dim calMod As New CalendarModule

    _item = calMod.GetEventByID(ItemID)
    If Not Page.IsPostBack Then                                              ②▼
      EditControls.Visible = False                                           ③▼
      SetText()

      SeeMoreLink.Text = SeeMoreLink.Text + " " + _item.ModuleInstance.Name  ④▼
      SeeMoreLink.NavigateUrl = "../../default.aspx?Module=" _
          _+ item.ModuleInstance.CommunityModule.PrimaryKey(0).ToString _
            + "&Instance=" + _item.ModuleInstance.PrimaryKey(0).ToString

      If Request.IsAuthenticated AndAlso _                                   ⑤▼
          _item.ModuleInstance.Member.PrimaryKey1 = _
            CType(Context.User, CommunityPrincipal).Member.PrimaryKey1 Then
        'the currently logged in member owns the item, so we can let them edit it

        EditControls.Visible = True
        EditCalendar.SelectedDate = _item.EventDate
        EditCalendar.VisibleDate = _item.EventDate
        NameTextbox.Text = _item.Name
        DescriptionTextBox.Text = _item.Description
      End If
    End If
  End If

End Sub
```

Adding a New Module

STEP-BY-STEP GUIDE: Implementing the View Item Control

1 ▲ The first thing we do is to check whether an item ID has been specified. If it has not, we should display an error message (although this has not been implemented yet). If there is an item ID, we get the item with the matching ID from the calendar module business service class.

2 ▲ Next, we check whether we are currently processing a postback. If we are, we will not need to do any more work in this method.

3 ▲ We then default the edit controls to invisible and call a method to set the text that is displayed for the event. We do this in a separate method because this code will need to be called from another event handler if the event is updated.

4 ▲ Now, we set up the See More In link, specifying both the text and the URL to use.

5 ▲ Finally, we check whether the currently logged-in user is the owner of the event. If he is, we make the edit controls visible and populate them with appropriate values.

4. Add code to set the displayed text.

Add the following method to the class:

```
Private Sub SetText()
   HeadingLabel.Text = _item.Name
   MemberLink.Text = _item.ModuleInstance.Member.Username
   MemberLink.NavigateUrl = "../../default.aspx?Member=" _
       + _item.ModuleInstance.Member.PrimaryKey(0).ToString

   DateLabel.Text = CType(_item.EventDate, DateTime).ToLongDateString
   BodyDiv.InnerHtml = FormatText(_item.Description)
End Sub
```

As mentioned before, we use a separate method to set these values because we will need to use this code from more than one place.

5. Add code to deal with the Update button being clicked.

Add the following event handler to the class:

```
Private Sub UpdateButton_Click(ByVal sender As System.Object, _
                               ByVal e As System.EventArgs) _
             Handles UpdateButton.Click
   Dim calMod As New CalendarModule
   _item = calMod.UpdateEvent(_item.PrimaryKey1, _
                    NameTextbox.Text, _
                    DescriptionTextBox.Text, _
```

```
                    EditCalendar.SelectedDate)
    SetText()
End Sub
```

We simply call the `UpdateEvent` method of the business service class and then reset the displayed text.

Making the Calendar Module Work

With all the controls implemented, the database table set up to hold events, an entry added to the repository, and the business service class ready for action, we should have a working Calendar module. There is just one more thing we need to do. In order for the module to work, we have to give the online community infrastructure some *metadata* about the module so that it will know how to use it. We will need to add an entry to the `tbl_Module` table for the module and some entries to the `tbl_ModuleView` table for the views.

The entry for tbl_Module is shown in Figure 10.8.

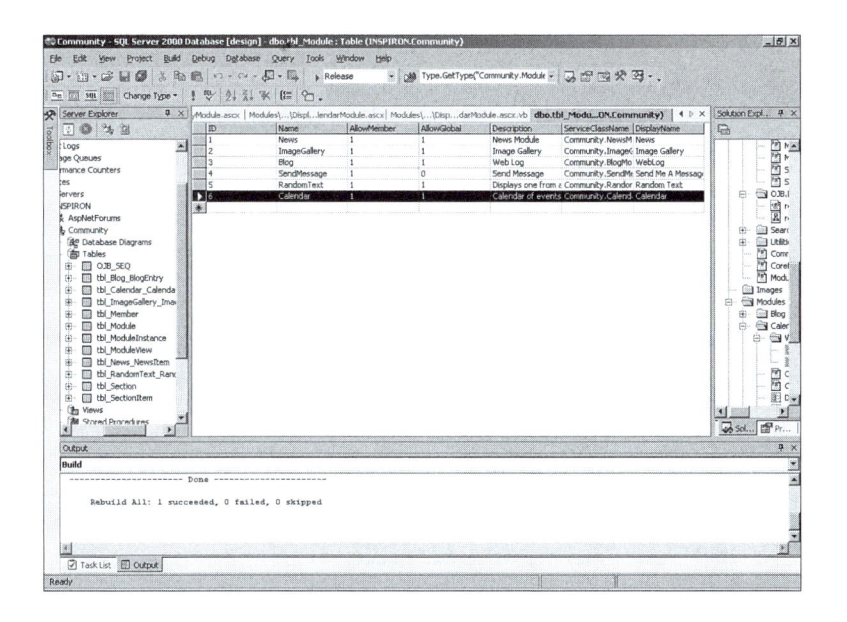

FIGURE 10.8
Entry in tbl_Module for the Calendar module.

The entries for tbl_ModuleView are shown in Figure 10.9.

Making the Calendar Module Work

FIGURE 10.9
Entries in tbl_ModuleView for the Calendar module.

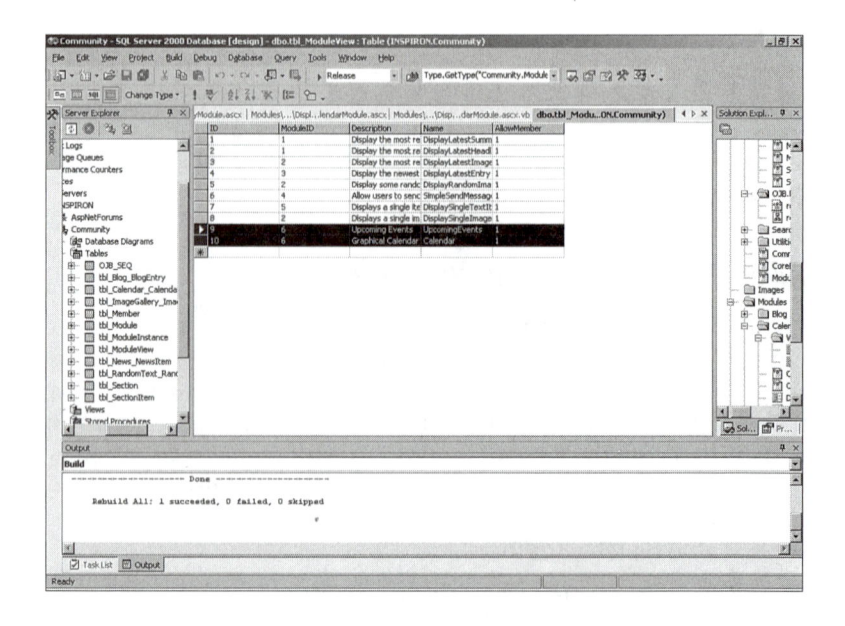

After these entries have been added, you should be able to create an instance of the Calendar module in the community and add the views to sections.

The graphical calendar control should look like that in Figure 10.10.

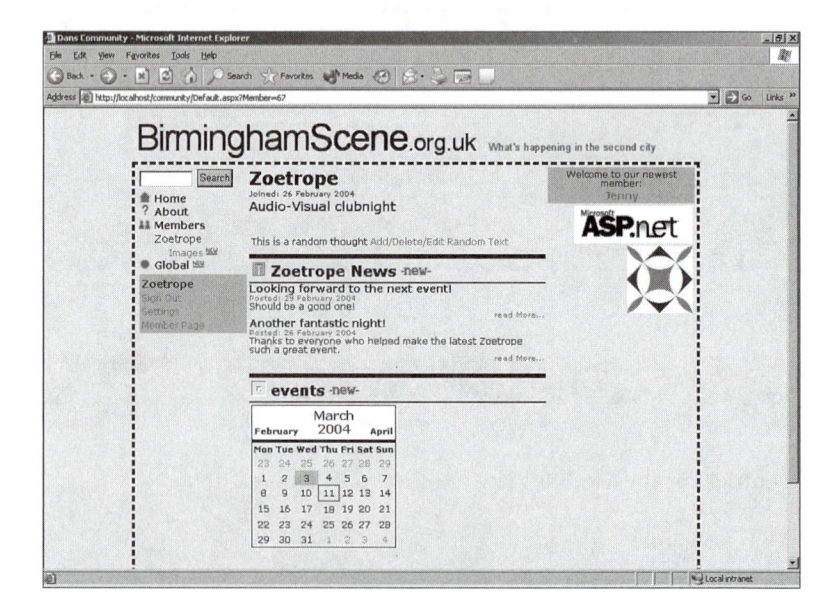

FIGURE 10.10
The graphical calendar view of the Calendar module.

CHALLENGE: **Displaying an Error Message**

When a day with an event is clicked, the names of the events for that day appear to the side of the calendar.

Clicking an event name will open the Display Item page, as shown in Figure 10.11.

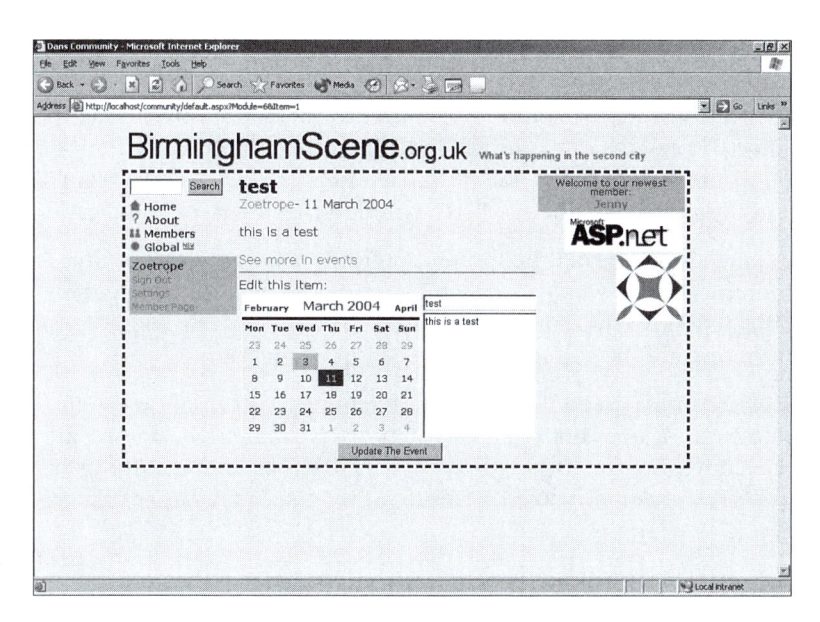

FIGURE 10.11
Viewing a single event in the Calendar module.

Notice that this is currently displaying the options for editing the event because we are logged in as the member who owns it.

CHALLENGE:
Adding a Delete Event Option

Currently, there is no way for members to delete an event completely. They can remove the text associated with it and move it to an old date, but it would be much nicer to provide a proper delete option.

CHALLENGE:
Displaying an Error Message

Change the code for the `DisplayItem` control so that an error message is displayed if no item ID is provided. You should also consider what should happen if the user supplies an ID, but no item with that ID exists.

Hint: If no event with the matching ID exists, nothing will be returned by the `GetEventByID` method of the business service class.

Integrating ASP.NET Forums with the Online Community Application

One major feature the community currently lacks is a forum system for members to discuss topics in which they share an interest. Fortunately, a good forum system has been built by members of the ASP.NET team at Microsoft and some others, which we are free to use in our applications.

We could simply install the forums application alongside our online community, but it would be much better if we were to integrate the forums properly with our community, so a member could log in to the community and be automatically logged in to the forums.

ASP.NET Forums uses a different architecture than our online community application—it does not use a persistence service. Instead, it uses data access components and stored procedures to persist and recover its data. Most strikingly of all, ASP.NET Forums is written in C# rather than in VB.NET.

These differences will not prevent us from integrating the two applications—provided both applications can accept the same authentication cookie, they will both recognize the same users.

STEP-BY-STEP GUIDE: Integrating ASP.NET Forums

Here are the steps we need to take to integrate ASP.NET Forums with our online community:

1. Install the database.
2. Create permissions on the database.
3. Install the `forums` Web folder.
4. Install the forums assembly.
5. Add configuration settings to `Web.config`.
6. Add a reference to the forums assembly to the community project.
7. Add code to insert new members in the forums database.
8. Add code to make community administrators forum administrators.

STEP-BY-STEP GUIDE: **Integrating ASP.NET Forums**

Install the database.

ASP.NET Forums uses a database of its own, separate from the main community database. It is possible to run them both from the same database, but it is much easier to keep them separate.

ASP.NET Forums comes with a SQL script that will install the database the forums use. Unfortunately, there are a couple of bugs in the script. However, there is a debugged version on the CD-ROM in this book that you can use to install the application.

Open Query Analyzer and connect to the database server. Load the `ASPNETForums.sql` script and execute it. You should see the various objects being created.

If you do not have Query Analyzer, you can use the `OSql` command-line tool that comes with MSDE. You will need to use a command like

```
OSql -E -I ASPNETForums.sql
```

from the folder where the script is located. This command uses Windows authentication to connect to the database and takes its commands from the specified file.

Create permissions on the database.

To use the database, ASP.NET will need to be able to access it. Use Enterprise Manager to set up the ASP.NET account with data reading and writing privileges on the forums database. You will also need to give the ASP.NET account execute privileges on all of the stored procedures that were created.

Install the `forums` Web folder.

Copy the `ASPNETForums` subfolder from inside the `ASPNETForums` folder on the CD-ROM to your online community folder in `Inetpub/wwwroot` (or wherever you have chosen to install the online community code). Rename it `forums`. This folder contains all the pages and user controls the forums need to run. It does not include code-behind classes or any other classes—these are stored in the compiled assembly for the forums.

Note that this version of the forums code has had some changes made to it from the version that was originally available for download. These changes were made to correct some problems that prevented some parts of the application from picking up the fact that the forums were configured to work in a subfolder of our application rather than be an application in its own right.

STEP-BY-STEP GUIDE: **Integrating ASP.NET Forums**

The files that were changed include

- `Engine/Componets/Globals.vb`
- `Engine/Controls/ForumGroupRepeater.vb`
- `Engine/Controls/BaseClasses/SkinnedForumWebControl.vb`

4 ▲ Install the forums assembly.

Copy `ASPNETForums.dll` from the bin subfolder of the new forums subfolder to the bin folder directly under your community application folder. We have to do this because ASP.NET expects to find assemblies with compiled code-behind in a bin folder under the root of the application. We want ASP.NET Forums to be a part of our online community application rather than an application in its own right.

5 ▲ Add configuration settings to `Web.config`.

We now need to add the configuration settings ASP.NET Forums needs. Add the following element to the top of the `Web.config` file:

```
<?xml version="1.0" encoding="utf-8" ?>
<configuration>

  <configSections>
    <section name="AspNetForumsSettings"
             type="System.Configuration.NameValueFileSectionHandler,
             ↪ System, Version=1.0.3300.0, Culture=neutral,
             ↪PublicKeyToken=b77a5c561934e089" />
  </configSections>
```

This defines a new settings section for the forums settings. We specify that it will consist of name value pairs (like the appsettings section does).

Now, add the section shown in Listing 10.8 within `<configuration>`, but outside of any other sections.

LISTING 10.8   ASP.NET Forums Configuration Section

```
<AspNetForumsSettings>
    <add key="DataProviderAssemblyPath" value="AspNetForums.dll" />

    <!--
    *******************************
    Application Settings
    *******************************
```

STEP-BY-STEP GUIDE: **Integrating ASP.NET Forums**

LISTING 10.8 ASP.NET Forums Configuration Section (continued)

```
    -->
    <add key="availableSkins" value="default;LightBlue"/>
    <add key="defaultPageSize" value="25"/>
    <add key="connectionString"
➥value="server=(local);Trusted_Connection=true;
➥database=ASPNETForums" />
    <add key="defaultDateFormat" value="dd MMM yyyy"/>
    <add key="defaultTimeFormat" value="hh:mm tt"/>
    <add key="pathToTransformationFile" value="/transform.txt" />
    <add key="smtpServer" value="default" />
<!-- Can specify SMTP Server to use to send out emails.
➥Use "default" to use the default Windows 2000 SMTP Server -->
    <add key="allowDuplicatePosts" value="false" />
<!-- Whether or not you wish to allow messages with duplicate
➥bodies being posted in various forums -->
    <add key="dbTimeZoneOffset" value="-6" />
<!-- The timezone offset of your database server.
➥ (GMT is +0; EST = -5;) -->
    <add key="siteName" value="ASP.NET Forums" />
<!-- The name of your AspNetForums.NET Web site. -->
    <add key="DataProviderClassName"
➥value="AspNetForums.Data.SqlDataProvider" />
    <add key="urlWebSite" value="http://localhost" />

    <!--
    If the ASP.NET Forums are configured to run in a directory
    that is not an IIS VRoot, provide the name of that directory here.
    -->
    <add key="forumsDirectory" value="/Forums" />


    <!--
    *****************************
    URL Resource Paths
    *****************************
    -->
    <add key="urlHome" value="/Default.aspx" />
    <add key="urlShowPost" value="/ShowPost.aspx?PostID=" />
```

STEP-BY-STEP GUIDE: **Integrating ASP.NET Forums**

LISTING 10.8   ASP.NET Forums Configuration Section
(continued)

```
    <add key="urlShowAllUsers" value="/User/ShowAllUsers.aspx" />
    <add key="urlSearch" value="/Search/default.aspx" />
    <add key="urlQuickSearch" value="/Search/default.aspx?searchText=" />
    <add key="urlSearchForPostsByUser"
➥value="/Search/default.aspx?SearchFor=1^SearchText=" />
    <add key="urlRegister" value="/User/CreateUser.aspx" />
    <add key="urlEditUserProfile" value="/User/EditUserProfile.aspx" />
    <add key="urlLogin" value="/login.aspx" />
    <add key="urlAdmin" value="/Admin/default.aspx" />
    <add key="urlAdminEditUser" value="/Admin/EditUser.aspx?Username=" />
    <add key="urlLogout" value="/logout.aspx" />
    <add key="urlShowForum" value="/ShowForum.aspx?ForumID=" />
    <add key="urlShowForumGroup" value="/ShowForumGroup.aspx?ForumGroupID=" />
    <add key="urlShowUserProfile" value="/User/UserProfile.aspx?UserName=" />
    <add key="urlReplyToPost" value="/AddPost.aspx?PostID=" />
    <add key="urlUserEditPost" value="/EditPost.aspx?PostID=" />
    <add key="urlAddNewPost" value="/AddPost.aspx?ForumID=" />
    <add key="urlMyForums" value="/User/MyForums.aspx" />
    <add key="urlChangePassword" value="/User/ChangePassword.aspx" />
    <add key="urlForgotPassword" value="/User/EmailForgottenPassword.aspx" />
    <add key="urlModeration" value="/Moderate/default.aspx" />
    <add key="urlModerateForumPosts" value="/Moderate/ModerateForum.aspx?ForumId=" />
    <add key="urlEditPost" value="/Moderate/EditPost.aspx?PostID=" />
    <add key="urlDeletePost" value="/Moderate/DeletePost.aspx?PostID=" />
    <add key="urlManageForumPosts" value="/Moderate/ManageForum.aspx?ForumId=" />
    <add key="urlMovePost" value="/Moderate/MovePost.aspx?PostID=" />
    <add key="urlModerateThread" value="/Moderate/ModerateThread.aspx?PostId=" />
    <add key="urlEditForum" value="/Admin/EditForum.aspx?ForumID=" />
    <add key="urlCreateForum" value="/Admin/CreateNewForum.aspx" />
    <add key="urlShowForumPostsForAdmin" value="/Admin/ShowPosts.aspx?ForumID=" />
    <add key="urlMessage" value="/Msgs/default.aspx?MessageId=" />
    <add key="urlModerationHistory" value="/Moderate/ModerationHistory.aspx?PostId=" />
</AspNetForumsSettings>
```

We also need to add a couple of new location elements to ensure that only logged-in members can add or edit posts:

```
<location path="Forums/AddPost.aspx">
  <system.web>
    <authorization>
```

```
        <deny users="?" />
      </authorization>
    </system.web>
</location>

<location path="Forums/EditPost.aspx">
  <system.web>
    <authorization>
      <deny users="?" />
    </authorization>
  </system.web>
</location>
```

We could completely deny anonymous users access to the forums, with a location element like this one:

```
<location path="Forums">
  <system.web>
    <authorization>
      <deny users="?" />
    </authorization>
  </system.web>
</location>
```

Add a reference to the forums assembly to the community project.

We want to be able to access the forums code from our community code so that we can add new members to the forums database and remove deleted members. In order to do this, we will need to add a reference to the forums assembly.

Right-click the community project in the Solution Explorer and select Add Reference. Browse to the bin folder of the application and select the `ASPNETForums.dll` assembly.

Add code to insert new members in the forums database.

When a new member registers with our community, we need to add him or her to the forums database. Open `CoreModule.vb` and find the `CreateMember` method we use to create new members. Add the following code:

```
Public Function CreateMember(ByVal pUsername As String, _
                             ByVal pPassword As String, _
                             ByVal pIntrotext As String, _
```

STEP-BY-STEP GUIDE: Integrating ASP.NET Forums

```
                                    ByVal pEmail As String, _
                                    ByVal pPublicEmail As Boolean) As Member

    Dim mem As Member = New Member(pUsername, _
                                   pPassword, _
                                   pIntrotext, _
                                   pEmail, _
                                   pPublicEmail)

    'add the member to the forums database
    Dim forumUser As New AspNetForums.Components.User
    forumUser.Username = pUsername
    forumUser.Password = pPassword
    forumUser.Email = pEmail
    forumUser.PublicEmail = pPublicEmail

    AspNetForums.Users.CreateNewUser(forumUser, False)

    Return mem
End Function
```

We create a new `User` object from the `AspNetForums.Components` namespace. This is the class that ASP.NET Forums uses to represent registered users. We then populate the new object with the same details we used to create our `Member` persistent object.

The `AspNetForums.Components.User` object is not a persistent object in it own right, however. To store the user in the forums database, we need to explicitly execute the forums data access code. We do this with a call to the `AspNetForums.Users.CreateNewUser` method.

8 ▲ Add code to make community administrators forum administrators.

To give all our administrators the privileges they need to administrate the forums, we must ensure that they have the correct role in their `CommunityPrincipal` object. We can do that with a simple change to `global.asax`:

```
Sub Application_AuthenticateRequest(ByVal sender As Object, _
                                    ByVal e As EventArgs)

    If Request.IsAuthenticated Then
       'we want to attach a CommmunityPrincipal
       'in place of the GenericPrincipal

       Dim coreMod As CoreModule = New CoreModule
```

STEP-BY-STEP GUIDE: **Integrating ASP.NET Forums**

```
    Dim member As Member = _
      coreMod.GetMemberByUserName(Context.User.Identity.Name)

    If Not member.IsActivated Then
      'the member is not activated,
      'so they should not be authenticated
      Dim id As New GenericIdentity("")
      Dim principal As New GenericPrincipal(id, New String() {})

      Context.User = principal
    Else

      Dim roles As String() = {}
      If member.IsAdmin Then
        ReDim roles(1)
        roles(0) = "administrator"
        roles(1) = "Forum-Administrators"
      End If


      Dim principal As CommunityPrincipal = _
        New CommunityPrincipal(member, Context.User.Identity, roles)

      Context.User = principal
    End If
  End If
End Sub
```

We make the roles array a two-element array and include the forums administration role in the second element. ASP.NET Forums will now recognize users with this role as administrators.

After you have made these changes, you should be able to browse to `Community/Forum` and see something like Figure 10.12.

Although the forums are integrated with our community codewise, they are not very integrated in terms of look and feel. Fortunately, the forums system is based on cascading style sheets in the same way as our main community application, so it is easy to change the forums to match the community.

ASP.NET Forums uses a system of "skins" to allow different users to have the forums display different appearances. The style sheet for the default skin can be found in `forums\skins\default\style`. It is well commented, so making changes to it is easy.

STEP-BY-STEP GUIDE: **Integrating ASP.NET Forums**

FIGURE 10.12
ASP.NET Forums in action as part of the online community.

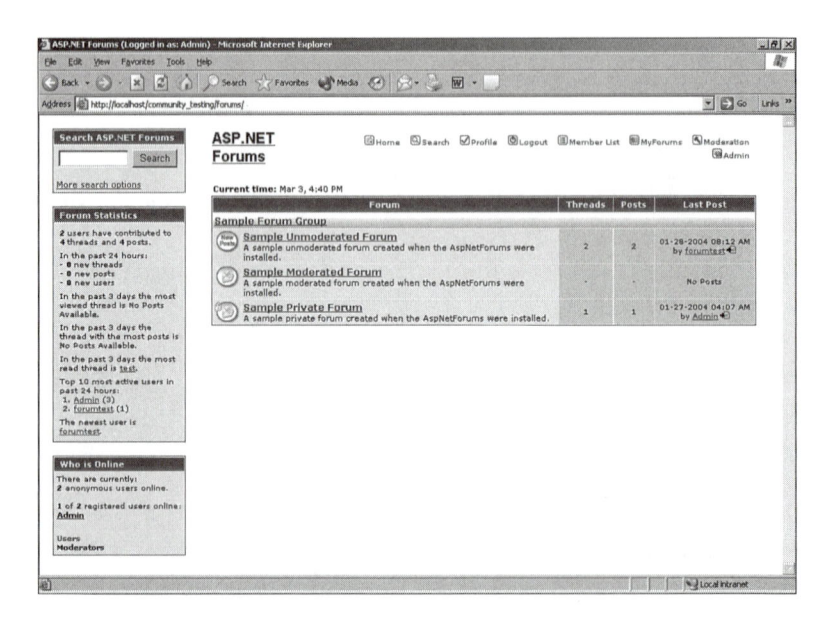

A full discussion of how to use the ASP.NET Forums application is beyond the scope of this book, but don't worry—it is pretty self-explanatory and there is plenty of help available online, especially at www.asp.net. I will also be happy to help you if you have any problems integrating the forums with the online community application.

Moving On

So, we reach the end of this book. Hopefully, this is not the end of your involvement with the online community application we have been playing with, though. There are plenty more features that could be implemented—both global application features and specific modules.

Here are some ideas for further improvements:

- ▶ The search system is currently pretty rudimentary. It could be improved by making the modules return search results with relevance values that have been calculated (for example, from the number of occurrences of the search term in the item).

- ▶ A polling module would be a good way to allow members to give their opinions on issues that interest the community.

- ▶ You might want to allow members to upload other content than images, such as video or music files.

- The Members page could be improved by having it display information about how many sections each member has, when they last added information, and so on.
- The Extras control could be used to add additional features to the site—you could even add a new kind of view to the modules that is designed to be displayed in the right column.
- Depending on the interests of your community, there will be different ideas for new modules. Sporting communities might like a League Table module, bird watchers might want a Log Book module to record the birds they spot, and a book group might want a module that provides links to an online book store for their favorite books. (Make sure to take advantage of affiliate schemes.)
- The community application provides an infrastructure you can build upon. Hopefully, you now understand enough about how the application works to add features of your own. If you want to learn more about the application, my best suggestion is to experiment with it. Play with the code and see what happens. Set a goal for yourself of implementing a feature and see how well you do.
- There is no substitute for getting hands-on with a real application and seeing what you can make it do.

Index

Symbols

& operator, string concatenation, 256
/bin folder, storing assemblies, 133
<div> elements, 152
_ (underscore), 43

A

A.NavigationItem class (CSS), 73
A.NavigationSubItem class (CSS), 73
A.NavigationSubSubItem class (CSS), 73
access
    data, efficient, 281-285
    denied, troubleshooting, 9
    online community applications, 5
accessors, property, 77
addresses, valid email, 139-142. *See also* IP addresses
admin subfolder, adding Web Forms, 173
administration system
    members
        Global/CommunityPrinciple.vb files, 171-172
        member management facilities, adding, 172-188
        protecting, 169-171
    online community applications, 23

administrators
    defined, 25
    forums, creating, 340-341
aligning navigation icons, 87
Anchor class (CSS), 74
applications. *See also* online community applications
    backgrounds, 70-72
    borders, 73
    breaking, 69
    design considerations, 70
    final, 4, 11
    starting-point, 4, 11-12
ASP.NET Forums, integrating, 334-342
ASP.NET pages, 27
assemblies
    forum, 336, 339
    storing, 133
attributes
    backgrounds, 70
    text, 74
    vertical-align, 87
AuthenticateRequest event handler, 170-171
automatic summaries, news items, 158

B

backgrounds, applications, 70-72
banning members, 224-226
base classes, CommunityPO inheritance, 301
Bin folder, 39
blocks, try/catch, 137
Blog module, GetResourceUsage function, 214-215
BlogEntrySummary class, 291
bold formatting, news items, 160
Boolean properties, check box columns, 180-181
borders, applications, 73
breaking applications, 69, 80-82
broken images, troubleshooting, 97
Build menu commands, Build Solution, 6
Build Solution command (Build menu), 6
business service classes, 28
    creating, modules, 306-314
    ModuleBase class, 37-38
Button, Edit Update Cancel command (Columns menu), 186
buttons, default, 134

C

C:\Inetpub\wwwroot\community\global\OJB.NET\repository.xml error, 9
caching
    module view controls, 250
    OJB.NET persistence service, 36
    refactoring code, 247
        dynamic controls, 251
        page output, 248-250
        partial pages, 250
        user controls, 250
Calendar modules, adding metadata, 331-333
CalendarEvent class, creating, 301
calendars, graphical, 320-325
calling methods, looping, 111
calls, Type.GetType, 270
cascading deleted members, 229-232

columns 347

Cascading Style Sheets (CSS)
    ASP.NET Forums, 341
    classes, 69-76
ChangePassword.aspx file, event handler, 197
check box columns, Boolean properties, 180-181
classes
    base, CommunityPO, 301
    BlogEntrySummary, 291
    business service, 28
        creating, modules, 306-314
        ModuleBase class, 37-38
    CalendarEvent, creating, 301
    CoreModule, methods, 238
    CSS (Cascading Style Sheets), 69-76
    Member
        fields, adding, 236
        persistence service repository, 236-238
        properties, adding, 236
    ModuleBase, 37-38, 208-209
    NewsItemSummary, 286-291
    RandomTextItem, removing, 269-270
    StringBuilder, string concatenation, 253-260
    utility, converting IList type, 173-176
cleanup method, implementing business service class, 310
client script files, WebControl (online community applications), 9
code
    adding, login controls, 238-239
    databinding, breaking out, 278-279
    Global/CommunityPrinciple.vb files, 171-172
    IL (Intermediate Language), 83
    IP addresses, viewing, 239-240
    markup, news items, 159-162

Modules/News/DisplayItem.ascx, 149-151
Modules/SendMessage/SimpleSendMessagebox.ascx, 137-139
navigation.ascx control, 77-85
online community applications
    CoreModule.vb file, 47-55
    default.aspx file, 40-47
    DisplayLatestHeadlines.ascx file, 55-57
    NewsModule.vb file, 57-60
refactoring
    caching, 247-251
    data access, efficient, 281-285
    file naming, 292-294
    magic numbers, eliminating, 260-264
    magic numbers, managing code, 271-279
    magic numbers, RandomTextItem class, 269-270
    magic numbers, thumbnail width, 264-269
    magic numbers, Type.GetType calls class, 270
    reusable code, creating, 279-281
    summary objects, 285-291
    viewstates, 251-260
reorganizing, 271-278
reusable, 133, 279-281
source code, 4-7
collections, SortedList, 110
color attribute (text), 74
colors
    backgrounds, 70
    links, navigation classes (CSS), 75
columns
    check box, Boolean properties, 180-181
    defining, 179-180

How can we make this index more useful? Email us at indexes@samspublishing.com

Columns menu commands, Button, Edit Update Cancel, 186

comments, CSS (Cascading Style Sheets) classes, 69

Community folder, 38

CommunityModule object, properties, 31-32

CommunityPO base class, inheritance, 301

compiling source code, 6-7

Computer Name command (Properties menu), 8

computers, names, 8

concatenation, strings, 253-260

configurations
    online community application, 8
    thumbnail widths, 264-269

confirmations, email (member registration), 205

constructors
    adding, persistence objects, 303
    implementing, business service classes, 307

controls, 28
    CustomValidator, news text limits, 157-158
    DataGrid
        adding, 176
        enabling editing, 186-188
        initializing, 176-178
        sorting, 185-186
    DefaultButtons, 133-134
    display module, implementing, 314-317
    DisplayItem, 149-155
    edit, visibility, 151
    image, creating, 296
    login
        code, adding, 238-239
        modules, 18
    module view, caching, 250

navigation.ascx, 77-85

NewestMember.ascx, 116-119

repeater, adding, 112-113

SectionItemHeader, 91-93
    icons, adding, 96-98
    image number, 94-95

user, 250, 296

view item, implementing, 326-331

Controls folder, 39

converting IList type, DataTable object, 173-176

cookies, persisted logins, 241-243

CoreModule class, adding methods, 238

CoreModule.vb file, 47-55

Could Not Load Type error, troubleshooting, 10

Criteria objects, CoreModule.vb files, 50

CSS (Cascading Style Sheets)
    ASP.NET Forums, 341
    classes, 69-76

custom images, members, 119-126

custom SQL, efficient data access, 283-285

CustomValidator controls, news text limits, 157-158

D

data access, efficient, 281-285

data files, online community application, 8

Data folder, 39

data quotas, setting (member resource usage), 207-223

databases
    entries, adding, 297
    forums, members, inserting, 339-340

installing, ASP.NET Forums, 335

setting up, online community applications, 7

SQL Server, 36

tables

    adding, 305

    IPAddress persistent objects, 235

databinding code, breaking out, 278-279

databinding subroutines, databinding code, 278-279

DataGrid control

    adding, 176

    editing, enabling, 186-188

    initializing, 176-178

    sorting, 185-186

DataTable objects, IList type, 173-176

deactivated member data, hiding, 226-228

default buttons, adding, 134

default.aspx files, 40-47

DefaultButtons control, 133-134

denied access, troubleshooting, 9

designing applications, considerations, 70

Details tab (members), 19

display module controls, implementing, 314-317

display text, 126

DisplayItem control, 149-155

DisplayLatestHeadlines.ascx files, 55-57

DisplaySection() method, default.aspx files, 44-46

DisplaySingleImage view, 299

downloading MSDE, 3

dynamic controls, caching (refactoring code), 251

E

edit controls, visibililty, 151

Edit Template menu commands, PublicEmail, 181

elements, <div>, 152

email

    confirmations, member registration, 205

    global SendMessage instances, allowing, 145-148

    Modules/SendMessage/SimpleSendMessageBox.ascx code, 137-139

    One-Use-Only Change Password, 197

    reminders, member registration, 205

    sending, troubleshooting, 142-144

    SendMessageModule.vb file, 135-137

    subject lines, 148

email addresses, valid, 139-142

encryption, one-way, 189-197

enumerators, searches (online community application), 63-65

error messages, displaying, 333

errors

    C:\Inetpub\wwwroot\community\global\OJB.NET\repository.xml, 9

    Could Not Load Type, 10

    Microsoft.Web.UI.WebControls, 9

    SQL Server Does Not Exist or Access Denied, 10

event handlers

    AutheticateRequest, 170-171

    ChangePassword.aspx file, 197

    Page_Load

        aspx.files, 41-44

        SectionItemHeader control, 92-94

How can we make this index more useful? Email us at indexes@samspublishing.com

event handlers

Request Button, 193-194
update, 187-188

events
adding, business service class, 310-311
deleting, modules, 333
retrieving, business service class, 311-314

expressions
regular
obtaining online, 141
searches, 256-257
valid email addresses, 139-141
values, 140-141
short-circuiting, 203

F

fields
adding, Member class, 236
private, adding, 302

file formats
Graphical Interchange Format (.gif), 87
Portable Network Graphic (.png), 87

files
ChangePassword.aspx, event handler, 197
online community applications, 9
CoreModule.vb, 47-55
data, online community application, 8
default.aspx, 40-47
DisplayLatestHeadlines.ascx, 55-57
ForgotPassword.aspx, 190-191
Global/CommunityPrinciple.vb, 171-172
jpeg, member images, 125
naming (code refactoring), 292-294

NewsModule.vb, 57-60
repository, online community application, 8
SendMessageModule.vb, 135-137
source code, files, 4
.vb, recompiling, 95
Web.config, configuration settings, 336-339

final applications, 4, 11

FindObject method, CoreModule.vb files, 49

folders
/bin, storing assemblies, 39, 133
Community, 38
Controls, 39
CoreObjects, 39
Data, 39
Global, 39
Images, 40
Modules, 40
OJB.NET, 40
online community application, 38-40
Search, 39
subfolders, admin, 173
Web folders, forums, 335

font attributes (text), 74

ForgotPassword.aspx file, 190-191

forgotten passwords, 190
hashing, 189-197
One-Use-Only Change Password emails, 197
secret questions, 189

formats. *See* file formats

formatting
bold, 160
news items, 152-155
style sheets, 86

forums
- ASP.NET Forums, 334-342
- administrators, creating, 340-341
- assemblies, 336, 339
- databases, inserting members, 339-340

forums Web folder, installing, 335

functions, GetResourceUsage
- Blog module, 214-215
- ImageGallery module, 210-214
- Member object, 217
- ModuleInstance object, 215-216
- News module, 209
- RandomText module, 209
- SendMessage module, 210

G

GetLatestGlobalNewsItems method, 57-60

GetResourceUsage function
- Blog module, 214-215
- ImageGallery module, 210-214
- Member object, 217
- ModuleInstance object, 215-216
- News module, 209
- RandomText module, 209
- SendMessage module, 210

GetResourceUsage method, implementing, 307-308

GetSearchResults method, 61-62, 308-309

.gif format (Graphical Interchange Format), 87

Global folder, 39

global instances
- allowing, Send Message module, 145-148
- defined, 26
- distinguishing with icons, 99

global modules, online community applications, 12, 16-18

global sections, 76, 87-88

Global/CommunityPrinciple.vb files, 171-172

graphical calendars, displaying, 320-325

Graphical Interchange Format (.gif) format, 87

graphics. See images

H

hashing forgotten passwords, 189-197

headers, SectionItemHeader control, 91-93
- icons, adding, 96-98
- image number, 94-95

hiding deactivated member data, 226-228

hyperlinks, news items, 160-161

I

icons
- adding
  - navigation, 86-88
  - SectionItemHeader control, 96-98
- global instances, distinguishing, 99
- navigation, 103-108
- tooltips, adding, 97-98
- updated instances, 99-103

How can we make this index more useful? Email us at indexes@samspublishing.com

352   IIS

IIS (Internet Information Services), community applications, 5
IL (Intermediate Language) code, 83
IList type, 31, 173-176
image controls, creating, 296
ImageGallery module
   GetResourceUsage function, 210-214
   image number, 94-95
   thumbnails, generating, 163-167
images
   backgrounds, 70-71
   broken, troubleshooting, 97
   checking before adding, 220-223
   custom, members, 119-126
   initializing, 296-297
   navigation icons, adding, 86-88
   thumbnails, generating, 163-167
   uploading, news items, 162
Images folder, 40
in place editing, 186
inheritance, CommunityPO base class, 301
initializing images, 296-297
installations
   forum assemblies, 336
   online community applications, 4
instances
   global
      allowing (Send Message module), 145-148
      defined, 26
      distinguishing with icons, 99
   modules
      adding to sections (members), 182-184
      defined, 25
      online community applications, 14, 18-19
   updated module, icons, adding, 99-103

integrating ASP.NET Forums, 334-342
Intermediate Language (IL) code, 83
Internet Information Services (IIS), online community applications, 5
IP addresses
   logging, 233-240
   updating, 240
   viewing, 239-240
IPAddress persistent object, 234-235

J-K-L

jpeg files, member images, 125

keys, primary (persistent objects), 30

layers, online community application, 27
   ASP.NET pages, 27
   business service classes, 28
   CommunityModule object, properites, 31-32
   controls, 28
   Member object, properites, 30-31
   ModuleInstance object, properites, 33
   ModuleView object, properites, 32-33
   persistent objects, 29-30, 35-36
   Section object, properites, 34-35
   SectionItem object, properites, 34
lazy loading, OJB.NET persistence service, 36
links
   adding, Member page, 182
   navigation classes, CSS (Cascading Style Sheets), 74-76
logging IP addresses, 233-240

login controls
    code, adding, 238-239
    modules, 18
logins, persisted (cookies), 241-243
looping method calls, 111

M

magic numbers
    code, reorganizing, 271-278
    databinding code, breaking out, 278-279
    eliminating, 260-264
    RandomTextItem class, removing, 269-270
    thumbnails, configuring width, 264-269
    Type.GetType calls, removing, 270
managing members. *See* member management
markup code, news items, 159-162
Member class, 236-238
member management
    administration system, 169
        Global/CommunityPrinciple.vb files, 171-172
        member management facilities, adding, 172-188
        protecting, 169-171
    forgotten passwords, 190
        hashing, 189-197
        One-Use-Only Change Password emails, 197
        secret questions, 189
    registration process
        email confirmations, 205
        email reminders, 205

        new user approval, 198-205
        terms and conditions agreements, 205
    resource usage
        data quotas, 207-223
        personal pages, 223
        personalized quotas, 223
    security
        persisted logins, 241-243
        private online communities, 243-246
        timeout periods, 241
    troubleshooting
        banning members, 224-226
        deactivated member data, hiding, 226-228
        deleting members, 228-233
        logging IP addresses, 233-240
        updating IP addresses, 240
Member object
    GetResourceUsage function, 217
    properties, 30-31
Member pages
    custom images, 119-126
    images/text, 223
    links, adding, 182
members
    adding module instances and sections, 182-184
    custom images, 119-126
    defined, 25
    inserting, forums databases, 339-340
    ModuleBase class, 38
    new, valid email address requirements, 142
    newest joined, displaying, 115-119
    online community applications, 13-14, 19-22
    private(_), 43

How can we make this index more useful? Email us at indexes@samspublishing.com

Members page, 13

messages. *See* email

MetaBuilders Web site, 133

metadata, adding, 331-333

methods
- adding, CoreModule class, 238
- calls, looping, 111
- cleanup, implementing, 310
- DisplaySection(), default.aspx files, 44-46
- FindObject, CoreModule.vb files, 49
- GetLatestGlobalNewsItems, 57-60
- GetResourceUsage, implementing, 307-308
- GetSearchResults, 61-62, 308-309
- Page_Load, 149-150
- SendMessage, 136

Microsoft.Web.UI.WebControls error, 9

MIME types, jpeg files, 125

module instances
- adding to sections (members), 182-184
- defined, 25
- updated, icons, adding, 99-103

module views
- controls, caching, 250
- defined, 26

ModuleBase class, 37-38, 208-209

ModuleInstance object
- GetResourceUsage function, 215-216
- properties, 33

modules
- adding, online community applications
  - business service classes, 306-314
  - calendar modules, 331-333
  - delete event option, 333
  - display module controls, 314-317
  - displaying error messages, 333
  - optional items, 300
  - persistent object implementations, 300-306
  - requirements, 299
  - view item controls, 326-331
  - views, 318-325
- Blog, GetResourceUsage function, 214-215
- Calendar, metadata, adding, 331-333
- defined, 25
- ImageGallery
  - GetResourceUsage function, 210-214
  - image number, 94-95
  - thumbnails, generating, 163-167
- ModuleBase class, 37-38
- name, configurable, 126-132
- News module, 148
  - automatic summaries, 155-158
  - formatting, 152-155
  - GetResourceUsage function, 209
  - markup code, 159-162
  - Modules/News/DisplayItem.ascx code, 149-151
  - text limits, 157-158
  - uploading images, 162
- online community applications, 11, 37
  - adding, 19
  - global, 12-18
  - instances, 14, 18-19
  - login controls, 18
- RandomText, GetResourceUsage function, 209
- Send Message module
  - GetResourceUsage function, 210
  - global instances, allowing, 145-148
  - Modules/SendMessage/SimpleSendMessageBox.ascx code, 137-139

SendMessageModule.vb file, 135-137
subject lines, 148
troubleshooting, 142-144
valid email address requirements, 139-142

views
adding, 295-299
configurable, 132
DisplaySingleImage view, 299
testing, 297-299

Modules folder, 40
Modules tab (members), 19-21
Modules/News/DisplayItem.ascx code, 149-151
Modules/SendMessage/SimpleSendMessagebox.ascx code, 137-139
ModuleView object, properties, 32-33
MSDE, downloading, 3

N

Name property, implementing, 309
names
computers, 8
modules, configurable, 126-132
usernames, changing, 179

naming files (code refactoring), 292-294
navigation, adding icons, 86-88, 103-108
navigation classes, CSS (Cascading Style Sheets), 73-76
navigation.ascx control, 77-85
New menu commands, Virtual Directory, 5
newest joined members, displaying, 115-119
NewestMember.ascx control, 116-119
news items, checking before adding, 217-218

News module, 148
formatting, 152-155
GetResourceUsage function, 209
Modules/News/DisplayItem.ascx code, 149-151

news items
automatic summaries, 158
editing/entering, 155-157
images, uploading, 162
markup code, 159-162
text limits, 157-158

NewsItemSummary class, 286-291
NewsModule.vb files, 57-60
non-global sections, showing, 115
null results, checking, 118

O

objects
CommunityModule, properties, 31-32
Criteria, CoreModule.vb files, 50
DataTable, IList type, converting, 173-176
Member
GetResourceUsage function, 217
properties, 30-31
ModuleInstance
GetResourceUsage function, 215-216
properties, 33
ModuleView, properties, 32-33
persistent, 29
implementing, 300-306
OJB.NET persistence service, 35-36
primary keys, 30
storing, 36

How can we make this index more useful? Email us at indexes@samspublishing.com

Section
    CoreModule.vb file, 51-53
    properties, 34-35
SectionItem, properties, 34
summary, 285
    BlogEntrySummary class, 291
    NewsItemSummary class, 286-291
OJB.NET folder, 40
OJB.NET persistence service, 35-36
One-Use-Only Change Password emails, forgotten passwords, 197
one-way encryption, forgotten passwords, 189-197
online community applications, 11
    accessing, 5
    administration system, 23
    benefits, 26
    breaking, 80-82
    code
        CoreModule.vb file, 47-55
        default.aspx file, 40-47
        DisplayLatestHeadlines.ascx file, 55-57
        NewsModule.vb file, 57-60
    configurations, 8
    CSS (Cascading Style Sheets), 69-76
    databases, setting up, 7
    data files, 8
    final applications, 4, 11
    folder structure, 38-40
    installing, 4
    layers
        ASP.NET pages, 27
        business service classes, 28
        CommunityModule object, properties, 31-32
        controls, 28

Member object, properties, 30-31
ModuleInstance object, properties, 33
ModuleView object, properties, 32-33
persistent objects, 29-30, 35-36
Section object, properties, 34-35
SectionItem object, properties, 34
members, 13-14, 19-22
modules, 11, 37
    global, 12, 16-18
    instances, 14, 18-19
    login controls, 18
    ModuleBase class, 37-38
modules, adding, 19
    business service classes, 306-314
    calendar modules, 331-333
    delete event option, 333
    display module controls, 314-317
    displaying error messages, 333
    optional items, 300
    persistent object implementations, 300-306
    requirements, 299
    view item controls, 326-331
    views, 318-325
navigation.ascx control, 77-85
navigation icons, adding, 86-88
private, creating, 243-246
repository files, 8
searches, 22-23, 60-65
security, 66
setting up, 5-6
SQL Server databases, 36
source code, 4-7
starting-point applications, 4, 11-12
system requirements, 3

terminology, 25-26
testing, 9
WebControl client script files, 9
Open Table menu commands, Return All Rows, 126
operators, & (string concatenation), 256

P

page output, caching (code refactoring), 248-250
pages
    ASP.NET, 27
    Members, 13
        adding links, 182
        custom images, 119-126
        images/test, 223
    modifying (members), 21
    partial, caching (refactoring code), 250
    What's New?
        adding, 108-115
        non-global sections, showing, 115
Pages tab (members), 19-21
Page_Load event handler
    default.aspx files, 41-44
    SectionItemHeader control, 92-94
Page_Load method, 149-150
paging global modules, 16
partial pages caching (refactoring code), 250
passwords, forgotten, 190
    hashing, 189-197
    One-Use-Only Change Password emails, 197
    secret questions, 189
permissions, databases (ASP.NET Forums), 335

persisted logins, cookies, 241-243
persistence service respository, adding entries, 305
persistent objects, 29
    CommunityModule, properties, 31-32
    implementing, 300-306
    IPAddress, 234-235
    Member, properties, 30-31
    ModuleInstance, properties, 33
    ModuleView, properties, 32-33
    OJB.NET persistence service, 35-36
    primary keys, 30
    Section, properties, 34-35
    SectionItem, properties, 34
    storing, 36
PersistentObjects folder, 39
Portable Network Graphic (.png) format, 87
primary keys, persistent objects, 30
private fields, adding, 302
private members, underscore (_), 43
private online communities, creating, 243-246
properties. *See also* attributes
    adding
        Member class, 236
        persistence objects, 303-304
    Boolean, check box properties, 180-181
    CommunityModule object, 31-32
    Member object, 30-31
    ModuleInstance object, 33
    ModuleView object, 32-33
    Name, implementing, 309
    Section object, 34-35
    SectionItem object, 34
Properties menu commands, Computer Name, 8

How can we make this index more useful? Email us at indexes@samspublishing.com

property accessors, 77

protecting member administration system, 169-171

psuedo code, news items, 159-162

PublicEmail command (Edit Template menu), 181

Q-R

quotas
    data, setting, 207-223
    personalized, member resource usage, 223

random text, checking before adding, 219-220

RandomText module, GetResourceUsage function, 209

RandomTextItem class, removing, 269-270

recompiling .vb files, 95

reconstructors, adding, 302

refactoring code
    caching, 247
        dynamic controls, 251
        page output, 248-250
        partial pages, 250
    data access, efficient, 281-285
    file naming, 292-294
    magic numbers
        databinding code, breaking out, 278-279
        eliminating, 260-264
        RandomTextItem class, removing, 269-270
        reorganizing code, 271-278
        thumbnail width, 264-269
        Type.GetType calls, removing, 270
    reusable code, creating, 279-281

summary objects, 285
    BlogEntrySummary class, 291
    NewsItemSummary class, 286-291

viewstates, 251
    minimizing, 252-253
    StringBuilder class, 253-260
    Trace feature, 252

registration process, members
    email confirmations, 205
    email reminders, 205
    new user approval, 198-205
    terms and conditions agreement, 205

regular expression validators, valid email addresses, 139-141

regular expressions
    obtaining online, 141
    searches, 256-257
    values, 140-141

reminders, email, 205

Repeater, DisplayLatestHeadlines.ascx file, 55-57

repeater controls, adding, 112-113

repository files, online community application, 8

Request Button, event handler, 193-194

resource usage, members
    data quotas, 207-223
    personal pages, 223
    personalized quotas, 223

results, null, 118

Return All Rows command (Open Table menu), 126

Return key, user interface, 132-134

reusable code, 133, 279-281

S

Search folder, 39

searches

    online community applications, 22-23, 60-65

    regular expressions, 256-257

secret questions, forgotten passwords, 189

section items, 91

    default buttons, adding, 134

    defined, 26

    icons

        global instances, distinguishing, 99

        navigation, 103-108

        updated instances, 99-103

    members, custom images, 119-126

    module names, configurable, 126-132

    module views, configurable, 132

    newest joined members, displaying, 115-119

    SectionItemHeader control, 91-93

        icons, adding, 96-98

        image number, 94-95

    troubleshooting, Return key, 132-134

    What's New? page, 108-115

Section object

    CoreModule.vb file, 51-53

    properties, 34-35

SectionItem object, properties, 34

SectionItemHeader control, 91-93

    icons, adding, 96-98

    image number, 94-95

sections

    adding to module instances (members), 182-184

    defined, 26

global

    navigation icons, 87-88

    navigation links, 76

security

    members

        persisted logins, 241-243

        private online communities, 243-246

        timeout periods, 241

    online community applications, 66

Send Message module

    global instances, allowing, 145-148

    Modules/SendMessage/SimpleSendMessageBox.ascx code, 137-139

    SendMessageModule.vb file, 135-137

    subject lines, 148

    troubleshooting, 142-144

    valid email address requirements, 139-142

SendMessage method, 136

SendMessage module, GetResourceUsage function, 210

SendMessageModule.vb file, 135-137

servers

    controls, 28

    SQL Server, 3, 36

short-circuiting expressions, 203

SiteBody class (CSS), 70-71

SiteTable class (CSS), 71-72

sites, MetaBuilders, 133

skins, ASP.NET Forums, 341

SortedList collection, 110

sorting DataGrid controls, 185-186

source code

    compiling, 6-7

    files, copying, 4

How can we make this index more useful? Email us at indexes@samspublishing.com

Source command (View menu), 251

SQL (Structured Query Language), custom, 283-285

SQL Server, 3, 36

SQL Server Does Not Exist or Access Denied error troubleshooting, 10

starting-point applications, 4, 11-12

storing
- assemblies, 133
- persistent objects, 36

StringBuilder class, string concatenation, 253-260

strings, concatenating, 253-260

Structured Query Language (SQL), custom, 283-285

style sheets, formatting, 86

subfolders, admin, 173

subject lines (email), 148

subroutines, databinding, 278-279

summaries, automatic, 158

summary objects, 285
- BlogEntrySummary class, 291
- NewsItemSummary class, 286-291

syntax. *See* code

system requirements, 3

system text, 126

T

table databases, IPAddress persistent objects, 235

tables, databases, 305

terminology, online community application, 25-26

testing
- online community applications, 9
- views, 297-299

text
- attributes, 74
- display, 126
- limits, news items, 157-158
- random, checking before adding, 219-220
- system, 126

text decoration attribute (text), 74

text indent attribute (text), 74

thumbnails
- generating, 163-167
- widths, configuring, 264-269

ticks values, 194

timeout periods, changing, 241

tooltips, adding, 97-98

Trace feature, 78-79, 252

transactional code, OJB.NET persistence service, 35-36

troubleshooting
- broken images, 97
- C:\Inetpub\wwwroot\community\global\OJB.NET\repository.xml error, 9
- Could Not Load Type error, 10
- email, sending, 142-144
- members
  - banning, 224-226
  - deactivated data, hiding, 226-228
  - deleting, 228-233
  - logging IP addresses, 233-240
  - updating IP addresses, 240
- Microsoft.Web.UI.WebControls error, 9
- SQL Server Does Not Exist or Access Denied error, 10
- user interface, Return key, 132-134

try/catch blocks, 137

Type.GetType calls, removing, 270

U

underscore (_), 43

update event handler, 187-188

updated module instances, adding icons, 99-103

updating IP addresses, 240

uploading images, news items, 162

user controls, 28

    caching, 250

    creating, 296

user interfaces

    configurable, 126-132

        newest joined members, displaying, 115-119

        troubleshooting, Return key, 132-134

        What's New? page, 108-115

    section items

        default buttons, adding, 134

        icons, 99-108

        members, custom images, 119-126

        SectionItemHeader control, 91-98

usernames, changing, 179

users, defined, 25

utility classes, IList type, 173-176

V

valid email addresses, requiring, 139-142

validators, regular expression, 139-141

values, ticks, 194

.vb files, recompiling, 95

vertical-align attribute, 87

view item controls, implementing, 326-331

View menu commands, Source, 251

viewing IP addresses, 239-240

views

    adding, modules, 295-299, 320-325

    database entries, adding, 297

    DisplaySingleImage, 299

    implementing, modules, 318-320

    modules

        configurable, 132

        defined, 26

    testing, 297-299

viewstates, 251

    minimizing, 252-253

    StringBuilder class, 253-260

    Trace feature, 252

Virtual Directory command (New menu), 5

visibility, edit controls, 151

visitors, defined, 25

Visual Studio, 3

VS.NET Solution Explorer, 116

W-Z

Web folders, forums, 335

Web Forms, adding, 173

Web sites, MetaBuilders, 133

Web.config files, configuration settings, 336-339

WebControl client script files, online community applications, 9

What's New? page, 108-115

Wouldn't it be great

if the world's leading technical publishers joined forces to deliver their best tech books in a common digital reference platform?

They have. Introducing **InformIT Online Books powered by Safari.**

POWERED BY **Safari**

informIT Online Books

- **Specific answers to specific questions.**
  InformIT Online Books' powerful search engine gives you relevance-ranked results in a matter of seconds.

- **Immediate results.**
  With InformIt Online Books, you can select the book you want and view the chapter or section you need immediately.

- **Cut, paste, and annotate.**
  Paste code to save time and eliminate typographical errors. Make notes on the material you find useful and choose whether or not to share them with your workgroup.

- **Customized for your enterprise.**
  Customize a library for you, your department, or your entire organization. You pay only for what you need.

Get your first 14 days **FREE!**

InformIT Online Books is offering its members a 10-book subscription risk free for 14 days. Visit **http://www.informit.com/onlinebooks** for details.

Your Guide to Computer Technology

informIT

www.informit.com

Sams has partnered with **InformIT.com** to bring technical information to your desktop. Drawing on Sams authors and reviewers to provide additional information on topics you're interested in, **InformIT.com** has free, in-depth information you won't find anywhere else.

ARTICLES

Keep your edge with thousands of free articles, in-depth features, interviews, and information technology reference recommendations—all written by experts you know and trust.

ONLINE BOOKS

POWERED BY **Safari**

Answers in an instant from **InformIT Online Books'** 600+ fully searchable online books. Sign up now and get your first 14 days **free**.

CATALOG

Review online sample chapters and author biographies to choose exactly the right book from a selection of more than 5,000 titles.

SAMS   www.samspublishing.com

What's on the CD-ROM

The companion CD-ROM contains all the source code for the examples developed in the book, and Microsoft's .NET Framework 1.1 Redistributable and Software Development Kit.

Windows Installation Instructions

1. Insert the disc into your CD-ROM drive.
2. From the Windows desktop, double-click the My Computer icon.
3. Double-click the icon representing your CD-ROM drive.
4. Double-click `start.exe`. Follow the onscreen prompts to access the CD-ROM information.

> **NOTE**
> If you have the AutoPlay feature enabled, `start.exe` will be launched automatically whenever you insert the disc into your CD-ROM drive.

License Agreement

By opening this package, you are also agreeing to be bound by the following agreement:

You may not copy or redistribute the entire CD-ROM as a whole. Copying and redistribution of individual software programs on the CD-ROM is governed by terms set by individual copyright holders.

The installer and code from the author(s) are copyrighted by the publisher and the author(s). Individual programs and other items on the CD-ROM are copyrighted or are under an Open Source license by their various authors or other copyright holders.

This software is sold as-is without warranty of any kind, either expressed or implied, including but not limited to the implied warranties of merchantability and fitness for a particular purpose. Neither the publisher nor its dealers or distributors assumes any liability for any alleged or actual damages arising from the use of this program. (Some states do not allow for the exclusion of implied warranties, so the exclusion may not apply to you.)

Microsoft .NET Framework 1.1 Redistributable and Software Development Kit

This program was reproduced by Sams Publishing under a special arrangement with Microsoft Corporation. For this reason, Sams Publishing is responsible for the product warranty and support. If your disc is defective, please return it to Sams Publishing, which will arrange for its replacement. PLEASE DO NOT RETURN IT TO MICROSOFT CORPORATION. Any product support will be provided, if at all, by Sams Publishing. PLEASE DO NOT CONTACT MICROSOFT CORPORATION FOR PRODUCT SUPPORT. End users of this Microsoft program shall not be considered "registered owners" of a Microsoft product and therefore shall not be eligible for upgrades, promotions or other benefits available to "registered owners" of Microsoft products.

NOTE: This CD-ROM uses long and mixed-case filenames requiring the use of a protected-mode CD-ROM Driver.